Work Abroad
The Complete Guide To Finding A Job Overseas

General Editor
Clay Hubbs

Contributing Editors
Susan Griffith, William Nolting

Transitions Abroad Publishing, Inc.
Amherst, Massachusetts
www.TransitionsAbroad.com

ISBN 1-886732-11-6
Library of Congress Control Number
2002109739
Fourth Edition

Editorial Assistant: Sian Wu • Production: Janis Sokol/Lisa Green
Cover photo (*Anzali Lagoon, Northern Iran*) by A.G. Ziaee

Introduction

Chapter 1

International Careers

Chapter 2

Short-Term International Jobs and Internships for Students and Recent Graduates

Chapter 3

Short-Term Jobs Abroad

Chapter 4

Volunteering Abroad

Chapter 5
Teaching English Abroad

Chapter 6
K-12 and University Teaching Abroad

How to Use This Book

Whether you are a professional planning to relocate, a student preparing for an international career, or a traveler looking to extend your trip, the thing you need most is reliable information.

The resource and program directories published here are continuously updated on our web site, www.TransitionsAbroad.com and www.working traveler.com. If a contact fails to respond, please check the web site for the most current information.

INTRODUCTION

Any individual with guts and gusto, from students to grandmothers, has the potential to support themselves as they travel to the corners of the globe. Those who have shed their unrealistic expectations are normally exhilarated by the novelty and challenge.

Work Abroad

Experience a Foreign Culture from the Inside

By Susan Griffith

In hopes of soothing the minds of the irresolute, here are some general guidelines to preface the unprecedented amount of specific information and contact addresses included in this fourth edition of *Work Abroad*.

Motives. Some travelers have future career prospects in view when they go abroad; a few go in search of highly paid jobs. Success is easier for people with acknowledged qualifications such as nurses and pipe-fitters, though cherry pickers and pot washers have been known to earn and save substantial sums. Those on open-ended trips may decide to postpone cashing their last traveler's check by looking around for ways of boosting their travel fund. They may find paid work, or they may decide to volunteer their labor in exchange for a bed and board. Most of the information in this volume concerns short-term work—12 months or less. For help on how to prepare for an international career and find a permanent job, see Chapter 1. Professionals should also consult their own trade's associations and journals.

Advance Planning. The aspiring working traveler either arranges a job before leaving home or gambles on finding something on the spot. Pre-arrangement is especially important for people who have never traveled abroad and who feel some trepidation at the prospect. Jobs can be pre-arranged either through private contacts or with the help of a mediating organization.

Some organizations accept a tiny handful of individuals who satisfy stringent requirements; others accept almost anyone who can pay the fee. Many work schemes and official exchanges require a lot of advance planning since it is not unusual for an application deadline to fall six or nine months before departure.

While it's easy to arrange a job to teach English in the former Soviet Union, the price you pay for this security is that you commit yourself to a new life, however temporary, sight unseen. Furthermore, a participation fee in some cases can be as expensive as booking a conventional vacation.

The alternative to these packaged arrangements is to wait until after arrival at your destination to explore local job possibilities. In the course of research for my book, *Work Your Way Around the World*, I have come across many examples of fearless travelers who are prepared to arrive in a foreign city with very little money, confident that a means by which they can earn money will present itself. In most cases it does, but not without a few moments of panic and desperation.

Like job-hunting in any context, it will be much easier to contend with the inevitable competition if prospective employers can meet you in the flesh and be assured that you are available to start work the minute a vacancy crops up. For casual work on farms or arranging a passage on a transatlantic yacht, a visit to a village pub frequented by farmers or yachties is worth dozens of speculative applications from home.

The more unusual and interesting the job the more competition it will attract. Less glamorous options can absorb an almost unlimited number of people. International workcamps, for example, mobilize thousands of volunteers from many countries every year who come together to build footpaths, work with disabled persons, etc.

Red Tape. Work permits and residence visas are not readily available in many countries and for many kinds of jobs. In most cases, job-seekers from overseas must find an employer willing to apply to the immigration authorities on their behalf well in advance of the job's starting date, while they are still in their home country. This is easier for nuclear physicists and foreign correspondents than for mere mortals, though in certain countries English teachers are welcomed by the authorities. In organized exchange programs, like the ones administered by Council on International Educational Exchange (see Chapter 2), the red tape is taken care of by the sponsoring organization.

Temporary jobs like apple picking and burger flipping will never qualify for a work permit, and unofficial employment can quite often lead to exploitative working conditions.

Improving Your Chances for a Short-Term Job. Preparation will improve your chances of convincing a potential employer of your superiority to the competition. For example, before leaving home you might take a short course in teaching English, cooking, word processing, or sailing—all skills that have been put to good use by working travelers. If you are serious, you might learn or improve your knowledge of a foreign language.

Even if you are not lucky enough to have friends and family scattered strategically throughout the world, it is always worth broadcasting your intentions to third cousins, pen friends, and visiting Asian professors. The more widely publicized your travel plans, the better your chance of a lead.

If you set off without an address book full of contacts, your fellow travelers are undoubtedly the best source of information on job prospects; most are surprisingly generous with their information and assistance. Youth hostels can be a gold mine for the job seeker. Jobs may even be advertised on the notice board. Any locals or expatriates you meet are a potential source of help. Any skill or hobby, from jazz music to motor car racing, can become the basis for pursuing contacts.

Local English language newspapers like Mexico City's *The News,* the *Bangkok Post,* or *Cairo Today* may carry job advertisements appropriate to your situation, or may be a good place for you to advertise your services. The most effective method of finding a job overseas is to walk in and ask. As in any job hunt, it helps to have a neat appearance and show keenness and persistence. If you want a job for which there appear to be no openings, volunteer. If you prove yourself competent, you will have an excellent chance of filling a vacancy if one does occur.

Seasonal jobs are most likely to go to itinerant foreigners. In times of recession the number of temporary jobs available may even increase since employers are not eager to expand their permanent staff but need extra help at busy times. Farmers and hotel/restaurant managers are the best potential sources of employment, and in most cases one setback leads to a success once you are on the track.

Young women and (increasingly) young men who want the security of a family placement and who may also wish to learn a European language may choose to live with a family, helping to look after the children in exchange for pocket money. Such positions can be found on the spot by means of advertisements or in advance through agencies, like Accord Cultural Exchange (www.cognitext.com/accord).

English teaching normally requires some experience and a 9-month commitment, though many travelers from Bangkok to Buenos Aires have used the yellow pages to direct them to local language schools willing to employ native speakers of English as conversational assistants.

Volunteering. Paid work in developing nations is rarely available, yet many travelers arrange to live for next to nothing while doing something positive. Charities and aid organizations offer a range of volunteer opportunities around the world. Many volunteer agencies require more than a curiosity about a country; they require a strong wish to become involved in a specific project and in many cases an ideological commitment to a cause. Almost without exception, volunteers must be self-funding.

For anyone with a green conscience, conservation organizations throughout the world welcome volunteers for short or long periods in projects ranging from tree planting to gibbon counting. Unfortunately, the more glamorous projects, such as accompanying scientific research expeditions into wild and woolly places, charge volunteers a great deal of money for the privilege of helping.

Whether you set off to work abroad with the help of a mediating organization or with the intention of living by your wits, you are bound to encounter interesting characters and lifestyles, collect a wealth of anecdotes, increase your self-reliance, and feel that you have achieved something. Inevitably there will be some surprises along the way.

Perspective

Making the Most of Being Overseas

By Laura Higgins Florand

You don't want to be just a tourist. You want to get to know the real people to experience what life is really like in this foreign country you've worked so hard and risked so much to live in. But you still feel like an outsider looking in. What can you do?

Accept the fact that you *are* an outsider and enjoy the benefits. When I lived in Tahiti, my light hair, blue eyes, and 5'3" build made it impossible for me to blend in with the black-haired, bronze-skinned, and generally much taller Tahitians. But having grown up where light brown hair, blue eyes, and small size were the most common of features, I enjoyed being "exotic." And I also made lots of friends, all with open minds and a strong interest in learning more about other countries and other cultures, in this case, mine.

Sign up to learn local arts or sports. In Tahiti, the sensual dancing seen in *South Pacific* is unarguably the most vital form of cultural expression for the *Ma'ohi*, as native Polynesians in Tahiti call themselves. I had my doubts about joining a class that would require me to bare my midriff and dance publicly in skimpy *pareus,* but by taking the risk I not only learned about but became a part of something quintessentially Tahitian. I also gained self-confidence. Since my return to the U.S. I have been teaching classes in dance to share this confidence and pleasure with others. In Spain I am now learning flamenco—completely different experience yet equally fascinating.

I have also tried outrigger canoeing, drumming, and cooking. For meeting people and learning about a culture, there is nothing like physically participating in something fundamental to that culture.

Intercambios. The word is Spanish, but the idea works everywhere. Meet a native of the country once a week at a café for conversation, alternating between your native language one week and his the next. You not only improve your language ability but the conversations you have can be fascinating and the friendships you develop will endure. I never became as fluent in *Reo Ma'ohi* (Tahitian) as I would have liked, but the fact that I tried led to my being surrounded with friendly, intrigued faces in the market and being invited to families' homes for weekends. Local universities are ideal places to put up notices.

Volunteer. You do it at home, why not abroad? A friend of mine always works with underprivileged children wherever she goes and another involves herself with women's shelters. Volunteering means being part of something that matters.

One nice thing about these "tricks" is that they work even for shy people like me. You live in another country because you are interested in its culture. All you have to do to immerse yourself in it is put a little energy into showing that interest.

Work Abroad Resources
Key Publishers

Selected and Reviewed by William Nolting

L ooking for international work, whether abroad or in the U.S. with an international organization, can be downright frustrating without good resources. There are many useful guides for almost any field in any country, but you won't find them all in your local bookstore. Some of the best guides (including the one you are reading) are made by small publishers and may lack mass distribution. The following key publishers' web sites and catalogs should be your first stop in your search for a job abroad.

CIEE (Council on International Educational Exchange), 633 3rd Ave., 20th Fl., New York, NY 10017; 888-COUNCIL, fax 212-822-2649; info@ciee.org, www.councilexchanges.org. CIEE administers the Council Work Abroad Program and Council Workcamps, as well as study abroad programs, and offers the Bowman Travel Grant scholarships.

Impact Publications, 9104-N Manassas Dr., Manassas Park, VA 20111-5211; 800-361-1055, 703-361-7300, fax 703-335-9486; info@impactpublications.com, www.impact publications.com. The best one-stop source for international career books published by Impact and many other publishers.

Institute of International Education (IIE), IIE Books, P.O. Box 371, Annapolis Junction, MD 20701-0371; 800-445-0443, fax 301-206-9789; iiebooks@pmds.com, www.iie.org, and www.iiepassport.org. Publisher of authoritative directories which list programs for studying, internships, and volunteering abroad. Also publishes a directory of scholarships for studying abroad. IIE's publications are available both as books and (free) online. IIE administers several of the Fulbright scholarship programs.

Intercultural Press, P.O. Box 700, Yarmouth, ME 04096; 800-370-2665 or 207-846-5168, fax 207-846-5181; books@interculturalpress.com, www.interculturalpress.com. Numerous publications dealing with cross-cultural issues, moving abroad, dealing with culture shock, and other issues related to working and/or studying abroad.

NAFSA Publications, P.O. Box 1020, Sewickley, PA 15143; 800-836-4994; fax 412-741-1142; www.nafsa.org. Essential publications for advisers and administrators in international educational exchange. For membership information, contact NAFSA: Association of International Educators, 1307 New York Avenue, NW, 8th Fl., Washington, DC 20005-4701, 202-737-3699, fax 202-737-3657; inbox@nafsa.org.

Peterson's, 202 Carnegie Center, P.O. Box 2123, Princeton, NJ 08543-2123; 800-338-3282, outside U.S. 609-243-9111, fax 609-243-9150; www.petersons.com. Publisher of guides to internships and careers, study abroad, and a U.S. distributor for many of the publications by Vacation Work (U.K.).

Reference Service Press, 5000 Windplay Dr., Suite 4, El Dorado Hills, CA 95762; 916-939-9620, fax 916-939-9626; webagent@rspfunding.com, www.rspfunding.com. Publisher of numerous directories for scholarships and financial aid.

Seven Hills Book Distributors, 1531 Tremont St., Cincinnati, OH 45214; 513-471-4300, fax 513-471-4311; www.sevenhillsbooks.com. U.S. distributor for Vacation Work (U.K.) publications and Survival Books. Also carries a wide range of travel books and maps from foreign and domestic publishers.

TESOL, (Teachers of English to Speakers of Other Languages, Inc.) 700 South Washington St., Alexandria, VA 22314; 703-836-0774, fax 703-836-6447; info@tesol.org, www.tesol.org. For orders from TESOL Publications: P.O. Box 753, Waldorf, MD 20604-0753; 888-891-0042, 301-638-4427 or 301-638-4428, fax 301-843-0159; tesolpubs@tascol.org, www.tesol.org. TESOL is the largest professional association for qualified teachers of English as a foreign or second language. TESOL's services include publications, job listings, and conferences.

Transitions Abroad, P.O. Box 1300, Amherst, MA 01004-1300; 800-293-0373, 413-256-3414, fax 413-256-0373; info@TransitionsAbroad.com, www.TransitionsAbroad.com. Publishes *Transitions Abroad* ($28/6 issues), the only U.S. periodical that covers work abroad, education

13

abroad, alternative and responsible travel, and living abroad. Also publishes *The Alternative Travel Directory,* which lists thousands of resources for seniors, the disabled, teens, families with children, and more. *Work Abroad* covers all aspects of international work, including short-term jobs, careers, teaching English volunteering, internships, and more.

Vacation Work Publications, 9 Park End St., Oxford, OX1 1HJ, U.K; 011-44-1865-241978, fax 011-44-1865-790885; www.vacationwork.

co.uk. Web site includes forum on work abroad. Publisher of numerous books on work abroad and international careers. Distributed in the U.S. by Peterson's or Seven Hills, depending on the particular book.

VGM Career Horizons. A division of NTC/Contemporary Publishing Group, 4255 West Touhy Ave., Lincolnwood, IL 60712-1975; 800-323-4900, fax 847-679-2494. Books on careers. Available through bookstores and Amazon.com.

Key Work Abroad Web Sites
Introduction and Search Strategies
Selected and Reviewed by William Nolting

Although the Internet contains enormous amounts of information for finding jobs, volunteer opportunities, and internships, it should be only part of your search. To find background and contact information for organizations with whom you would like to work, use the online information as a starting place. Find out more about the organization via phone calls, letters, and meetings. Many parts of the world are still not online, so supplement your search by consulting books and newspapers targeted to international opportunity seekers.

Your search will probably proceed in two overlapping stages:

1. Information Search and Compilation: During this stage, pull together as much information as you can on potential opportunities that interest you. This stage should involve online resources (web search engines, online databases, and discussion lists), as well as international opportunity books and newspapers.

Start out researching as widely as possible and narrow down as you discover opportunities more closely matching your interests. Follow links, search on key words, and generally try to gather as much information as you can handle at first. Then go through it all and sort out what you need. *The most valuable information you can gain for job hunting is a contact name and number.*

2. Narrowing Down and Networking: Learn the details about a small list of organizations that interest you through email and discussion lists, phone calls, letters, and face-to-face meetings.

Email Discussion Lists
Email lists are email groups with many subscribers (sometimes in the hundreds) who share an interest in a specific topic—whether a country, a region, or an issue such as human rights. Once you sign up, don't be afraid to broadcast a question or ask for advice; but follow the list's rules or you will not be very happy with the responses you get. Occasionally, list members will send out information on just what you are looking for, or they may be connected to an organization you want to work with. An excellent database of Internet discussion lists is **www.liszt.com**. To find usenet groups specifically, go to **www.dejanews.com**.

CHAPTER 1

INTERNATIONAL CAREERS

*There is, literally, a world of opportunity for job seekers
who are already pursuing an international career or
are serious about doing so. Whether you are an entry-
level college graduate or mid-career professional, it is
possible to find your niche by thoroughly researching
the job market, identifying the relevant skills you
already have, and acquiring the skills you may lack.*

Getting Ready

Developing Global Skills for an International Career

By Debra Peters-Behrens

As an international careers adviser, I receive questions daily from people of varied backgrounds who hope to try their luck in the global marketplace. Many job seekers mistakenly believe that they can't begin an international career until their feet are on foreign soil. They overlook their own backyard for resources and training opportunities.

The Most Sought-After Skills

What do international employers really look for in employees and what skills will be needed by professionals to perform successfully in the global marketplace?

A study commissioned by the College Placement Council Foundation surveyed 32 international employers and colleges to determine what international employers seek in prospective employees. They identified the following areas of required knowledge and skills:

Domain knowledge. Colleges in the U.S. are presently preparing their graduates well in domain knowledge, or knowledge in one's academic discipline, although employers expressed concern that increasingly greater demands and higher standards may soon result in inadequately prepared graduates.

The three most important skills were cognitive skills, social skills, and "personal traits." Problem-solving ability, decision making, and knowing how to learn are highly prized generic skills. Social skills were described as the ability to work effectively in group settings, particularly with diverse populations. Personal traits mentioned frequently included flexibility, adaptability, and the capacity to be innovative. Employers often mentioned that colleges do not adequately address this type of skill development.

Cross-cultural competence. Students must make a concerted effort to acquire the knowledge, skills, and traits gained through cross-cultural interaction because we are more geographically and linguistically insulated than most other countries.

On-the-job training and prior work experience. Employers seek applicants who have been successful in applying their domain knowledge or academic studies and generic skills in the workplace. They say that colleges do not place sufficient emphasis on work experience.

Acquiring the Skills

Get Experience. An internship or a stint as a volunteer can be invaluable to recent graduates or career changers. Locate organizations at the local level which have similar goals to those of larger international organizations. Service organizations address issues of health, housing, economic development, and employment—all of which are local as well as global concerns.

For example, one client wanted to find a position in development work in the Third World. I suggested that she research local human service organizations to find an internship that would provide her with opportunities to work with on-going projects. She found an internship as an interagency liaison with a relief organization that distributed medicine, food, and supplies to countries affected by war or natural disasters.

Many job seekers plan to teach English as a second language with little or no experience beforehand. Even a brief stint as a volunteer language assistant can provide insight into the challenges and rewards of the work. Testing a field in familiar settings can make for a smoother transition abroad.

Build Your Resume. Job seekers often do not have the time or the money to pursue a degree program, but in some instances a few courses may sufficiently augment the experience and education you already have. Consult a career counselor to help you assess your skills and identify approaches for strengthening your background. A counselor can also help you determine an optimum strategy for meeting your goals. Investigate extension and continuing education programs offered by local colleges and universities for courses in computer science, graphic design, and foreign languages.

Research the Job Market. Gather information by researching a variety of sources: trade publications, journals, professional associations, and electronic bulletin boards. The public library is a treasure trove of information. Many university libraries will issue a community user card for a nominal annual fee.

After you have a grasp of key issues and trends you may want to get the perspective of people who are active in the field. Use your alumni directory and professional associations as resources for networking and information interviewing. Do not set up an information interview and then ask your informant for a job. People generally resent the imposition. Instead, use the time to ask questions that are not covered in print material, including "If you were me, what would you do next?," "If you had to do it all over again, is there anything you would do differently?," and "What strategies did you use that were most successful?"

With a focused and well-organized approach, you can be on the path to developing skills for a global career.

Go Where the Action Is. Many U.S. cities are becoming global in population and perspective as people with diverse linguistic, national, and cultural backgrounds converge to live and work. Living in these locales can help you acquire cross-cultural competence and find work in fields such as business, cultural exchange, and health and human services with a focus on certain regions of the world. All major cities have world trade centers which support international commerce, as do some mid-sized and smaller cities.

If you're interested in the Asian Pacific Rim, for example, a job with a multinational organization in Seattle, Portland, or San Francisco may be a good starting point. Miami, Houston, and San Diego hold great potential for international trade between the U.S. and Latin America. New York and Los Angeles are centers of international business, diplomacy, and cultural affairs. Washington, DC provides a strong base for finding international employment, particularly in government and nonprofit organizations.

Setting Out
What You Do Here, You Can Probably Do Overseas

By Bryan J. Estep and Becky Youman

You can land just about any job abroad that you can in the United States; the secret is to go there. While a few lucky souls move with a U.S. contract in hand—including attractive expatriate benefits—many of us go without any guarantee of work on the other side.

The payoffs are worth the gamble. More than likely you will peg in at a higher responsibility level with greater mobility than with your job at home. This doesn't necessarily translate into higher earnings, but nonmonetary benefits include development of language and cross-cultural skills and a global perception.

We are frequently amazed at the positions our friends hold and the activity stemming from their work. The people we know are no different from the people we studied with in college, except that they made the decision to work abroad. The professional community abroad is smaller, the contacts are at higher levels—and things just seem to happen.

Admittedly, the transcontinental jump is a challenge. Pulling up roots, convincing your family to accept a move to a foreign country, then sacrificing part of your savings for airfare and the job hunt is difficult. But through adaptability and determination, most of us succeed in making the transition.

Typical Work Arrangements
Work abroad falls into one of three categories: 1) U.S. contract, paid in dollars by a U.S. company, usually with expatriate benefits; 2) national contract, paid in local currency as a resident of the country; and 3) self-employed and freelance.

U.S. Contract. The most desirable situation is to work as a U.S. contracted employee. The company will usually pay for your move and perhaps even include airfare home for the holidays. It may also subsidize rent, buy household appliances, pay foreign taxes, arrange working papers, and provide other expat benefits. Sometimes the most important aspect of the arrangement is payment in dollars, which adds stability in countries with shaky currencies.

Working as a national in a foreign country means being paid in the local currency and in line with similar positions there. In developing countries this usually translates to much less than you would receive in the U.S. for similar work; however, the cost of living is usually lower. In developed countries compensation is usually comparable with similar work in the U.S., but the entry barriers are likely to be higher because of a ready supply of nationals with similar education levels and the difficulty of obtaining a work visa.

The self-employed either start a business in the foreign country or freelance as consultants, journalists, and models. Many have at least a few years of experience in their field and begin generating income immediately.

Targeting Your Country

The first step is picking a deadline six to 12 months down the road to make the move if the stateside search doesn't produce results. In this time you can collect a lot of useful information that will help you choose your target country. Equally important tasks include making contacts in the target country, improving your language skills, and saving money.

Begin with the region that interests you, then narrow down the countries by available opportunities. You can glean macro-economic information from the international sections of periodicals like *Business Week* and the *Wall Street Journal*. As with all secondary research, your web browser and local librarian are your best friends. Personal interests can be as important as macro-ecomonics.

The Search From Home

Interestingly enough, you use the same tools and strategies in an international job search that you would use in a regular job search, the most of important of which is getting the word of your interest out through your personal contacts.

Let's say you've picked Seoul, South Korea as your prospective destination. If in every social occasion you mention off-handedly, "I'm hoping to make a job move to Korea in about six months," you will be amazed at the references you get. The contacts may range from a friend to show you around the city, a prospective host to stay with upon arrival (this is a huge benefit), or perhaps even an employer.

If the referenced person seems worthwhile, you should send a cover letter and resume informing her/him of your goals and requesting an informational interview. If that person doesn't feel responsible for giving you the job, the meeting will probably be more productive.

Internships

Real jobs frequently start with internships. One frequently tried avenue to overseas employment is to look up companies that have operations in the target country and send resumes to their personnel departments. However, the likelihood of this even leading to an interview is small. It is worthwhile, however, to learn all you can about business activity in your target country and to bring along a list of companies to contact upon arrival. (See Krannich and Krannich, *International Jobs Directory*, Impact Publications, under Key Publishers.)

Another route is to take a job in any capacity with a multinational corporation in the U.S. and try to work your way into an international slot from the inside. Many large companies fill overseas positions from within the organization, but there is no guarantee you will be moved abroad.

Making the Move

Few people land a job without first going to their target country, usually on a tourist visa. Working papers are arranged once a job is found. Before you fly into town with nothing more than a couple of suitcases, some savings, and gutsy ambition, try to talk to enough people to know the cost of sustaining a 2- to 3-month job hunt. Your budget should include roundtrip airfare, initial hotel costs, rent, food, transport, and health insurance.

The first priority is to avoid an expensive hotel stay. Ideally, before leaving you will have lined up a personal contact with whom you can stay for a few days. If not, the first task at hand is to find a place to unpack your suitcases at a monthly rather than daily rate. The English language newspapers often have classified ads from people looking for roommates. You'll also want to check the want ads.

As much as you may want to "go local" immediately and completely immerse yourself in the new culture, meeting other expats is helpful. Look for the watering holes and gyms where they congregate and start the personal networking immediately. This is the most likely way to find a place to live and a job.

Finding the Job

The most efficient onsite job search follows a 2-pronged strategy: The first is the direct route of targeting firms in your area of interest and leaving resumes with decision-makers contacted in earlier phone calls. The second is letting as many people as possible know that you are looking for work and eager to get to it. You should be well practiced at this because you did it when you started your search from home.

The American Chamber of Commerce sometimes has a bulletin board of companies that have contacted them looking for bilingual personnel. The member companies themselves are good targets.

Starting out on a student visa in the foreign country is another option for gaining a longer-term legal status. A few manage to transform the study experience into a job experience.

Working for Yourself

The self-employed—entrepreneurs, journalists, consultants, models—follow much the same route as those looking for national contracts. Most are freelancers who live from assignment to assignment and struggle until their business base is established. Their previous experience usually helps them beat down the learning curve a bit. But stubborn determination remains the biggest asset.

Remember that if you are self-employed you have the added challenge of setting up an office. That means wrestling with business taxes, lawyers, and accountants— the same as for entrepreneurs at home, but more difficult in a foreign environment.

The possibility of working overseas is not a pipe dream. In fact, with the globalization of the world's economies, U.S. employers are in a position to benefit from professionals with cross-cultural experience. If you make the move successfully, all the talk about global strategies, trade wars, and common market begins to involve you. Amazingly, you realize that you are one of the actors.

Perspective

Working in Western Europe
Skilled Foreign Workers are in Demand

By Charlie Morris

W estern Europe welcomes foreign workers who have skills that are in demand, as long as they play by the rules. Nonresident workers are required to have a work permit. While thousands work there illegally and some employers may encourage you to work "black" to save them tax money and paperwork, don't do it. If you are caught, you can be hit with hefty fines or even barred from the country. An acquaintance of mine fell afoul of the U.K. immigration authorities because he was honest (or foolish) enough to admit that he was entering the country to work and had no work permit. His passport now sports a "black mark," and he will never be able to enter Britain again without proving that he will be staying only a short while.

Misinformation abounds, and calling the immigration authorities may leave you more confused than before. The best way to get the facts is from a lawyer who specializes in immigration law.

Work permits are generally issued for specific jobs. Technically, you are not allowed to enter a country to look for work, although you can't help it if someone happens to offer you a position while you're on vacation.

In Western Europe, the process usually works this way:

1. An employer agrees to hire you subject to a work permit being approved.

2. The employer applies for a work permit for you; this may be a simple process or very complex, depending on what country the job is in, what country you are from, and what your skills and salary level are.

3. If the permit is approved, you will probably receive a document to take to an official for processing and the payment of a fee.

4. Upon arrival at your place of employment, you may be required to register with the local police and perhaps pay another fee.

If you change jobs you must start the process all over again.

Work Permits for Short-Term Jobs
Perhaps the best place to look for short-term work in Europe is Switzerland (and the other countries that have seasonal tourist industries). Those with special skills, like photographers and ski instructors, have the best chance of success, but I've met

Americans behind the bar, in the kitchen, and working the ski lifts. Wages are good, and many jobs include room and board.

Getting a work permit is usually straightforward once you have a job offer. The Swiss Hotel Association (Monbijoustrasse, 130 P.O. Box 3001, Bern, Switzerland; www.swisshotels.ch) publishes a directory of hotels every year, a valuable resource for those seeking seasonal work. Send your resume to the larger hotels in resorts like Davos, Klosters, St. Moritz, Zermatt, Grindelwald, and Gstaad. Call the local tourist office verkehrsverein and ask for the numbers of the local ski lift operators.

Generally, a European employer who wants to hire a non-European Union citizen must demonstrate that they can't fill the position with an EU citizen. (Switzerland is not a member of the EU.) Those with valuable skills stand a good chance of getting a permit, while those in lower-paid lines of work will not get one, except possibly for seasonal jobs in resort areas.

The employer does not have to prove that there is not a single qualified person in all of the EU, just that they have made a diligent effort to find one. This usually means that they have to advertise the position in a local newspaper for two to four weeks before the job can be offered to a foreigner.

Immigration law in the U.K. is complex, and much depends on what country you are from. If you are a citizen of a Commonwealth country (including Canada and Australia) and if your grandfather was born in the U.K., then you may not need a work permit. Citizens of non-EU and non-Commonwealth countries need a work permit, and your chances of getting one depend on your skills and salary level. Those seeking unskilled jobs can basically forget about working in the U.K.

Work Permits for Professionals

Even for those in high-paying professions, the paperwork and hassle involved can be a deal-killer. Fortunately, there are agencies that will handle the whole process for a fee. One good one is BCL Immigration Services (11 Bolt Court, Fleet St., London EC4A3DQ, UK; 011-44-2074-953999, fax 011-44-2074-953991; bcl@workpermit. com; www.workpermit.com.) They will see you through the whole process for around £800 (1999) and offer specific advice for a reasonable fee. Many employers assume that getting a work permit is tougher than it actually is, so knowing about a service like BCL beforehand and mentioning it to your prospective employer can improve your prospects. The employer can make a phone call to the agency and get a good assessment of what your chances are.

I have worked in several European countries and have almost never encountered hostility because of it. But keep in mind this is a controversial issue for some people. Also keep in mind that the U.S. is one of the most restrictive countries in the world in issuing work permits to nonresidents, so you may meet people who resent that you can work in their country but they can't work in yours. Be sensitive.

Work regulations can change often; the above is not the definitive word and certainly not legal advice. You'll have to research your particular situation to make sure you're in compliance. If you make a good-faith effort with your employer to comply with the law, you're unlikely to get in trouble.

Perspective

Attorneys in Paradise

Explore Enchanting Foreign Cultures in Micronesia

By Robert Diemer

Help-wanted ads in the legal press tempt stateside lawyers with visions of hammocks strung between palm trees and tropical drinks in coconut shells. But ask almost any American attorney who has worked in Micronesia and they're likely to say the reality is quite different—and vastly more rewarding.

Practicing law in Micronesia is challenging. Lawyers might find themselves negotiating international treaties or constitutional amendments. It's exciting, too, to work on islands of postcard beauty where the pace of life is quite different from that of the mainland. Best of all is the chance to explore enchanting—and frequently frustrating—foreign cultures, where the people just happen to speak English as well as their native tongues.

Specialists are in demand for many positions. Experts in international law, environmental regulation, and government contracts are always needed. Legislatures have an ongoing need for those versed in preparing and editing bills and resolutions. Lawyers with experience in several different fields are needed as well, particularly at the states' attorney general offices. As anywhere, experienced attorneys have an edge, but lawyers right out of law school find jobs on the islands in both government and private practice.

As on the mainland, no one is likely to consider an unsolicited resume unless a position is vacant or will soon open. Likewise, do not travel to Micronesia in hopes of getting an interview or job. The 30-day tourist visa is strictly enforced.

Daily legal newspapers, particularly in Hawaii and on the west coast, like the *Recorder* or the *Daily Journal*, often carry advertisements, as does the *National Employment Monthly*, which specializes in government attorney jobs. Some web sites below have links to employment pages listing open positions. Many Americans in Micronesia learn about jobs through word of mouth. Patience is critical.

Remember that a little knowledge can go a long way. Candidates should educate themselves about current island issues.

Salaries are low by U.S. standards, but higher than in other developing nations. Taxes are minimal and the cost of living is low. A housing allowance is included in almost every contract. And few jobs anywhere can beat the fringe benefits: Micronesia ranks among the finest scuba dive locales on the planet, and for kayaking, snorkeling, and deep-sea fishing it can't be beat. Local food, especially fresh fruit and fish, is terrific. The frequently minimal time demands of some jobs means expatriates may have plenty of time for hobbies, exploration, and reading. Bring that copy of *War and Peace*.

For More Info

Web Sites: The FSM and Marshall Islands embassies maintain excellent web sites with many links. Both are good sources for general information and issues, although some information is dated. Go to www.rmiembassyus.org and www.fsmembassy.org. The

FSM Government web site links to an employment page with current listings. Palau National Communication Company's web site is the best for that country: www.palaunet.com. For the CNMI, www.mariana-islands.gov.mp is incomplete. A good general information site is www.micronesia-center.com.

Newspapers: Island newspapers come and go, but Guam's *Pacific Daily News* sets the standard. The online edition is www.guampdn.com. Palau and the CNMI have their own newspapers. *Tia Belau News* is written in both English and Palauan. The *Saipan Tribune* covers the Northern Mariana Islands. The online edition is www.tribune.co.mp.

Perspective

Financial Services Jobs Abroad
Investment Research Offers Attractive Benefits

By Steven Ayers

For those with financial skills looking for their first experience living abroad, or for those already overseas looking to switch from English teaching, journalism, or development work, investment research offers very attractive benefits. While pay scales vary widely by country, base salaries are often from 50 to 100 percent higher for financial professionals than for those in other fields popular with expatriates. Bonuses can occasionally equal or exceed annual salaries.

Types of Jobs Available

Research Editor: Working as a research editor is an ideal transition from English teaching or journalism into the financial field. Editors prepare research reports for final publication and dissemination to the bank's clients, many of whom are American- or European-based investment fund managers who communicate in English. The skills needed for effective English teaching, including a mastery of correct grammar and usage and a grasp of common errors made by non-native speakers, are most important. Like journalism, research editing can be deadline-sensitive and pressure-packed at times.

Research Analyst: Research analysts study companies whose stocks trade on the local stock market and write reports detailing their recommendations. While previous financial experience is a distinct advantage, many research analysts have been able to get their first positions without it. Applicants with local language skills and specialized expertise (such as engineering or software design) are in great demand. First-time research analysts, particularly those with no previous finance experience, are often teamed with more experienced analysts as assistants. Research analysts work very long hours (50- to 70-hour weeks are typical) and the beginning pay may seem low, but advancement and pay increases can come very quickly. Most research analysts who stay in the field find the intellectual challenge of the job fascinating.

Research Salesperson: The salesperson is the frontline interface between the bank and the investment client. Clients encompass a wide variety of investors, from pension and mutual fund companies to wealthy individuals and families. The main "product" being sold is the bank's research, written by its various analysts. Clients buy and sell stocks with a particular bank in exchange for access to written research and in many cases to the analysts themselves. Office hours are shorter than for editors and analysts, but salespeople face greater demands in entertaining clients and travel. Language skills and a wide range of business and social contacts are definite advantages. Many large banks in American and European cities have sales desks that specialize in international stocks.

Finding the First Job

Networking is essential to finding the decision makers who can offer you a job. Meet people at the American Chamber of Commerce in your target country (see Web link below). Many alumni associations at larger universities have chapters abroad, some of whose members work in investment research and sales. While banks may hire you directly, most use the services of professional recruiters. Two of the best-known international finance recruiters are Korn/Ferry International and Michael Page International (below). Smaller local recruiters may specialize in placements in your country of interest.

Be sure to learn everything you can about investing before you begin interviewing. While working as an English teacher in Taipei, I found Peter Lynch's book *Beating the Street* a useful introduction to the fundamentals of good investing.

Contacts

Association for Investment Management and Research (800-247-8132, 434-951-5499; info@aimr.org, www.aimr.org). The premier organization for research analysts, AIMR awards the Chartered Financial Analyst (CFA) designation. The local societies and chapters page (www.aimr.org/socservices/societies.asp) has local contact and event information for AIMR chapters in 27 countries outside North America.

American Chapters of Commerce (AmCham). Go to www.uschamber.com/International/Chambers+Abroad/default.htm for a country-by-country list of AmCham organizations which sponsor events for professionals.

Korn/Ferry International. Go to www.kornferry.com and click on "Offices Worldwide" for local office contacts in Latin America, Europe, and Asia/Pacific.

Michael Page International. Pulldown bar on home page, www.michaelpage.com, has national offices for 14 countries outside the U.S.

Key Work Abroad Print Resources

International Careers and International Job Listings

Selected and Reviewed by William Nolting

L ooking for international work, with an international organization, whether abroad or in the U.S. can be daunting. Fortunately, some excellent books, organizations, and web sites can provide real help. Here, we separate the best from the rest in several categories:

• **International Careers** resources offer help in continuing your career abroad or in planning for a "global" lifetime.

• **International Job Listings** include newsletters specializing in worldwide job openings, but advertised jobs tend to be only a fraction of those actually available.

*The rating codes are as follows: **Essential; *Outstanding and of broad interest. For ordering information, if not included below, see Key Publishers, page 13.*

INTERNATIONAL CAREERS

Accounting Jobs Worldwide by Ian Collier. 1998. 190 pp. Vacation Work (U.K.). Available for $19.95 from Seven Hills. A guide to accounting and bookkeeping employment opportunities throughout the world.

*The Adventure of Working Abroad: Hero Tales From the Global Frontier by Joyce Sautters Osland. 1995. 269 pp. $25 from Jossey-Bass, 350 Sansome St., 5th Fl., San Francisco, CA 94104; 800-956-7739. Thirty-five American expatriates assigned abroad tell about the perils and opportunities of working in a new culture. Suggestions for employers and employees for preparation, support, and reentry.

*Best Resumes and CVs For International Jobs: Your Passport to the Global Job Market by Ronald L. Krannich and Wendy S. Enelow. 2002. $24.95 from Impact Publications. Definitive new guide includes over 100 examples of professionally produced international resumes and CVs for a variety of occupations and experience levels.

Building an Import/Export Business by Kenneth D. Weiss. 1997. $19.95 from John Wiley & Sons. Detailed guide to entering the import/export business.

*The Canadian Guide to Working and Living Overseas by Jean-Marc Hachey. 1998 edition. 1000 pp. U.S.$34, CAN$54.40. Save 30 percent on web order. Order by phone 800-267-0105, fax 800-221-9985; www.workingoverseas.com. Not only for Canadians, this directory provides one of the most comprehensive and up-to-date overview of work abroad and interna-

tional careers available. Profiles tend to focus on Canadian organizations, so U.S. readers should use this book along with one of the U.S. books recommended here. Covers every facet of international work and living overseas. Features 1,870 profiles, 1,670 web sites, and 700 resources in 58 bibliographies, web updates until the year 2003.

*Careers for Foreign Language Aficionados and Other Multilingual Types by Ned Seelye and Laurence Day. 1992. 128 pp. $14.95 hardcover/$9.95 paperback from VGM Career Horizons. Mainstream and offbeat jobs for those who want to use a foreign language. One of the better books on this topic. Includes profiles of various career fields.

**Careers in International Affairs edited by Maria Pinto Carland and Michael Trucano. 1996. 6th ed. 282 pp. $17.95 from Georgetown Univ. Press, P.O. Box 4866, Hampden Station, Baltimore, MD 21211-0866; 800-246-9606, fax 410-516-6998. A comprehensive overview of international career fields. Provides survey-based specifics on major organizations in all international sectors and insightful first-hand essays by practitioners. Developed by the Georgetown Univ. School of Foreign Service, this book is highly recommended for those serious about entering an international career.

Careers In International Business by Edward J. Halloran. 1996. 112 pp. $17.95 hardcover/$13.95 paperback from VGM Career Horizons. Overview of education for international business, and types of opportunities from start-ups to Fortune 500 companies.

Careers in International Law edited by Mark W. Janis and Salli A. Schwartz. 2001. 224 pp. $64.95 ($34.95 for students) from American Bar Association, ABA Orders and Billing Services, P.O. Box 10892, Chicago, IL 60611; 312-988-5522; www.abanet.org. Essays on how to plan for a career in international law by lawyers in the field. Also lists ABA-approved study abroad programs.

**The Complete Guide to International Jobs and Careers by Ronald L. Krannich and Caryl R. Krannich. 1993. 349 pp. $24.95 from Impact Publications. An excellent introduction to strategies and skills for landing an international job. Should be used with its companion volume, *The International Jobs Directory.*

Connected: Careers for the Future. This 30-minute video, anchored by Charlayne Hunter-Gault in 1997, features on-site interviews with African Americans, Latinos, Asian Americans, and Native Americans who are working in international settings. Available for $75 plus $4 s/h (must receive check before sending the video) from The Global Center, 1600 Broadway, Suite 700, New York, NY 10019; 212-246-0202, fax 212-246-2677; globaltv@igc.org, www.globalvision.org/globalvision.

Directory of American Firms Operating in Foreign Countries. 2001. $325 plus $13.50 s/h from Uniworld, 257 Central Park West, Suite 10A, New York, NY 10024-4110; 212-496-2448, fax 212-769-0413; www.uniworld.com. CD Rom 1-year subscription $975, 2-year subscription $1,500 plus s/h. Lists 2,500 American companies with 34,500 subsidiaries and affiliates in 190 foreign countries. Check your local library for this and dozens of other expensive specialized international directories that are beyond the scope of this bibliography. Impact Publications carries this and many more directories.

Directory of International Organizations by Hans-Albrecht Schraepler. 1997. 456 pp. Paperback, $29.95 from Georgetown Univ. Press, P.O. Box 4886, Hampden Station, Baltimore, MD 21211-0866; 800-246-9606, fax 410-516-6998. Comprehensive reference to international organizations.

*The Directory of Jobs and Careers Abroad by Elisabeth Roberts. 2000. 415 pp. Vacation Work (U.K.). $16.95 from Peterson's Guides. The only career guide with country-by-country (50) coverage of everything from professional fields to short-term and volunteer possibilities. British publication, but usually includes relevant U.S. organizations.

**The Directory of Websites for International Jobs by Ronald L. Krannich and Caryl R. Krannich. 2002. 147 pp. $19.95 from Impact Publications. Identifies more than 1,400 web sites for launching a global job search. The authors (renowned for their extensive career publications) also cover strategies for organizing an effective online job search.

Employment Abroad: Facts and Fallacies. Edited by Rachel Theus. 1993. $7.50 plus $3 shipping from the International Division of the U.S. Chamber of Commerce, 1615 H St. NW, Washington, DC 20062; 202-463-5460, fax 202-463-3114; www.uschamber.com/ International/default.htm. Booklet stresses the realities of international employment.

Global Health Directory 2000: U.S. Based Agencies Working in International Health. 2000. 108 pp (oversize). $70 ($35 members) postpaid from Global Health Council, 1701 K St. NW, Suite 600, Washington, DC 20006-1503; 202-833-5900, fax 202-833-0075; ghc@globalhealthcouncil.org, www.global healthcouncil.org. Lists organizations in international health fields by specialty and location. Includes a listing of those organizations which offer volunteer opportunities abroad. Career Network ($120 non-members, $60 members per year) is a job bulletin published by GHC.

**Global Resume and CV Guide by Mary Anne Thompson. 2001. Goinglobal.com; 251-342-9811. (Also available: Country Career Guides.) Going Global provides extensive career information for 23 countries on topics such as: job resources, resume/CV writing guidelines, industry trends, work permit/visa regulations, business resources, interviews, and cultural advice. In-country researchers have compiled more than 1,500 pages of content. More than 500 employment and career resources listed in each Country Career Guide. Global Career Advisors available to provide one-on-one career counseling.

The Good Cook's Guide to Working Abroad by Katherine Parry. 1998. Vacation Work (U.K.). Available for $19.95 from Seven Hills. Worldwide opportunities for chefs, servers, etc. in a variety of locales and establishments.

Great Jobs Abroad by Arthur H. Bell. 1997. 378 pp. McGraw-Hill. $14.95 from Impact Publications. Describes strategies for getting hired with corporations based in the U.S., in hopes of being assigned abroad. Tips on research, resumes, interviewing, and using the Internet. Most of this book consists of information available elsewhere in directories, such as U.S. corporations with international operations, U.S. embassies and consulates abroad, etc.

Great Jobs for Foreign Language Majors by Julie DeGalan and Stephen Lambert. 2001. 260 pp. VGM Career Horizons. $14.95. Covers careers in all sectors that use foreign languages either directly or as an auxiliary skill. Also discusses career strategies.

Health Professionals Abroad by Tim Ryder. 2000. 256 pp. Vacation Work. Available for $17.95 from Seven Hills. Book provides the first overview (from a British perspective) of working abroad in all areas of health care, from volunteer to career. Professions include doctors, nurses, pharmacists, physiotherapists, and others.

*****How to Get a Job in Europe: The Insider's Guide** by Robert Sanborn and Cheryl Matherly. 5th ed. 2001. 556 pp. $22.95 plus $3 shipping from Surrey Books, Inc., 230 E Ohio St., Suite 120, Chicago, IL 60611; 800-326-4430, fax 312-751-7334; www.surreybooks.com. Names and addresses of over 2,000 companies in 39 countries plus general suggestions on how to conduct an international job hunt.

*****Inside a U.S. Embassy: How the Foreign Service Works for America** edited by Karen Krebsbach. 1996. 98 pp. American Foreign Service Association. $5 from AFSA, 2101 E Street NW, Washington, DC 20037; 202-338-4045, fax 202-338-6820; www.afsa.org. In-depth, first-hand descriptions of what foreign service officers do. One chapter provides reports about individual's roles in international crises.

*****InterAction Member Profiles 2000-2001.** 400 pp. $60/$50 ($30 members). Up-to-date information on 160 U.S. private voluntary organizations in relief and development work. Details which agencies are doing what in which countries. Also: Monday Developments, $65 per year (individuals), the best biweekly job listing in this field. Available from Interaction, Publications Department, 1717 Massachusetts Ave. NW, Suite 801, Washington, DC 20036; 202-667-8227, fax 202-667-8236; publications@interaction.org, www.interaction.org.

*****International Job Finder** by Daniel Lauber. 2002. 200 pp. $19.95 plus $5.50 s/h from Planning/Communications, 7215 Oak Ave., River Forest, IL 60305; orders toll-free 888-366-5200; dl@jobfindersonline.com, www.jobfindersonline.com. Book by a leading career expert promises to provide useful information on the best sources for an international job search, including: specialty and trade periodicals, job hotlines, Internet job and resume databases, job placement services, directories, and salary surveys. Free updates to purchasers of this book will be available online, plus a free copy of *American Jobs Abroad.*

*****The International Jobs Directory: A Guide to Over 1001 Employers.** Ronald L. Krannich and Caryl R. Krannich. 1999. 334 pp. $19.95 from Impact Publications. This is a comprehensive source of hard-to-find information, tips on other resources including hundreds of web sites, and trends in international employment for Americans. It provides the most up-to-date and extensive overview of international employers from a U.S. perspective. Highly recommended. Should be used with its companion volume on strategies, *The Complete Guide to International Jobs and Careers.*

*****International Jobs: Where They Are and How to Get Them** by Eric Kocher with Nina Segal. 1999. 400 pp. Harper Collins. $17 plus 5% handling charge from Harper Collins, Direct Mail Dept, P.O. Box 588, Scranton, PA 18512, 800-331-3761; www.harpercollins.com. New, completely revised edition of a classic overview of international career fields and how to prepare for them, by authors associated with Columbia Univ.'s School of International and Public Affairs (SIPA). This is the best 1-volume introduction to international careers.

*****Jobs For People Who Love to Travel** by Ronald L. Krannich and Caryl R. Krannich. 1999. 285 pp. $15.95 from Impact Publications. Information for those who want to work the world before settling down, including but going far beyond the travel industry. Explores motivations; 50 myths about jobs involving travel; includes internet sites, teaching abroad, and internships.

Kennedy's International Directory of Executive Recruiters. 2002. $149. Kennedy Information 800-531-0007, 603-585-6544, fax 603-585-9555; bookstore@kennedyinfo.com, www.kennedyinfo.com. Identify recruiters around the globe with this comprehensive source profiling 1,627 firms in 67 countries. For those with considerable professional experience only.

New titles: Live and Work in Scotland (2001) by Nicola Taylor and **Live and Work Abroad: A Guide for Modern Nomads** (2001) by Huw Francis and Michelyne Callan. 300 plus pp each. Prices $18-20. (Available in the U.S. from Seven Hills). British series for long-term stays gives in-depth information on employment, residence, home buying, daily life, retirement, and starting a business. More useful for those on overseas assignment than for those looking for a job.

NAFSA's Guide to Education Abroad. William Hoffa and John Pearson, eds. 2nd ed., 1997. 494 pp. NAFSA, www.nafsa.org. $45 (nonmembers), $36 (members) plus $5 s/h. An indispensable manual for those working in the profession of study abroad advising and administration, published by the largest association in this field.

Opportunities in Foreign Language Careers by Wilga Rivers, Maguerite Duffy. 1998. 151 pp. $11.95 paperback from VGM Career Horizons. Harvard professor emerita discusses the use of languages as an auxiliary skill; also covers teaching languages and working as a translator or interpreter.

Opportunities in International Business Careers by Jeffry Arpan. 1996. 160 pp. $11.95 paperback from VGM Career Horizons. General overview of careers in international business, with discussion of types of international business degrees and specific business schools.

Special Career Opportunities for Linguists/Translators/Interpreters. Free pamphlet from U.S. Department of State, Office of Language Services, Interpreting Division, Room 2212, Washington, DC 20520; 202-647-3492, fax 202-647-3881.

Tax Guide for U.S. Citizens Abroad. (Publication 54). Free from Forms Distribution Center, P.O. Box 25866, Richmond, VA 23260. Available on the web at the U.S. Department of Treasury/IRS web site. www.irs.ustreas.gov/prod/forms_pubs/pubs/p549901.htm.

*U.S. Department of State. Application for the Foreign Service Officer Exam. This is the primary way to apply for a career position in U.S. diplomacy (U.S. citizens only). Application for the (free) exam is available from: U.S. Department of State, HR/REE SA-1, 2401 E. Street NW 5A, Washington DC 20522—but online application is preferred, via www.state.gov/employment. Register by August 2001 for next exam. To prepare, order Study Guide using form in exam application, or order it online.

*Work Worldwide: International Career Strategies for the Adventurous Job Seeker by Nancy Mueller. 2000. 231 pp. $14.95. Avalon Travel Publishing (available in bookstores). An in-depth look at strategies for finding international jobs. Covers topics such as researching, networking, resumes and job applications, interviewing, working abroad, and readjustment upon returning home. From an American perspective.

Working with Animals: The U.K., Europe, and Worldwide by Victoria Pybus. 1998. Vacation Work (U.K.). Available for $19.95 from Seven Hills. Opportunities for individuals to work with animals in zoos, nature preserves, and out in the wild.

Working with the Environment by Tim Ryder and Elizabeth Roberts. 2000. 254 pp. Vacation Work (U.K.). Available for $19.95 from Seven Hills. This book surveys international environmental work possibilities, from volunteer to career. Intended for a British audience, it provides in-depth coverage of Great Britain and Ireland, but also includes organizations (including U.S.-based ones) offering placements worldwide.

*The World on a String: How to Become a Freelance Foreign Correspondent by Alan Goodman and John Pollack. 1997. 198 pp. Henry Holt. $12.95 from most bookstores. Two experienced American freelancers based overseas give lots of first-hand advice on how to break into the field and survive financially.

INTERNATIONAL JOB LISTINGS

*The Guide to Internet Job Searching by Margaret Riley Dikel and Frances E. Roehm. 2000. 344 pp. $14.95 from VGM Career Horizons. The best book on job search resources on the internet, by the author of the respected web site The Riley Guide, www.rileyguide.com. Book includes 30 pages on international jobs web sites.

International Career Employment Weekly. Weekly listings of 500 international job openings (about 70 percent located overseas) organized by career fields: international education, foreign policy, international commerce, environment, development, program administration, health care. Most listings are for professionals, typically asking for 2 to 5 years or more experience. One section in each issue covers internships; these are nearly all in U.S. Subscriptions available from 6 issues ($26 individuals) to 49 issues ($149 individuals, $195 institutions) from International Employment Weekly, Carlyle Corporation, 1088 Middle River Rd., Stanardsville, VA 22973; 804-985-6444, fax 804-985-6828; Lisa@internationaljobs.org, www.internationaljobs.org.

International Employment Gazette. Each biweekly issue includes more than 400 overseas job openings by region and field. Good for private-sector business and technical jobs, although many of these require extensive experience, as well as teaching and volunteer positions. Subscriptions available from $40 for 3 months (6 issues); $75 for 6 months (13 issues); $95 for 1 year (26 issues) from International Employment Gazette, 423 Townes St., Greenville, SC 29601; 800-882-9188, fax 864-235-3369; intljobs@aol.com, www.intemployment.com. Also publishes *The International Directory of Employment Agencies and Recruiters,* which contains information on nearly 200 international recruiters, including complete contact information as well as the occupations and geographic regions for which they recruit. Available for $29.95, including shipping and handling.

*International Employment Hotline. Subscriptions available from $21 for 3 months to $129 for 2 years from International Employment Hotline, Carlyle Corporation, 1088 Middle River Rd., Stanardsville, VA 22973; 800-291-4618, fax 804-985-6828; Hotline@internationaljobs.org, www.internationaljobs.org. Monthly reports on who's hiring now in private companies, government, and nonprofit organizations. Lists entry-level and mid-career jobs located overseas and in the U.S. A bargain.

Job Registry, NAFSA: Association of International Educators. Free (email only) from NAFSA Job Registry, NAFSA: Association of International Educators, 1307 New York Ave. NW, 8th Fl., Washington, DC 20005-4701; 202-737-3699, fax 202-737-3657; jr@nafsa.org, www.nafsa.org. The best job listing for those interested in the field of international educational exchange.

The Key Web Sites

International Careers and International Job Listings

Selected and Reviewed by William Nolting

Web sites in this section list mainly career positions, most of which require previous experience. These sites rarely include listings of exchange programs for work abroad, internships, volunteering, or teaching abroad.
****Essential; *Outstanding and of broad interest.*
(I) Informational site with directories or databases
(P) Site for a specific work abroad program
(S) Scholarships or fellowships

ALL COUNTRIES, PROFESSIONS

(I) The Canadian Guide to Working and Living Overseas, www.workingoverseas.com by Jean-Marc Hachey. Essentially a promotional site for his book (see Print Resources above). You'll have to buy the book to benefit from the hundreds of web sites listed therein.

*(I) Career Mosaic, www.careermosaic.com. Links to thousands of international jobs, virtually all requiring previous experience. Engineering and business jobs predominate.

(I) Career Web, www.cweb.com lists thousands of professional, technical and managerial jobs in the private sector, virtually all requiring previous experience.

(I) Career Office of Brandeis Univ., www.brandeis.edu/hiatt includes sections for internships and international jobs.

**Wall Street Journal, www.careers.wsj.com. An outstanding site, though most jobs are in business and require previous experience. Check the "Working Globally" section for excellent articles about international careers.

*(I) Chronicle of Higher Education, thisweek.chronicle.com is the best source of job listings for the well-qualified academicians. Much of site accessible only to subscribers. Also check with discipline-specific professional associations.

(I) College Grad Job Hunter, www.collegegrad.com is a well-designed site

29

with lots of listings of internships, entry-level jobs, and jobs for those with experience; few if any overseas positions.

(I) Dave's ESL Café, www.eslcafe.com, ESL Cafe's Web Guide, Jobs: **www.eslcafe.com/search/Jobs** by Dave Sperling. Site has a staggering amount of well-organized information about teaching and other types of work abroad; links to hundreds of job databases of particular interest to teachers, college students, and liberal arts graduates. A highly recommended resource for anyone interested in working abroad.

*Dickinson College, Web Guide to International Employment, www.dickinson. edu/career/international.htm** by Dr. Kate Brooks. One of the few sites on the web to provide an overview of international careers and how to plan for one.

Escape Artist, Escape from America Overseas Jobs Pages, www.escapeartist.com/jobs/overseas1.htm by Roger Gallo. This site is one of the best overall for those looking for overseas jobs. It links to hundreds of job bank sites listed by country and region. There's also lots of other useful information for anyone working, studying, or living abroad, with one of the best online bookstores for this purpose.

(I) Impact Publications, www.impact publications.com by Ronald L. Krannich and Caryl R. Krannich. This publisher carries one of the most extensive selections of books on working abroad and international careers. The Krannichs' own *International Jobs Directory* lists hundreds of web sites and gives an outstanding overview of international jobs and careers.

(I) International Career Employment Center (Carlyle Corporation), www. internationaljobs.org. Not a jobs web site, this nonprofit organization publishes 2 of the best listings of international jobs: *International Career Employment Opportunities* (weekly) and *International Employment Hotline*. The site gives examples of their listings but does not list current openings.

(I) IRS: Tax Information for Aliens and U.S. Citizens Living Abroad, www.irs.ustreas. gov/prod/tax_edu/faq/faqg.html. Essential information from the U.S. Internal Revenue Service for anyone working abroad.

(P, I) JETAA Job Guide, cheno.com/job. Site by alumni of the JET (Japan Exchange and Teaching) Program, one of the largest of all work abroad programs, includes a guide to international career issues and links to job web sites listed by country.

Job Source Network, www.jobsourcenetwork. com/intl.html. Includes links to job web sites and businesses offering employment in many countries; most positions require previous experience.

Jobtrak, www.jobtrak.com. This site is associated with hundreds of U.S. college and university career offices (access by password), so may be useful for students and alumni.

*(I) Jobweb (National Association of Colleges and Employers), www.jobweb.org**. One of the more useful sites for college students and recent graduates, has sections for international jobs, **www.jobweb.org/catapult/interntl.htm** and internships and summer jobs, **www.jobweb.org/catapult/jintern.htm**.

(I) The Monster Board, www.monster.com. Jobs by international location: **http://international.monster.com**. Links to job databases for specific countries. Thousands of jobs listed, most for engineers or managers and virtually all requiring previous experience.

(I) Overseas Jobs Express, www.overseasjobs. com. British-based site claims to list vacancies that are open to non-citizens of the target country. It has databases of career positions for specific countries or regions.

(I,P) Peace Corps Career TRACK, www. peacecorps.gov/rpcv/careertrack. Even if you're not interested in the Peace Corps, this web site has lots of information about international work and careers.

(I) Purdue Univ.'s Center for International Career Opportunities, www.cco.purdue.edu/student/InternInternational.html. Two outstanding sets of links to web site job banks arranged by country or region. Check both sites, since they are not entirely identical.

(I) The Riley Guide: Resources for International Job Opportunities, www.dbm.com/jobguide/internat.html. Alternative Work and Career Options **www.dbm.com/jobguide/misc.html** by Margaret Dickel. Classic guide provides an excellent country-by-country compilation of employment resources on the web.

PROFESSION-SPECIFIC SITES

All Professions

(I) The Riley Guide, www.dbm.com/jobguide/jobs.html by Margaret Dickel. An excellent compilation of profession-specific resources on the web. See "Resources for Specific Industries and Occupations."

Academia

**(I) Chronicle of Higher Education,
http://thisweek.chronicle.com/jobs. The best
source of job listings for well-qualified
academians (most positions require a PhD or
professional degree). Much of site accessible
only to subscribers. Also check with
discipline-specific professional associations.

Arts, Architecture

(I, S) Arts International, www.arts
international.org. Grants, events, and an
excellent region-by-region compilation of arts
web sites worldwide.

(I) National Endowment for the Arts,
www.arts.endow.gov/partner/International.
html. The NEA's International Partnerships
Office site has links to organizations that may
consider applications for internships or may
offer funding for international activities.

Business

Most overseas job sites list plenty of business
jobs, though most require experience.

**(P) AIESEC-USA, www.us.aiesec.org.
AIESEC (from the French acronym for the
International Association of Students in
Economic and Business Management) is an
international student-run organization which
offers approximately 5,000 paid internships
each year in business and other fields in over
80 countries. Site has links to chapters worldwide. Note that application for AIESEC
internships is possible only through campus
chapters. Students who have no AIESEC chapter at their university should see the programs
listed in "Worldwide Short-Term Paid Work
Abroad Programs," all of which have great
opportunities for those interested in business.

**(I) Working Globally (Wall Street Journal),
www.careers.wsj.com. An outstanding site for
those interested in business. Most jobs require
previous experience.

*U.S. Chamber of Commerce: International
Division, www.uschamber.com International.
Not a jobs site, but an essential organization
for anyone interested in international trade.

Engineering and Computer Science

Most overseas job sites list plenty of engineering
and computer science jobs. Students of
engineering and computer science should
definitely look into the overseas internship
programs of the following organizations see
International Internships, Directory of Programs
(page 68) for more information:

**(P) American-Scandinavian Foundation,
www.amscan.org/training.htm

**(P) CDS International, www.cdsintl.org

**(P) IAESTE, www.aipt.org/iaeste.html

**(P) International Cooperative Education
Program, www.icemenlo.com

Environment and Natural Resources

*(I) Envirolink: The Online Environmental
Community, www.envirolink.org. Site has
links to hundreds of environmental
organizations. There are good links for finding
jobs and internships; however, the site does
want you to sign up and become a member
before using their resources.

*(I) SD Gateway (Sustainable Development),
http://sdgateway.net. Not only environmental,
this outstanding site will be of interest to
people in a number of fields, from policy and
international relations to development and
nongovernmental organizations. Searches
using "internship" or desired location bring up
plenty of internationally-related positions.

Health: Dentistry, Medicine, Nursing, Public Health, Social Work

*(I) American Medical Student Association,
www.amsa.org/gh.html. AMSA's site lists
overseas internship and volunteer programs,
including options for premed and other health
sciences—see International Health
Opportunities section. Site includes an
excellent online guide to fundraising, *Creative*
Funding Guide, useful for all students.

*(I) Global Health Council (formerly
National Council for International Health),
www.globalhealth.org. NCIH is one of the
main professional associations for U.S.
organizations working in international health.
It publishes (in hard copy only) *The Directory*
of Global Health which lists the health fields
and locations in which each organization is
active, and Internship and Volunteer
Opportunities. Web site includes an online
article on "Career Opportunities in Global
Health", information for students and
internships, and extensive links to member
organizations.

(P, S) Minority International Research
Training Grant (MIRT), www.nih.gov/fic/
programs/mirt.html. Program of the Fogarty
International Center, National Institutes of
Health, sends minority undergraduates and
medical students abroad to do health-related
research.

*(I) Social Work and Social Services Jobs
Online, Washington Univ., George Warren
Brown School of Social Work, http://gwbweb.
wustl.edu/jobs by Carol Doelling. This

outstanding site has specific job listings and automatic links to other job web sites. Search provisions make it easy to find jobs by type of work or location, including a good number of overseas listings.

Information and Library Science

(I) **Human-Computer Interaction Resources Network, www.hcirn.com.** A top resource for students and professionals in user interface design, usability and other HCI-related fields. Job bank includes some international jobs and site links to other international HCI employment sites.

*(I) **Library Job Postings on the Internet, Bridgewater State College, webhost.bridgew. edu/snesbeitt/libraryjobs.htm** by Sara Nesbitt. Best meta-site for library jobs is viewable by regions, including good international links. Well-organized and up-to-date.

International Educational Exchange

*NAFSA: Association of International Educators www.nafsa.org.** The largest and most helpful professional association for those interested in careers in international educational exchange. NAFSA publishes a hard-copy *Job Bulletin*, and also announces jobs through email lists which can be subscribed to from their web site.

*(I) **Overseas Teachers Digest & Expat Exchange For Americans www.overseasdigest. com.** This site contains valuable information for Americans working abroad. Be sure to see the Better Business Bureau article made available by this site, "Overseas Job Scams," http://overseasdigest.com/scams.htm.

International Relations, International Organizations, Public Policy

*(I) **APSIA (Association of Professional Schools of International Affairs) www.apsia. org.** These are some of the top graduate schools offering advanced degrees in preparation for international careers. Web site links to these schools, but offers little information about international work—try the Career Services offices of the individual schools.

(I, P) **U.S. Department of State, www.state.gov/www/careers. How to work for the U.S. diplomatic services. The State Department offers 1,000 internships annually, student work programs, and special fellowship/internship programs such as the Foreign Affairs Fellowship and Fascell Fellowship. Site also shows how to apply for career positions.

(I) **UN and International Organization Employment Information (site of the U.S. Department of State), www.state.gov/www/ issues/ioemployment.html.** An extensive overview of employment with the UN and other multigovernment international organizations, with links and job announcements.

(I) **The WWW Virtual Library: International Affairs Resources, www.etown.edu/v/.** While not designed as an employment site, this web site has the most comprehensive set of links for international relations.

(S, P) **Woodrow Wilson International Fellowship Foundation, www.woodrow.org/ public-policy.** Information on several multi-year scholarship-internship programs for students, especially women and minorities, interested in careers in international affairs.

Law

*(I, P) **American Bar Association, Section of International Law, www.abanet.org/intlaw.** The ABA's site offers an extraordinary number of links, as well as the International Legal Exchange Program.

(I, P) **International Law Students Association, www.ilsa.org.** ILSA administers an internship abroad program for law students. Site has many useful links.

(I) **Legal Study Abroad Headquarters, www.studylaw.com.** Comprehensive guide to study abroad and internships for law students.

Nongovernmental and Volunteer Organizations

(I) **Idealist, www.idealist.org. This site's claim of tens of thousands of organizations "under one roof" says it all. Excellent search provisions give useful results using "internship" or "volunteer." Also has lists of volunteer, internship and job opportunities. Search possible by country, type of work, and many other variables. The "browse by country" section lists organizations according to their work focus. Site includes organizations worldwide, not only U.S.-based ones.

(I) **InterAction: American Council for Voluntary International Action, www.inter action.org.** InterAction is a coalition of over 150 private, U.S.-based voluntary organizations engaged in international humanitarian efforts, including disaster relief, sustainable development, refugee assistance, advocacy, and education. Their web site includes links to their members and an online *Guide to Volunteer Opportunities* (most of which require professional skills). InterAction also publishes in hard copy *Global Work* (organizations seeking volunteers), *InterAction Member Profiles*, and *Monday Developments* (biweekly job announcements).

REGION-SPECIFIC SITES

Africa and Middle East

(I) **Africa South of the Sahara, African Studies Association, www-sul.stanford.edu/depts/ ssrg/africa/guide.html**. Karen Fung, ed. Site is not intended primarily for study and work abroad, but offers a huge number of links to web sites of organizations concerned with Africa, arranged by topics such as development, health, human rights. Try a search using "work," "internship," "volunteer," or "research."

(I) **African Studies, Univ. of Pennsylvania, www.sas.upenn.edu/African_Studies/AS.htm l**. Ali Ali-Dinar, ed. Site is not intended primarily for work abroad, but offers a huge number of links for information about Africa. Look on the Bulletin Board for the "Job and Grant Opportunities" section. A search on the main site using "internship" or "volunteer" produces useful results.

*(I) **AMIDEAST's Guide to Study Abroad, www.amideast.org**. Nonprofit site provides complete listing of study abroad and internship programs throughout the Middle East. AMIDEAST may consider applications for internships at its overseas offices.

*(I) **National Consortium for Study in Africa (based at Michigan State Univ.), www.isp.msu.edu/NCSA/volteer.htm**. Includes a section on volunteer, research and work in Africa.

(P, I) **Peace Corps, www.peacecorps.gov/ countries/africa.html. More U.S. citizens work in Africa through the Peace Corps than through any other organization.

*(I) **World Zionist Organization, www.wzo.org.il, Complete Guide to the Israel Experience www.israelexperience.org**. Directories of study and volunteer opportunities in Israel, along with offices in the U.S. that can provide information and advice.

Latin America and Canada

*(P) **AIPT, www.aipt.org/prog_cde.html**. Nonprofit AIPT's Career Development Program can assist university graduates who find their own position abroad with work permits for up to 18 months in Mexico.

(P) **COUNCIL Work in Canada and Costa Rica Programs, www.ciee.org. Work exchange program for students and recent graduates issues work permits and provides job search assistance.

(I) **HISPANIC Online, Career Links, www.hisp.com/carlinks.html** by *Hispanic* magazine. Lots of information about jobs and careers for Spanish speakers, though this site's job bank lists few overseas positions.

*(P) **International Cooperative Education Program, http://www.icemenlo.com**. ICEP and Foothill College offer paid summer internships in Argentina, Brazil, or Chile for students and recent graduates who have studied Spanish or Portuguese. Apply by January.

*(P) **IIE Internship in Mexico City, www.iie.org/latinamerica/admin.htm**. The Institute of International Education (IIE) offers 3-month paid internships at its advising center in Mexico City. Email to iie@profmexis.sar.net for details.

(I) **LatPro: Latin America's Professional Network, www.latpro.com**. Positions in Latin America and the U.S. for professionals who are bilingual in Spanish or Portuguese. All positions require previous experience.

(P, I) **Peace Corps, www.peacecorps.gov/ countries/americas.html. More U.S. citizens work in Latin American and the Caribbean through the Peace Corps than through any other organization.

*(I) **South American Explorer's, www.sam explo.org**. Nonprofit organization produces a guide to volunteering in South America (hard copy only, but inexpensive). Site includes links to volunteer organizations as well as employment opportunities.

*(I) **Univ. of Pittsburgh, Center for Latin American Studies, www.pitt.edu/~clas/ english/finassist.htm**. This Center's "Guide to Financial Assistance and Internships" has good information for graduate students and graduates, though few overseas listings.

Asia

(P) **AIPT, www.aipt.org/prog_cde.html**. Nonprofit AIPT's Career Development Program can assist university graduates who find their own position abroad with work permits for up to 18 months in Japan and Malaysia.

*(I) **Asia-Net, www.asia-net.com** lists internships and professional jobs for people who speak Japanese, Chinese, or Korean as well as English. Has search categories for internships and first full-time positions.

*(I) **Association for Asian Studies,
www.aasianst.org**. Professional association
web site includes sections on employment
listings, study abroad, and grants and
fellowships. Comprehensive links to other sites
on all regions of Asia.

(P, I) **JETAA Job Guide, www.jet.org/job.
Site by alumni of the JET (Japan Exchange
and Teaching) Program, one of the largest of
all work abroad programs. Site includes a
guide to international career issues and links
to job web sites listed by country.

*(P) **International Cooperative Education
Program, www.icemenlo.com** offers
internships in Japan, Singapore and Malaysia
for students and recent graduates who have
studied Japanese or Chinese.

**(P, I) **Peace Corps, www.peacecorps.gov/
countries/asia.html, www.peacecorps.gov/
countries/pacific.html**. More U.S. citizens
work in Central, South and Southeast Asia
and the Pacific through the Peace Corps than
through any other organization.

(I) **Singapore Economic Development Board,
www.sebd.com.sq/index1.html**. The Singapore
government's site for career jobs in Singapore
lists positions mainly for engineers and
managers.

Australia and New Zealand

(I) **Australian Job Search, http://job-
search.dewrsb.gov.au**. Government site lists
jobs by occupational category. "Traineeships"
indicate entry-level or internship positions.

**(P) **BUNAC Work in Australia and New
Zealand Program, www.bunac.org**. Work
exchange program for students and recent
graduates issues work-permits and provides
job search assistance.

**(P) **Camp Counselors USA, Outbound
Program, www.campcounselors.com/
americans.html**. Work exchange program for
students and non-students issues work
permits and provides job search assistance
for Australia and (students only) New
Zealand.

**(P) **COUNCIL Work in Australia and New
Zealand Programs, www.ciee.org**. Work
exchange program for students and recent
graduates issues work-permits and provides
job search assistance.

(I) **Employment Opportunities in Australia
www.employment.com.au**. Jobs mostly for
experienced professionals, except for
"graduates" section—where most listings
specify Australian residents.

Central and Eastern Europe and the Former USSR

(P) **AIPT, www.aipt.org/prog_cde.html**.
Nonprofit AIPT's Career Development
Program can assist university graduates who
find their own position abroad with work
permits for up to 18 months in Hungary and
the Slovak Republic.

(I) **American Association of Teachers of
Slavic & East European Languages, http://
clover.slavic.pitt.edu/~aatseel**. Professional
association web site includes internships,
scholarships and career information related to
Central and East European Studies.

*(I) **Indiana University, Russian & East
European Institute—Employment Resources,
www.indiana.edu/~reeiweb/indemp.html**.
Site has extensive section on employment, as
well as sections on academic programs (both
in the U.S. and abroad), language programs,
scholarships, and links to dozens of centers for
Russian and East European studies.

**(P, I) **Peace Corps, www.peacecorps.gov/
countries/europe.html**. More U.S. citizens
work in Central and Eastern Europe, Russia,
and the NIS through the Peace Corps than
through any other organization.

*(I) **Univ. of Washington, Center for Civil
Society, http://solar.rtd.utk.edu/~ccsi/
announce.htm, http://solar.rtd.utk.edu/
~ccsi/jobs**. Site has extensive listings of
internships, volunteer, and career positions
throughout Russia and the Newly Independent
States (i.e. entire former USSR) and facilitates
NGO development throughout the region.

Western Europe

(P) **AIPT, www.aipt.org/prog_cde.html.
Nonprofit AIPT's Career Development
Program assists university graduates who find
their own position abroad with work permits
for up to 18 months in Austria (11 months
max.), Britain (12 months max.), Finland,
France, Germany, Ireland, Sweden,and
Switzerland. Current students have access to
these and other countries through the
AIPT/IAESTE Student Exchanges program.

*(I, P) **American-Scandinavian Foundation,
www.amscan.org/work.htm**. Web site
includes a comprehensive directory of study,
language, and work abroad programs
throughout Scandinavia. ASF offers placements for technical internships and teaching
English. ASF can also provide work permits
for those who find their own internships.

**(I) **British Information Services,
www.britain-info.org**. British government site

provides official information on employment options for foreigners in Britain, with links to work and internship programs.

**(P) BUNAC Work in Britain Program, www.bunac.org. Work exchange program for students and recent graduates issues work-permits and provides job search assistance.

**(P) Council Work in Ireland, France, and Germany Programs, www.ciee.org. Work-exchange program for students and recent graduates issues work-permits and provides job search assistance.

*(P) CDS International, www.cdsintl.org. Government supported nonprofit organ-ization offers paid study-internship programs in Germany for students, graduates, and pro-fessionals. Site provides program information and listings of current internship openings, plus links for information about Germany.

(I, S) German Academic Exchange Service (DAAD), www.daad.org. Deutscher Akademischer Austauschdienst (DAAD) site provides official information about study abroad (direct enrollment), degree study, and scholarships for Germany. Site also has information about the Deutscher Bundestag/ Humboldt Univ. of Berlin Internship Program and an internship program for law graduates.

**(P) International Cooperative Education Program, www.icemenlo.com. ICEP offers paid summer internships in Switzerland, Germany, Belgium, or Finland for students and recent graduates who have studied the appropriate language: German, French, Italian, Finnish, Dutch, Japanese, or Chinese. Apply by January.

**(P) InterExchange, www.inter-exchange.org. Nonprofit organization offers low-cost placements for internships and work abroad in several Western and Eastern European countries.

TEACH AND TRAVEL WITH TRANSWORLD SCHOOLS

DUBAI . WESTERN · EUROPE . SHANGHAI . SANTIAGO . PRAGUE . MILAN . PARIS

ISTANBUL . MIDDLE · EAST . JAPAN . SOUTH · AMERICA . BRAZIL . VIETNAM

Approved and Accredited Internationally Recognized Certificate in Teaching English to Speakers of Other Languages – CTESOL

> California State Approved (BPPVE) and ACCET Accredited CTESOL Courses

> Highest quality courses at lowest tuition

> Proven job placement record both throughout USA and overseas, including W. Europe

> Courses include Teaching Children and Adults, Business English, and Computer Assisted Language Learning

> On-site practical teaching with foreign students

> Expert Instructors with overseas teaching and training experience

> Bi-monthly start dates, full and part-time, and distance learning courses available

> Maximum 14 trainees per class, 6 per group

> Job preparation courses and lifetime access to job database and placement

> No second language, teaching or computer experience required

> Beautiful school, conveniently located in downtown San Francisco

701 Sutter Street, 2nd Floor,
San Francisco, CA 94109 USA
Tel: 1-415-928-2835 or 1-800-588-8335
Fax: 1-415-928-0261
email: transwd@aol.com

Visit our website: www.transworldschools.com

CHAPTER 2

SHORT-TERM JOBS AND INTERNSHIPS FOR STUDENTS AND RECENT GRADUATES

The best time to seek work overseas and to prepare for an international career is while you are a student or soon after graduation. Numerous special work abroad programs are available only to students and recent graduates up to around age 30.

Work Abroad Overview
Overseas Jobs and How to Find Them

By William Nolting

You may be considering an overseas work experience for many reasons: an adventure, a chance to gain in-depth knowledge of another culture and of yourself, an inexpensive way to improve foreign language proficiency, or as preparation for an international career.

Keep in mind what you want from working abroad: Will an unpaid internship working with Americans in a U.S. embassy do as much for your French as working in an ice cream shop in Paris? Or would the State Department internship be the best choice if your long-term goal is an international career?

Also, keep in mind how extraordinarily difficult it is to be hired into a career position abroad unless you have a scarce skill and professional experience.

Visas and Work Permits

One major obstacle to working abroad is the law. All countries require special permission for foreigners to either work or reside for long periods of time. Whereas short-term tourists sometimes do not need a visa and student visas are granted relatively easily, work permit visas are normally available only through application by an employer who has offered you a job. The employer must show that you have unique skills and abilities not possessed by local citizens.

This is expensive and time-consuming to prove, so most employers, who are subject to heavy fines if they hire illegally, will not offer a job to a foreigner who does not possess a work permit. Work exchange programs are one of the few legal ways around this. Note: it is also possible to work illegally; i.e., without a work permit. Such jobs may turn up in restaurants and agriculture as well as in teaching English. We cannot recommend working illegally because it puts you at risk of immediate deportation, possible fines, lowest wages (or no wages at all), and lack of legal protection or insurance in case of injury or illness.

Study, Work, and the Cost of Living Abroad

Study abroad programs provide logistical assistance and a structured learning environment, which can be especially valuable if you are going abroad for the first time. They provide the quickest way to achieve fluency in a foreign language, a prerequisite for many international careers. For those interested in working abroad, the study abroad program can also provide a secure base from which to explore job possibilities and make contacts with potential employers. Credit towards your degree is available as long as you check with the proper offices before going.

Cost ranges from about the same to considerably more than the cost of study at home. If you don't need the academic credit towards a degree, study abroad might simply be impractical. Scholarships for undergraduate study abroad are fairly rare. Even fewer scholarships support work abroad (except for graduate students), and students report more success with fundraising through family, friends, and hometown associations (such as Rotary, Kiwanis, etc.).

Work abroad *can* be combined with study (before, during, or after), helping you to defray the cost and gain experience in a very different environment from academia. But two caveats:

1. **Do not expect to finance study with part-time work.** At best, it can provide extra spending money. Savings can usually be accumulated more quickly by working in the U.S.

2. **You must carefully investigate whether and under what circumstances work is allowed for American students in a particular country.** Most countries do not allow students to work and may deport those who work without a work permit. However, student work-permit programs for some popular European destinations allow work in combination with study. You have to enter the country with a special work permit provided by the work exchange program, which can only be obtained by applying in advance. Finally, a few countries (e.g., Australia, Britain, and some locales in Germany) permit part-time work for students who are directly enrolled in local universities. Other countries (e.g., France) will generally not allow students to work unless they participate in a special student work exchange program.

Study and Work Abroad After Graduation

Fulbright, Rotary, and other scholarships are available to support a year of overseas study (not necessarily for a degree) after graduation. These prestigious awards and the contacts they open up are often stepping-stones to international careers.

Direct enrollment in a foreign university is another postgraduate possibility. Tuitions for direct enrollment are low in some countries but relatively high in Britain, Ireland, and Australia. Student status may allow you to work part time or during vacations in some countries. However, the main disadvantage of attempting to "work your way" through an overseas university is that you may find yourself marking time, neither making headway towards a degree nor progress in a career. You also want to be sure that a degree earned from an overseas university would be recognized as well in the U.S. as one from a U.S. university.

Types of Work Abroad Programs

Numerous special programs offer placements in specific jobs (paid or unpaid) along with a work permit or assist you in procuring a short-term work permit and help with a job search once overseas. Work abroad programs are limited in duration, lasting from two weeks for short-term volunteer programs, to a summer or six months, or as long as one or two years for programs for teaching abroad or long-term volunteering such as the Peace Corps. There are four types of work abroad programs.

1. International Internships. Internships offer the most direct connection to international careers. Available in a wide range of locations and disciplines, internships are equaled in this respect only by volunteer options. Internships for academic credit are plentiful (they charge tuition); paid internships are rare. "International" internships may be located abroad or in the U.S. with international organizations. Typical duration is a summer or semester.

2. Short-Term Paid Work Abroad. Typical types of short-term paid work abroad include restaurant work, temping, childcare (au pair) and farm work, though enterprising students do find work of a professional nature. (For a list of employers for short-term jobs and au pair placements, see Chapter 3.) Short-term paid work abroad programs for students or recent graduates offer the best chance for you to earn your way abroad; however, there are up-front costs for program fees, airfare, and initial spending money. These programs are located primarily in Europe, Australia, New Zealand, and Canada, with a small number of programs offering other locations. The typical duration is up to six months.

3. Volunteering Abroad. Volunteers usually work and live together with ordinary local citizens. Types of work range from archaeology digs to social services in locations worldwide. Volunteering is excellent career preparation for those interested in work in developing countries or careers with non-governmental organizations. (See Chapter 4.)

4. Teaching Abroad. Teaching English as a Foreign Language (TEFL or ESL) is one of the most accessible options for long-term (one to two years) work abroad. (See Chapter 5.) Most programs require a college degree. Jobs are typically in Asia or Eastern Europe (few such jobs are available in Western Europe for Americans, with the notable exceptions of Austria, Finland, and France). Experience in tutoring or teaching is recommended. Additional teaching abroad options are available for those with teaching qualifications at the K-12 or university level. (See Chapter 6.)

Work Abroad Calendar: When to Apply

Internships. September-November for study abroad internships for winter term. This is also the best time to contact organizations if you are lining up your own job. November 1: Deadline for summer U.S. State Department internships. December: IAESTE, American-Scandinavian Foundation (engineering and sciences), CDS Congress-Bundestag Program (Germany). January-April: deadlines for study abroad internships for spring, summer, fall terms. March 1: Deadline for State Department internships for fall semester. July 1: Deadline for State Department internships for winter semester.

Short-Term Paid Work Abroad. Apply in the fall term for International Cooperative Education Program paid summer internships. Apply three to four months in advance for InterExchange and other placement programs. Apply one month in advance for BUNAC and CIEE Work Permit programs.

Volunteering Abroad. Apply at least nine months in advance for Peace Corps and other long-term volunteer programs; apply in March-May for short-term "work-camps."

Teaching English Abroad. Apply at least nine months in advance for Peace Corps; September-October for Fulbright English Teaching Assistantship positions; December for major TESL programs in Asia, including JET, Princeton-in-Asia, Earlham College; January-March for various other TESL programs, but best to apply early.

Short-Term Paid Work Abroad

Exchange Programs for Students and Recent Graduates

By William Nolting

The bad news about working abroad is that you can't just hop a plane to any country and start looking for a paid job. To work would be illegal without a permit, which you cannot acquire without a job offer, and—Catch 22—very few employers will offer you a job if you don't already have a work permit. The good news is that a number of organizations can help you cut the red tape and acquire a legal work permit or place you in a job.

If you're looking for an inexpensive way to experience total cultural immersion, or to simply earn your way through an adventure abroad, here's a good place to start. The emphasis is on exchange, since your participation in most of these programs enables someone from abroad to have the equivalent experience in the U.S.

The two main program types are 1) the CIEE and BUNAC Work Abroad exchanges, which enable students to get a work permit in advance, then look for a job on site with assistance from overseas offices, and 2) overseas job placement programs offered by a number of U.S.-based work exchange organizations.

Work Permit Programs for Students

Over 6,000 U.S. students and recent graduates work abroad each year in programs administered by the Council on International Educational Exchange (CIEE) and BUNAC, the most popular option for working abroad and one of the few which does not require applying far in advance. You can get a work permit without a job offer, you can work at any job you find, and the application process is non-competitive.

BUNAC or CIEE can get you a work permit—otherwise virtually impossible for Americans to obtain—any time of the year for Australia, Britain, New Zealand, Canada (BUNAC only), Ireland, France, China, Ghana, Brazil, and Germany (CIEE only). Without a work permit, you could only work illegally, seriously limiting your options. The cost of the program ranges from $250 (for Britain) to $500.

To be eligible, you must be a U.S. citizen (or permanent resident) and an undergraduate or graduate student studying in the U.S. and taking at least eight credit hours. Non-students under age 30 may participate in the Australia and New Zealand programs. (Student status as defined by the program continues for one semester after you leave school: spring and summer graduates have until the following December 31 to enter the country in which they will work, and December graduates have until June 30.) Participants in the France and Germany programs must have had two years' study of the appropriate language.

This is a do-it-yourself program—you find your own job and apartment using listings provided by the overseas program office. The average time for finding jobs is around one week, depending upon the country. The initial investment includes the program fee, roundtrip airfare, and enough money ($1,000), to tide you over until you get the first paycheck. Most students report that they can cover their expenses.

The typical CIEE/BUNAC job is in restaurant, hotel, clerical, or sales work—but even these ordinary jobs provide a total immersion experience in the daily life of another culture, resulting in cross-cultural insights, friendships, and personal growth.

According to BUNAC and CIEE, less than a quarter of their participants arrange for a job or an interview in advance—not necessary for ordinary jobs such as pub and temp work, but a good strategy for getting a career-related internship.

As explained elsewhere, internships are available through special organizations such as AIESEC or IAESTE (see below), as well as universities, but these are competitive, have early deadlines, or require paying tuition in the case of "academic" credit-granting internships.

Career-Related Jobs

Rather than paying for someone else to place them, many students use their own initiative, combined with work permits from BUNAC or CIEE, to find a career-related job. You can email firms well in advance to request an interview upon your arrival. Try to be neither too general nor overly specific in your work objective. Send a one-page resume outlining your education, work experience, computer skills or organizational talents, and interests. Include a cover letter clearly stating that you will arrive with a valid student exchange work permit. Even if you have been unable to arrange for an interview or job in advance, contact the company again by phone just before or after you arrive and try again—chances are good that your persistence will be rewarded.

Come prepared. Bring your resume and references from previous employers or professors and a suit for interviews.

For applications and more information, contact: CIEE Work Abroad, 633 3rd Ave., 20th Fl., New York, NY 10017; 888-COUNCIL, fax 212-822-2649; info@councilexchanges.org, http://us.councilexchanges.org. BUNAC USA, P.O. Box 430, Southbury, CT 06488; 800-GO BUNAC or 203-264-0901, fax 203-264-0251; wib@bunacusa.org, www.bunac.org.

Accommodations. Take advantage of optional room reservation services offered by most programs. Otherwise, reserve a youth hostel ($15-$30 per night) in advance. Contact the American Youth Hostel headquarters 202-783-6161; hiayhserv@hiayh.

org, www.hiayh.org to find out how. You should find an apartment after you get your job to minimize commuting time. Some jobs include housing.

Insurance. Most programs require you to have your own health insurance. The International Student ID (ISIC) card, available from STA Travel, 800-777-0112; www.statravel.com for $22, provides travel discounts and minimal health insurance. We recommend everyone get one. More comprehensive coverage is available from special agencies starting at $60 per month, essential if you have no other health insurance. Agencies include HTH Worldwide (800-242-4178, www.hth worldwide.com), Seabury and Smith (800-282-4495, www.gateway.com), or Wallach and Company (800-237-6615, www.wallach.com).

Study and Work. If you are going on a study abroad program, you may be able to combine it with a BUNAC or CIEE permit, allowing work before, during, or sometimes after studying. However, don't expect to finance your studies this way. American students studying in Britain for more than six months are officially allowed to work part-time during the term and full-time during vacations. Those studying for only one semester still need the BUNAC work permit to work legally. In Britain you can only work before or during study abroad (i.e. during the first six months when you are in the country), but not after.

Getting a work permit overseas. This is nearly impossible unless you already have a job offer. Get the work permit before you leave, or use one of the job placement programs below which also arrange for work permits.

Other Work Permit Programs

The BUNAC/CIEE work permits cannot be extended or renewed, but the following organizations may be able to assist with a different permit—if you already have a job offer.

The Association for International Practical Training (AIPT, Work Exchanges, 10400 Little Patuxent Pkwy., Columbia, MD 21044-3510; 410-992-3924; iaeste@aipt. org, www.aipt.org). AIPT can get you a permit for up to 18 months for current students or college graduates to work in dozens of countries.

Work permit and placement programs are also offered by the **American-Scandinavian Foundation** and **CDS** (see below).

Placement Programs

If you would you rather be placed in a job than find your own, or if you want a certain type of job, these programs may make it easier. Agencies should be willing to furnish you with names and telephone numbers of past participants.

AIESEC, 734-662-1690, fax 734-662-0126; aiesec.info@umich.edu, www.aiesecmichigan. org. AIESEC is a worldwide student-run organization which generates over 6,000 paid internships each year in nearly 90 countries. The internships range from those with a business or technical focus to teaching English. You can only apply through campus chapters.

American-Scandinavian Foundation, 15 E. 65th St., New York, NY 10021; 212-879-9779; fax 212-249-3444; trainscan@amscan.org, www.amscan.org. Offers placements in Finland for teachers of English as a foreign language. Teachers work in public schools, private institutes, or private firms. Time commitment is from 2 months to an academic year. Eligibility: native English-speaking U.S. university students or graduates age 21-30 who have completed at least their junior year in college. Salary: FIM5,000-8,000 per month

($900-1,550). Housing is arranged but participants are responsible for rent ($200-300 per month). Application deadline: March 1. Application fee is $50, plus a $200 refundable deposit when position accepted. ASF also offers placements for engineering, business, and agriculture students throughout Scandinavia (apply by January 1). ASF can also assist with work permits for those who have a job offer.

Camp Counselors USA, Outbound Program, 2330 Marinship Way, Suite 250, Sausalito, CA 94965; 800-999-2267, fax 415-339-2744; outbound@campcounselors.com, www.camp counselors.com. Offers programs in Australia and New Zealand which are similar to those of BUNAC and Council. The Australian program requires student status while the New Zealand program does not. Program fee is $365. An "educational work-travel program" in camps and orphanages all across Russia and countries of the former Soviet Union. Placement in camp with full room and board and a symbolic stipend (not enough to cover program fee). Minimum requirements include experience with children, knowledge of the appropriate foreign language desirable but not always required, and teaching/coaching experience. Fee of $1,600 includes roundtrip airfare from New York, visa, travel insurance, orientations (not training) in New York and Moscow, and support during the 4- or 8-week program. Application deadline: April 1.

CDS International, Inc., 871 United Nations Plaza, 15th Fl., New York, NY 10017-1814; 212-497-3500; fax 212-497-3535; info@cdsintl.org, www.cdsintl.org. CDS offers many different paid internship programs in Germany, Singapore, and Turkey (unpaid internships are also offered in Argentina). For programs in Germany, at least some knowledge of German is a prerequisite upon start of the program. Check the CDS web site for most updated listings of program offerings.

Congress-Bundestag Youth Exchange for Young Professionals. Contact CDS International, 871 United Nations Plaza, New York, NY 10017; 212-497-3500, fax 212-497-3535; info@cdsintl.org, www.cdsintl.org. Consists of 2 months of intensive German, 4 months attending a technical school, and a 5-month internship. All expenses paid; no application fee. Specified age of participants is 18-24. Application deadline is mid-December for the following academic year. 60 participants are selected.

• **The Robert Bosch foundation Fellowship Program** offers a 9-month professional internship program to individuals with graduate degrees in the fields of Business Administration, Economics, Law, Political Science, Public Administration/Policy, and Mass Communication/Journalism. All expenses paid; no application fee. Application deadline is mid-October for the program beginning the following September. Twenty participants are selected. Internship Program is for seniors or graduates and arranges paid internships for 6-24 months in Germany or Singapore. Participation fee for the 6-month program is $500. Summer Internship Program in Germany offers paid 3-month internships to juniors, seniors, and recent graduates. Administration fee for the program is $500. Summer Internship program in Turkey offers paid 3-month internships to juniors, seniors, and recent graduates. Administration fee for the program is $500. Summer internship Program in Argentina offers unpaid 3-month internships to juniors, seniors, and recent graduates or a combination 1-month Spanish language course followed by a 2-month internship. Administration fees are $700 and $1,165 respectively.

Center for Interim Programs. West of the Mississippi: Sam Bull, Director, Western Branch Office, 2143 Pine Street #1, Boulder, CO 80302; 303-447-8320, fax 303-447-3765; SamuelBull@aol.com. East of the Mississippi: Center for INTERIM Programs, P.O. Box 2347, Cambridge, MA 02238; 617-547-0980; fax 617-661-2864; Interimcip@aol.com, www.interim programs.com. The Center for INTERIM Programs was founded in 1980 to match clients' interests with a database of over 3,000 non-academic but structured opportunities worldwide (from art to zoology, Australia to Zimbabwe) many of which provide room and board. They have arranged such opportunities for some 3,000 people between the ages of 16 and 70 over the past 15 years. INTERIM charges a $1,500 basic fee, plus program fees.

IAESTE, info@iaeste.org, www.iaeste.org. Offers paid internships in 70+ countries for students of engineering and science. Application deadline January 1. Lowest fees of any placement program.

InterExchange, 161 6th Ave., New York, NY 10013; 212-924-0446, fax 212-924-0575; workabroad@interexchange.org, www.interex change.org. InterExchange was founded in 1971 and has official non-profit status. InterExchange offers the following kinds of placements. Contact the program for more specifics.

• **English Teaching in Spain or Bulgaria.** Those

with experience teaching or tutoring English as a foreign language are strongly preferred (volunteer experience usually available in your community). Only room and board or small stipend provided in Spain and Italy. Apply at least 3 months prior to desired starting date. Fees: $400 (Spain) or $500 (Bulgaria).

• **Work in rural Australia or Norway.** Work 2-3 months year round on family-run farms. Stipend is provided. Apply at least 4 months before preferred starting date. Fees: $400 (Norway), $795 (Australia).

• **Au Pair.** Placements in France, Germany, and Spain for those with some knowledge of the language of the host country. No foreign language necessary for placements in the Netherlands. Women only eligible for most positions. Summer placements possible in Spain but at least a 6-month commitment wanted elsewhere. Apply at least 3 months prior to desired starting date ($400).

• **Unpaid internships in London and France.** Apply four months before preferred starting date. Placement fee $1,650 (London) or $1,000 (France).

• **Paid summer jobs in Belgium.** Apply 4 months before preferred starting date. Placement fee $700. Applicants must have working knowledge of French or Dutch/Flemish.

• **Summer Camp Counselors in Russia, Latvia, Lithuania, Belarus, or Ukraine.** Basic knowledge of Russian or relevant language required. Placement fee is $400.

International Cooperative Education Program, Drs. Guenter and Ellen Seefeld, 15 Spiros Way, Menlo Park, CA 94025; 650-323-4944. Please call after 10 a.m. Eastern time, fax 650-323-1104; ICEmenlo@aol.com, www.icemenlo.com. In existence since 1971, this program places several hundred students each summer into paid, not-for-credit internships. This program is more structured than most and seems to take care to provide individualized placements. Some of the jobs pay well enough to allow modest savings, and others pay enough to cover living expenses. ICEP internships last 2-4 months and are offered in Switzerland, Germany, France (Bordeaux region), Belgium, Argentina, Chile, Japan, and Singapore. Type of work ranges from ordinary jobs to demanding internships in retail sales, supermarkets, hotels/restaurants, agriculture, offices, hospitals, banks, computer science, engineering and many more areas. Applicants must have studied the appropriate foreign language for at least one academic year—note that ICEP's director interviews you in the foreign language! Relevant foreign languages include German, French, Italian, Dutch, Finnish, Chinese or Japanese. Participants must be between the ages of 18-30. Citizens of most countries are eligible. Best to apply in the fall, or no later than February. Fees: After the initial interview, there is a $200 fee for the extensive application process. The application fee is refunded if no placement can be found, but you forfeit the fee if you turn down a placement offered to you. There is a $600 participation fee if you accept the placement (i.e. fees total $800). Airfare, health insurance, and $800 reserve are the participant's responsibility.

Internships International, Judy Tilson, Director, 1612 Oberlin Rd., Raleigh, NC 27608; Dec-May: 919-832-1575; Jun-Nov: 207-443-3019; intintl@aol.com, www.studyabroad.com. A nonprofit program, directed by an experienced study abroad administrator. Unpaid, not-for-credit internships are offered in London, Paris, Stuttgart, Florence, Dresden, Dublin, Budapest, Bangkok, Shanghai, Glasgow, Moscow, Melbourne, and Santiago from 6 weeks to 6 months, mostly in summer. Open only to college graduates and graduate students. The $700 fee ($800 for London, $1,000 for Dublin) is refunded if satisfactory placement cannot be found. Placements are highly individualized, and applicants must submit a detailed statement of what they want.

Short-Term Volunteer Projects ("Workcamps")

Volunteer projects known as workcamps, which last two to four weeks, usually in the summer, and "pay" only room and board, provide invaluable opportunities for international experience. Hundreds are available, located in most European countries, as well as a few in Africa, Asia, and Latin America. You can work for social causes—unlikely as a paid job. And workcamps are group experiences, often with nearly every participant coming from a different country. The best time to apply is in early April, when you'll have the greatest choice. Student status not required.

Registration fees are typically around $200-$300 but much more for locations in Africa or Asia. Americans can register for workcamps through:

• **Council International Volunteer Projects**, 205 E 42nd St., New York, NY 10017-5706; 888-COUNCIL; info@ciee.org, **www.ciee.org**. Over 600 projects in more than 20 countries. Fee typically $300.

• **Operation Crossroads Africa,** 475 Riverside Dr., Suite 1366, New York, NY 10027; 212-870-2106; oca@igc.apc.org, **www.igc.org/oca**. Seven-week volunteer projects in Africa and Brazil; $25 application fee, $3,500 program fee (includes airfare), which many participants fundraise.

• **SCI-IVS**, 5474 Walnut Level Rd., Crozet, VA 22932; 804-823-1826, fax 804-823-5027; sciivsusa@igc.apc.org, **www.wworks.com/~sciivs**. Fee typically $125.

• **Volunteers for Peace** (VFP), 43 Tiffany Rd., Belmont VT 05730, 802-259-2759, fax 802-259-2922; vfp@vfp.org, **www.vfp.org**. Over 1,200 projects offered in more than 65 countries. Fee typically $200.

For further exploration of short-term work abroad options, see back issues of *Transitions Abroad* magazine and Susan Griffith's classic book, *Work Your Way Around the World* (available from Peterson's Guides, 800-338-3282).

Work Abroad Checklist

To help ensure a succesful job search, follow this checklist compiled by Jane Cary for her students at Amherst College.

Before Leaving

• Make a list of alumni living in the city and country where you'll be.

• Talk with students who are back from your future study site. Did any work or perform an internship while there? How did they arrange it?

• Read the sections of all work abroad books that mention the country or city where you'll be.

• Read back issues of *Transitions Abroad* magazine.

While Abroad

• Maintain a "contacts" notebook. Include the name, address, phone number, email address of every interesting professional you meet.

• Contact alumni. Meet them at their place of business or socially. Express your interest in staying on after your program of study ends, or your interest in returning after graduation.

• Check the local Yellow Pages and the daily paper want ads for future reference.

• Look for schools that teach in English. What qualifications do their teachers have?

• If in a homestay, take every opportunity to meet the family's friends and extended family. Network.

• Practice the local language. Meet the "natives" in all walks of life, constantly. Read the local and national papers and periodicals.

• Introduce yourself to older Americans living locally. Learn about where they are or were employed and how they obtained their positions.

• Pay attention to living costs of the country and figure out how much money you would need.

• Have a standby friend at home pick up and save summer job and internship information for you.

• If graduate study in that country is an option, get information while you're there.

After Returning

• Visit your Career Center early and often to learn about its services for job-hunting seniors; attend all relevant job-seekers workshops.

• Find out if firms with offices abroad recruit on campus. Don't be distressed to learn that you might have to work in the U.S. first.

• Ascertain whether you will need a higher degree to obtain the job you want. What graduate entrance exams are required? Where in the U.S. or abroad can that degree be earned? Make time to gather and pursue short-term and more permanent work-abroad resources.

• Prepare your resume. Make sure it describes your experience abroad and all the skills you acquired, including language competency.

• Keep in touch with all the contacts you gathered abroad. Write to them, stating your serious interest in returning to work in that country after graduation (if you are serious).

• Investigate short-session programs that teach the Teaching of English as a Second Language. Do they help with job placement?

• Assess your financial situation. How much money must you earn before you go? How long can you afford to live abroad?

• Find a friend to job hunt with. Two heads are better than one: you can share leads and contacts.

<u>Perspective</u>

Work in Britain
A Veteran's Tale of the BUNAC Program

By Lori Cloutier

During the summer following my college sophomore year, my friend and I wanted to go overseas. The problem was age-old—money. How were we to fund a whole summer abroad and survive? The answer was BUNAC, The British Universities North America Club, which provides British work visas for students from the U.S. for up to six months.

The visa made it legal for me to work anywhere in Britain. The administrative cost of $250 was very reasonable. Planning to leave for Britain in mid-May, we applied for the work permits in March and received them in mid-April. BUNAC also sent us a whole packet of prep materials to help us get ready.

Preparations: We attended an information session about BUNAC and heard tips from past participants and what their trips and jobs entailed. We bought International Student Identification Cards for $22 that offered basic insurance and allowed us to get a great discount on a flight from Council Travel. The BUNAC handbook also listed a few hostels that could guarantee a place to stay for BUNACers but you must call about a week ahead.

Settling Down in London: My friend and I said a tearful goodbye to our families and were off on our journey. We rounded up our luggage at Gatwick airport and somehow got a train to Victoria Station. Never had I felt so free—an ocean away from home, all my belongings with me, and able to go anywhere. It was the best.

The city was beautiful and strange: black "cabbies," as taxis are called in Britain, double decker buses, uniform townhouses, and drivers on the left. We had so much to discover and a whole summer to do it! We settled into our hotel and went out to look for a flat. We found that most apartments charge rent by the week, and some wanted a month plus the first week's rent down as a deposit. If the flat was 100 pounds per week ($150—average to inexpensive), that would have been 400 pounds ($600) down, plus the first week which would be a total of 500 pounds ($750) just for the first payment. As a flat proved to be far too expensive for us, we decided to look for work with housing included, like some pub or hotel jobs.

Finding a Job and Housing: At the BUNAC orientation the next day, we learned how to register with the Jobcentre and a few other simple things to make sure we were legal to work. There were about 20 other students at the orientation, all BUNACers, all as jobless and homeless as we were. It was comforting to meet others in the same situation. The BUNAC office had many listings of employers wanting to hire BUNACers and of available apartments. We called dozens of places for jobs, mostly pubs and restaurants. Some positions were already filled; others wanted us to bring them a resume and they would conduct a short interview. After the interviews, they kept our resumes and wanted to call us back. We quickly learned that you need a stable contact number during the job search.

After calling and interviewing at about four more places, we were both offered jobs at a pub located near the London Bridge. It was exactly what you would think of as a traditional English pub. Our manager, his wife, and their two small children had come over from Ireland and they lived above the pub. My friend and I would share a room in their apartment, and essentially become part of the family. We could move in and start immediately. The entire job and house search process took us about five days.

Working in Britain: Our manager wanted my friend and I to run the pub together during the day and then alternate working at night with another bartender. On our first day they put me behind the bar and told me to just do my best and ask lots of questions. Everything was fine until in came the lunch-time crowd. All I remember is loud music, many voices, and people throwing orders at me through the noise and in various accents. But I made it without any major problems, and it took only about a week of on-the-job training before I felt comfortable in my bartender's job and could really start to enjoy it.

As we settled into our jobs and new home, we found more time to go out and see the great city of London. I benefitted so much from the museums, historical sites, and cultural events because I could enjoy them at a slow pace due to my long stay in the city.

As the summer went on, we found it a bit difficult to travel because we worked almost every day, so my friend and I decided to quit work two weeks early. At the beginning of May, we traveled to Paris and then went on a tour all over Scotland. Finally, we had three more days in London which we spent taking our last admiring impressions of the wonderful city we called home for three months.

Work Abroad vs. Study Abroad: I learned many things by being a part of the British work force. I have studied abroad as well. And in comparing the two experiences, I felt I learned more factual information from study abroad, but I gained better insight into the country's culture and social system by working overseas.

I was immediately aware of a larger division between the social classes in Britain compared to the U.S. This also translated to the workplace where people are very formal when speaking to their superiors. One man who had just started working for an American company said he was absolutely astounded when the American boss came right up to him, introduced himself, and asked him all kinds of friendly, casual questions. His comment was, "This would never happen in Britain. You can't be that casual with your company superiors if they even speak to you at all."

There was also the famous British reserve that I noticed right away. People were less apt to begin a conversation, but I found every British person with whom I did speak to be incredibly polite and friendly. The British are also less likely to complain about customer service. My boss said that from a British perspective, complaining, even though the service may be really bad, is seen as rude and inappropriate. Even as a novice bartender I never had one complaint.

The British people I met were curious about America and asked many questions. I found that a few of them had quite strange views of American culture, associating the U.S. with Hollywood and the Old West. I also found that the British get a lot of American talk shows, and I was asked many times if our society is really that corrupt. I tried to give everyone the most accurate perspective possible, which is all part of the learning experience. I found I learned not only about British culture, but also much about myself, how others view my culture, and why I do things the way I do. This all came from being in another culture and seeing the world from a different perspective. Working in London really changed me and widened my view of the world. It was a priceless experience.

Contact: BUNAC USA, P.O. Box 430, Southbury, CT 06488; 800-GO-BUNAC or 203-264-0901, www.bunac.org; BUNAC U.K., Incoming Programmes, 16 Bowling Greene Ln., London, ECIR OQH, England; 011-44-20-7251-3472, fax 011-44-20-7251-0215; enquiries@bunac.org.uk, www.bunac.org.

Perspective

Working Holidays in Australia
If You're Under 30, You Have Many Choices

By Judy Van Rhijn

Those from Canada, the U.K., and parts of Europe and Asia who wish to work in Australia are eligible for the Working Holiday Maker's Scheme. Asians and Europeans must be between 18 and 30 years of age. U.S. passport holders are eligible for restricted working visas if they hold a student visa. There is no age limit for student visas.

With permission to work granted, the traveler faces the same decision I did: What sort of work and where? I wanted to avoid resort work and cities, preferring physical work in the countryside. I didn't want to climb ladders for apples or oranges. I didn't want to scrabble on the ground for macadamia nuts or small crops. Grapepicking sounded attractive. It would also mean spending time in one of the winegrowing areas.

Just north of Sydney lies the Hunter Valley. Its grapepicking season starts in the height of summer, December to January which coincides with the longer summer holiday (so students can make the most of their work visa) but also with sizzling sunny days. In Australia the summer slogan is "Slip, slop, slap." Slip on a shirt, slop on some sunscreen, and slap on a hat!

Your consolation at the end of a long, hot working day will be the many good restaurants and retreats along the Hunter River. On the weekends you can enjoy fantastic beaches at nearby Newcastle or escape to the cooler temperatures of the Barrington Tops or Wollemi National Parks.

My next stop was the beautiful Barossa Valley in South Australia. The vintage starts there in February after the worst of the heat is over and continues into autumn. Although the weather was my first consideration, I might just as well have chosen the area for its beauty and culture.

The Barossa was settled in 1842 by pioneers from Silesia, a wine-growing region of Germany. They built their Lutheran churches of pale stone with tall spires. They also built small stone cottages and furnished them with distinctively plain furniture and housewares that are now eagerly sought by collectors. The valley itself is lined with bleached hills that overlook a grid of vines and pasture. Patches of shadow and sunlight pass over fields dotted with golden shocks of hay. Many of the winery buildings have peaks and turrets resembling German castles.

We worked all day from Monday to Friday, unless the heat became extreme or the rain too heavy. There were two stops for "smoko" under the gum trees during which we ate sandwiches and drank water in companionable silence. At the end of the day I was filthy and exhausted. My back ached so badly at first I thought I'd cracked a disc. It took until the middle of the third week for my backache to disappear. My speed picked up until I reached the $100-a-day mark.

Besides visiting the wineries, I browsed through the antique stores and relaxed at German-style cafes. Then I hiked in the rocky ridges of the Kaiser Stuhl

Conservation Park and located the lost town of Hoffnungstahl. I also attended many of the events and ceremonies associated with the vintage: wine shows, jazz evenings, and gourmet weekends abound.

As a worker, I felt part of all the celebrations and not merely a visitor. The locals were welcoming and there was camaraderie amongst the ever-changing teams of pickers. By the end of the season I had more physical strength and stamina than I've ever had in my life. More importantly, I had enjoyed beauty and ceremony, friendship and fun. As I drifted up and over the valley in a balloon and saw the leaves turning to autumn gold, I felt replenished in every way.

Contacts: BUNAC USA: 800-GO-BUNAC or 203-264-0901; www.bunac.org. Australian Consulates: Los Angeles 310-229-4840, New York 212-408-8460; Tourism Newcastle: Margo Chapman, 011-61-2492-99299, Tourism@ ncc.nsw.gov.au; Sunraysia Tourism: Kris Harrington, 011-61-3502-14424, Krish@ mildura.vic.gov.au; Margaret River Tourism Bureau: Sue Jackman, 011-61-8975-72911, Suejackman@mrwia.org.au; Barossa Valley Info Center: Rachel@barossa-region.org; Centrelink; Australian Employment Agency: www.centrelink.com; Department of Immigration (Australia): www. immigov.au.

International Jobs For Students and Recent Graduates
The Key Print Resources

Selected and Reviewed by William Nolting

The following resources focus on casual work abroad that is often, though not always, for students and recent graduates. The positions are generally not career-related and last from a summer to six months. Typical locations are Western Europe. Look into these a few months before traveling.

**Essential; *Outstanding and of broad interest.
For ordering information, if not included below, see Key Publishers page 13.

WORLDWIDE WORK AND STUDY ABROAD

**Academic Year Abroad edited by Marie O'Sullivan. 2002 (Annual). 693 pp. Institute of International Education (IIE). $46.95 plus $6 shipping from IIE. Also available online and free at www.iiepassport.org. This is the most comprehensive and authoritative directory of semester and academic year programs abroad for college students and adults. Lists nearly 2,700 programs offered by U.S. and foreign universities and private organizations. Indexed for fields of study and location, with special indexes for cost; graduate, professional, teacher and adult courses. More than 850 of

the programs include work or practical experience, and are listed under indexes for internships (400), practical training (250), student teaching (60), and volunteer/service (140). Companion volume to *Short-Term Study Abroad.* Can be found in most college libraries and study abroad offices.

**Advisory List of International Educational Travel & Exchange Programs. Annual. $17.50. Council on Standards for International Educational Travel, 212 S Henry St., Alexandria, VA 22314; 703-739-9050, fax 703-739-9035; www.csiet.org. Lists programs for high school students which adhere to CSIET's standards. The most valuable single resource for locating programs for high school students.

**The Back Door Guide to Short Term Job Adventures by Michael Landes. 2001. 336 pp. Ten Speed Press. $19.95 plus $3.50 s/h from Ten Speed Press, P.O. Box 7123, Berkeley, CA 94710; 800-841-2665, fax 510-559-1629; www.backdoorjobs.com. A guide to internships, "extraordinary experiences," seasonal jobs, and volunteering for everyone from college students through senior citizens. Most listings are in the U.S., but one section lists 60 programs and resources for overseas work and educational travel.

*Charting a Hero's Journey by Linda A. Chisholm. 2000. 328 pp. $23.95 postpaid from Partnership for Service Learning, 815 2nd Ave., Suite 315, New York, NY 10017; 212-986-0989, fax 212-986-5039; pslny@aol.com, www.ipsl.org. Based on the work of Joseph Campbell and using excerpts from journals of famous authors, this is a guide to the writing of a journal for college students engaged in study abroad, off-campus study, and/or service learning. Not a directory of opportunities (for program listings, see the IIE and Peterson's publications).

**Fellowships in International Affairs: A Guide to Opportunities in the United States and Abroad by Women in International Security. 1994. 196 pp. $10 plus $3.50 shipping Lynne Rienner Publishers, 1800 30th St., Suite 314, Boulder CO 80301; 303-444-6684; www.rienner.com. Well-researched directory of fellowships and grants for students, scholar and practitioners. Most are for graduate students, postdoctorates, or professionals. Indexes for level of study and geographic specialization. Visit WIIS's comprehensive web site at www.wiis.org, which includes an Online International Internship Directory.

*Financial Aid for Research and Creative Activities Abroad 2002-2004 edited by Gail Ann Schlachter and R. David Weber. 2002. 350 pp. $45 plus $5 shipping from Reference Service Press. Lists over 1,200 funding sources available to support research, professional development, teaching assignments, or creative activities. Useful for graduate students, postdocs, and professionals. Relatively few funding opportunities (ca. 50) listed are available for high school and undergraduate students. Indexes for level of study, location, and subject.

**Financial Aid for Study and Training Abroad 2001-2003 edited by Gail Ann Schlachter and R. David Weber. 2001 (revised every 2 years). 398 pp. $39.50 plus $5 shipping from Reference Service Press. Lists almost 1,000 funding sources available to support for-mal educational programs such as study abroad, training, internships, workshops, or seminars. Most useful for high school, undergraduate and graduate students, postdocs; some listings for professionals. Indexes for level of study, location, and subject. This is the most up-to-date and comprehensive directory of scholarships for study abroad currently available. Highly recommended.

**Financial Resources for International Study: A Guide for U.S. Nationals edited by Marie O' Sullivan and Sara Steen. 1996. 300 pp. $39.95 plus $6 shipping from IIE. Also available free as a searchable document on IIE's web site, at www.iie.org/help/search.htm. Comprehensive and authoritative directory of almost 700 funding sources based on a survey of over 5,000 organizations and universities in the U.S. and abroad. Lists funding sources available to support undergraduate, graduate, postdoctorate, and professional learning abroad, from study and research to internships, training and teaching. Indexes for level of study, subject, and organization.

**Impact Press Catalog Great International Job and Travel Resources. Free from Impact Publications, see www.impactpublications. com. Catalog of hard-to-find books on international jobs and careers which can be ordered from Impact or downloaded from their web site.

**Intercultural Press Catalog Updated quarterly. Free from Intercultural Press, see www.interculturalpress.com. Catalog of practical books on cross-cultural issues, moving abroad, dealing with culture shock, and other issues related to working and/or studying abroad.

**Peterson's Study Abroad. Peterson's. 2002 (Annual). 1,171 pp. $29.95, plus shipping from Peterson's. Detailed information on over 1,800 semester and academic year study abroad programs worldwide for college students, of which nearly 560 offer internships (from 180 institutions), listed in a special index. Includes essays on credit, financial aid, nontraditional destinations, internships and volunteering, and traveling. Indexes for field of study, location, host institutions, and internships (internships for academic credit).

**Peterson's Summer Study Abroad. Peterson's. 2002 (Annual). 760 pp. $29.95 plus shipping from Peterson's. Detailed information on over 1,600 summer and short-term (up to 6 weeks) study abroad programs worldwide, of which around 260 offer internships (from 100 institutions), listed in a special index. Other indexes for field of study and host institutions.

**Short-Term Study Abroad. (formerly titled Vacation Study Abroad) edited by Marie O'Sullivan. 2002. (Annual). 504 pp. Institute of International Education (IIE). $44.95 plus $6 shipping from IIE. Also available online and free, at www.iiepassport.org. This is the most comprehensive and authoritative directory of summer and short-term (less than a semester) programs abroad for college students and adults. Lists over 2,200 programs offered by U.S. and foreign universities and private organizations. Indexed for fields of study and location, with special indexes for cost; graduate, professional, teacher and adult courses. More than 500 of the programs include work or practical experience and are listed under indexes for internships (130), practical training (220), student teaching (40), and volunteer/service (110). Companion volume to *Academic Year Abroad.* Can be found in most college libraries and study abroad offices.

*Study Abroad: A Parent's Guide by William A. Hoffa. 1998. 112 pp. $15 from NAFSA. The only guide to respond to parents' questions and concerns about safety, academic credit, financial aid, program evaluation, travel documents, insurance, banking, and other issues related to study abroad. Not a directory of programs (for program listings, see the IIE and Peterson's publications).

Studying and Working in Spain: A Student Guide by Michael T. Newton and Graham J. Shields. 2002. 300 pp. $24.95. Manchester University Press. Provides background information on contemporary Spain and practical advice on preparing a study abroad with a major section devoted to working in Spain. Directory of Spain's 67 universities with contact numbers, teaching centers, student services, and courses in Spanish language and culture.

Taking Time Off by Collin Hall and Ron Lieber. 1996. 289 pp. Noonday. $10 at www.amazon.com. Thoughtful book that gives reports of individuals who studied abroad or interned, worked, volunteered, or traveled both abroad and in the U.S., but listings now dated.

**Transitions Abroad. Available from Transitions Abroad. $28/6 issues. Also available in bulk at reduced price for educators. Published 6 times a year, this is the only U.S. periodical which gives extensive coverage to work abroad options in addition to all other varieties of education abroad. And don't miss the great Transitions Abroad web site, www.TransitionsAbroad.com.

**The Unofficial Guide to Study Abroad by Ann M. Moore. 2000. 416 pp. $14.95. Arco/IDG Books, 800-762-2974 (Arco) 800-723-0448 (Study Abroad Advisor) study abroadadvisor@yahoo.com, www.study abroadadvisor.com. This book provides an excellent introduction to all aspects of studying and working abroad. Not a directory of programs.

**What in the World is Going On? A Guide for Canadians Wishing to Work, Volunteer or Study in Other Countries by Alan Cumyn. 2001. (Available free on CBIE web site at www.cbie.ca/work.html). Includes a comprehensive listing of work abroad possibilities, organized according to location and level of skills and education required. Invaluable for Canadians.

*A World of Options edited by Christa Bucks. 3rd ed., 1997. 658 pp. Mobility International USA. $35 individual, $45 organizations, members receive a 10% discount, from MIUSA, P.O. Box 10767, Eugene, OR 97440; 541-343-1284, fax 541-343-6812; info@miusa.org, www.miusa.org. A comprehensive guide to international exchange, study, and volunteer opportunities for people with disabilities.

REGIONAL WORK AND STUDY ABROAD

*After Latin American Studies: A Guide to Graduate Study and Employment for Latin Americanists by Shirley A. Kregar and Jorge Nallim. 2000. $15 (check payable to Univ. of Pittsburgh) postpaid from: Center for Latin American Studies (CLAS), 4E Posvar Hall, Univ. of Pittsburgh, Pittsburgh, PA 15260; 412-648-7392, fax 412-648-2199; clas@ucis.pitt.edu, www.ucis.pitt.edu/clas. An essential resource for anyone with career or scholarly interests in this region, but few listings for overseas opportunities. Extensive bibliography. Also available on the CLAS web site.

Directory of Work and Study In Developing Countries edited by Toby Milner. 1997. 256 pp. Vacation Work (U.K.). $16.95 from Seven Hills. Comprehensive guide to employment, voluntary work, and academic opportunities (with over 400 organizations) in developing countries. Chapters on Work, Voluntary Work, and Study, with subsections about specific professional fields and geographic areas. Intended primarily for a British audience, it omits some organizations of interest to Americans.

www.birthrightisrael.com, a comprehensive listing of study, volunteer, and travel programs in Israel for high school, college students, and other young adults. Also listed are offices in the U.S., which can provide information and advice. Full text also on the web site.

*Living in China: A Guide to Teaching and Studying in China Including Taiwan by Rebecca Weiner, Margaret Murphy, and Albert Li. 1997. 284 pp. $19.95 from China Books and Periodicals, Inc., 2929 24th St., San Francisco, CA 94110; 415-282-2994, fax 415-282-0994; info@chinabooks.com, www.chinabooks.com. Comprehensive advice on topics such as "Adjusting: How Not to be a Foreign Barbarian." Has extensive directories of schools and colleges as well as organizations which offer study abroad or teacher placement.

*Living, Studying, and Working in France: Everything You Need to Know to Fulfill Your Dreams of Living Abroad by Saskia Reilly and Lorin David Kalisky. 1999. 304 pp. $14.95. Owl Book, Henry Holt and Co., 115 West 18th St., New York, NY 10011; 888-330-8477, fax 212-647-1874; academic@hholt.com. The only book on this topic from an American perspective provides useful, very comprehensive advice for anyone wishing to study, work or live in France.

*Living, Studying, and Working in Italy: Everything You Need to Know to Fulfill Your Dreams of Living Abroad by Travis Neighbor and Monica Larner. 1998. 340 pp. $14.95. Owl Book, Henry Holt and Co., 115 West 18th St., New York, NY 10011; 888-330-8477, fax 212-647-1874; academic@hholt.com. The only book on this topic from an American perspective provides useful, very comprehensive advice for anyone wishing to study, work or live in Italy.

**The Peace Corps and More: 175 Ways to Work, Study, and Travel at Home and Abroad by Medea Benjamin and Miya Rodolfo-Sioson. 1997. 126 pp. $8.95 from Global Exchange, 2017 Mission St., # 303, San Francisco, CA 94110; Book orders 800-497-1994, 415-255-7296, fax 415-255-7498; www.globalexchange.org. Describes 175 programs that allow anyone to gain Third World experience while promoting the ideals of social justice and sustainable development.

*The Post-Soviet Handbook: A Guide to Grassroots Organizations and Internet Resources in the Newly Independent States by M. Holt Ruffin, Joan McCarter, and Richard Upjohn. 1999. 416 pp. Univ. of Washington Press. $19.95 plus $4 shipping from Center for Civil Society International, 2929 NE Blakely St., Seattle, WA 98105; 206-523-4755, fax 206-523-1974; ccsi@u.washington.edu, www.friends-partners.org/~ccsi. The best guide to independent, non-governmental ("third sector") organizations in Russia and the NIS. Up-to-date source for organizations, both U.S.-based and local, that may welcome volunteers. Includes listings of U.S. study abroad programs and academic area studies centers. CCSI's web site and listserv (CivilSoc) are the best single sources for announcements of jobs located in this region.

*Working in Asia by Nicki Grihault. In Print Publishing Ltd. (U.K.). 1996. 488 pp. $16.95 from Amazon.com or bookstores. This is the only book which gives an overview of all work options, from volunteer to teaching to career opportunities, throughout Asia—from the Indian subcontinent to Southeast Asia to Northern Asia. Includes specifics on U.S. and other organizations.

SHORT-TERM PAID WORK ABROAD

(U.S. citizens need work permits to work legally in other countries. The officially-recognized work exchange programs listed here can help. See also Chapter 3.)

**The Au Pair & Nanny's Guide to Working Abroad by Susan Griffith and Sharon Legg. 2002. 320 pp. Vacation Work (U.K.). $16.95 from Seven Hills. Practical, insightful advice on how to prepare for and find a child care job in another country. Lists agencies worldwide.

*The British Council: Internships/Work Experience in the U.K. Students and Employment in the U.K. Free from The British Council, 3100 Massachusetts Ave, NW, Washington DC 20008-3600; 202-588-7830, fax 202-588-7918; www.studyintheuk.org. Official information on work regulations and work-exchange programs.

**BUNAC Work Abroad Programs, (for Britain, Australia, New Zealand). Application from BUNAC USA, P.O. Box 430, Southbury, CT 06488; 800-GO-BUNAC or 203-264-0901, fax 203-264-0251; www.bunac.org. Nonprofit work abroad organization provides a work permit for up to 6 months and job-hunting assistance. Program fee of $250 (Britain) or somewhat more for Australia or New Zealand. U.S. college students and recent grads (within 1 semester) eligible for Britain. Non-students aged 18-30 eligible for Australia & New Zealand. No other program makes it as easy for

U.S. citizens to work in Britain. The invaluable **BUNAC Work in Britain Participant's Handbook* may be requested by college study abroad and career offices; otherwise for program participants only (not for sale).

*Directory of Overseas Summer Jobs edited by David Woodworth and Ian Collier. 2002. (revised annually) 288 pp. Vacation Work (U.K.). $17.95 from Peterson's. Lists more than 30,000 temporary jobs, paid and volunteer, in over 50 countries: who to contact, pay rates, how and when to apply. Contact information includes email addresses and web sites. Valuable information on work permits required by each country.

*Directory of Summer Jobs Britain edited by David Woodworth. 2002. (revised annually) 271 pp. Vacation Work (U.K.). $17.95 from Peterson's. Lists more than 30,000 jobs, ranging from internships ("traineeships") to casual jobs, farming, hotel work, and volunteering. Each listing includes wages, qualifications, and contact information including email addresses and web sites. U.S. citizens need a work permit—contact BUNAC or AIPT.

*French Cultural Services: Employment in France for Students. Free information from French Cultural Services, 972 5th Ave., New York, NY 10021; 212-439-1400, fax 212-439-1455; www.frenchculture.org. Work regulations and work possibilities. Also free: Teaching Assistant Program; Au Pair Work in France.

*How to Get a Job with a Cruise Line by Mary Fallon Miller. 2001. 352 pp. $16.95 ($29 foreign) from Ticket to Adventure, Inc., P.O. Box 41005, St. Petersburg, FL 33743; 800-929-7447 or 727-822-5029; cruisechooser@yahoo.com, www.cruiseserver.net/travelpage/other/jobs_overview.asp. Detailed information on how to apply plus tips from cruise line employees. Bibliography. Recommended by the cruise industry.

*InterExchange Work Abroad Programs. Free brochure from InterExchange, Inc., 161 6th Ave., New York, NY 10013; 212-924-0446, fax 212-924-0575; info@interexchange.org, www.interexchange.org. Nonprofit program offers placements for paid work abroad, internships, English teaching, and au pair in Europe.

**Work Your Way Around The World by Susan Griffith. 2001 (10th edition). 531 pp. Vacation Work (U.K.). $17.95 from Peterson's Guides. The authoritative (and only) guide to looking for short-term jobs while abroad, by the Work Abroad editor for *Transitions Abroad*. Extensive country-by-country narratives include first-hand reports.

*Working in Ski Resorts-Europe and North America by Victoria Pybus. 1998. 320 pp. Vacation Work (U.K.). $16.95 from Seven Hills. Available jobs plus reports from resorts.

**Working in Tourism: For Seasonal and Permanent Staff by Verite Reily Collins. 1999. 320 pp. Vacation Work (U.K.). $16.95 from Petersons. How to find jobs in tourism, country-by-country listings, and a directory of travel companies with staff requirements.

International Internships
Cover Expenses, Gain Career Experience

By William Nolting

Why do you want an international internship—to live and work abroad, or to gain specific career-related work experience? If the former, many other work abroad opportunities may be easier to get or less expensive. These include short-term paid work abroad programs, teaching English abroad, or volunteering abroad.

Where. Many internships related to international careers, especially ones with international organizations, are actually located here in the U.S.—especially in centers of international activity such as Washington DC or New York. But it is often possible to combine an international internship with an overseas location.

How. *Tuition-based study abroad internships* sponsored by universities provide credit towards your degree. Financial aid can usually be used to help meet expenses. Tuition costs range widely. *Unpaid, non-academic* internships account for the majority of internships, both in the U.S. and abroad. If living costs are high, these may be as expensive as tuition-charging internships but without the benefits of credit and financial aid. The main benefit of such internships will be professionally-related experience and better prospects for career positions.

Volunteer positions abroad sometimes provide room and board, which can make them less expensive than unpaid internships. The Peace Corps pays well, although this is a two-year commitment. Repayment of educational loans can often be deferred during volunteer work (check with your lender and the volunteer agency). Volunteer positions may be the best option for those interested in careers having to do with developing countries.

Paid internships are somewhat rare abroad and are available mainly in applied fields such as business and engineering. See the resource section of this chapter for a directory of internships.

When to Apply. For summer internships, it's best to apply in the fall. Some programs, such as the U.S. State Department, have deadlines as early as November 1. IAESTE and others have deadlines in early December. Study abroad internships usually have application deadlines the semester before the term of the internship.

Types of Internships and International Organizations

1. Study Abroad Internships. Hundreds of overseas internships are sponsored by universities and for undergraduates are the most easily available option. Advantages include credit, applicability of financial aid, and a variety of subjects and locations. Disadvantages are cost and sometimes unpredictability of placement. Some of the best web sites for finding study abroad internships are Transitions Abroad www.transitionsabroad.com, www.iiepassport.org (use the "format" search), www.goabroad.com, and www.studyabroad.com.

2. Internship Exchange/Work Permit Programs. A few reciprocal exchange programs offer paying internships in applied fields. If you find your own internship abroad, these organizations can also assist in obtaining a work permit. Best web sites for finding these programs are Transitions Abroad, www.transitionsabroad.com, and Univ. of Michigan's International Center, www.umich.edu/~icenter/overseas.

AIESEC (80-plus countries), a student-run international organization with chapters on many campuses, offers business-related internships open to all majors. AIESEC members have preference in getting these internships. See AIESEC's web site. The CIEE and BUNAC work abroad programs are the only ways to get a work permit without a job offer. The programs are available for Britain, Ireland, France, Germany, Canada, Australia, and New Zealand. (See page 46.)

IAESTE (70 plus countries) and the American-Scandinavian Foundation (Scandinavian countries) have placements in engineering and natural sciences, while AIPT offers hotel and culinary programs.

CDS (Germany) has several programs in business and technical fields for undergraduates, graduates, and professionals. These organizations accept applications directly from students. (See page 67.)

The International Cooperative Education Program (ICEP) offers paid placements in a number of fields. Knowledge of a foreign language is required (e.g., German, French, Spanish, Dutch, Japanese, Chinese). (See page 67.) Internships International, the Center for Interim Programs, and others offer low-cost placements in unpaid internships. (See page 67.)

3. Internships Directly with International Organizations. Some organizations in international sectors offer internship programs with a centralized formal application process. Many do not have formal internships but often respond positively to applications from individuals who propose their own "internship." In general, the larger and better-known the organization, the more competitive the application process for internships will be. Smaller and more locally-based organizations, often overlooked by applicants, may offer some of the best internship experiences.

A) Government. The U.S. State Department and other federal agencies overseas and in the U.S. offer internships (usually unpaid) for undergraduates and graduate students. Application is competitive. Apply by November 1 for summer, March 1 for fall, July 1 for winter. State and city governments have many internship possibilities, often overlooked by applicants, in their international trade offices. Internships with members of Congress who sit on international committees are also possible. A U.S. State Department Internship is a great way to see if a career in diplomacy is for you. Most are unpaid, but free housing may be provided. Eligibility: U.S. citizens who are undergraduates (junior or senior) or graduate students who will continue as students. Apply via the State Department's web site, www.careers.state.gov.

You may also apply for career positions with the U.S. State Department from the same web site.

The U.S. Peace Corps is possibly the best (and best-paying) entry-level job for anyone interested in grassroots development work overseas. Unlike in a State Department job, you live and work with ordinary local people. Eligibility: U.S. citizens, generally for those with at least a bachelor's degree; two-year commitment. Peace Corps pays all expenses plus over $6,000 ("resettlement allowance") at the end of service. Full training and support is provided. Educational loans can be deferred and some partially canceled. Some tuition support is available for later graduate study. Contact: Peace Corps, P.O. Box 948, Washington DC 20526; 800-424-8580; www.peacecorps.gov.

The Woodrow Wilson Foundation administers several scholarship/internship programs related to U.S. government agencies, for which women and minorities are especially encouraged to apply. Most of these scholarships fund several years of study and include summer institutes and internships. Applicants must apply as sophomores (for 3-year scholarships) or as seniors (for graduate school scholarships, for a shorter period of time).

For the most up-to-date information and applications, see the Woodrow Wilson web site, www.woodrow.org/public-policy. Other U.S. government departments that offer international internships and career positions include the U.S. Agency for International Development (USAID), www.usaid.gov, the U.S. Commercial Service, www.usatrade.gov, and the U.S. Department of Commerce http://ohrm.doc. gov/jobs.

B) Public Multinationals (also known as "international organizations"). Multi-government giants like the United Nations, the European Community and the World

Bank offer internships. They are often unpaid and highly competitive (paid positions are usually reserved for graduate students), and most positions for Americans are in the U.S. Most internships in the "Key Resources" list that follows have information on internships with these organizations. Some organizations are designated as officially recognized international organizations. Work permits for these employers are easier to get. The U.S. State Department's web site, www.careers.state.gov, has links to the job sites of many major international organizations.

C) **Private Enterprise.** Organized international internship programs are sponsored by Proctor & Gamble, Coca-Cola, and others. These are sometimes restricted to students in MBA programs. Many undergraduates, however, have arranged overseas internships with U.S. or host-country companies, especially by using the CIEE or BUNAC programs. Most internships with private industry pay enough to cover basic living expenses, though usually not the cost of transatlantic airfare. Try web sites such as Monster.com, or try Google searches www.google.com for specific companies—using search terms such as "company name + internship." In fact, Google works amazingly well for most types of organizations, assuming you have specific ones in mind.

D) **Non-Government Organizations** (NGOs), typically nonprofit, include humanitarian or human-rights watchdogs like Amnesty International, health care providers like CARE, research institutes like the Bermuda Biological Station, and organizations supporting international educational exchange such as the Institute of International Education. NGOs typically welcome interns in their U.S.-based offices and sometimes by direct application to overseas offices. Internships with NGOs are often unpaid. Two excellent web sites for exploring internship and job opportunities with NGOs are Idealist.org, www.idealist.org (some 30,000 orgnizations worldwide) and the Women in International Security Online Internship Directory (www.puaf.umd.edu/WIS/intern).

E) **Educational Organizations.** Teachers are needed worldwide. Positions fall into two categories: Teaching English as a foreign language, for which no other credential than a bachelor's degree is usually needed, and teaching K-12 in overseas schools taught in English, for which teaching certification is usually required. Most teaching positions require a commitment of at least one academic year. Teaching at the university level nearly always requires an advanced degree. See Chapters 5 and 6 for specific organizations. See also the web sites of Transitions Abroad, www.transitionsabroad.com, Univ. of Michigan's International Center, www.umich.edu/~icenter/overseas, and Dave's ESL Café, www.eslcafe.com.

F) **Private Voluntary Organizations** (PVOs) offer many overseas placements and are one of the only possibilities for work in developing countries. Positions are typically designated as "volunteer" or service positions, rather than internships. These range from secular organizations, such as Amigos de las Americas or WorldTeach, to religious-sponsored groups. While some religious groups insist on affiliation, others, such as the Brethren or the American Friends Service Committee, do not. Short-term placements (of less than one year) will often charge fees, or at best provide room and board. A few long-term placements provide for all the expenses of the volunteer, most notably the Peace Corps (a U.S. government program which funds positions with host-country voluntary organizations). Again, "volunteer" positions offer the possible benefit of deferring educational loan repayments during the volunteer assignment. For more information see Chapter 4. See the web site of the International Volunteer Programs Association, www.volunteerinternational.org, www.transitionsabroad.com, www.goabroad.com, and especially the great new book, *How to Live Your Dream of Volunteering Overseas* (authors Collins, DeZerega, and Heckscher).

Tips on Having a Successful International Internship

By Kristin Stewart

For starters, don't assume that our concept of an internship is meaningful abroad. You may be viewed as a regular employee, or your supervisor may not know what to do with you. Take the first week or so to get acclimated and learn the ropes, then work on implementing the following suggestions:

1. Try to set up a workplan with your boss. Elements include: time schedule of work to be done, different departments or areas you want to gain experience in, setting up regular meetings to check progress, and flexible but realistic deadlines for completing projects.

2. Let your boss know what your skills are, what you can offer, and what you are not comfortable doing.

3. Make yourself useful and do things your supervisor needs to get done. If you take on some of the grunt work, you're also more likely to get assigned challenging tasks. Ask your supervisor to let you help them with what they're doing.

4. Arrange informational interviews with people in other parts of the organization to learn what they are doing.

5. Have a set of skills or job experiences you hope to accomplish during the summer and check them off a list. Be flexible, and be prepared to add new things or modify your initial expectations.

6. You may want to take on one major long-term project such as program planning and work on this all summer. Couple it with day trips to other program sites or short-term projects in other parts of the office.

7. If overcoming language barriers or language acquisition is a goal of your internship, state this clearly in the beginning to your boss.

8. Let your boss know upfront if you need any time off and what your travel plans are. Leave a copy of your passport (visa if necessary) and travel itinerary with your supervisor for safe keeping.

9. Communicate often with your faculty adviser or department, before and during your overseas internship, and don't forget to communicate frequently and on a regular basis with your family and friends.

10. Have fun!

Perspective

Work in Washington

International Education Internships Lead to Careers

By Heather Powers

While the job market in your area may be depressed, Washington, DC continues to offer internships and entry-level job opportunities in the field of international education. With planning and persistence, you may land an internship that will get you started in your desired career.

College graduates sometimes dismiss internships because a steady income is needed to pay off accumulated debt—student loans, car payments, or credit cards. But when job leads are scarce, an internship may provide the experience that will help you break into the field while giving you the opportunity to get to know the players. An internship also lets an organization learn what you have to offer, and as an internal candidate you get first crack at job openings. Other benefits of an internship are the ability to openly conduct a job search, after-hours use of computers and printers to produce cover letters and resumes, and work experience that will immediately be recognized by other not-for-profits in DC.

The Search

So how do you begin? Some nonprofits, like the Institute of International Education and Meridian International Center, try to reach prospective interns through flyers sent to career placement offices. I discovered NAFSA *Job Registry*, a bimonthly publication of job openings, in my alma mater's international center. This opened my eyes to the wide range of positions available in international education—from credentials evaluation to international student advising to grant administration.

Two sources that will reveal the wealth of potential employers awaiting you in Washington are *International Education Career Information*, produced by NAFSA (NAFSA Item #1680; 800-836-4994, $10 plus s/h), and the *International Exchange Locator: 2000 Edition* published by IIE New York (IIE Books; 800-445-0443, $19.95 plus $6 s/h; www.alliance-exchange.org/store). The first is an excellent introduction to the field of international education, with an overview of the qualifications required. Also listed are career resources to assist you with informational interviewing and networking in DC. *The Exchange Locator* contains overviews of organizations involved in international educational exchange. While not all-inclusive, it does provide information critical to a job search, such as the organization's mission, branch offices if any, and the number of staff.

Not-for-profit organizations such as Youth for Understanding, NAFSA, and the Institute of International Education welcome interns and rely on volunteers to meet their objectives. Personalize your resumes and cover letters to convince human resource personnel they have a good match. Call to determine to whom your resume should be sent, if writing samples and transcripts are required, and if there is a hiring cycle for interns. A bachelor's degree, demonstrated interest in international education, and writing samples are usually all that is required to secure an internship.

Compensation ranges from nothing to stipends of $500 per month. Your survival during this time requires careful budgeting. Once you obtain your internship, contact your student loan provider about a temporary hardship deferment; it won't affect your credit rating and the six-month deferment of payments on the principal will help you pay your bills.

Networking Is the Key

Only 20 percent of job vacancies are advertised, so networking is the key to success. This is especially true of international nonprofits where position descriptions are distributed to similar organizations. Asking your colleagues to keep their eyes open is important. Your chances of getting the job increase enormously when you have a contact or you are an internal candidate. Typical minimum requirements are a BA, foreign language study, experience abroad, and good communication skills. Computer skills are recommended. Salaries in the field are low and there is no overtime, but most organizations offer excellent benefits: health insurance, retirement, sick leave, and ample paid vacation time.

The circle of international educational exchange in Washington is relatively small; after a year in the city you will recognize names and begin to run into familiar people. Participating in career roundtables, after-work happy hours, office sports leagues, and an occasional embassy reception will give you sufficient opportunity to mingle with your colleagues and advance your new career.

Perspective

Work in the Middle Kingdom
Internship Opportunities for Students in China

By Christopher Moore

Adding work on top of study abroad experience demonstrates to employers that one can function professionally in a foreign environment and an overseas job can be the stepping stone to a life of foreign work and adventure. At the least, it will be an exciting time of learning and challenge.

My job destination was China. As it has gained full membership in the World Trade Organization, China offers the student or recent graduate a wealth of possibilities to gain international work experience.

Many positions in multinational organizations in China do not require a knowledge of the language. In addition, many opportunities for English teachers, writers, and editors are advertised in publications targeted at the foreign community in China. I recently saw the following statement on a Chinese web site: "There are more English speakers in China than in America." True or not, there are many Chinese who speak English and many more who want to learn.

The best place to start a job search in China is at the American Chamber of Commerce. Here you can network and find out about job availability throughout the country (the Chamber also offers its own internships). You can order the

Chamber's directory of companies in China that employ foreigners and possibly nail down an internship before you leave the U.S. (see below).

How I Did It

I went to my adviser and announced my plan to intern in Beijing. What kind of academic credit, if any, could I get?

Surprisingly, my adviser accepted this vague proposal without questioning how I would implement it. Now the pressure was on me: I had to go to Beijing and find an internship.

When I arrived in Beijing I looked for jobs advertised in the local expat publications to get a feel for the job market and contacted whomever I could think of for possible leads. I looked at Internet sites for promising openings; I went to the Chamber of Commerce and looked through their directory of U.S. companies operating in China; I made a list of potential employers in which I was interested and contacted the most attractive ones-whether they had advertised openings or not. Then I sent cover letters and resumes to the eight organizations I especially liked. From these first contacts I obtained five interviews and in the end I had four offers to choose from.

At first I worked in the market research division of Unisono, a Dutch company whose focus is the Chinese marketplace. I am now interning with UNESCO in Beijing.

Living and working in China and taking part in its daily life is exhilarating. I enjoy the Chinese and love the expatriate environment, which permits one to get to know and make friends with people from around the world.

How You Can Do It

All you need is a resume, a positive attitude, and an appropriate work uniform. Be prepared with these necessities and you'll lose no time. I have talked with many student interns in Beijing and can safely say that an internship can begin—if one searches diligently—within two to four weeks after arrival in China.

Finding a position in China is similar to a job search anywhere. My experience has been concentrated in Beijing. But one could easily find similar possibilities in all business-oriented areas of China.

Internship Contacts

• The Department of State has several student employment programs, some in Washington, DC and others in embassies overseas. For info write: Attn: Student Programs, U.S. Department of State, Recruitment Division, SA-1, 2401 E St., NW, 5th Fl., Washington, DC 20522; www.state.gov.

• MOGPA, a nonprofit organization that arranges 6- to 12-month professional work assignments and internships for corporations in Asia with U.S. students and recent graduates, operates in China and Japan. Proficiency in the language is required. Contact: 2345 Rice St., Suite 200, Saint Paul, MN 55113; info@mogpa.org, www.Mogpa.org.

• The American Chamber of Commerce, a great launching point for networking and researching companies, publishes a directory of all U.S. companies operating in

China and hosts a monthly social. It offers a resume service in which you can advertise to companies in China that you are looking for an internship. Contact: Room 1903, China Resource Bldg., 8 Jianguomenbei Dajie, Beijing 100005, China; 011-86-10-8519-1920; AmCham@AmCham-China.org.cn, www.AmCham-China.org.cn.

• Canada-China Business Council offers services similar to the American Chamber of Commerce and also hosts a social every month that is good for networking and finding out about job availability. Contact: Suite 1802 CITIC Bldg., 19 Jianguomenwai Dajie, Beijing 100004, China; 011-86-10-6512-6120, fax 011-86-10-6512-6125; www.ccbc.com.

• The U.S.-China Business Council, a useful source for company information, has a human resource link to many Asian job sites. This is the principal organization of U.S. companies engaged in trade and investment in the Peoples Republic of China. It offers its own internships. Contact: 1818 N St., NW, Suite 200, Washington, DC 20036; 202-429-0340, fax 202-775-2476; www.uschina.org.

• The United Nations has various internship and fellowship programs. Each department has a separate internship administration, so you must contact the department you are interested in. For information on the UN Development Fund in China contact: UNDP China, 2 Liangmahe Nan Lu, Beijing 100600, China; 011-86-10-6532-3731; registry.cn@undp.org, www.un.org.

Web Sites

• Teach in China www.cbw.com/teaching describes conditions for teachers and contains articles from people who have taught in China. It will match you with a position for up to six months at no cost.

• www.JobOK.com is a Hong Kong, Macau, Mainland China job site.

• www.ChinaNow.com, a general China information site, has a classified section where one can search for housing and jobs wanted and offered, including teaching.

• Expat Publications: City Weekend, Full Link Plaza Tower B, Suite 1212, Chaoyangmenwai Dajie 18, Beijing 100020, China; 011-86-10-6588-1341, www.city weekend.com.cn.

Perspective

You Can Have It All

A Synergistic Program for Young Professionals

By Matthew M. Pierle

During college I worked as a peer adviser in a well-equipped overseas opportunities office. When students searching for personalized international experience came through our door we'd usually ask if they wanted to work, study, or travel abroad. Their interests varied but were often specific: "This guy at a party told me you can get a job working at ski resorts in Chile. . . . Sign me up!"

Occasionally, however, someone wants everything: to study a foreign language, enroll at an institution of higher education, work or intern with a foreign organization, and travel on the side with little or no personal cost. The Congress-Bundestag Youth Exchange for Young Professionals (CBYX) program is one exceptional program that offers it all. (CBYX also offers two other unique programs worth looking into: a high school exchange and a vocational school exchange. Visit their web site, below, for information on these two under-18 programs.)

The CBYX program, or Parlamentarisches Patenschafts-Programm (PPP) as it is known auf Deutsch, was founded 18 years ago to commemorate the 300th anniversary of the first German emigrants arriving in America. This multifaceted exchange of young professionals between Germany and the U.S. is administered on the U.S. side by CDS International, Inc. (formerly the Carl Duisberg Society) and on the German side by the Carl Duisberg Gesellschaft (CDG). Currently, about 60 Americans and 100 Germans participate annually.

Program participants from the U.S. range in age from 18-24 at the time of departure. While a high school degree is the minimum educational requirement for U.S. outbounds, a high proportion of the participants are either presently enrolled in or recent graduates of U.S. universities, community colleges, or technical schools. No prior language experience is necessary. Applicants do, however, need to be able to express their career objectives, exhibit flexibility, and have an outgoing personality. They must also demonstrate a curiosity and desire for learning German language and engaging directly in the culture.

When I discovered this synergistic program I knew it would allow me to discover modern Germany in ways impossible as a participant in a study abroad program or as a short-term employee or a vagabond traveler. I applied, and two months later I interviewed for the scholarship.

Much of the beauty of the CBYX program is its individual nature. After an intensive language instruction phase, each CBYX scholar moves to an assigned Bundesland (state) where they enroll for a semester of study within a German institution of higher education. From that point on CBYXers generally have limited contact with the other American participants. Participants encounter German culture head-on and learn about the subtle and the stark differences between American and German academic systems, public and private institutions, language, and everyday life.

A monthly stipend covers basic living and study expenses. Although it is recommended that participants have access to $300-$350 per month for discretionary purchases and travel, a few frugal participants have come home without having spent an additional dollar or Euro.

For me, one of the greatest fringe benefits of studying German in Saarbrücken (August through September) was the chance to meet over 100 scholars and professionals from all over the world. The scholarship holders study in Germany for periods of three months to two years and are sponsored primarily by the German Ministry of Economic Cooperation. Because of these connections, CBYXers enjoy an international experience within a German context.

After the 2-month German course, CBYXers study at a German university, technical college, or training school (mid-October through January). Housing arrangements depend upon the participant's preference and local availability of housing options. Transferable academic credit may in some cases be arranged.

I studied in the former East Bloc city of Erfurt at the satellite campus for Horticulture and Landscape Architecture of the Fachhochschule Erfurt. My housing was in an externally drab but lively cooperative apartment.

The CBYX program allows each participant to engage in one or more internships (February through June). The practical workplace training can take the form of pure or applied research or the application of hands-on skills. Financial compensation varies. My American colleagues and I studied and carried out Praktika all over Germany in fields ranging from forestry to marketing, culinary arts to auto body painting and repair, chemistry to music, computer science to wine making, engineering to beer brewing, industrial welding to law.

Although not officially a traveling program, there is enough built-in travel time in the form of obligation-free weekends and required seminars throughout the year to satisfy almost everyone. The last few weeks of the program are free for reisen und wandern.

I spent my weekends touring by rail, bike, and thumb. I enjoyed bike trips throughout Germany and to neighboring France, the Czech Republic, and Poland. I particularly enjoyed attending the earthy medieval and Renaissance gatherings and folk music festivals.

For More Info

For a downloadable CBYX application from the New York office go to www.cdsintl.org. Applications are generally due in December for programs beginning the following August. Contact: Program Officer, Rebecca Reagan Delfino, CDS Intl., Inc., 871 United Nations Plaza, 15th Fl., New York, NY 10017-1814; 212-497-3500, fax 212-497-3535; rdelfino@cdsintl.org.

Perspective

Foreign Service in Florence

Interning for the U.S. Department of State

By Victoria Grisanti

A s the taxi crossed over Ponte Della Vittoria and made its way onto Lungarno Amerigo Vespucci, I got my first glimpse of Palazzo Canevaro. The Palazzo looked out over the Arno, just two bridges down from the Ponte Vecchio. This large, lemon-colored villa is home to the American Consulate in Florence and would be my home for the next three months. My summer internship would not only introduce me to a new culture and language but provide a first hand look at American operations abroad.

Applicants must be college or university juniors, seniors, or graduate students. The internships range in location from Washington, DC to an overseas embassy and are offered during the spring, summer, and fall. Positions are generally unpaid, but the Department will consider financial aid requests. If you apply for an internship during a college semester you may also be eligible to receive credit at your university. In this case plan to meet with an advisor or professor to work out the requirements to receive credit for the internship.

The application process provides an opportunity to be specific and provide detailed information. Applicants may choose two locations of interest from the list of participating posts. Select locations that are familiar to you. I had spent a semester studying in Florence and knew the language and the city itself rather well. I was not fluent in Italian, but was able to speak and understand general conversation. I included all this information in my application and explained that I was extremely interested in a position in Italy.

Another point to keep in mind as you complete the application is the reason you are seeking this internship. Beyond spending time in a foreign city or experiencing a new culture, why do you want to work for the U.S. Department of State? The answer was relatively easy for me. I had applied to graduate school at several universities to study international relations. I had a keen interest in U.S. foreign policy and diplomacy abroad and wanted to learn more first-hand about the Foreign Service.

The application usually takes about six to eight months to process. I applied in October and received a call in December to say that I had been tentatively chosen for the position. In January I received and sent back paperwork to authorize the agency to perform a security check. Once I passed the security clearance, I received an official offer to begin in April. My position was unpaid, but fortunately the Consulate in Florence did offer to pay for housing and expenses. I accepted immediately.

Home Away from Home

Preparing for a 3-month sojourn overseas is not as easy as it may seem, especially when you know very little about your new position and even less about where you will be living.

Before they travel to a post abroad, the Department of State requires that interns have adequate international medical coverage.

In Florence, interns had use of the third floor of the Consulate, which has several bedrooms and bathrooms and even a kitchen and laundry room with a washer and dryer. I was able to do my own cooking (which kept my food expenses low), leaving weekend travel as my only other big expense.

I had a large room with two windows, one of which looked out on the Ponte Vecchio and the other on a magnificent view of the Duomo.

Getting to Work

The Department of State offers a range of positions and accepts students from many different educational backgrounds. The Consulate in Florence offered internship positions in the consular section, economic section, business development, and office technology. In the economic section interns research business issues of interest to the Consul General, while others work on formatting new web pages or promote U.S. business interests abroad.

I had been assigned to the consular section, which meant aiding the full-time, 2-person staff with requests from American citizens either residing in or traveling through this region of Italy. Tuscany is a popular destination for American tourists, and Florence offers more than 35 university programs that enroll American students. The influx of travelers and students ensured a hectic summer in the consular section.

Interns work alongside the full-time staff, Monday-Friday from 8 a.m. to 5 p.m. Day to day activities in the consular section included aiding travelers with passport requests, helping couples looking to get married in Italy work their way through Italian bureaucracy, and documenting births of American citizens abroad. Computer and typing skills are important.

Our responsibilities did not end in the office. Interns also help plan and attend any receptions or festivities held at the Consulate and are highly encouraged to attend various events in Florence when Consular staff is invited-free rein to enjoy the festivities and represent the U.S. on foreign ground.

Surprising Encounters

Meetings with famous personalities, like Andrea Boccelli, were not uncommon, and each event I attended was a wonderful opportunity to interact with people of a different culture and lifestyle.

Applications can be found by logging onto www.state.gov and following the links to Student Programs. For information regarding the American Embassy and Consulates in Italy log onto www.usembassy.it.

International Internships

The Key Print Resources

Selected and Reviewed by William Nolting

L ike the international careers they can help open up, internships may be either located in the U.S. with international organizations or overseas. They are often unpaid. Start your search early, as applications can be due three to nine months in advance.

**Essential; *Outstanding and of broad interest.
For ordering information, if not included below, see Key Publishers, page 13.

**Academic Year Abroad and Short-Term Study Abroad. These are the most comprehensive and authoritative directories of study abroad, listing over 4,900 programs offered year round and summer. Indexes for internships, practical training, volunteering, and student teaching list over 1,300 programs, most of which charge tuition and give academic credit. Available free online at www.iiepassport.org.

*American-Scandinavian Foundation: "Study in Scandinavia". 2001 (annual). 54 pp. Free

from ASF, 58 Park Ave., New York, NY 10016; 212-879-9779, fax 212-249-3444; www.amscan.org. Web site lists both study and work programs. This nonprofit organization offers paid internships in Scandinavia in engineering, teaching English as a foreign language, business, and agricultural fields. Apply for internships by late Dec. Fee $50. (If accepted a $200 refundable deposit is required to hold position.) ASF also assists with obtaining work permits for Scandinavia. "Study in Scandinavia" is now available only on the ASF web site, no longer in hard copy.

*CDS International, Inc. Free booklet and applications available from CDS, 871 United Nations Plaza, 15th Fl., New York, NY 10017-1814; 212-497-3500, fax 212-497-3535; info@cdsintl.org, www.cdsintl.org. CDS International, a nonprofit organization, offers overseas practical training internships for Americans in a variety of fields including business, engineering and technology. Programs are offered in Germany, Argentina, Singapore, Turkey, and Switzerland, and are intended for young professionals seeking to gain international work experience. Some language proficiency is usually required, as well as some relevant experience. CDS also assists and sponsors work permits, and charges a fee of $300-$500. Most internships are paid. The CDS web site provides more information on each program.

**Directory of International Internships: A World of Opportunities edited by Charles A. Gliozzo and Vernicka K. Tyson. 2002. 5th edition. 162 pp. Michigan State Univ. Career Services and Placement. $25 postpaid from Michigan State Univ., Career Services and Placement, Attn: Directory of International Internships, 113 Student Services Bldg., East Lansing, MI 48824; 517-353-5589 ext. 146, fax 517-353-7254; gliozzo@pilot.msu.edu, www.isp.msu.edu/InternationalInternships. This is the most comprehensive directory of both academic and non-academic internships located abroad. Describes experiential educational opportunities offered through educational institutions, governmental, and private organizations—for academic credit, for pay, or simply for experience. In-depth profiles of more than 200 internship programs offered by over 160 organizations. Very useful cross-indexes by subject and country. Highly recommended.

A Handbook for Creating Your Own Internship in International Development by Natalie Foster and Nicole Howell. Just Act: Youth Action for Global Justice, 333 Valencia St., #101, San Francisco, CA 94110; 415-431-4204, fax 415-431-5953; info@justact.org, www.justact.org. The handbook includes a workbook to help evaluate your skills, motivations, and learning objectives, as well as practical advice. See Just Act's directory of opportunities in the volunteer section below.

*International Cooperative Education Program. Free information from ICE, 15 Spiros Way, Menlo Park, CA 94025; 650-323-4944, fax 650-323-1104; ICEmenlo@aol.com, www.icemenlo.com. Organization offers 450 paid summer internships for students with

knowledge of foreign languages (German, Finnish, French, Italian, Chinese, Japanese) in Europe and Asia. U.S. or Canadian citizens preferred. Apply by February. Fee of $800.

International Health Electives for Medical Students. American Medical Student Association. $15 from AMSA Resource Center, 1902 Association Dr., Reston, VA 20191; 703-620-6600 ext. 217 800-767-2266, fax 703-620-5873; amsarc@www.amsa.org, www.amsa.org. Overseas internships for third- or fourth-year medical students. Related titles: A Student's Guide to International Health ($8), and Cross-Cultural Medicine: What to Know Before You Go ($8), Creative Funding for International Health Electives ($5) also available from AMSA. Most publications available free on AMSA web site.

*The Internship Bible by Mark Oldman and Samer Hamadeh. 2002 (Annual). 621 pp. $25. Princeton Review, distributed by Random House, available through Velarde Publicity; 212-572-2870, fax 212-572-6026; www.review.com. Directory describes in detail paid and unpaid internships offered by nearly 900 mostly non-academic organizations. Around 120 of these organizations have overseas branches, listed in an index for location, though it's often not made clear which of these actually offer internships abroad. Other indexes for field, benefits, level of study, minority programs, and deadlines.

Internships International. Free information from Judy Tilson, Director, P.O. Box 480, Woolwich, ME 04579-0408; 207-443-3019, fax 207-442-7942; intintl@aol.com, http://rtpnet.org/~intintl. Organization offers unpaid, not-for-credit internship placements for college graduates (or seniors who need an internship for graduation) in London, Paris, Dresden, Florence, Dublin, Santiago, Budapest, Glasgow, Melbourne, and Cape Town. Fee of $800 ($1,000 for Dublin). The internships are in all fields.

LEAPNow: Lifelong Education Alternatives & Programs. Download brochure available from web site or available from LEAPNow, P.O. Box 1817, Sebastopol, CA 95473; 707-829-1142, fax 707-829-1132; info@leapnow.org, www.leapnow.org. LEAPNow is a leading source for low-cost internships, volunteer positions, work exchanges, and experiential academic programs in 129 countries and the U.S. Over 20,000 options and 20 years experience tailoring custom programs for people of all ages and backgrounds. Academic credit available for all programs.

*Peterson's Study Abroad (2002, 9th ed.) & Summer Study Abroad. (2002, 5th ed.) Both $29.95, available on their web site, www.petersons.com. Study abroad directories list over 3,500 programs, over 800 of which offer internships, listed in a special index. Most are for academic credit.

*U.S. Department of State Student Intern Program. Free brochure and application from U.S. Department of State, Intern Coordinator, HR/REE SA-1, 2401 E St., NW 5th Fl., Washington, DC 20522; Email for hard-copy application: internbook@socent.org. Apply online: www.state.gov/employment. Nearly 1,000 mostly unpaid and paid internships in international relations annually, in Washington and abroad. Only for currently-enrolled undergraduate and graduate students who will continue studies after the internship. Competitive. Deadlines: Nov 1 (Summer), Mar 1 (Fall), Jul 1 (Spring).

*Women in International Security: Online International Internships Directory by Women in International Security. 1999 (continuously updated), info@wiis.org, www.wiis.org. Web site includes detailed descriptions of internships offered by more than 250 international organizations, primarily in the Washington, DC area as well as a few overseas locations.

International Internships
Directory of Programs

By Transitions Abroad Editors

For the most up-to-date information on international internship programs check the *Transitions Abroad* web site [www.TransitionsAbroad.com], or contact the program directors. Please tell them you read about their program in this book. Programs based in more than one country or region are listed under "Worldwide."

ARGENTINA

Study and Intern in Argentina
COINED Argentina is offering a complete program of Spanish language classes and internships in Argentinian companies and institutions of many fields in Buenos Aires and Cordoba, Argentina. COINED has been active in international education since 1971. Thousands of students from Europe, North America and other countries have joined our programs and most of them studied Spanish in their language school.

Dates: Year round. Cost: Spanish course $165 per week. Internship placment fee: $500. Ask for special promotions. Contact: Marcelo Cuestas, COINED Argentina, Artigas 220, P.A. 5000 Cordoba, Argentina; Tel./fax 011-54-351-4299402.

AUSTRALIA

Australian Internships
Interns are placed with research teams, Australian employers, political administrations, etc., for periods ranging from 6 weeks to a year. The positions are unpaid. Homestay accommodations are included. Placement is arranged to suit the individual provided 4 months notice is given. Most placements are in Queensland or New South Wales. Fields: marine and wildlife biology, business, etc. No academic credit offered. Unlimited internships. Prerequisites: a) High School Graduates, b) Professional Development for Graduates and Junior/Senior college students.

Dates: Year round. Application deadline: Four months before start date. Cost: $2,990 (includes room and board) for 6-week professional development program. Application fee: $500. Contact: Dr. Maurice A. Howe, Education Australia, P.O. Box 2233, Amherst, MA 01004; 800-344-6741, fax 413-549-0741; edaust@javanet.com.

Custom Designed Internsips
AustraLearn will facilitate enriching and educational internships in Australia. Focus: diversity of fields such as International Business, Sports and Fitness, Marine Biology, Education, Public Policy, Public Relations, and more. Available to all interested students (undergraduate and graduate) and working professionals. Academic credit can be arranged through home university.

Dates: Year round, from 6-week minimum to 52 weeks maximum. Lead-time must be at least 4 months prior to intended date of departure. **Cost:** Starts at $2,990 for 6-week program. Prices are adjusted based on desired length of internship. Includes internship placement, homestay with 2 meals or shared accommodations without meals, liaison services in Australia, and airport transfers. Call for more information. **Contact:** AustraLearn: North American Center for Australian Universities. CSU Denver Center, 110 16th St., Denver, CO 80202; 800-980-0033, fax 303-446-2214; studyabroad@aus tralearn.org, www.australearn.org.

Univ. of the Sunshine Coast

Australia's newest university offers students a truly Australian experience. Located 1 hour from Brisbane, on the Sunshine Coast, USC offers courses in a wide range of disciplines, outstanding faculty, small classes, individualized attention, strong program of support services and cultural activities. Internships available with the required prior academic preparation. Student apartments adjacent to campus.

Dates: Session I: early Feb-late Jun; Session II: mid-Jul-early Dec. **Cost:** Approx. $5,056 per semester includes orienation in the U.S. and Australia, 20 weeks of housing with food allowance, Australian health insurance, USC tuition, administrative fees. Airfare and SUNY tuition not included. **Contact:** Office of International Programs, P.O. Box 2000, SUNY Cortland, Cortland, NY 13045; 607-753-2209, fax 607-753-5989; koppl@cortland.edu, www.studyabroad.com/suny/cortland.

BELIZE

Internships in Belize

Experience living and working in an English-speaking developing country. Internships are available in most disciplines. Interns live with host families. Following a 1-week orientation, participants work full time with various agencies and organizations. Must be self-starters. Journals and written projects are submitted for assessment at the end of program. Academic credit offered: 15-16 credits per semester. Required: 2.5 cumulative GPA, strong performance in major, maturity, and adaptability. Junior or senior status.

Dates: Fall and spring, 16-17 weeks each. **Cost:** Estimate: $4,400 includes internship supervision, room and board, health insurance, local transportation, international airfare, full-day orientation prior to departure in Cortland, and 1-week orientation upon arrival in Belize. SUNY tuition not included. **Contact:** Office of International Programs, P.O. Box 2000, SUNY Cortland, Cortland, NY 13045; 607-753-2209, fax 607-753-5989; studyabroad@cort land.edu, www.studyabroad.com/suny/cortland.

COSTA RICA

Learn Spanish While Volunteering

Assist with the training of Costa Rican public school teachers in ESL and computers. Assist local health clinic, social service agencies, and environmental projects. Enjoy learning Spanish in the morning, volunteer work in the afternoon/evening. Spanish classes of 2-4 students plus group learning activities; conversations with middle class homestay families (1 student or couple per family). Homestays and most volunteer projects are in a small town near the capital, San José.

Dates: Year round, all levels. Classes begin every Monday (except Mar 25-29 and Dec 14-Jan 5), volunteer program is continuous. **Cost:** $345 per week for 26 hours of classes and group activities including Costa Rican dance and cooking classes. Includes tuition, meals, homestay, laundry, all materials, weekly 3-hour cultural tour, and airport transportation. $25 one-time registration fee. **Contact:** Susan Shores, Registrar, Latin American Language Center, P.M.B 123, 7485 Rush River Dr., Suite 710, Sacramento, CA 95831-5260; 916-447-0938, fax 916-428-9542; lalc@madre.com, www.madre.com/~lalc.

EUROPE

Internship Program

CCI's Discovery Abroad Internship Program gives students (18-25) the opportunity to participate in a volunteer internship in France, Germany, Ireland, Italy, or the U.K. Internships provide exciting opportunities for language and cross-cultural immersion and valuable work experience. Participants live with a host family for the duration of the program and will be placed in an internship related to their course of study.

Dates: Year round. **Cost:** One month approx. $2,000, 2 months approx. $2,900, 3 months approx. $3,400. **Contact:** Outbound Department, Center for Cultural Interchange, 17 N 2nd Ave., St. Charles, IL 60174; 888-ABROAD1, fax 630-377-2307; karen@cci-exchange.com, www.cci-exchange.com.

Internships in Europe/E.P.A.

The Univ. of Rochester and Educational Programs Abroad sponsor programs in London, Bonn, Brussels, Madrid, and Paris that combine coursework with unpaid internships for academic credit. Fields include politics, law, business, health science, and the arts. Available to juniors, seniors, and recent graduates. Requirements: 3.0 GPA or better, and at least 2 years of college-level language study where appropriate.

Dates: Sep-Dec, Jan-Apr; 2 summer terms of 8

69

weeks each. **Cost:** Semester programs range from $6,700-$9,850; summer $5,400. **Contact:** Jacqueline Levine, Director, Center for Study Abroad, Univ. of Rochester, Rochester, NY 14627; 716-275-7532, fax 716-461-5131; abroad@mail.rochester.edu, www.rochester.edu/College/study-abroad/europe/index.html.

Prehistoric and Tribal Art

Apprenticeship in prehistoric and tribal art: research, editing, international relations, museums, and exhibitions planning, evaluation and definition of rock art and of art objects. Minimum stay: 3 months; stage 6 months or 12 months. Specialization courses and field school. Details upon request.

Dates: Year round. **Cost:** Contact sponsor. **Contact:** Prof. Emmanuel Anati, Centro Camuno di Studi Preistorici (CCSP), 25044 Capo di Ponte, BS, Italy; www.rockart-ccsp.com.

GERMANY

Internship Programs

This program is designed for American college seniors or recent graduates in business, hotel management, engineering, or technical fields who want 6-12 months of practical on-the-job training in an international environment. Individuals are placed in paid internships with companies that match their professional interests.

Dates: Programs begin the first day of each month. **Cost:** Application fee: Participants responsible for airfare, housing, and living expenses. **Contact:** Isabell Kowalk, CDS International, Inc., 871 United Nations Plaza, 15th Fl., New York, NY 10017; 212-497-3500; info@cdsintl.org, www.cdsintl.org.

LATIN AMERICA

Internship Positions

In Costa Rica, Mexico, Guatemala, Ecuador, Argentina, Peru, Bolivia. Various positions in the fields of health care, education, tourism, ESL, business, law, marketing, administrative, environmental, and social work. Additional customized options available. Four weeks to 6 months. Inexpensive lodging in homestays or dorms. Some positions provide free room and board.

Dates: Year round. Flexible start dates. **Cost:** $350 placement and application fee. Travel insurance and pre-departure preparation included. Lodging costs depend on location. **Contact:** AmeriSpan Unlimited, P.O. Box 40007, Philadelphia, PA 19106; 800-879-6640, fax 215-751-1100; info@amerispan.com, www.amerispan.com.

RUSSIA AND THE NIS

ACTR Business Russian Language and Internship Program

This program combines a curriculum focusing on the language of Russian business communication with a 20-hour per week internship in a U.S. or Russian business, NGO, or government agency. The program emphasizes speaking and reading skills for business communications, commercial document preparation, and reading the Russian business press.

Dates: Summer term, academic year, fall and spring. **Cost:** Summer $6,000, fall/spring terms $9,000, academic year $15,000. **Contact:** Graham Hettlinger, Gabriel Coleman, or Terrence Graham, Program Officer, ACTR, 1776 Massachusetts Ave., NW, Suite 700, Washington, DC 20036; 202-833-7522, fax 202-833-7523; hettlinger@actr.org, www.actr.org.

SCANDINAVIA

Training Program

Two- to 6-month positions in engineering, chemistry, computer science, agriculture, business, TEFOL. Most positions are in Finland and Sweden.

Dates: Contact organization for details. **Cost:** $50 application fee. **Contact:** Training, The American-Scandinavian Foundation, 58 Park Ave., New York, NY 10016; 212-879-9779, fax 212-686-2115; training@amscan.org, www.amscan.org.

UNITED KINGDOM AND IRELAND

AIFS International Internship Program in London

A 1-semester program awarding 12 to 18 credits for an unpaid internship in London. Placements are in international business, finance, marketing, international relations, education, media, museums and galleries, art and design firms, theater and entertainment, and politics. Individual attention given to clarify and set goals as well as support during placement.

Dates: Sep-Dec; Jan-May. **Cost:** $11,000 includes tuition, housing, and one way flight to London from any of 32 U.S. cities. **Contact:** AIFS, River Plaza, 9 West Broad St., Stamford, CT 06902-3788; college info@aifs.com, www.aifs.com/.

AIU London Study and Internship Program

AIU's central London campus offers a U.S.-accredited curriculum and a multicultural

population. Study abroad students take courses in International Business, Communication, Liberal Arts, Fashion Design/Marketing, Interior Design, Visual Communication, and Media Production. Program features include comprehensive student services, activities/travel, furnished apartment accommodations, and scholarships and financial aid.

Dates: Five regular academic quarters: fall (Oct-Dec); winter (Jan-Mar); spring (Mar-May); summer I (Jun-Jul); summer II (Aug-Sep). Special 4-week summer sessions as well. **Cost:** Three classes $4,900; 4 classes $5,700; 2 classes and internship $4,900. **Contact:** American InterContinental Univ., 6600 Peachtree-Dunwoody Rd., 500 Embassy Row, Atlanta, GA 30328; 800-255-6839, fax 404-965-8006; studyabroad@aiuniv.edu, http://studyabroad.aiuniv.edu.

Dublin Internships

The opportunity to work in a supervised setting and live in Dublin provides students both rare insight into Irish Culture and practical training in their field. Internships organized according to requirements of Cooperative Education Program at Cortland, which necessitates developing a project with home-campus faculty adviser. Internships unpaid except those in financial institutions, which require 6 months lead time and appropriate academic preparation. Possible internships in anthropology, archaeology, architecture, broadcasting, business, communications, economics, education, ESL, fine, visual, and performing arts, health science professions and technologies, interior design, journalism, library sciences, linguistics, nutrition, physical education, practical classroom experience, special education, social sciences, and sport science. Housing in flats or with families.

Dates: Fall: late Aug-mid-Dec; spring: early Jan-mid-May. **Cost:** $4,700 per semester; summer $3,950. Estimates include full-day orientation in the U.S., application fee, apartment rentals, meals, weekly bus pass, insurance, roundtrip airfare from NY, placement and supervision, biweekly cultural seminar, passport, books, and supplies, administrative fees. SUNY tuition and spending money not included. **Contact:** Office of International Programs, Box 2000, SUNY Cortland, Cortland, NY 13045; 607-753-2209, fax 607-753-5989; studyabroad@cortland.edu, www.studyabroad.com/suny/cortland.

Hansard Scholars Program

An opportunity for students to become involved in the workings of the British government and British politics, accompanied by a comprehensive study of British politics and British public policy. Students are mainly assigned internships with members of Parliament, but also to political parties, think tanks, and pressure groups. Prerequisites: 2 or more years of college. Application materials: transcript, 2 letters of recommendation, an essay, and a personal statement.

Dates: Spring: mid-Jan-early Apr; summer: mid-May-late Jul; fall: late-Sep-mid-Dec. **Cost:** £5,350 per semester (includes housing and London travel costs, and a series of study visits and social events). **Contact:** Melanie Rimmer, Program Coordinator, The Hansard Society, St. Philips, Building North, Sheffield St., London WC2A 2EX, U.K.; 011-44-171-955-7713, fax 011-44-171-955-7492; hansard@lse.ac.uk, www.hansard-society.org.uk.

Internship Program

We personally design internship packages, both in New York and London to suit individual needs and career interests. Internships are available year round in just about any field imaginable.

Dates: Year round. **Cost:** From $995 year round internship to $4,995 London summer internship packages (4 weeks). Includes program, theater, trips, room and partial board. **Contact:** Janet Kollek Evans, Director, American Assn. of Overseas Studies, 51 Drayton Gardens, Suite 4, London SW10 9RX, U.K.; 800-EDU-BRIT; aaos2000@hotmail.com, www.worldwide.edu/uk/aaos.

Internship Program in Wales

A semester or year in Latin America at Friends World Center in San José suburb of Heredia, incorporates seminars, field study, travel, and independent projects. Seminars to introduce students into Latin America and its culture include Central American realities today, intensive Spanish for any level student, ecology and development, women's studies in Latin America. Independent work has included: ecology, community development, peace studies, health and agriculture studies. Students may earn 12-18 credits per semester.

Dates: Summer 2002, late May-mid Jun. **Cost:** Approx. $2,000 includes accommodations. **Contact:** Emma Frearson, American Studies Exchange Office, Univ. of Wales Swansea, Singleton Park, Swansea SA2 8PP, Wales, U.K.; 011-44-1-792-295135, fax 011-44-1-792-295719; e.frearson@swansea.ac.uk, www.swan.ac.uk/sao.

London Internship Program

A pioneer of supervised work experience, Middlesex Univ. offers one of the widest range of internships in the U.K. Year-long opportunities are available to gain experience in business, politics, community, and health, amongst others. All internships are project-based, academically supervised, and carry academic credit. Internships can be taken alongside other university courses.

Dates: Fall, spring, or summer semester. **Cost:** Approx. $1,950 (tuition and internship). **Contact:** Valdev Chaggar, Registry Admissions, Middlesex Univ., White Hart Ln., London N17 8HR, U.K.; 011-44-203-362-5782, fax 011-44-208-362-5649; admissions@mdx.ac.uk.

Univ. of North London

SUNY Cortland celebrates its 30th consecutive year at UNL. Over 400 courses are offered. Fields of study include education, natural sciences, humanities, communications, social sciences, business, health, theater arts, fine arts, and others. Direct enrollment with British students. Credits per semester: 12-16. Pre-arranged housing in flats in Central London district. Full- and part-time internships available.

Dates: Fall: late-Sep-mid Dec; spring: late Jan-mid-May. **Cost:** Estimates: Fall $7,015; spring $7,715 (longer semester). Estimates include full-day orientation in the U.S., application fee, pre-arranged apartment rental, meals, commuter ticket on underground, London tour and Thames cruise, insurance, roundtrip airfare from NY, transportation from airport to downtown London upon arrival, passport, books and supplies, various cultural activities, administrative fees. SUNY tuition and spending money not included. **Contact:** Office of International Programs, P.O. Box 2000, SUNY Cortland, Cortland, NY 13045; 607-753-2209, fax 607-753-5989; studyabroad@cortland.edu, www.studyabroad.com/suny/cortland.

WESTERN EUROPE

First Choice/Ski Bound

First Choice leases and runs 30 hotels and 40 chalets in European ski resorts. Recruits over 850 staff to work in resorts each year. Positions include hotel/bar/restaurant managers, chefs (all grades), kitchen porters/night porters, bar staff, general assistants maintenance staff. A job with First Choice provides the opportunity to travel, meet many new friends, improve language skills, and learn to ski while gaining valuable job experience. Training is carried out in house either prior to departure or while in resort. Offers attractive package that includes travel to and from resort, medical insurance, personal belonging insurance, food, accommodations, and either a free or subsidized lift pass (dependent on position).

Dates: Contact organization for details. **Cost:** Contact organization for details. **Contact:** Applications should be made in writing with a resume: First Choice Ski Lakes and Mountains Division, Olivier House, 18 Marine Parade, Brighton BN2 1TL, U.K.; 011-44-1273-677777, fax 011-44-1273-600486.

WORLDWIDE

Association for Int'l. Practical Training (AIPT)

AIPT is the foremost provider of worldwide on-the-job training programs for students and professionals seeking international career development and life-changing experiences. AIPT arranges workplace exchanges in hundreds of professional fields, bringing employers and trainees together from around the world. AIPT's online placement service PINPOINT matches individuals seeking training opportunities with appropriate training positions in their field.

Dates: Year round. **Cost:** Vary. **Contact:** Customer Service Representative, AIPT, 10400 Little Patuxent Pkwy., Suite 250, Columbia, MD 21044-3519; 410-997-2200, fax 410-992-3924; aipt@aipt.org, www.aipt.org.

Boston Univ. International Programs

Offering internships in language/liberal arts, fine arts, archaeology, engineering, and tropical ecology programs in 40 locations on 6 continents and in 9 different languages. Course offerings range from intermediate-level language and liberal arts study through advanced-level, direct enrollment in local universities. Internship programs combine coursework with participation in local work life. Application materials: 2 references, transcript, essays, and academic approval.

Dates: Fall, spring, and summer (length varies). **Cost:** $5,000-$18,010; application fee: $45. **Contact:** Boston Univ., International Programs, 232 Bay State Rd., 5th Fl., Boston, MA 02215; 617-353-9888, fax 617-353-5402; abroad@bu.edu, www.bu.edu/abroad.

Directory of International Internships

The Directory is a comprehensive guide to international internships sponsored by educational institutions, government agencies, and private organizations. The Directory's 170 pages include subject and location indexes, international internship opportunities, and a bibliography.

Dates: Up-to-date, 4th ed., revised in late 1998. **Cost:** $25 includes s/h. **Contact:** Charles Gliozzo, Michigan State Univ., Rm. 209, International Center, E. Lansing, MI 48824; 517-353-5589, fax 517-353-7254; gliozzo@pilot.msu.edu, www.isp.msu.edu.

Global Service Corps (GSC)

A project of Earth Island Institute creates opportunities for adult participants to live in homes in Tanzania and Thailand while volunteering on health, education, sustainable agriculture, HIV/AIDS awareness and environment community service and development projects. These service-learning programs emphasize grass-roots collaboration on the local level, mutual transfer of skills, and cross-cultural understanding. Undergraduate and graduate level credits qualifying for financial aid available.

Dates: Year round. Contact GSC office or check the web site for specific starting dates **Cost:** Approx. $1,900-$2,000 for 23-28 day project trips; $3,255-$4,305 for summer and semester college internships. Long-term 3-6 month placements also available. Includes pre-departure preparations and in-country expenses (hotel and homestay room and board, orientation, training, language lessons, project expenses, transportation, and weekend safari). Airfare not included. **Contact:** Global Service Corps., 300 Broadway, Suite 28, San Francisco, CA 94133; 415-788-3666 ext 128, fax 415-788-7324; gsc@earthisland.org, www.globalservicecorps.org.

IAESTE (United States)

Founded in 1948, the International Association for the Exchange of Students for Technical Experience (IAESTE) is an international network that coordinates paid international internships for students in technical fields such as engineering, computer science, mathematics, natural/physical sciences, architecture, and agricultural science. IAESTE United States has represented IAESTE in America since 1950.

Dates: Application deadline for 2003 internships is January 1, 2003. **Cost:** $25 application fee, $175 participation fee. **Contact:** Customer Service Representative, 10400 Little Patuxent Pkwy., Suite 250, Columbia, MD 21044-3519; 410-997-3069, fax 410-997-5168; aipt@aipt.org, www.aipt.org/subpages/iaeste_us/index.php.

Internships International

Quality, nonpaying internships in London, Paris, Dublin, Dresden, Santiago, Budapest, Melbourne, Bangkok, Glasgow, Ho Chi Minh City, and Capetown. Internships in all fields, from 8 weeks to 6 months. Open to college graduates and seniors requiring an internship to graduate.

Dates: Based on individual's needs. **Cost:** $800 program fee for all cities except Dublin ($1,500) and London ($1,000). **Contact:** Judy Tilson, Director, Internships International, P.O. Box 480, Woolwich, ME 04579-0480; 207-443-3019, fax 207-442-7942; intintl@aol.com, http://rtpnet.org/~intintl.

Marist International Internships

Internship and study abroad programs in Australia, England, Ireland, Italy, and Spain. Programs combine internships and course work at host institutions. Homestays are available at select sites.

Dates: Fall and spring semesters and full academic year. **Cost:** Average program fee is $11,500. **Contact:** Carol Toufali, Marist College, 3399 North Rd., Poughkeepsie, NY 12601; 845-575-3330, fax 845-575-3294; international@marist.edu, www.marist.edu/international.

MAST Experience Abroad

A chance to learn first-hand under the guidance of innovative and successful farmers, agribusiness operators, and horticulturists around the world. Spend 2 to 12 months training on a farm or agricultural, horticultural, or forestry business in one of 15 countries. Develop lifelong friendships with your host family and colleagues. Gain a personal and professional learning experience that will shape your life. Single men and women between the ages of 18 and 30.

Dates: Jan, Mar, Jun, Sep. Other dates available. **Cost:** $400 program fee. **Contact:** Susan VonBank, MAST International, Univ. of Minnesota, 1954 Buford Ave., #395, St. Paul, MN 55108; 800-346-6278, 612-624-3740; mast@tc.umn.edu, http://mast.coafes.umn.edu.

The Best Web Sites

Internet Resources for Finding Scholarships and Internships

Selected and Reviewed by William Nolting

These are the best sites we've seen for work abroad and international careers, but for different reasons. Sites designated (I) for *Information* contain lists or databases of work abroad programs, information about working abroad, links to many other work abroad sites, or actual job listings. The (I) sites are some of the best starting places for overseas job hunters.

Sites designated (P) for *Program*, belong to a few selected work abroad programs chosen for their large size, longevity, or other unique qualities. Examples include the JET Program, the Peace Corps, and those official work exchange programs in the "Short-Term Paid Work" section.

Sites designated (S) for *Scholarship* provide funding for international exchange or provide information on how to fundraise.

Scholarships for undergraduates and for nonacademic work abroad are relatively rare; funding for graduate students, postdocs, and professionals tends to be more readily available. For other options, fundraising through job savings, family, friends, hometown organizations such as Rotary, Kiwanis, Optimist, and religious organizations may be more effective than scholarships. The sites of AMSA and WorldTeach have "non-traditional" fundraising suggestions useful for anyone.
**Essential; *Outstanding and of broad interest.*
(I) Informational site with directories or databases
(P) Site for a specific work abroad program
(S) Scholarships or fellowships

*(I) **American Medical Student Association,** www.amsa.org lists overseas internship and volunteer programs, including options for premed and other health sciences—see International Health Opportunities section. Site includes an excellent online guide to fundraising, *Creative Funding Guide*, useful for all students.

(S) **Council Bowman Scholarship, www.ciee.org. CIEE's undergraduate scholarship funds the cost of airfare and can be used for study, work, volunteering, or research in developing countries (i.e. excluding Australia, Canada, Europe, Israel, Japan, Korea, New Zealand, Russia, Singapore). Students at CIEE member institutions, participants in CIEE programs, and students at institutions which sell ISIC cards are eligible. Application deadlines are twice a year, typically in October and March or early April.

(S) **Fulbright Scholarships and Teaching Programs, www.iie.org/fulbright. All the Fulbright programs—official exchange pro-

grams for teaching, study or research—are described here; Fulbright Student programs (including scholarships and English Teaching Assistantships) are for graduating seniors, graduate students, and alumni; Fulbright Scholar programs are for university faculty and international education administrators. The Fulbright Teacher Exchange is for currently employed K-12 and community college teachers.

*(I) **The Electronic Embassy,** www.embassy.org contains links to the home pages of all U.S.-based embassies. Many countries provide cultural and educational exchange information, as well as essential information for travel and work (visas, etc.) on their sites. Note, however, that these sites rarely mention the internship, volunteer, and work exchange programs found in the other resources mentioned here.

(I, P) **GoAbroad.com www.goabroad.com by Troy Peden. A very comprehensive and up-to-date web site with excellent search provisions. Site's design allows continuous updates by program providers. Most listings give extensive information. Search possible by country or subject. Provides addresses, telephone numbers, and email addresses for all programs and links to web sites for some programs. Listings also bring up country-specific travel information. One of the best sites for those looking for a broad range of education abroad options.

**(I, S, P) Institute of International Education, www.iie.org, Financial Resources for International Study and Funding for United States Study, Marie O'Sullivan and Sara Steen, editors. IIE publishes some of the best hard-copy directories of scholarships for overseas opportunities, which include grants for all levels of students as well as for postdoctorates and professionals. IIE's databases are available on its site. Search terms "work," "internship," "practical," "teach," "research" all yield a good number of listings. Full texts are available only to those at IIE member institutions with password provided by IIE (for password, email: membership@iie.org). Or, use the search with book in hand; most college libraries have these books.

*International Volunteer Programs Association (IVPA), www.volunteer international.org by Christine Victorino. IVPA is a professional association for administrators of international volunteer programs, as well as advisers and students interested in this type of international experience. The site lists programs for volunteering abroad, some of which offer academic credit, and has extensive links to relevant resources.

*(I) National Association of Financial Aid Administrators, www.finaid.org. Site of the main U.S. professional association for financial aid administrators. Search using terms such as "study abroad" or "work abroad."

(S, P) Minority International Research Training Grant (MIRT), www.nih.gov/fic/ programs/mirt.html. Program of the Fogarty International Center/National Institutes of Health sends minority undergraduates and medical students abroad to do health-related research. Apply through one of the centers listed.

(I) Studyabroad.com, www.studyabroad.com by Mark Landon. Site's databases list approximately 5,000 programs. Has special databases for language courses and experiential programs. Information limited to location and subjects (does not provide cost information, for example). Contains

addresses, phone numbers, email addresses. Links to program web sites for only some programs. Search by country, academic subject, or both, but no other variables.

**(I) Reference Service Press, Financial Aid for Study and Training Abroad and Financial Aid for Research and Creative Activities Abroad, www.rspfunding.com. RSP publishes of some of the best hard-copy directories of scholarships for overseas opportunities, which include grants for all levels of students as well as for postdoctorates and professionals. Its databases are available to America Online subscribers (keyword RSP), or through some university libraries to their own students.

**(S) Rotary Foundation Ambassadorial Scholarships, www.rotary.org. The Rotary Foundation provides the largest single U.S. scholarship program for study abroad. Scholarships are available for all levels of study, from highschool, undergraduate, and graduate students to alumni and professionals. Generally not for use with study abroad programs sponsored by U.S. institutions. Application possible only through local Rotary Clubs. Deadlines (locally-determined) may be as much as one and one-half years in advance. Web site provides scholarship information and lists Rotary clubs worldwide.

**(I) Transitions Abroad, www.transitions abroad.com. *Transitions Abroad* magazine is unique in its coverage of all education abroad options, from study and work abroad to educational travel. The online version includes annotated guides to resources and country-by-country listings of programs for study, work, internships, volunteering, language study, etc. Includes up-to-date list of short-term employers worldwide. Search functions available for entire site. The major sections of this site include Study Abroad, Work Abroad, International Travel, and Living Abroad Resources.

(I) Univ. of California-Irvine, International Opportunities Program, www.cie.uci.edu/~cie/iop. Concept by Ruth Sylte, now edited by IOP's Sharon Parks. Extensive directories (not databases) for internships, research, teaching, volunteering and work abroad programs, as well as study abroad and summer programs. Contains links to many useful sites. Information on both academic and nonacademic internships. See also **The World at Your Fingertips, www.cie.uci.edu/~cie/world, which is not a directory, but an instructional site—how students and advisers can use the Internet to research options for education abroad.

(I) Univ. of Michigan, International Center's Overseas Opportunities Office, www.umich.edu/~icenter/overseas by William Nolting, Anthony Hand, and students. Not a database, but a collection of articles, annotated links, and print resources for study, work, and travel abroad, including in-depth reports on work abroad options—the most singular feature of this site.

(I, P) U.S. Department of State, www.state.gov. While not a directory of programs, this site provides essential information from the diplomatic branch of the U.S. government for everything from travel safety advisories to crisis assistance for U.S. citizens abroad and contact information for all U.S. embassies and consulates. Also lists foreign embassies and consulates in the U.S. The Department of State offers 1,000 internships annually as well as career positions. Country background notes, travel advisories, and countless other articles make this site one of the most valuable sources of international information on the web. Other frequently consulted parts of this very comprehensive web site include Travel Warnings and Information, Travel Tips for Students, Services for U.S. Citizens Abroad, Passport services, Publications, and Background Notes (country information).

(I) Univ. of Minnesota, International Study and Travel Center Scholarships Database, www.istc.umn.edu/html/default_wi.html. An excellent, free online database of scholarships. Search categories include study, research and internships as well as location and other variables.

*(S) U.S. State Department "International Information Programs,"** www.usinfo.state.gov in the **Bureau of Educational and Cultural Affairs,** http://exchanges.state.gov. Official information about Fulbright and other US-sponsored programs for study, research, and teaching abroad.

*(I) U.S. Department of Education: Student Financial Assistance Programs,** www.ed.gov/offices/OSFAP/Students and **The Student Guide to Financial Aid,** www.ed.gov/prog_info/SFA/StudentGuide. The federal government's official guide to financial aid (which can be used only for academic study, including study-internship or study-volunteer programs).

(I) Washington and Lee Univ., Office of International Education, http://internationaleducation.wlu.edu/main by William Klingelhofer. This site, by an expert on work abroad formerly at Harvard Univ., provides an excellent overview of working abroad, including internships, teaching, and volunteering, with links to hundreds of programs. Good section on study opportunities.

(S) **Woodrow Wilson International Fellowship Foundation,** www.woodrow.org/public-policy. Information on several multi-year scholarship-internship programs for students, especially women and minorities, interested in careers in international affairs.

*(I) **WorldTeach,** www.worldteach.org funds.html. Contains ideas for non-traditional fundraising.

Checklist for Working, Interning, And Volunteering Abroad

By William Nolting

Before You Leave

- Assess potential health, safety, crime, and political instability factors in the countries (and areas within a country) where you intend to travel. Regularly recheck the U.S. State Department Travel Advisories at http://travel.state.gov/travel_warnings.html.

- Communicate with students who have participated in the program you are considering or have decided upon. Programs should be willing to furnish you with email and phone numbers of past participants.

- If you are interested in academic credit for your work abroad, see your academic adviser.

- Communicate with the program's office in advance to ask questions about the internship placement (if known), whether a work permit is needed, assistance with finding housing, and other matters. If possible, communicate in advance with your supervisor abroad concerning expectations about the internship and other matters.

- Immunizations/inoculations are needed for certain destinations in Africa, Asia, or Latin America. Start early, one to several months in advance, since some immunizations require several shots over time. Be sure to get a vaccination certificate listing your inoculations, since some countries (especially in tropical areas) require it at the border. Travel clinics can also recommend and prescribe medications appropriate for your destination, such as malaria pills.

- Medications and personal care items. If you need prescription drugs on a regular basis, ask your physician to prescribe enough to last the entire duration of your stay abroad. Be sure to take copies of the prescription with you for checks at borders. Consider taking personal care items such as non-prescription drugs (as with prescription drugs, the same brands or formulas may be unavailable abroad), spare glasses or contact lenses, sunscreen, insect repellant, contraceptives, feminine hygiene products, etc.

- Passport. This is your most important means of identification abroad—allow 2-4 weeks for arrival. You will need to build in another 2-6 weeks if you need a visa and/or work permit (below).

- Visas. This is a stamp in your passport which gives you permission from a foreign government to enter the country. You must have your passport first. Many countries may require visas even for tourists, depending on the country and your citizenship. To get a visa, you may need to show that you have adequate means to support yourself for the duration of your stay. If you are working for pay in another country, you will need a Work Permit or Work Authorization (a special type of visa), without which you risk deportation. Be sure to ask your employer whether a work permit is needed, and check with the host country's embassy at www.embassy.org. If you need a work permit, inquire whether the employer can help you obtain one. The organization IAESTE may be able to help you get a work permit for many countries, if you have a written internship offer: 410-997-3068; iaeste@aipt.org, www.aipt.org/iaeste.html. Special student work permit programs are available for Britain, Ireland, France, Germany, Canada, Australia and New Zealand. See "Short Term Paid Work Abroad."

- Housing. Your best bet will be to work with your overseas employer or program to find housing. Cities with universities may have student dorms available in the summer. If you cannot pre-arrange housing, you will want to arrive a week or two early to look for housing onsite. Be cautious about making any commitments to a lease sight-unseen. Use Google.com to search for housing listings with terms such as "student."

- International Student ID Card (ISIC). This card makes you eligible for a broad range of discounts for airfare and overseas. Available at your international studies office.

- Transportation. For airfares between the U.S. and your foreign destination (you must have a round-trip ticket), you will save money by buying weeks in advance from student-rate specialists such as STA Travel. Railpasses may save money in some destinations such as Europe and Japan, and cannot be bought once you get there—get railpasses from STA Travel or other travel agencies.

- Guidebooks. Take one with you geared to your own travel style and itinerary. Some of the best guidebook series for student budgets are Lonely Planet, Let's Go, and Rough Guides.

- Foreign language/advance reading. If your language skills are weak, learn key phrases for conversation and emergencies, and consider enrolling in language classes onsite. Read current books and or see movies about your destination.

- Means of Communication. Plan for multiple means of communication: Internet cafes; cell phones (you will have to buy a special phone abroad or from your cell phone company); phone cards for regular phones; ISIC card phone service; regular mail—people still like to get postcards and letters! Also, discuss with family members and your department/faculty contact how often you expect to communicate, and communicate with them as soon as possible after you reach your destination.

- Photocopy important documents. Make two copies of your passport, plane ticket, traveler's checks, rail pass, credit card numbers, and prescriptions. Be sure to take one set of copies with you and leave another set in the U.S. with family or a friend.

- Money in multiple forms. Take cash in new $20 and $50 bills, traveler's checks in dollars, credit cards (make sure you've made arrangements to pay these bills while you're gone), ATM cards (only 4-digit PIN numbers work overseas.)

- Money belt. The type that can be worn under your clothes is the most secure. Keep photocopies of your passport, visa, insurance and emergency contact information, travelers checks, extra ATM / credit cards in your money belt.

- Luggage. Take as little as possible. An internal frame backpack is easiest to carry and to handle on trains; if you take a suitcase, be sure it has wheels! You should not take any more than you can carry, since shipping abroad is extremely expensive. Check your airline for special weight limits for overseas flights.

- Computers. It's best to leave your laptop in the U.S. to prevent theft and damage. If you must take it, mark down serial numbers, bring copies of receipts to avoid duty taxes, make sure insurance and warranties are up to date, check to see if your home or renters' insurance covers computers abroad, and be aware of differences between American and foreign current—it can be easily damaged by the wrong current.

- Avoid bringing unnecessary electrical devices (hair dryers, curlers, computers). If you do bring such items, buy your current converters in the U.S. as they can be difficult to find abroad.

- Make reservations for your first night abroad and information on traveling to and from the airport (consult your guidebook for inexpensive options).

- If possible, register yourself with the U.S. embassy or consulate abroad at http://usembassy.state.gov (non-US citizens should register themselves with their own country's embassy; see www.embassy.org). Include your itinerary (dates, places, and addresses abroad) and emergency contact information. If this cannot be done online, then register yourself once you arrive in the host country by phone, fax, or in-person. Keep the embassy/consulate contact information with you in case of emergency.

Once You Are There

• Communicate with family and friends ASAP after you arrive, and on a regular basis thereafter. Set up regular times (say, specific days each week) when your contacts can expect to hear from you. If possible, have multiple means for communications: regular phone, cell phone, email.

• Be careful of water and food in less-developed countries. See guidebooks for detailed tips such as drinking only bottled water, avoiding ice cubes, etc.

• Be careful when seeking medical care abroad in less-developed countries—needles may be unsterilized or re-used. Ask the U.S. embassy for recommended health-care providers.

• Register with the closest U.S. embassy or consulate (or your own embassy if not a U.S. citizen) if you have not already done so before leaving.

• Register with local authorities if this is required—it is in many countries.

• Develop local contacts at your internship site and living quarters. They can be your best source of information and assistance in case of any crisis. If you travel, be sure to inform them about your itinerary, and leave your emergency contact information with them. Your local hosts will also be your best guides to the local culture, courtesies, and customs.

• Monitor local news sources.

CHAPTER 3

SHORT-TERM JOBS ABROAD

The major fields of temporary employment abroad are tourism and agriculture, au pairing, English teaching, and volunteer work in exchange for room and board. The more you research before you go abroad the better; however, available information is often misleading. Remain determined in the face of discouragement and use the reliable resources updated each year by Bill Nolting and published in the September/October issue of Transitions Abroad and on www.TransitionsAbroad.com to clarify what you want to do and determine what is possible.

Key Employers
Short-Term Jobs Abroad

Compiled by Susan Griffith

As a first step in finding short-term work, contact the embassy or consulate and the tourist office of the countries in which you want to work to find out the official line on visas, etc. In the old days, some job-seekers visited embassy libraries or reading rooms to check the "situations vacant" columns of national and preferably local newspapers or to consult the telephone directories and yellow pages for lists of English language schools or other potential employers in their field. Increasingly, this information is available on the Internet.

If you are searching for a specific kind of job you might get leads by consulting the specialist press. Professionals should consult their own associations and journals. For example, teachers should look at The International Educator, P.O. Box 513, Cummaquid, MA 02637; www.tieonline.com.

AFRICA

Travelers sometimes negotiate teaching contracts in East Africa and casual tutoring in Cairo on the spot. It may also be possible to join conservation or scientific research trips for a fee. Additional contacts include:

American Language Center, 4 Zankat Tanja, Rabat, 10000 Morocco; 011-212-37-767103, fax 011-212-37-766255; alcrabat@mtds.com.

The largest of 10 ALCs in Morocco which hires EFL teachers for 1 year or longer.

American Universities Preparation Institute Mrs. Muchori, Director, P.O. Box 14842, Westlands Rd., Chiromo Ln., Nairobi, Kenya; aupi@africaonline.co.ke. Volunteer teachers may apply for a 6-month period.

Azafady, Studio 7, 1A Beethoven St., London W10 4LG, U.K.; 011-44-208-960-6629;

www.madagascar.co.uk. This 10-week Pioneer Madagascar program allows volunteers to work on a grassroots level to combat deforestation and extreme poverty in Madagascar. Fundraising target is £1,750 excluding flights.

CADO (Community Animation & Development Organization), 1 Ross Rd., P.M.B. 1317, Cline town, Freetown, Sierra Leone; 011-232-22-226162; cado@sierratel.sl. Volunteers needed for social projects.

Care for Others, P.O. Box 73, Soroti, Uganda. NGO helps deprived children and their communities in war-ravaged area by teaching vocational skills.

Care of the Needy (COTN), P.O. Box 2247, Mwanza, Tanzania; 011-255-811-218364; cotn@raha.com. NGO working with homeless children uses volunteers, including on Lake Victoria environmental project.

Cross-Cultural Solutions, 47 Potter Ave., New Rochelle, NY 10801; 800-380-4777, 914-632-0022; info@crossculturalsolutions.org, www.crossculturalsolutions.org. Volunteer vacations in eastern Ghana (as well as India, Russia, Peru, and China). Volunteers spend 3 weeks teaching, providing skills training, and direction in arts, and recreation. Program fee is $1,950.

CYTFWEA, Charity Youth Travel for Working Experience Abroad, P.O. Box MA30, Ho V/R, Ghana. Self-funding international volunteers are placed in range of development projects.

Frontier Conservation Expeditions, 50-52 Rivington Str., London EC2A 3QP, England; 011-44-207-613-2422; info@frontier.ac.uk, www.frontier.ac.uk. Frontier is an international conservation and research NGO which works in threatened tropical environments in Madagascar, Tanzania, and Vietnam to protect endangered habitats and wildlife through research and practical projects. Offers self-funding volunteers the opportunity to work on overseas projects for 10 or 20 weeks. Full training is provided, leading to a qualification.

Global Citizens Network/Harambee, 130 N Howell St., St. Paul, MN 55104; 651-644-0960; gcn@mtn.org, www.globalcitizens.org. Sends paying volunteers for 3 weeks to rural Kenya (among other countries worldwide). $1,650 plus airfares.

G-NETT, Global Youth Travel Network, P.O. Box M542, Kumasi-Ghana (011-233-51-26880; goldlink@ghana.com. Hosts international volunteers for 3 weeks to 6 months to assist with the English syllabus in junior and senior secondary schools.

Green Fingers, G.P.O. Box 5200, Brikama, Gambia; fax 011-220-393999. NGO has broadened its range of programs to include the promotion of sustainable agriculture, education, health, and environmental protection in Kombo Central Region.

Health Action Promotion Association, Volunteer Africa, www.volunteerafrica.org. Newly formed NGO working with village projects in the Singida Region of Tanzania. Start dates for 3-month projects Jun-Sep 2002. Hoping to appoint recruitment coordinator in U.S. or Canada soon.

International Intercultural Students Exchange, P.O. Box OS 1053, Osu-Accra, Ghana; 011-233-27-560225; nbenneh@ghana.com. Voluntary internships in various fields including teaching, forestry, etc.

Operation Crossroads Africa, Inc. 475 Riverside Dr., Suite 1366, New York, NY 10115-0050; 212-870-2106; oca@igc.org, www.igc.org/oca. Runs 7-week summer projects in rural Africa, and Bahia, Brazil, staffed by self-financing volunteers from the U.S. and Canada. Also runs 13-week project in Namibia in both fall and spring.

Overland Adventure Tours. A number of overland adventure tour operators require expedition leaders aged 25-40 for at least 1 year. These include Guerba Expeditions, 40 Station Rd., Westbury, Wiltshire BA13 3JN, U.K.; info@guerba.co.uk, www.guerba.com.

PASACOFAAS, Pa Santigie Conteh Farmers' Community Development Association, 5a City Rd., Wellington, P.M.B. 686, Freetown, Sierra Leone; pasacofaas84@hotmail.com. Needs manual and administrative help for its projects in the Bombali District of Sierra Leone.

Public Affairs Department, U.S. Embassy, Madagascar English Teaching Program, 4 Lalana Dr. Razafindratandra Ambohidahy, Antananarivo, Madagascar; 011-261-20-22-202-38, fax 011-261-20-22-213-97; etptana@compro.mg, www.usmission.mg/etp.htm. Occasionally hires native speakers of English for short-term work on local pay scale.

Regal Holidays, info.sharm@emperordivers.com or info.hurghada@emperordivers.com. Divers employed by British-managed tour company to work at Red Sea dive resorts of Sharm el Sheikh and Hurghada, especially November-January.

S & S Human Resources Development, P.O. Box TN 1501, Teshie-Nungua Estates, Accra, Ghana; 011-233-21-713391/7011154;

hrdev@ighmail.com. Paid and unpaid internships with organizations and institutions in Accra, Kumasi, Cape Coast, Tema, Ho and Takoradi.

Save the Earth Network, P.O. Box CT 3635, Cantonments-Accra, Ghana; 011-233-21-236362; eben_sten@hotmail.com. Voluntary positions as English and maths teachers in primary and junior secondary schools, in rainforest conservation projects, youth work, agro-forestry in or near Accra.

SCORE (Sports Coaches' OutReach), Sports Science Institute of South Africa, Boundary Rd., Newlands, South Africa 7700 or P.O. Box 13177, Mowbray, South Africa; 011-27-21-689-7395, fax 011-27-21-689-7486; score@iafrica.com. Program for self-funding volunteers to live in host families and coach sports, teach physical education, and set up clubs in deprived communities. Minimum 6 months from January or July. Programs in South Africa and Namibia. Internships available.

SHUMAS (Strategic Humanitarian Services), P.O. Box 5047, Nkwen, Bamenda, Northwest Province, Cameroon; Tel./fax 237-362682; shumas@bamenda.org. Development NGO that places volunteers aged over 21 for 3-6 months in social and environmental projects in Cameroon. Volunteers are asked to contribute £75 for each month of their stay.

Teachers for Africa, IFESH 5040 East Shea Blvd., Suite 260, Phoenix, AZ 85254-4687; 480-443-1800, 800-835-3530, fax 480-443-1824; teachers@ifesh.org, www.ifesh.org. Arranges for teachers and college instructors to teach TESL, teacher training, education and other subjects at schools and colleges in Ethiopia, Benin, Guinea, Malawi, Ghana and Namibia. Expenses covered during 10-month program.

Traveling Seminars Abroad, Inc., 1037 Society Hill, Cherry Hill, NJ 08003; 609-424-7630. Summer and longer term programs for students and others in village in northern Ghana helping to build Habitat for Humanity homes. Estimated cost for 3-month stay is $1,200.

United Children's Fund, P.O. Box 20341, Boulder, CO 80308-3341; 888-343-3199; www.unchildren.org. Volunteers work in Ugandan clinics, schools, farms, etc. for 1 or 2 months. Fees are $1,850 or $2,950. Airfare not included.

Visions in Action, 2710 Ontario Rd., NW, Washington, DC 20009; 202-588-9344; visions@visionsinaction.org, www. visionsinaction.org. Range of volunteer projects in Mexico, Uganda, Zimbabwe, Burkina Faso, South Africa, and Tanzania. Volunteers must raise $6,000-$8,000 and commit themselves to stay from 6-12 months. A shorter summer program is also available in northern Tanzania.

Workcamps in Africa. The following organizations arrange workcamps in Africa, though applications should normally be sent to the partner organization in the U.S. (see Voluntary Service, below):
• **Mouvement Twiza,** A.M.T., 23 rue Echiguer Hammand, Hay Salam, B.P. 77, 15000 Khemisset, Morocco;
• **Tunisian Assn. of Voluntary Work,** Maison du RCD, Blvd. 9 Avril, 1938, 1002 Tunis, Tunisia. (For Morocco and Tunisia, a knowledge of French is very useful.)
• **Christian Welfare and Social Project Organization,** 39 Soldier St., Freetown, Sierra Leone; 011-232-22-229779.
• **Voluntary Development Assn.,** P.O. Box 48902, Nairobi, Kenya.
• **Lesotho Workcamps Assn.,** P.O. Box 6, Linare Rd., Maseru 100, Lesotho.
• **Swaziland Workcamps Assn.,** P.O. Box 1430, Mbabane, Swaziland.
• **Zimbabwe Workcamps Assn.,** P.O. Box CY 2039, Causeway, Harare, Zimbabwe. AJUPE (Mozambique), Avenida Marion Ngouabi No. 1506, C.P. 1406, Maputo, Mozambique.
• **Southern African Student Volunteers (SASVO),** Centre for Human Rights, Univ. of Pretoria, Pretoria 0002, South Africa.
• **Uganda Volunteers for Peace and Development,** P.O. Box 3312, Kampala, Uganda; 011-256-077 402201; uvpeace@yahoo.co.uk.
• **WWOOF-Ghana,** c/o Ebenezer Nortey-Mensah, P.O. Box 154, Trade Fair Site, La-Accra, Ghana places volunteers on traditional farms and bicycle workshops in Ghana.
• **WWOOF Togo, Prosper Agbeko,** B.P. 25 Agou-Gare, Togo; 011-228-471036. Places volunteers on organic farms, forest projects, etc. in Togo.

WorldTeach. Center for International Development, Harvard Univ., 79 John F. Kennedy St., Cambridge, MA 02138; 800-4-TEACH-0 or 617-495-5527, fax 617-495-1599. For year long program recruits college graduates to teach science, English, etc. in Namibia. For summer programs recruits volunteers who are at least 18 years old to teach information technology in Namibia.

ANTARCTICA

Raytheon Polar Services. Polar Services, 7400 S Tuscon Way, Centennial, CO 80112; 303-790-8606 or 800-688-8000; www.rpsc. raytheon.com. Hires 800 U.S. citizens for U..S Antarctic Program including both general assistants and skilled staff for 4, 6, or 12 months.

ASIA

Bangladesh Work Camps Association (BWCA). BWCA is a Volunteers Organization which organizes Work Camps accommodating participants with a combination of different nationalist on 7 to 15 days through health, environment and community development projects within Bangladesh between October and February. BWCA also accommodates overseas volunteers on a medium-term (3 or more months) basis at its rural projects. Participation fee is $150 for each program.

Center for Coordination of Voluntary Works and Research, 9 Raja Design Nagar, Desurpattai Rd., Gingee Villupuram, 604 202, Tamil Nadu, South India. Organizes workcamps and longer term projects which volunteers can join for $150 per month plus a non-refundable $50 registration fee.

Colorado China Council, 4556 Apple Way, Boulder, CO 80301; 303-443-1108; fax 303-443-1107; www.AsiaCouncil.org. Places 20-35 teachers per year at institutes throughout China, including Mongolia.

Cultural Destination Nepal, P.O. Box 11535, Kathmandu, Nepal; 011-977-1-426996; www.volunteernepal.org.np. Placements last 2-4 months starting February, April, August and October; $650 fee includes language training and homestay.

Dakshinayan, c/o Siddharth Sanyal, F-1169, Ground Fl., Chittaranjan Park, New Delhi 110019, INDIA; Tel./fax 011-91-11-6276645; sid@linkindia.com, www.linkindia.com. Volunteers to help with grassroots educational medical projects in tribal lands in remote areas of Bihar state.

DPCA Sikkim (Denjong Padme Cheoling Academy), c/o 53 Blenheim Crescent, London W11 2EG; 011-44-207-29-4774; jjulesstewart@ cs.com. Foreign volunteers assist in classrooms of this school in the restricted Indian area of Sikkim for up to 45 days.

ECC (Thailand), 430/17-24 Chula Soi 64, Siam Square, Bangkok 10330, Thailand; 011-66-2-253-3312; fax 011-66-2-254-2243; jobs@ecc.ac.th, www.eccthai.com. Chain of language schools with 60 branches employs 500 native speaker teachers, preferably with TEFL certification.

Educate the Children, P.O. Box 414, Ithaca, NY 14851-0414; 607-272-1176, fax 607-275-0932; info@etc-nepal.org, www.etc-nepal.org. Provides educational opportunities for low-income women and children in Nepal. Arranges 3-month internships; fee of $500.

ELS International/YBM, 649-1 Yeoksam-dong, Kangnam-gu, Seoul 135-081, Korea; 011-82-2-552-1492, fax 011-82-2-501-2478; teach@ybmsisa.co.kr, www.ybmsisa.com. Employs 100 native English teachers for English conversation centers and other kinds of schools institute throughout Korea.

GEOS Corporation, Simpson Tower 2424, 401 Bay St., Toronto, Ontario M5H 2Y4, Canada; 416-777-0109, fax 416-777-0110; geos@istar.ca, www.geoscareer.com. One of Japan's largest English language institutions employing 1,800 teachers for 450 schools, all of whom are hired outside Japan

Global Action Nepal, P.O. Box 2717, Ganeshchowk, Budhanilkantha, Kathmandu, Nepal; 011-977-1-370977; info@gannepal.org, www.gannepal.org. A charity which provides dynamic volunteers to support village teachers in their work and also to improve school environments by building toilets, wells, etc.

Grahung Kalika, Southwestern Nepal, Dol Raj Subedi, c/o Mr. Tara Prasad Subedi, P.O. Box 11272, Kathmandu, Nepal; 011-977-1-532674, fax 011-977-1-527317; mail@multcon.wlink. com.np. Volunteers help pupils and teachers improve their English in local schools in Walling, a municipality in the remote Syangja District of western Nepal. Volunteers stay with local families for the duration of their placements (between August and May) and are asked to contribute RS4,000 ($60) plus a monthly fee of RS3000 ($45) to the host family for food and accommodations.

Helping Hand Club Nepal (HHCN), Mangalpur V.D.C. 8, Bijayanagar, Chitwan, Nepal; hhcnepal@yahoo.com. English teaching in rural schools, environmental and business consulting projects, demographic research, and healthcare work. Average stay 3 months at any time of the year; $150 per month or $50 a week if staying less than a month.

Hess Educational Organization, 419 Chung Shan Rd., Sec. 2, No. 419, Chung Ho City,

Taipei County, Taiwan; 011-886-2-3234-6188; ext 1053; fax 011-886-2-3234-9499; hesswork@hess.com.tw, www.hess.com.tw. Employs 250 Native Speaking Teachers (NSTs) in more than 100 branches. Very structured teaching program and curriculum for children. Quarterly intake of teachers in September, December, March, and June.

Himalayan Explorers, P.O. Box 3665, Boulder, CO 80307; 888-420-8822; info@hec.org, www.hec.org. Runs Nepal Volunteer Program from September-December and February-May ($120 per month plus travel expenses). Volunteer teachers placed in Sherpa village schools while living with local families.

Himalayan Volunteers (RCDP Nepal), c/o Murali Adhikari, 232 "C", Mark Twain Cir., Athens, GA 30506; rcdpnepal@hotmail.com, www.rcdpnepal.com. Paying volunteers work on various programs while living with a Nepalese family

Hostelling International Thailand, International Community Service Program, 25/14 Phitsanulok Rd., Si Sao Thewet, Dusit, Bangkok, 10300 Thailand; 011-66-2-628-7413, fax 011-66-2-628-7416; snesbitt_tyha@yahoo.com. Volunteers with basic TEFL experience spend 3-5 months teaching 4 hours a day in different locations around Thailand.

IEF Education Foundation, fax 626-965-1675; mwurmlinger@ief-usa.org. Recruits mainly Americans with at least 2 years of college education to spend 6 months teaching English to junior high and high-school aged students in many Chinese cities.

Insight Nepal, P.O. Box 489, Pokhara, Kaski, Nepal; insight@mos.com.np; www.insightnepal.org. Volunteer placements for 1-4 months in Nepali schools. Must be high school graduate. $400 fee for 4-6 week placements, $800 for longer ones.

International Avenue Consulting, Penthouse 01, 1889 Alberni St., Vancouver, BC, Canada V6G 3G7; 604-642-4199; service@iacc.com.tw, www.iacc.com.tw. Agency places North Americans in teaching vacancies throughout Taiwan.

JAFFE International Education Service, Kunnuparambil Buildings, Kurichy, Kottayam 686549, India; tel./fax 011-91-481-430470. Placement agency for young foreign volunteers to teach in English-language high schools, vocational institutes, summer camps, etc. in Kerala and elsewhere in India.

Joint Assistance Centre (JAC), G 17/3 DLF Qutab Enclave, Phase 1, Gurgaon, Haryana 122002, India; fax 011-91-124-351-308; nkjain@jac.unv.ernet.in, www.jacindia.org. Community service organization near Delhi. Volunteers pay $230 for the first month and $130 for each subsequent month.

Korean International Volunteer Association (KIVA), 1102, Sekwang B/D, 202 Sejong-ro, Chongro-ku, Seoul, South Korea 110-050; kiva21@hotmail.com, www.kiva.or.kr. Work placements throughout Korea for international volunteers for a minimum of 4 weeks. Board and lodging provided.

Lotus Children's Centre, P.O. Box 1018, Central Post Office, Ulaanbaatar, Mongolia; lotuschild@magicnet.mn, http://members.nbci.com/lotuscentre/home.htm. Maintenance and gardening volunteers are needed for this center for deprived children.

Missionaries of Charity, 54A A.J.C. Bose Rd., Kolkata 16, India. Runs Mother Teresa's homes for destitute people in Calcutta. Skilled or unskilled volunteers can work for short periods.

MOGPA/Intern in Asia, recruiter@interninasia.com, www.InternInAsia.com. Professional work assignments of 6-12 month in Asia for American (U.S.) students and recent graduates who have knowledge of Japanese or Chinese.

Mondo Challenge, 8 Milton Ct., Milton Malsor, Northampton NN7 3AX, U.K.; 011-44-1604-858225; businesslink1@compuserve.com, www.yangrima.org. Volunteers sent to the Helambu area of Nepal and Kathmandu to teach basic English to primary aged pupils. £700 contribution to the school's running costs plus £200 to cover board and lodging. Start dates in February, April, June and September/October.

National Meditation Center for World Peace, Rt. 7, Box 252-D, Jacksonville, TX 75766, www.nationalmeditation.org. Sends volunteers to various projects and workcamps. The cost is $200 per week in addition to the airfare. It offers a few internships as well as running cultural tours.

NAVA Language Schools, 34 Paholyothin 7, Phayathai, Bangkok 10400, Thailand; 011-66-2-617-1391; navaoperations@nls.ac.th. Teachers needed; experience and TESOL certificate not required.

New International Friendship Club, Post Box 11276, Maharajgunj, Kathmandu, Nepal; 011-977-1-427406, fax 011-977-1-429176; fcn@ccsl.com.np. Places 40 English-speaking university graduates placed in schools or colleges. Volunteer teachers should contribute $150 per month for their keep (unless they become a project expert).

Rural Organization for Social Elevation (ROSE), Social Awareness Centre, Village Son-argaon, P.O. Box Kanda, Dist. Bageshwar, U.A. 263631, India; 011-91-5963-41081. Grassroots development projects in Uttaramchal.

Sarvodaya International Division, Sarvodaya Shramadana Movement, 98 Rawatawatte Rd., Moratuwa, Sri Lanka; 011-94-1-647159/ 655255, fax 011-94-1-65612; volunteer@ itmin.com, jdg@itmin.com, general@ itmin.com. Internship programs for university students. Receiving volunteers and foreign groups. Promote ecotourism and cultural tourism; conduct study on voluntary team work in villages; carry out social development programs in 15,000 villages in Sri Lanka.

The Japan Times and Korea Times. English-language newspapers that carry teaching advertisements (especially Mondays); www.japantimes.co.jp, www.koreatimes.com.

WWOOF Japan. Contact: Glenn Burns, Akebono, 5-jo, 3-chome, 19-17, Teine-ku, Sapporo 006-0835, Japan or in U.S.: Randal Irwin, 2922 SW 153rd Dr., Beaverton, OR 97006; wwoofjapan@thejapangroup.com. Short-term opportunities to experience life on farms in Japan. WWOOF Japan is a smaller list compared to WWOOF Australia, etc.

WWOOF Korea, Seoul, Korea; 011-82-2-723 4458; www.wwoofkorea.com. Forty member farms. Membership costs $12.

Youth Charitable Organization (YCO), 20/14 Urban Bank St, Post Office No. 3, Yellamanchili 531055, Vizag.Dt., Andhra Pradesh, India. Foreign volunteers work on soil conservation, irrigation and community development programs lasting 2-6 months. Daily charge of 320 rupees ($7.50).

AUSTRALIA AND
NEW ZEALAND

Affordable Au Pairs & Nannies 3/62A Trafalgar St., Annandale, NSW 2038, Australia; 011-61-2-9557-6644; aapn@nanny.net.au, www.nanny.net.au. Network of placement offices throughout Australia.

Au Pair Australia, 6 Wilford St, Corrimal, NSW 2518, Australia; 011-61-2-42-846412, fax 011-2-42-854896. Places young women with work visas in live-in childcare positions for a minimum of 3 months.

Australian Tropical Research Foundation, Cape Tribulation Tropical Research Station, Cape Tribulation, Queensland 4873, Australia; 011-61-7-4098-0063; hugh@austrop.org.au, www.austrop.org.au. Rainforest/reef environment. Volunteers, interns, and students over the age of 23 preferred for a variety of tasks and study areas (from biology to appropriate technology). Contribution $20 per day includes food and lodging.

Australian Trust for Conservation Volunteers, P.O. Box 423, Ballarat, Victoria 3350, Australia; 011-61-353-331483; info@atcv.com.au, www.actv.com.au. Organizes short- and long-term voluntary conservation projects in Australia. Overseas volunteers participate in a 6-week package costing from AUS$840.

Backpacker's Resource Centre 167 Franklin St., Melbourne, Vic 3000; 011-61-3-9329-7525, fax 011-61-3-9329-7667; brc@btg.net.au. Agency with offices in Melbourne, Sydney, and Brisbane helps people with the working holiday visa set up work. Also provides a range of other back-up services for a fee of $250. Another agency which assists working holiday makers is Travellers Contact Point, Level 7, Dymocks Building, 428 George St., Sydney 2000 (011-61-2-9221-8744; www.travellers-contact.com.au). Services for members include job search, mail forwarding, etc.

BUNAC USA P.O. Box 430, Southbury, CT 06488; 1-800-GO-BUNAC; www.bunac.org. Administers Work in Australia program (maximum 4 months) and Work in New Zealand program (maximum 12 months); open to students and non-students.

CALM (Conservation and Land Management), Department of Western Australia, Locked Bag 104, Bentley Delivery Centre, WA 6893, Australia; 011-61-8-9334 0251; www.calm.wa.gov.au. Volunteer program open to anyone, though accommodation not necessarily provided.

CCUSA (Camp Counselors USA), 2330 Marinship Way, Suite 250, Sausalito, CA 94965; 800-999-CAMP; outbound@camp counselors.com, www.campcounselors.com. Sends American students aged 18-30 to Australia and New Zealand between June and September. Program fee is $365.

Conservation Volunteers Australia, P.O. Box 423, Ballarat, Victoria 3350, Australia; 011-61-353-331483; info@conservationvolunteers.

com.au, www.conservationvolunteers.com.au. Organizes short- and long-term voluntary conservation projects throughout Australia. Overseas volunteers participate in a 6-week package costing from AUS$966.

Council Exchanges, 20th Fl., 633 3rd Ave., New York, NY 10017; 1-888-COUNCIL; www.councilexchanges.org. Work abroad programs in Australia and New Zealand.

Department of Conservation (DOC) New Zealand, 59 Boulcott St., Wellington, New Zealand; 011-64-4-471-0726. Runs conservation projects such as kiwi monitoring in a national park. Addresses and Calendar of Volunteer opportunities listed on web site www.doc.govt.nz/commu/volunteers/calendar.htm. Many short-term projects such as counting bats and cleaning up remote beaches.

Earthwise Living Foundation (NZ), Box 108, Thames 2815, New Zealand; U.S. voicemail/fax 435-408-4123; www.elfnz.com. Volunteers placed on wilderness ecology and conservation projects. Registration fee of $200 plus $175 per week

Farm Helpers in New Zealand, 50 Bright St., Eketahuna 5480, New Zealand; Tel./fax 011-64-6-375 8955; fhinz@xtra.co.nz, www.fhinz.co.nz. NZ$25 membership includes booklet listing farmers looking for helpers in exchange for room and board.

HELP Exchange www.helpx.net. Free info exchange for people who want to work for free accommodations and meals in Australia and New Zealand.

Internship Programs Australia, 800-704-4880; www.advc.com/internships. Up to 100 interns placed in career-related field in Australia. Fees typically $5,000 for a 12-week internship.

Northern Victoria Fruitgrowers' Assn., P.O. Box 394, Shepparton, Victoria 3632, Australia; 011-61-3-5725-3700; nvfa@mcmedia.com.au, www.nvfa.com.au. Actively recruits fruit pickers from January to March. Also Victorian Peach and Apricot Growers' Assn., 30A Bank St., P.O. Box 39, Cobram, VIC 3644, Australia.

Rocky Creek Farm, Isis Hwy., M.S. 698, Biggenden, Queensland 4621, Australia; 011-61-741-271377; worsley@isisol.com.au, www.isisol.com.au/rockycrkfarmstay. Offers 1-week course for jackaroos and jillaroos (farm hands) for AUS$330. Those with working holiday visas can be placed on a Queensland property for an extra $110.

Stablemate Staff Agency, 1 Bullridge Rd., E. Kurrajong, NSW 2758, Australia; 011-61-2457-6444; info@stablemate.net.au, www.stablemate. net.au. Supplies staff to the horse industry. Operates exchange program with the U.S.

Troys Hospitality Staff Sydney, 011-61-2-9290 2955, fax 011-61-2-9290 1955; robyn@troys.com.au, www.troys.com.au. Places casual staff in the hospitality industry in Sydney.

WWOOF-Australia, Mt. Murrindal Co-operative, Buchan, Victoria 3885, Australia; 011-61-3-5155-0218; wwoof@ozemail.com.au, www.wwoof.com.au. Distributes the "Auslist," with the addresses of 1,300 member farms in Australia looking for short- or long-term voluntary help. AUS$40 (which includes accident insurance) if bought outside Australia. Also publishes worldwide list of farms and volunteer work opportunities for US$20.

WWOOF-New Zealand, P.O. Box 1172, Nelson, New Zealand; Tel./fax 011-64-3-5449890; a&j@wwoof.co.nz, www.wwoof.co.nz. Their list of about 600 organic growers costs $20.

VisitOz Scheme, Springbrook, MS 188 Via Goomeri, Queensland 4601, Australia; 011-61-7-4168-6106; www.visitoz.org. Station (i.e. ranch) runs short courses in outback working techniques and then directs participants with working holiday visas to paid jobs on the land and in the hospitality industry. Wages earned should cover cost of course.

CENTRAL AND EASTERN EUROPE

Many opportunities, especially in English language teaching, have become available in the Baltic, Russia, and the Republics.

Adriatic Dolphin Project Croatia, http://adp.hpm.hr. Paying volunteers join researchers for 12 days in the ancient village of Veli Losinj.

American Academy of Foreign Languages, Dmitreva Sat 16, Office 16, Kiev, Ukraine. Tel./fax 011-380-44-227 07 82. Also has large English institutes in Moscow; aafl@rui.ru, www.college.ru/english/academy.html, which employ TEFL qualified teachers.

Association for Educational, Cultural and Work International Exchange Programs (AIEP), 011-374-1-584-733, fax 011-374-1-5292; aiep@arminco.com, www.aiep.com. Sponsors camps to restore and maintain medieval buildings in Armenia. Runs internship and training program in the field of technical experience.

Bridges for Education, 94 Lamarck Dr., Buffalo, NY 14226; 716-839-0180, fax 716-839-9493; jbc@buffalo.edu, www.bridges4edu. org. Organizes international summer peace camps in which 180 volunteers teach English for 3 weeks in July followed by 1 week of travel in Belarus, Hungary, Poland, and Romania. Volunteers receive basic ESL training before departure. Participants pay airfare and administrative fee.

Caledonian School, Vlatavska 24, 150 00 Prague 5, Czech Republic; Tel./fax 011-42-2-57-31-36-50; jobs@caledonianschool.com, www.caledonianschool.com. Employs 80 teachers with TEFL background to teach English in a large Prague language institute. Canadian recruitment agent: Thomas Norris, 6 Greenmount Court, Toronto, ON, M8Y 1Y1, Canada; fax 416-231-1730; norr-cal@sympatico.ca.

Central European Teaching Program, Beloit College, 700 College St., Beloit, WI 53511; 608-363-2619; dunlopa@beloit.edu, www.beloit. edu/~cetp. Supplies nearly 100 English teachers to Hungary and Romania plus Poland and Lithuania. Placement fee of $2,000.

City University Slovakia, International Headquarters: 335 116th Ave. SE, Bellevue, WA 98004; 800-426-5596, 425-637-1010, fax 425-709-7699, TTY: (Hearing Impaired) 425-450-4660; info@cityu.edu, www.cityu.edu. Language Assistance Programs, 919 SW Grady Way, Renton, WA 98055; www.cityu.sk. Bratislava Site: Drienova 34, P.O. Box 78, 820 09 Bratislava 29, Slovakia; Tel./fax 011-421-7293-114; Bratislava@cityu.edu. Trencin Site: Bezrucova 64, 911 01 Trencin, Slovakia; Tel./fax 011-421-8315-293-37; Trencin@cityu.edu. Recruits 30-35 native English-speaking teachers per year (must have Master's degree and teaching experience) for Slovakia. IEP and BSBA programs. Slovakia; must have TEFL certification and international living experience.

CJO-International House, 4 IH schools situated in southern Poland. Great opportunities for support and development. Ideal for newly qualified and experienced teachers alike. The group comprises IH Bielsko, IH Katowice, IH Opole, and IH Wroclaw, www.ih.com.pl.

Czech Academic Information Agency, Dum Zahranicnich Sluzeb, Senovázné Námesti 26, 11121 Prague, Czech Republic; 011-42-2-24-22-9698; aia@dzs.cz, www.dzs.cz/aia/lektori. htm. Helps prospective English teachers find posts mainly in state schools but also in private institutes.

Ecologia Trust, The Park, Forres, Moray IV36 3TZ; 011-44 1309 690995; all@ecologin. org.uk, http://atschool.eduweb.co.uk/ecoliza. Student volunteers needed for at least 1 month at children's home in Kaluga region of Russia. Fee is $1,000+ for up to 2 months excluding airfares.

English for Everybody, c/o ITC, Kaprova 14, 110 00 Prague 1, Czech Republic; Tel./fax 011-42-2-2481 4791; info@itc-training.com, www. itc-training.com. EFL placement agency affiliated to U.S.-owned TEFL training company.

English School Sunny Plus, 1-Aeroportoskaya St, Bldg. 1/3, P.O. Box 23, 125057 Moscow, Russia; Tel./fax 011-7-095-129 7303; www.sunnyplus.ru. Hires university-educated Americans with some teaching experience.

Galindo Skola (Sava Centar), Milentija Popovica 9, 11070 Novi Beograd, Yugoslavia; 011-381-11-311-4568; galindo@net.yu. English teachers to work with children and adolescents for at least 3 months.

Goloustnoye Center for Ecology, Culture and Information ("USTYE") ul. Sverdlova 20, 664515 Bolshoye Goloustnoye, Irkutskaya Oblast, Russia; 011-7-3952-510-069; hank@irk.ru. Volunteer opportunities in conservation, English teaching, ecotourism, etc. at this center in Siberia affiliated with the new Baikal Center for Conservation of Biodiversity.

INEX Czech Republic, National Centre, Senovzne nam, 24, 116 47 Prague 1; 011-420-2 241 02 527; inex@czn.cz, www.czex.cz/inex. Forty-five projects in Czech Republic for international volunteers in social, cultural and environmental fields.

INEX Slovakia, Prazska 11, 814 13 Bratislava; 011-421-7 524 96 249, fax 011-421-7 524 94 707; inexsk@nextra.sk, www.inex.sk. Partner organization in Slovakia for workcamps.

International Exchange Center, 2 Republic Sq., LV-1010 Riga, Latvia; fax 011-371-783 0257; iec@mail.eunet.lv. Recruits English-speaking volunteers for summer projects in Latvia and Russia that may involve camp counseling, au pairing, etc. Basic knowledge of Russian or local language required.

Language Link Russia, Novoslobodskaya ul. 5 bld. 2, 103030 Moscow; Tel./fax 011-7-095-

250-8935; jobs@language.ru, www.language. ru. Places 400 native-English teachers in schools throughout Russia.

Ormansag Foundation, Arany Janos u. 4, 7967 Dravafok, Hungary; Tel./fax 011-36-73-352 333. Unpaid gardening work in orchard, herb garden, etc. at sustainable farm. Also coordinates volunteers for neighboring farms. Free accommodations. Minimum stay 1 week.

Petro-Teach Program, c/o Prof. Wallace J. Sherlcok, Dept. of Curriculum and Instruction, Univ. of Wisconsin, Whitewater, WI 53190; sherlocw@mail.uww.edu, www.semlab2.sbs.sunysb.edu/Users/jbailyn.Pe tro.html. Petro-Teach program in St. Petersburg places candidates in state secondary schools and private institutes. Application process begins in February and March for September 1 start date.

Project Harmony, 6 Irasville Common, Waitsfield, VT 05673; 802-496-4545, www. projectharmony.org. Teaching Intern Program places teachers in Russia and Ukraine (Odessa). Recent college graduates accepted.

REAP (Rural Enterprise Adaptation Program), 1109 31st St., NE, Cedar Rapids, IA 52402; 319-366-4230; REAP@reapintl.com, www.reapintl.com. Village volunteer programs and internships of 3-4 weeks in Lake Baikal region of Russia. $2,100 fee includes flight Chicago-Irkutsk.

Russia Camp Program, c/o Camp Counselors USA, 2330 Marinship Way, Suite 250, Sausalito, CA 94965; 800-999-CAMP; outbound@campcounselors.com, www.ccusa. com. American counselors spend 4 or 8 weeks volunteering at Russian youth camps. Program fee of $1,600 including return airfare New York-Moscow, visa, insurance, and orientation.

SCI Slovenia-Voluntariat, Breg 12, 1000 Ljubljana, Slovenia; 011-386-1-425-8067, fax 011-386-1-251-7208; placement@ zavod-voluntariat.si, www.zavod-voluntariat. si. Sponsors 15 international workcamps in Slovenia for volunteers, mostly building renovation, ecological, agricultural, or social projects.

Services for Open Learning, North Devon Professional Centre, Vicarage St., Barnstable, Devon EX32 7HB, U.K.; 011-44-1271-327319; www.sol.org.uk. Recruits graduates to teach in schools in Belarus, Croatia, Czech Republic, Hungary, Romania, and Slovakia. Interviews in Eastern Central Europe or U.K.

Soros Professional English Language

Teaching (SPELT), Open Society Institute, 400 W. 59th St., 4th Fl., New York, NY 10019. English as a Foreign Language teaching and teacher training positions. Master's degree in TESL/TEFL/ Applied Linguistics and/or CELTA required. Visit web site for more information and an application: www.soros.org/spelt.

Svezhy Veter Travel Agency, 426076 Izhevsk Pushkinskaya 154, 426000 Izhevsk, P.O. Box 2040, Russia 011-7-3412-512500, fax 011-7-3412-752268; www.sv-agency.udm.ru. Native speakers teach evening course (15 hours a week) at a secondary school in Izhevsk in exchange for homestay with meals and visa support.

Teachers for Central and Eastern Europe, 21 V 5 Rakovski Blvd., Dimitrovgrad 6400, Bulgaria; Tel./fax 011-359-391-24787; U.S.: 707-276-4571; tfcee@usa.net, www.tfcee. 8m.com. Appoints 80 native speakers to teach in English language secondary schools for 1 academic year in Bulgaria, and also in Czech Republic, Hungary, Poland, and Slovakia. Details also available from InterExchange see Worldwide Jobs, below).

Travel Teach, St. James's Building, 79 Oxford St., Manchester M1 6FR; UK premium line: 011-44-870-789-8100; www.travelteach.com. Working holiday opportunities teaching English in Moldova and Lithuania. Placement fees £445 (Moldova-minimum 2 weeks) and £495 (Lithuania-minimum 7 weeks).

Union Forum Ukraine, Lychakivska Str. P.O. 5327, Lviv 10, 79010 Ukraine; Tel./fax 011-38-0322-759488; ukrforum@ipm.lviv.ua, www.eastlinks.net/members/forum.html. Invited enthusiastic individuals to participate in Voluntary International Exchange Service Program in the summer.

FRANCE

American Church, 65 quai d'Orsay, Paris and the **American Cathedral,** 23 Ave George V, Paris 75008; www.us.net/amcathedral-paris. Both churches feature notice boards you should consult while in Paris. The latter offers volunteering opportunities in its own programs as well as career forums for job seekers.

APARE/GEC, Groupement Européen des Campus 41 cours Jean Jaurès, 84000 Avignon, France; 011-33-4-90-85-51-15; gec@apare-gec.org, www.apare-gec.org/. Runs volunteer camps at historic sites in Greece, Italy, Spain, Gemany, Bulgaria, Austria, Romania, Ireland, Great Britain, Poland, Portugal, Tunisia, and

Morocco (as well as France and Europe).

Bombard Balloon Adventures, SRO Ground Crew, Chateau de LaBorde, 21200 Beaune, France; 011-33-3-80-26-63-30. U.S. contact fax: 240-384-7107; mike@bombardsociety. com, www.bombardsociety.com/jobs. Hot-air balloon ground crew for summer season, mainly in France (winter season in Swiss Alps).

Butterfly et Papillon, 5 Av de Genève, F-74000 Annecy, France; 011-33-450-67-0133; aupair.france@wanadoo.fr, www.butterfly-papillon.com. All nationalities placed as au pairs in French families for 3-18 months.

Centre International d'Antibes (CIA), 28 Avenue du Chateau, 06600 Antibes; 011-33-4-92-90-71-70; direct1@cia-france.com, www.cia-france.com. Work exchange program offered by French language school on the Cote d'Azur. Volunteers with the right to work in Europe do administrative or domestic work in exchange for board and lodging and/or French tuition.

Centres d'Information et de Documentation Jeunesse (CIDJ), 101 Quai Branly, 75740, Cedex 15, Paris; fax 011-33-1-40-65-02-61; www.cidj.asso.fr. Advisory centers for young people throughout France. Paris branch distributes leaflets *(fiches)* on work, study, etc. in France. Send 4 IRCs to receive the catalog.

Club du Vieux Manoir, 10 rue de la Cossonerie, 75001 Paris; 011-33-3-44-72-33-98; http://clubduvieuxmanoir.asso.fr. Workcamps to restore ancient monuments. Board and lodging cost FF80 per day.

Council Exchanges Paris, 112, ter rue Cardinet, Paris 75017, France; 011-33-1-58-57-20-50; www.councilexchanges-fr.org. Support office to "Work in France" participants (through Council Exchanges; see Worldwide Jobs below). Program allows students to work in France for up to 3 months.

Fédération Unie des Auberges de Jeunesse, 27 rue Pajol, 75018 Paris, France; 011-33-144-89-87-27. Short-term work (catering, reception, sports, instruction, etc.) at youth hostels throughout France. Applications must be sent to individual hostels. FUAJ also organizes voluntary workcamps to renovate hostels; volunteers pay Euro 67 per week. Another chain of youth accommodation is Ucrif Etapes Jeunes, 27 rue de Turbigo, BP 6407, 75064 Paris cedex 2; 001-33-1-40-26-57-64; www.ucrif.asso.fr.

France-USA Contacts (FUSAC), P.O. Box 15, Coopers Station, New York, NY 10276; 212-777-5553, fax 212-777-5554; franceusa@aol.

com, www.fusac.com. This publication in Paris carries job ads. You can place an ad before arrival. $20 for 20 words.

French American Chamber of Commerce, 6th Fl., 1350 Ave. of the Americas, New York, NY 10019; 212-765-4460. Exchange Visitor Program. Offers internships in business are open to graduates with relevant professional experience. The 6-month visa can be renewed twice.

The French Cultural Service, 972 5th Ave., New York, NY 10021; fax 212-439-1455/1482; new-york.culture@diplomatic.fr, www.info-france-usa.org/culture. English Teaching Assistantship program, SCULE, runs from October 1 to April 30. Must have working knowledge of French. Stipend of Euro 915 a month.

La Sabranenque, Centre International, rue de la Tour de l'Oume, 30290 Saint Victor la Coste, France; 011-33-466-50-05-05. Volunteers needed to help preserve and restore monuments in France (and Italy). Inquiries to Jacqueline Simon, 124 Bondcroft Dr., Buffalo, NY 14226; 716-836-8698; info@ sabranenque.com, www.sabranenque.com.

Also consult in person the notice boards at the American Church, 65 quai d'Orsay, Paris or at the American Cathedral, 23 Ave. George V, Paris 75008; www.us.net/amcathedral-paris. The latter offers volunteering opportunities in its own programs as well as career forums for job seekers.

Ministry of Culture, Sous-Direction de l'Archéologie, 4 rue d'Aboukir, 75002 Paris, France; 011-33-1-40-15-77-81; www. culture.fr/fouilles. Government department which deals with archaeological digs. Every May they publish a list of excavations throughout France that accept volunteers.

REMPART, 1 rue des Guillemites, 75004 Paris, France; 011-33-1-42-71-96-55; contact@ rempart.com, www.rempart.com. Needs volunteers to care for endangered monuments. Most projects charge Euro 6-8 per day, plus membership of Euro 35.

Star Crew, The Office, Gallerie du Port, 8 Boulevard d'Aguillon, 06600 Antibes, France; info@starcrew.com, www.starcrew.com. Crewing agency for private yachts. Located in building with other crewing agencies.

GERMANY, SWITZERLAND, AUSTRIA

AGABUR Foundation Inc., 9 Eastwood Rd., Storrs, CT 06268; 860-429-1279;

austynas@hotmail.com, http://.mannheim-program.necaweb.com. Professional program: language training, university study, and optional paid internships in Germany.

Agroimpuls, Laustrasse, 5201 Brugg, Switzerland; 011-41-56-462-51-44; www.agroimpuls. ch. Swiss Farmer's Union runs a program for trainees in agriculture and horticulture.

Arbeitskreis Denkmalpflege, Goetheplatz 9B, D-99423 Weimar, Germany; 011-49-643-502390; akdenkmalpflege@t-online.de. Volunteers restore historic buildings year round.

Bergwald Projekt, (Mountain Forest Project/MFP), Hauptstrasse 24. CH-7014 Switzerland; 011-41-81-630-41-45; www.berg waldprojekt.ch. Educational and practical workcamps in alpine forests of Switzerland, Germany and Austria. Send 12 International Response Coupons for info. Must already be in Europe to participate

Compagna, Unterer Graben 29, 8400 Winterthur, Switzerland; 011-41-52-212 5530. Also Compagna Lausanne, Rue du Simplon 2, 1006 Lausanne; 011-41-21-616 2985; Compagna Luzern, Reckenbuhlstrasse 21, 6005 Luzern; 011-41-41 312 1173; compagna-Luzern@bluewin.ch. Au pair placements for minimum of 1 year throughout Switzerland. Registration and placement fee total SFR190.

Council Exchanges Germany, Oranienburger Str. 13-14, 10178 Berlin, Germany; 011-49-30-28 48 59-0; fax 011-49-30-28 09 61 80; InfoGermany@councilexchanges.de, www.council.de. Support office for "Work in Germany" participants through Council Exchanges. (See Worldwide Jobs below). Program allows students of German to work for up to 3 months and those who organize a career-related job in Germany for 6 months.

English for Children, Kanalstrasse 44, P.O. Box 160, 1220 Vienna, Austria; 011-43-1-282-77-17; english.for.children@eunet.at. TEFL-trained teachers needed for residential summer camps or for academic year. Should be resident in Austria. Also: English for Kids, A. Baumgartnerstr. 44/A 7042, 1230 Vienna, Austria; 011-43-1-667 45 79; www.e4kids. co.at. EFL teachers and camp counsellors for summer language camp. Must have pre-arranged work permit.

First Choice/Skibound, Olivier House, Ski Lakes & Mountains Division, 18 Marine Parade, Brighton, East Sussex BN2 1TL, U.K.; 011-44-1273-677777; min@fcski.co.uk, www.fcski.co.uk. Domestic and kitchen staff needed to work winter season for tour opera-tor which runs hotels in Alpine resorts in Austria (and also France).

GIJK Gesellschaft fur Internationale, Jugendkontakte, Baunscheidtstr. 11, 53113 Bonn, Germany; 011-49-228-95-73-00; gijk@gijk.de, www.gijk.de (in German). Au pair placements for people of all nationalities under the age of 24.

Gruppo Volontari, della Svizzera Italiana, C.P. 12, 6517 Arbedo, Switzerland; 011-41-77-3540161, 011-41-91-8574520, fax 011-41-91-6829272; www.adonet.org. Conservation workcamps to help mountain communities. Participants pay SFR15 per day to cover expenses.

Happy Hands, Working Holidays in Germany, Römerberg 8, 60311 Frankfurt/Main, Germany (also Frankfurt) 011-49-69-293733; Anne.Gleichen@t-online.de, www.workingholidays.de. Farm assistants live and work on farms and estates, work in on-site shops and restaurants, and care for horses and other animals for 6 or more weeks. Must have prior permission to work in Germany.

Haut-Lac International Centre, 1669 Les Sciernes, Switzerland; 011-41-26-928-4200; info@haut-lac.ch, www.haut-lac.ch. Teachers and monitors needed for summer and winter language programs.

Hiking Sheep Guesthouse, Villa La Joux, 1854 Leysin, Switerland; Tel./fax 011-41-24-494-3535; hikingsheep@leysin.net, www.keysin. net/hikingsheep/uk. Hostel needs good linguists for reception and general duties.

IBG, Schlosserstrasse 28, D-70180 Stuttgart, Germany; 011-49-711-649-11-28; ibg-work camps@t-online.de. Organizes voluntary workcamps throughout Germany.

Involvement Volunteers-Deutschland, Naturbadstr. 50, 91056 Erlangen, Germany; Tel./fax 011-49-9135-8075; ivde@t-online.de. Conservation organization allied to Involvement Volunteers in Australia.

Ökista, Garnisongasse 7, 1090 Vienna, Austria; 011-43-1-401-48-220; www.oekista.co.at. Live-in childcare positions throughout Austria. Pocket money 700 Austrian schillings per week.

Pro Filia, 241G Rte d'Hermance, 1246 Corsier/Geneva; 011-41-22-751-02-95. Places live-in babysitters with French-speaking families for a minimum of 1 year. The office at Beckenhofstrasse 16, 8035 Zurich; Tel./fax 011-41-1-361-53-31; profilia@dplanet.ch, www.profilia.ch, deals with German-speaking Switzerland.

Pro International e.V, Bahnhofstraße 26 A, 35037 Marburg, Germany; 011-49-6421-65277; pro-international@lahn.net, www.pro-international.de. International work-camps last 2-3 weeks March-November.

Swiss Travel Service, Bridge House, 55-59 High Rd., Broxbourne, Hertfordshire EN10 7DT, England; www.swisstravel.co.uk. Winter and summer resort representatives needed April to end of September. Interviews held in U.K.

TASIS (The American School in Switzerland), Summer Language Programs, 6926 Montagnola-Lugano, Switzerland; 011-41-91-994-64-71; administration@tasis.ch, www.tasis.ch. U.S. address: 1640 Wisconsin Ave., NW, Washington, DC 20007; 202-965-5800. Work as English teachers and children's counselors at summer camp.

U.S. Military Bases throughout Germany have Civilian Personnel Offices (CPOs) that are responsible for recruiting auxiliary staff to work in bars, shops, etc., on base and as ski instructors. Heidelberg is the HQ for the U.S. Army in Europe, which creates long-term jobs for secretaries, clerks, etc. The best bet is at the **Armed Forces Recreational Centers** at Garmisch-Partenkirchen and Chiemsee, AFRC Europe, Unit 24501, APO AE 09053; 011-49-8821-750707; cpo@afrc.garmisch.army.mil, www.afrceurope.com/empl.htm.

Vereinigung Junger Freiwilliger (VJF), Hans-Otto-Str. 7, 10407 Berlin, Germany; 011-49-30-428-506-03; office@vjf.de. Workcamps held in former East Germany. Registration fee Euro 112.

WWOOF-Austria, c/o Hildegard Gottlieb, Langegg 155, 8511 St Stefan ob Stainz, Austria; Tel./fax 011-43-3463-82270; wwoof/welcome@telering.at. Membership costs $25 per year and comes with list of 90 Austrian organic farms looking for work-for-keep volunteer helpers. Combined Swiss-Austrian list is $35; combined German-Swiss-Austrian list is $50.

WWOOF-Germany, (Willing Workers on Organic Farms), Postfach 210 259, D-01263, Dresden, Germany; info@wwoof.de; www.wwoof.de. Volunteer openings on organic farms. Membership fee of Euro 30 gives access to 160 farms.

WWOOF-Switzerland, Postfach 59, 8124 Maur, Switzerland; wwoof@dataway.ch, www.dataway.ch/~reini/wwoof. For details on working for your keep on an organic farm, send $15. Includes 45 addresses in Switzerland plus a handful elsewhere.

Young Austria Summer Camps, Ferienhofe GmbH, Alpenstrasse 108a, A-5020 Salzburg, Austria; 011-43-662-62 57 58-0; office@camps.at, www.camps.at. Monitors and EFL teachers for summer language and sports camps near Salzburg. Application deadline end of February.

Zentralstelle für Arbeitsvermittlung (ZAV), Villemombler Str. 76, 53123 Bonn, Germany 011-49-228-713-0, fax 011-49-228-713-1111; www.arbeitsamt.de/zav. Federal employment bureau handles student applications from abroad. Applicants must speak German. Majority of jobs are in hotels and restaurants, in industry and agriculture.

GREECE AND THE MEDITERRANEAN

Adriatic Dolphin Project Croatia, Zad Bone 11, Veli Losing, 51551 Croatia; 011-385-51-236 406; adp@adp.hr, http://adp.hpm.hr. Paying volunteers join dolphin research project for 12 days on the Croatian island of Losinj.

American Language Center Damascus, P.O. Box 20, Damascus, Syria; 011-963-11-333 7936, fax 011-963-11-331 9327. Native speaker teachers employed after local interview.

Anglo Nannies, 2 St. Marks Pl., London SW19 7ND, England; 011-44-20-8944-6677; nannies@anglonannies.com, www.anglonannies.com. Places mother's helpers and nannies in wealthy Istanbul households. Must be available for interview in U.K. or Istanbul.

Archelon, Sea Turtle Protection Society of Greece, Solomou 57, 10423 Athens, Greece; Tel./fax 011-30-1-523 1342; stps@archelon.gr, www.archelon.gr. Can advise volunteers on locations where they are needed over the summer to conserve and research the loggerhead turtle population.

Arcturos, Victor Hugo 3, 546 25 Thessaloniki; 011-30-31-55 46 23, www.forthnet.gr/arcturos. Accepts short-term volunteers at its bear protection center at Ag. Mina 3, 546 25 Thessaloniki.

Athanassopoulus Language Schools, 6 Einstein St., 18757 Keratsini-Piraeus, Greece; 011-30-1-43-14-921. Eight-month teaching contracts in Greece.

Athenian Nanny Agency, P.O. Box 51181,

Kifissia, Athens 145 10, Greece; Tel./fax 011-30-1-808-1005; mskiniti@groovy.gr. Places nannies and experienced nurses in private families in Greece.

Au Pair Activities. Placement service for au pairs. Also offers positions in the tourist industry. P.O. Box 76080,17110 Nea Smyrni, Athens, Greece; Tel./fax 011-30-1-932-6016; porae@iname.com.

Balkan Sunflowers. Volunteers for Social Reconstruction in the Balkans Kosovo/Macedonia/Albania), Central Office, Postfach 1219, D-14806 Belzig, Germany; 011-49-33841 30670; www.ddh.nl/org/balkan sunflower. U.S. contact: Katarzyna Wargan, 3701 16th St, NW, Suite 500, Washington, DC 20010; 202-726-3317; kate@usbsf.org. Various volunteer projects in the Balkans.

Centre for Cultural Initiative and Communications, Pavlou Mela Kai Bizaniou St., 59100 Veria, Greece; 011-30-331-62548. Restoration of the historic town of Veria in Western Macedonia may be able to use willing volunteers.

Conservation Volunteers in Greece, 15 Omirou St., 14562 Kifissia, Greece; fax 011-30-1-801-1489; cvgpeep@otenet.gr, www.cvgpeep.org. Projects include work in protected landscapes, conservation of traditional buildings and work in archaeological sites.

Consolas Travel, 100 Eolou St., 105 59 Athens, Greece; 011-30-1-821-9228 or 322-6657; info@consolas.gr, www.consolas.gr. Possibility of work in hostels, etc. in Athens and islands of Paros and Gavdos.

Earth, Sea and Sky, P.O. Box 308, Lincoln LN4 2GQ, U.K.; anna@earthseasky.org, www.earthseasky.org. Volunteers carry out summer projects like cleaning up wildlife habitats in Greece.

Global Children's Organization, 10524 W Pico Blvd., Suite 216, Los Angeles, CA 90064; 310-842-9235; gco@globalchild.org, www.globalchild.org. Volunteer camp counselors for camps held in areas of world conflict; e.g., Badija, Croatia.

Hellenic American Union, 22 Massalias St., 106 80 Athens, Greece; 011-30-1-362 9886; fax 011-30-1-363 3174; admin@hau.gr, www.hau.gr. Needs 45 TEFL-qualified teachers.

L'Aquilone Service Agency, Via Giovanni Pascoli 15, 20129 Milan, Italy; 011-39-02-2952-9639; aquilone@azienda.com. Summer and year-long placements of au pairs.

Sani Beach Holiday Resort, Sani SA, 63077

Kassandra, Halkidiki, Greece; 011-30-374 31231; hrdtrain@saniresrot.gr, www.saniresort.gr. Hospitality industry trainees aged 18-20 needed to work at this eco-resort south of Thessaloniki for at least 5 months.

Skyros, 92 Prince of Wales Rd., London NW5 3NE, U.K; 011-44-207-267-4424; www.skyros.com. Work scholars recruited to assist at Atsitsa alternative holiday center on Greek island of Skyros. Volunteers must be nurses, chefs, or experienced maintenance people. Board and lodging costs £40 per week. Workers can participate in courses offered at center from abseiling to windsurfing.

Sunsail USA, Annapolis Landing Marina, 980 Awald Dr., Suite 302, Annapolis, MD 21403; 800-327-2276; sunsailusa@sunsail.com, www.sunsail.com. Sunsail U.K.: Sunsail Ltd, The Port House, Port Solent, Portsmouth, Hampshire, PO6 4TH, U.K.; 011-44-870-777-0313, fax 011-44-23-9221-9827; sales@sunsail.com. Hires sailors, hostesses, clubhouse staff, cooks, and nannies for Greece and Turkey.

Sunworld Sailing Ltd., 120 St. Georges Rd., Brighton, E. Sussex BN2 1EA, U.K.; www.sunworld-sailing.co.uk. Employs instructors, maintenance staff, crew and other staff for sailing and windsurfing holidays in Spain, Greece, and Turkey.

UNIPAL (Universities Trust for Educational Exchange with Palestinians), BCM Unipal, London WC1N 3XX, U.K.; Tel./fax. 011-44-207-771-7368; www.unipal.org.uk (written enquiries preferred). Runs a summer program of teaching in the West Bank, Gaza, and Lebanon. Volunteers teach children in refugee camps. Volunteers must be native English speakers and based in the U.K.

ITALY

A.C.L.E. Summer and City Camps, Via Roma 54, 18038 San Remo, Italy; Tel./fax 011-39-0184-506070; info@acle.org, www.acle.org. Need counselors and EFL teachers for multi-activity and English-language camps in northern Italy for 4, 8 or 12 weeks. Compulsory 3-day training course.

Abruzzo National Park, Viale Tito Livio 12, 00136 Rome, Italy; 011-39-06-3540 3331; fax 011-39-06-3540 3253. Volunteers carry out research and protection of flora and fauna in remote locations. For details contact the local park office in Pescasseroli (011-39-0863-1955) or Villetta Barrea (011-39-0864-9102, fax 011-39-0864-9132).

Archeoclub d'Italia, Via Sicilia 235, 00100 Rome, Italy; 011-39-06-488 1821, fax 011-39-06-428 81 810, www.gruppiarcheologici.org. Accepts paying volunteers on archaeological digs.

Byron Language Development, Via Sicilia 125, 00187 Rome, Italy; 011-39-06-42 01 44 36, fax 011-39-06-42 01 25 37; byron.lang@flashnet.it, www.byronschool.it. TEFL-qualified teachers needed.

English Language Schools in Italy may be found in the Italian yellow pages under *Scuole di Lingue.*

Gruppi Archeologici d'Italia, Via Degli Scipioni 30/A, 00192 Rome, Italy; 011-39-06-39 73 36 37; gruppiarch@tiscalinet.it; www.gruppiarcheologici.org. Regional archaeological units coordinate 2-week digs which paying volunteers can join. The web site (with an English version) gives contact details for archaeological projects throughout Italy.

Interlingue School of Languages, Via E.Q. Visconti 20, 00193 Rome, Italy; 011-390-6-321-5740; info@interlingue-it.com, www.interlingue-it.com. Native speaker English teachers needed; degree in education or TEFL background required.

Jolly Italian Au Pair Agency, Via Giovanni XXIII°, 20 - 36050 Monteviale (VI), Italy; Tel./fax 011-39-0444 552426; jolly@golden.it, www.goldnet.it/~jolly. Au pair agency.

L'Aquilone Service Agency, Via Giovanni Pascoli 15, 20129 Milan, Italy; 011-39-02-2952-9639; aquilone@azienda.com. Summer and year-long placements of au pairs.

LIPU (Lega Italiana Protezione Uccelli), Via Trento 49, 43100 Parma, Italy; 011-39-0521-273043; www.lipu.it. Long-established environmental and bird conservation association. Catalog of projects including short summary in English sent on request. Volunteer camps cost Euro 130 per week.

Oikos Protezione Ambientale, Via Paolo Renzi 55, 00128 Rome, Italy; 011-39-06-508-0280; oilos@oikos.org. Environmental volunteers needed especially for fire prevention near Rome.

Romana Musicisti, Via La Spezia 100, 00055 Ladispoli, Rome, Italy; Tel./fax 011-39-06-9922-1766; www.caerenet.it/romus. Recruits Italian-speaking musicians, singers, DJs and entertainers for summer jobs around Italy. Registration fee must be paid.

Smile, Via Vigmolese 454, 41100 Modena, Italy; Tel./fax 011-39-059-363868. Tutors and counselors needed for summer language camps.

WWOOF Italia, c/o Bridget Matthews, 109 Via Casavecchia, 57022 Castagneto Carducci (LI), Italy; wwoof@oliveoil.net. Membership costs Euro 10 to obtain list of organic farmers in Italy looking for volunteers.

KENYA

Future in Our Hands Kenya, P.O. Box 4037, Kisumu, Kenya; 011-254-35-40522; FIOHK@hotmail.com. Volunteers needed for 5 weeks to 6 months.

LATIN AMERICA

AFP Languages, Av. Colón 2277 & Ulloa Fierro, Bldg. Apa 2B, Quito, Ecuador; 011-593-2-234268; info@apf-languages.com, www.apf-languages.com. Spanish tuition plus choice of ecological or humanitarian voluntary projects.

American Friends Service Committee, 1501 Cherry St., Philadelphia, PA 19102; 215-241-7000/7295; afscinfo@afsc.org, www.afsc.org. Sends paying volunteers who speak Spanish to community projects in Mexico during the summer. Program fee about $1,000 plus travel expenses.

AmeriSpan Unlimited, P.O. Box 40007, Philadelphia, PA 19106-0007; 800-879-6640; www.amerispan.com/volunteer. Runs volunteer and internship programs as well as language immersion courses in Latin America.

Amigos de las Americas, 5618 Star Lane, Houston, TX 77057; 800-231-7796; info@amigoslink.org, www.amigoslink.org. AMIGOS provides students an opportunity to experience hands-on cross cultural understanding and leadership by means of living with host families in rural communities or underserved semi-urban neighborhoods and volunteering as public health and community development workers. AMIGOS volunteers typically partner in teams of 2 or 3, and spend 4-8 weeks living and working in 1 of 8 Latin American countries: Bolivia, Brazil, Costa Rica, Dominican Republic, Honduras, Mexico, Nicaragua, or Paraguay. Collaborating with local sponsoring agencies and community members, volunteers usually propose asset assessment projects in their community's schools, health clinics, and house-to-house. AMIGOS programs in the past have included: community-based initiatives, sanitation and development, environmental education, family nutrition, health education, home improvement, rabies vaccinations, youth groups, education and leadership.

Amity Volunteer Teachers Abroad, 10671 Roselle St., Suite 101, San Diego, CA 92121-1525; 858-455-6364; avta@amity.org, www.amity.org. Volunteers needed to teach English in Argentina, Peru, Mexico and the Dominican Republic while living with local families. Also active in other countries (see Worldwide Jobs below).

Amizade Volunteer Vacations, 367 S Graham St, Pittsburgh, PA 15232; 888-973-4443; volunteer@amizade.org; www.amizade.org. Short-term community service volunteer programs in Brazil and Bolivia (plus Montana, Navajo Nation, Australia and Nepal). Participation fees vary according to program, $1,000-$2,600.

Artemis Cloud Forest Preserve, Apdo. 937 San Pedro Montes de Oca, 2050 Costa Rica. Volunteers pay $175 per week. Tasks include trail building and tree planting. Minimum stay 1 month.

Benedict School of Languages, Mercedes de Elizalde, P.O. Box 09-01-8916 Guayaquil, Ecuador; 011-593-4-244-4418; benecent@telconet.net, www.worldwide.edu/ci/ecuador/schools/14556.html. College-educated native speakers needed for several Benedict schools in Ecuador.

Bermuda Biological Station for Research, Inc., 17 Biological Ln., St. George's, GE01 Bermuda; 441-297-1880; www.bbsr.edu. Volunteer interns help scientists conduct research; apply 4 months in advance.

Bospas Forest Farm, c/o Casa Dobronski, Calle Guanhuiltagua N34-457 Quito, Ecuador; bospas@hotmail.com. Farm assistants with experience in gardening needed for fruit farm in subtropical valley in Northwest Ecuador. Monthly charge of $200.

Caledonia Languages Abroad, The Clockhouse, Bonnington Mill, 72 Newhaven Rd., Edinburgh EH6 5QG, U.K.; 011-44-131-621-7721; www.caledonialanguages.co.uk. Spanish and voluntary work programs organized in Peru and Costa Rica year round. Community and environmental projects and teaching English, depending on skills and level of language ability.

Casa de los Amigos, Ignacio Mariscal 132, 06030 Mexico, D.F., Mexico; 011-52-5-705-0521; friends@avantel.net, www.casadelosamigos.org. Quaker-run service center in Mexico City with information on volunteers opportu-nities throughout Mexico and Central America.

Casa Guatemala, 14th Calle 10-63, Zona 1, Guatemala City; 011-502-232-5517/221-1851; casaguatemal@guate.net. Runs orphanage in the Petén region that needs volunteer medical staff, teachers, and nannies.

Casa Xelaju Guatemala, Callejon 15, Diagonal 13-02, Zona 1, Quetzaltenango, Guatemala; 502-761-5955; info@ casaxelaju.com, www.casaxelaju.com. Supervised internships in and around Quetzaltenango. Minimum stay 2 months. Must have good knowledge of Spanish. Cost of participation is $120 per week. U.S. contact: Casa Xelaju, 3034 47th Ave. S, Minneapolis, MN 55406; 888-796-CASA.

Centro Cultural Colombo Americano, Carrera 43, 51-95 Apartado Aereo 2097, Barranquilla, Colombia; 011-57-53-408084; colombo@b-quilla.cetcol.net.co. Recruits native speaker teachers. Similar centers in Cali, Bogota, Medellin, etc.

Centro Mexicano Internacional (CMI), Fray Antonio de San Miguel 173, Morelia, Michoacan, Mexico or Apartado Postal 56, Morelia, Michoacan 58000; 011-52-43-12-4596; cmi.spanish-language.com, www.spanish-language.com. Intern placement program with Spanish language tuition in Mexico. $370 per week. Web site lists various voluntary projects in Mexico education, camp counseling, social, etc). U.S. contact: Victor Padelford, International Director, 14427 Brookhollow, P.M.B. 279, San Antonio, TX 78232; vwpadelford@spanish-language.com.

Centro Venezolano Americano (CVA), Apartado 61715 Del Este, Caracas 1060-A, Venezuela; or Avenida Jose Marti, Edif. CVA, Urb. Mercedes, Caracas 1060-A, Venezuela; 011-58-2-993-7911; infocva@cva.org.ve, www.cva.org.ve. Internships of at least 6 months for English teachers. In the U.S. this Pasante Internacional program is represented by Nancy Carapaica, 1408 NW 82nd Ave., C-525, Miami, FL 33126; fax 582-993-6812.

CIS-MAM Language School, Boulevard Universitario #4, Colonia El Roble, San Salvador, El Salvador; 011 503-226-2623; www.cis-elsalvador.org. Volunteer English teachers to work part-time with members of the Salvadorean opposition.

Conservation International, Eco-Escuela de Español, c/o Conservation International, 2501 M St. NW, Suite 200, Washington, DC 20037; 202-973-2238; ecoescuela@conservation.org;

also c/o G.A.P. Adventures, 19 Duncan St, Suite 401, Toronto M5H 3H1, Canada; www.gap.ca/ can/eco. Students live in Guatemalan village in Peten region and help with development work while studying Spanish. Fee of $200 per week covers tuition and homestay.

Cuban Studies Institute, Center for Latin American Studies, Tulane Univ., Caroline Richardson Bldg., New Orleans, LA 70118-5698; 504-862-8629; http://intern.tulane.edu. Internships and rural homestays in Ecuador, Mexico, and Cuba. Six weeks costs $3,600.

Darwin Foundation, External Relations Unit, Casilla Postal 17-0103891, Quito, Ecuador; 011-593-5-526 146/7; volunteer@darwin foundation.org, www.darwinfoundation.org. International volunteer porgram on the Galapagos Islands.

EcoLogic Development Fund, P.O. Box 383405, Cambridge MA 02238-3405; 617-441-6300, www.ecologic.org. Recruits university students and professionals to work as interns and volunteers in Central America in the fields of conservation, community development and social justice. Relevant expertise is normally needed for minimum 3-month attachments to partner organizations.

Foundation for Sustainable Development, 5547 Mitcham Ct., Springfield, VA 22151; 703-764-0859; fsd@interconnection.org. Summer and longer term internships in all areas of development in Nicaragua and Bolivia (as well as South Africa and Tanzania).

Fundación Jatun Sacha, Eugenio de Santillán N34 248 y Maurián, Casilla 17 12 867, Quito, Ecuador; 011-593-2-432240/432246; volunteer@jatunsacha.org. Volunteer interns participate in research, plant conservation, agroforestry, etc. at four reserves in Amazonian Ecuador. Reserve fees including lodging and meals are $225-$250 per month.

Fundación Planeta Azul, Cuero y Caicedo 1036 y Carvajal, Quito, Ecuador; 011-573-2-226732; planetaazul@earthling.net. Partner organization of Ecuadorian Ministry of the Environment authorized to send volunteers (preferably aged 25-35) to 25 national parks and reserves plus the Galapagos National Park. Fee of $150-$250 per month depending on park.

Genesis Project, Horacio Gostalle 402 and Padre Laenen St., Bahia de Caráquez, Manabi, Ecuador; 011-593-5-692400; vladivr@ hotmail.com. Volunteers needed to spend 2 hours a day teaching English in a junior

school in return for free local accommodation near the beach.

Grant Foundation, 8466 N Lockwood Ridge Rd., #111, Sarasota, FL 34243; 941-355-2805, fax 941-351-0735. Work team projects use voluntary input to help at the Hopital Albert Schweizer in Haiti.

IFISA, Calle 4 Cruce con Carrera 4, Lecherias 6016, Venezuela; 011-58-81-817651. Undergraduates needed to teach ESL to all ages in Venezuela.

ICADS (Institute for Central American Development Studies), Apartado 300-2050, San Pedro de Montes de Oca, Costa Rica; 011-506-225-0508; icads@netbox.com, www.icad-scr.com. In U.S.: Dept. 826, P.O. Box 025216, Miami, FL, 33102-5216. One-month Spanish course combined with voluntary service in Costa Rica, Nicaragua, or Belize, $1,500. 10-week summer internships $3,400.

IMARC (Instituto Mexicano Norteamericano de Relaciones Culturales), Pres. Cardenas 840, Satillo, Coahuila 25000, Mexico; 011-52-84-14 84 22; academ@imarc.edu.mx. Experienced EFL teachers needed.

International Student Exchange Center (ISEC), 35 Ivor Place, London NW1 6EA, U.K.; 011-44-20-7724 4493, fax 011-44-20-7224 8234; isec@btconnect.com, www. isecworld.co.uk. Cultural exchanges with large range of countries in Europe and worldwide, including au pairing, volunteering, paid work, etc.

International Voluntary Expeditions, P.O. Box 189518, Sacramento, CA 95818-9518; 916-444-6856; oakland2@ix.netcom.com. Unskilled manual labor needed for Antigua, Barbados, Mexico, Ecuador, St. Lucia, Montserrat, and Dominica.

Just Act-Youth Action for Global Justice, 333 Valencia St., Suite 101, San Francisco, CA 94103; 415-431-4204, fax 415-431-5953; info@justact.org, www.justact.org. Publishes material on work and internships working for global justice. Formerly Overseas Development Network.

Language Link, 21 Harrington Rd., London SW7 3EU, England; 011-44-20-7225 1065; www.languagelink.co.uk. Places TEFL Certificate holders in its network of affiliated schools in Eastern and Central Europe, Germany, Vietnam, and China.

Latin Link STEP Programme, 175 Tower Bridge Rd., London SE1 2AB, U.K.; 011-44-207-939 9014; step.uk@latinlink.org, www.latinlink.org. Self-funded team-based program for committed Christians. Work is on small-scale building projects in Argentina, Bolivia, Brazil, Ecuador, Mexico, and Peru. Four months in spring (March to July) or 7 weeks in summer (July to August).

Mangrove Action Project, P.O. Box 1854, Port Angeles, WA 98362-0279; Tel./fax 360-452-5866; mangroveap@olympus.net, www. earthisland.org/map/map.html. Short mangrove-replanting project on the Pacific coast of Esmeraldes Province, Ecuador during the month of November.

Mojanda Foundation, Casa Mojanda, Apartado 160, Otavalo, Ecuador; Tel./fax 011-593-9-731737; mojanda@uio.telconet, www.casamojanda.com. Minimum stay for skilled volunteer interns at this environment awareness center is 6-12 months.

Na Bolom Volunteer Program, Na Bolom Cultural Institute, Av. Vicente Guerrero No. 33, San Cristóbal de Las Casas, C.P. 29220 Chiapas, Mexico; Tel./fax 011-52-967-8-14-18; nabolom@sclc.ecosur.mx, www.ecosur.mx/nabolom. Variety of voluntary opportunities for at least 3 or 6 months with association working to preserve indigenous culture.

Opening English School, Via Augusta 238, 08021 Barcelona, Spain; 011-34-93-241 89 00; awesterman@openingschool.com. Recruits 450 teachers for schools in Spain, France, Greece, Brazil, and Portugal.

Persohotel International, Mexico; persohotel@usa.net. Recruitment agency for the hospitality industry in the Caribbean looking for resort "animateurs" willing to spend 6 months in Cancun, Playa del Carmen, or Cozumel, Mexico.

Polyglot, Villavicencio 361 Of. 102, Santiago, Chile; 011-56-2-639-8078; application@polyglot.cl, www.polyglot.co.uk. Hires 40-50 English teachers with TEFL background each year.

Programa de Voluntariado Internacional, Servicio de Parques Nacionales, Apdo. 11384-1000/10104-1000, San Jose, Costa Rica; 011-506-257-0922. Spanish-speaking volunteers work in national parks for at least 45 days. Cost is $10 a day.

Pronatura Chiapas, Av. Benita Juarez 11-B, Apartado Postal 219, San Cristobal de Las Casas, Chiapas, C.P. 29200 Mexico. Tel./fax 011-52-967-85000; pronaturach@laneta. apc.org, www.pronatura.org. Rainforest conservation, environmental education and sustainable agriculture projects. Volunteers must be Spanish-speaking. Accommodations provided.

Tambopata Jungle Lodge, P.O. Box 454, Cusco, Peru; Tel./fax 011-51-84-245695; www. tambopatalodge.com. Takes on guides for a minimum of 6 months. They must have studied natural sciences and preferably speak Spanish.

MIDDLE EAST

Active English, Ataturk Bulvari 127/701, Selcan Han, Bakanliklar, 06640 Ankara, Turkey; 011-90-312-418 7973; www.acteng.com. Teachers for small chain of private language schools, interviews in Ankara or London.

Au Pair International, 2 Desler St, Bnei Brak 51507, Israel; 011-972-3-619 0423; www.aupair-international.co.il. Placement agency for full-time nannies and housekeepers of all nationalities. Must have full health insurance and HIV test certificate.

Christian Information Centre in Jerusalem, P.O. Box 14308, 91142 Jerusalem, Israel; 011-972-2-627 2692; cicinfo@cicts.org. Keeps a list of schools and institutes, mainly for people with disabilities, that take on volunteers.

ELS Language Centers/Middle East, P.O. Box 3079, Abu Dhabi, U.A.E.; 011-971-2-665-1516; elsme@emirates.net.ae, www.elsme.com. Employs many EFL-trained teachers full- and part-time throughout the Middle East.

Friends of Birzeit Univ., 21 Collingham Rd., London SW5 0NU, U.K.; 011-44-207-373 8414; fobzu@fobzu.org, www.fobzu.org. International summer workcamps near Ramallah in the West Bank.

Gençtur, Istiklal Cad. Zambak Sok. 15/5, 80080 Beyoglu, Istanbul, Turkey; fax 011-90-212-249-2554; workcamps.in@genctur.com, www.genctur.com. Student travel organization that arranges about 30 2-week international workcamps where volunteers work 6 hours a day and 6 days a week. Full board accommodations are supplied in return for voluntary work. Applications through partner organizations in each country.

GSM Youth Services Centre, Bayindir Sokak No. 45/9, 06650 Kizilay, Ankara, Turkey; 011-90-312-417-1124; gsm@gsm-youth.org, www.gwm-youth.org. Arranges 2-week workcamps in Anatolia.

Hilma's Au Pair Intermediary, Mrs. Hilma Shmoshkovitz, P.O. Box 91, Rishon-le-Zion 75100, Israel; 011-972-3-965-9937;

hilma@netvision.net.il. Well-established au pair and nanny agency for Israel. Also has an office in Jerusalem.

ICEP, Ugur Mumcu Cd. Kahramankadin Sk. 18-8, GOP-Ankara, Turkey; 011-90-312-446 4245; kultur@icep.org.tr, www.icep.org.tr. Au pair in Turkey program for 3-12 months. Pays monthly pocket money.

Internship in Israel Program, Israeli Ministry of Foreign Affairs; www.mfa.gov.il/mfa/go.asp?MFAH0egz0. Young Jewish professionals under 30 or students in their final year of college can be placed in government or public and private institutions in Israel from October.

Kent English Istanbul, Bahariye Arayicibasi Sok. No. 4, 81300 Kadikoy, Istanbul, Turkey; 011-90-216-347 2791; www.kent-english.com. Also in Ankara at Mithatpasa Caddesi No. 46 Kat. 3,4,5, 06420 Kizilay, Ankara, Turkey; 011-90-312-433 6010; kentenglishankara@yahoo.com. Many native speaker teachers employed; should have university degree certificate and TEFL certificate.

Kibbutz Program Center, Volunteer Dept., 18 Frishman St., 90 Ben Yehuda St., Tel Aviv 61030, Israel; 011-972-3-527-8874; kpcvol@inter.net.il. This office can place you on a kibbutz for a fee of $60, although it is better to arrive with a letter of introduction from Kibbutz Aliya Desk, 633 3rd Ave., 21st Fl., New York, NY 10017; 800-247-7852; kibbutzdsk@aol.com, www.kibbutz.org.il/eng (which acts as a clearinghouse for American volunteers). Minimum stay 2 months. Summer is the busiest time.

Malta Youth Hostels Association, 17 Triq Tal-Borg, Pawla PLA 06, Malta; 011-356-693957; myha@keyworld.net. Volunteers who spend a minimum of 21 hours a week doing hostel maintenance and administration receive free bed and breakfast for 2 weeks to 3 months. For detailed information and application form please send 3 IRC's from the post office. Inquires by email also answered.

Meira's Volunteers, 73 Ben Yehuda St., 1st Fl., Tel Aviv 63435, Israel; 011-972-3-523-7369, fax 011-972-3-524-1604. Agent for kibbutzim and moshavim for volunteers already in Israel.

Moshav Volunteer Center, 19 Leonardo da Vinci St., Tel Aviv 64733, Israel; 011-972-3-696-8335, fax 011-972-3-696 0139. Places volunteers who are already in Tel Aviv on moshavim throughout Israel.

Ottoman & Ottoman, Gaziosmanpasa Bulvari No. 9, Esen Han Kat: 5/506, 35210 Izmir, Turkey; 011-90-232-445 0599; ottomanyouth@superonline.com. Conservation camps on Turkish coasts.

Weizmann Institute of Science, P.O. Box 26, Rehovat 76100, Israel; 011-972-8-957 1667; www.weizmann.ac.il. Research students (with a minimum of 2 years university study) assist with interdisciplinary scientific projects for 10-16 weeks in the summer, earning a small stipend.

Yemen-American Language Institute (YALI), P.O. Box 22347, Sana'a, Yemen; 011-967-1-416-973/4; yaliroy@y.net.ye; www.yali.org.ye. Educated Americans with good knowledge of American culture needed to teach, preferably for a year. Also in Sana'a, try American School, Box 16003; Tel./fax 011-967-1-417119; and Modern American Language Institute (MALI), P.O. Box 11727, Sana'a; Tel./fax 011-967-1-241561.

NETHERLANDS, BELGIUM, LUXEMBOURG

L'Administration de L'Emploi, 10 rue Bender, 1229 Luxembourg; 011-352-478-53-00; www.etat.lu/adem. Operates a Service Vacances for students seeking summer jobs in warehouses, restaurants, etc. Non-European students must visit the office in person.

Activity International, P.O. Box 7097, 9701 JB Groningen, Netherlands; 011-31-50-3130666; info@activity.aupair.nl, www.activity.aupair.nl. Au pair placements throughout Holland.

Archeolo-j, Ave. Paul Terlinden 23, 1330 Rixensart, Belgium; 011-32-2-653 8268, fax 011-32-2-673 40 85; www.skene.be. Residential archaeological digs accept paying volunteers in July.

Au Pair Discover Holland, C. Barendregtlaan 9-F, 3161 HA Rhoon; and the international exchange organization.

The Bulletin, 1038 Chaussée de Waterloo, 1110 Brussels. A weekly English-language magazine in Brussels which carries job ads. Published on Thursdays.

Call International, Boulevard de la Cense 41, 1410 Waterloo and Avenue des Drapiers 25, 1050 Brussels, Belgium; Tel./fax 011-32-2-644-95-95; callinter@skynet.be. Needs 40 teachers with good communication skills to teach flexible hours.

Centre Information Jeunes (CIJ), 26 Place de la Gare, Gelerie Kons, L-1616 Luxembourg; 011-352-26 29 3-200. Run holiday job service between January and August, primarily for people with a European Union passport.

Euro Business Languages, Leuvensesteenweg 325, 1932 Zavantem, Belgium; 011-32-2-720-15-10; euro.business.languages@skynet.be. Experienced TEFL teachers needed to run business English courses.

Interexchange, www.interexchange.org. Applicants over 18 with a working knowledge of French (or Dutch) can be placed in a summer job, internship, or teaching position in Belgian companies or organizations for between 1 and 3 months. The program fee is $700; the application deadline is late April.

Natuur 2000, Bervoetstraat 33, 2000 Antwerp, Belgium; fax 011-32-3-231-26-04; http://home.planetinternet.be/~n2000. Organizes summer conservation workcamps and study projects throughout Belgium, which cost from Euro 37.

NJBG (Nederlandse Jeugdbond voor Geschiedenis), Prins Willem Alexanderhof 5, 2595 BE Den Haag, Netherlands; fax 011-31-70-335 2536; www.njbg.nl (partially in English). Archaeological and building restoration camps.

Phone Languages, Rue des Echevins, 65, Schepenenstraat, Brussels 1050, Belgium; 011-32-2-647-40-20, fax 011-32-2-647-40-55; belgium@phonelanguages.com, www.phonelanguages.com. Telephone teachers recruited for clients throughout Belgium and Luxembourg.

Stufam VZW, Vierwindenlaan 7, 1780 Wemmel, Belgium; 011-32-2-460-3395; aupair.stufam@pi.be. Places au pairs in Belgium.

Travel Active, P.O. Box 107, 5800 Venray; 011-31-478-551900; info@travelactive.nl. Arranges au pair stays in the Netherlands.

SCANDINAVIA

Allianssi Youth Exchanges, Olympiastadion, Etelakaarre, 00250 Helskini, Finland; 011-358-9-34824 312; www.alli.fi/nuorisovaihto. Coordinates workcamps in Finland; enquiries should be sent to partner organizations in the U.S.

American-Scandinavian Foundation, 58 Park Ave., New York, NY 10016; 212-879-9779; trainscan@amscan.org, www.amscan.org. Places summer trainees in engineering, chemistry, or computer science throughout Scandinavia, mainly Finland and Sweden. Also places American students and graduates in schools and companies in Finland to teach English from August to May.

APØG, Norsk Økologisk Landbrukslag, Langeveien 18, N-5003 Bergen, Norway; fax 011-47-55 32 02 45; organic@online.no. Service for volunteers who want to work on organic farms in Norway; send $20 for list of 50+ farm addresses.

Atlantis Youth Exchange, Kirkegata 32, 0153 Oslo, Norway; 011-47-22-47-71-70; post@atlantis-u.no. Arranges summer working guest positions on farms for 2 to 6 months. Also recruits au pairs for a minimum of 6 months. Applications can be sent direct or via InterExchange in New York.

Center for International Mobility (CIMO), Postbox 343, 00531 Helsinki, Finland; 011-358-9-7747-7033; cimoinfo@cimo.fi, www.cimo.fi. Arranges short- and long-term traineeships with Finnish companies. (The Finnish Family Program is now open only to those who are studying Finnish at university.)

Exis, Postbox 291, 6400 Sonderborg, Denmark; 011-45-74-42-97-49; info@exis.dk; www.exis.dk. Increasing number of au pair placements throughout Scandinavia, especially Denmark.

IAL/Internationella Arbetslag, Barnängsgatan 23, 116 41 Stockholm, Sweden; 011-46-8-643-0889; fax 011-46-8-641-8188. Peace and conservation camps organized through the Swedish branch of Service Civil International.

Scandinavian Institute, Box 3085, 200 22 Malmø, Sweden; 011-46-40-93-94-40; www.scandinavianinst.com and the **Scandinavian Service Center,** Lilla Strandgatan 2, 252 23 Helsingborg, Sweden; 011-46-42-12 33 45; scandinavian.aupair@telia.com. Au pair agencies in Sweden.

Stifelsen Stjarnsund, 770 71 Stjarnsund, Sweden; 011-46-225-80001; michael@stdi.w.se. Swedish community aims to encourage personal, social and spiritual development. Operates an international working guest program, 1 week to 3 months, mostly between May and September but winter visits possible.

VHH, c/o Inga Nielsen, Asenvej 35, 9881 Bindslev, Denmark. For $10 publishes a list of English-speaking organic farmers in Denmark looking for volunteers.

Village Camps S.A., Dept. 800, 14 rue de la Morache, 1260 Nyon, Switzerland; 011-41-22-990-9405, fax 011-41-22-990-9494; personnel@villagecamps.ch, www.

villagescamps.com. Recruits monitors, counselors, and medical staff to work for the summer or winter seasons at international children's activity camps in several Swiss resorts, France, U.K., and Austria.

Vista Cultural & Educational Travel Laekjargata 4, 101 Reykjavik, Iceland; 011-354-562 2362; vista@skima.is. Au pair agency placing foreign young people for 6-12 months in Icelandic households.

WWOOF-Finland, c/o Anne Konsti, Partala Information Services for Organic Agriculture, Huttulantie 1, 51900 Juva, Finland; 011-358-15-321 2380. Finnish organic farm organization. Send 2 IRCs to get list of 30 farmers looking for volunteers over the summer.

SPAIN, PORTUGAL

Acorn Adventure Ltd., 22 Worcester St., Stourbridge, West Midlands DY8 1AN, England; 011-44-1384-378827; topstaff@ acornadventure.co.uk, www.acorn-venture. com. Activity instructors and support staff for holiday center on the Costa Brava of Spain.

Castrum Lenguas Cultures y Turismo, Ctra. de Reudas 33, 47008 Valladolid; 011-34-983-222213; www.terra.es/personal2/castrum spain. Places young people with families in Castille and Leon where they exchange 3-4 hours of English lessons per day for room and board. They also enroll in a Spanish course.

Centros Europeos Principe, Calle Principe 12-6ºA, 28012 Madrid, Spain; 011-34-91-532-7230, fax 011-34-91-521-6076; ceprincipe@ inicia.es. Au pair placements in Spain. Language assistants for short time. Non paid work in Spanish companies. Full immersion with families, young exchanges programs, Spanish lessons.

Club de Relaciones Culturales, Calle Ferraz 82, 28008 Madrid, Spain; 011-34-91-5417103; rci_ic@mad.servicom.es, www.clubrci.es. Places American and European au pairs and live-in language assistants in Madrid and elsewhere in Spain. Registration fee is Euro 120.

Deya Archaeological Museum and Research Centre, Deya, Mallorca, Baleares, Spain; Tel./fax 011-34-71-639001. Participants join this long-established research project and excavation for 2 weeks at a time. Room, board and tuition cost $600 for the fortnight.

Instituto da Português, Juventude, Av. da Liberdade 194, 1259-015 Lisbon, Portugal; 011-351-21-317-9200; ipj.infor@ mail.telepac.pt. Arranges workcamps,

including archaeological digs, throughout Portugal. Applications should be sent to workcamp agency in home country.

Manga del Mar Menor Restoration and Research Project, Instituto de Ciencias Sociales y Ambientales and Amigos de la UNESCO, Paseo Marques de Corvera 33, 4BA A, Apartado de Correos 4.661 Murcia, Spain; Tel./fax 011-34-968-22-05-96; www.ctv.es/ USERS/murban/volunt.htm. Volunteers stay 15 days to 3 months at this coastal wetlands center collecting data and working with the public. Two-month working stay costs Euro 150.

Proyecto Ambiental Tenerife, 59 St. Martin's Ln., Covent Garden, London WC2, England; fax 011-44-207-240-5795; www.interbook.net/ personal/delfinc. Volunteers needed to work 2-6 weeks on whale and dolphin projects based in Tenerife, Spain. Must contribute £75 per week toward expenses.

Sunseed Trust, Apdo 9, 04270 Sorbas, Almeria, Spain; tel/fax 011-34-950-525 770; www.sunseed.org.uk. Invites volunteers to a remote research project on the south coast of Spain to help subsidize their stay costing from about $150 per week.

Vigvatten Natur Klubb, Apartado 3253, 01002 Vitoria Gasteiz, Spain; 011-34-945-28 17 94. Monitors and teachers needed for sports camps in the Basque country, Pyrenees, and Sierra de Urbion.

UNITED KINGDOM AND IRELAND

Acorn Adventure Ltd., 22 Worcester St., Stourbridge, West Midlands DY8 1AN, England; 011-44-1384-378827; topstaff@ acornadventure.co.uk, www.acorn-venture. com. Activity holiday centers in North Wales and the Lake District of England that need instructors and catering staff for full season (April-September).

Aillwee Cave Co., Ltd., Ballyvaughan, Co. Clare, Ireland; 011-353-65-77036; www. aillweecave.ie. Cave tour guides and catering/sales staff taken on for summer season at this busy tourist attraction open March to November.

An Oige, 61 Mountjoy St., Dublin 1, Ireland; 011-353-1-830-4555. The Irish Youth Hostels Association makes use of voluntary assistant wardens in the summer months.

Atlantis Community, Burtonport, Co.

Donegal, Ireland; 011-353-75-42304; afan69@hotmail.com. Volunteers with skills will receive bed and board to help restore a 50-foot wooden sailboat.

British Trust for Conservation Volunteers, 36 Saint Mary's St., Wallingford, Oxfordshire OX10 0EU, England; 011-44-1491-839766; www.btcv.org.uk. Organizes 1- or 2-week working breaks throughout Britain for environmentally concerned volunteers.

BUNAC (British Universities North America Club), operates the "Work in Britain" program enabling U.S. university students and recent graduates to take virtually any job in Britain for up to 6 months. BUNAC, info@bunacusa. org, www.bunac.org, also offers work/travel programs to Australia and New Zealand for U.S. citizens aged 18-30. Participants can work for up to 4 months in Australia and up to 12 months in New Zealand. Support resource centers for job and accommodations in London and Edinburgh, plus social program.

Children's Holiday Companies recruit large numbers of summer staff. PGL Travel, Alton Court, Penyard Ln., Ross-on-Wye, Herefordshire HR9 5NR, England; 011-44-1989-764211; enquiries@pgl.co.uk, www.pgl.co.uk/online. Hires over 500 people as sports instructors, counselors, and general staff for activity centers throughout Britain. Other children's holiday companies include: Prime Leisure Activity Holidays, Ltd., 4A Chawley Ln., Cumnor Hill, Oxford OX2 9PX, England; Camp Beaumont, Linton House, 164/180 Union St., London SE1 OLH, England; Buckswood International Summer School, Uckfield, Sussex TN22 3PU, England; and Conquest Tours Ltd., 13 Victoria Rd., Bath BA2 3QY, England.

Community Service Volunteers, 237 Pentonville Rd., London N1 9NJ, England; 011-44-207-278-6601; volunteer@csv.org.uk, www.csv.org.uk. Places full-time volunteers (age 18-35) in community settings from 4-12 months throughout Britain, supporting a variety of people including children with special needs, adults with learning difficulties, homeless people. Free accommodations and food plus £26.50 weekly allowance. No minimum qualifications needed. Overseas placement fee applies.

Conservation Volunteers Ireland, P.O. Box 3836, Ballsbridge, Dublin 4, or Green Griffith College, South Circular Rd., Dublin 8, Ireland; 011-353-1-454-7185; info@cvi.ie, www.cvi.ie. Coordinates unpaid environmental working

holidays throughout Ireland. Membership is Euro23/Euro 29.

Council for British Archaeology, Bowes Morrell House, 111 Walmgate, York Y01 9WA, England; 011-44-1904-671-417; info@britarch.ac.uk, www.britarch.ac.uk. Publishes *British Archaeology* 6 times a year with details of upcoming excavations in Britain. Membership costs £24, student discount available.

Dublin Internships, 8 Orlagh Lawn, Scholarstown Rd., Dublin 16, Ireland; Tel./fax 011-353-1-494-5277; mhrieke@eircom.ne, http://homepage.eircom.net/~dublinternships/. Places American undergraduates, graduate students and graduates in professional level internships in the spring, fall, and summer across the spectrum of majors, minors, and career options. Internships are non-salaried and a fee is charged. Advisable to forward application documentation 3 months in advance.

Hostel Assistants for Cork, Kerry, and Wexford for people with work permits. Email plat@indigo.ie.

Independent Living Alternatives, Trafalgar House, Grenville Pl., London NW7 3SA, U.K.; 011-44-20-8906 9265; ILA@cwcom.net. Volunteers needed to provide support for people with disabilities, to enable them to live independently in their own homes. Volunteers receive £63.50 per week plus free accommodation, usually in the London area.

Irish Job Search, www.irishjobsearch.com. Register of international job-seekers for hospitality and leisure industry in Ireland. Advice given on work permits.

Kingswood Group, Old Bembridge School, Hillway Rd., Bembridge, Isle of Wight PO35 5PH; 011-44-1983 875353; jobs@kingswood. co.uk offers jobs at holiday centers in Staffordshire, Isle of Wight and north Norfolk coast.

Barracudas Summer Activity Camps, Graphic House, Ferrars Rd., Huntingdon, Cambs. PE18 6EE; 011-44-1480-435090. Residential and day camps in southern England.

National Trust. One-week outdoor conservation camps throughout the U.K. year round. Volunteers pay £51-£62 per week. Minimum age for overseas applicants 18. Must have good conversational English. Brochure requests and bookings to open contact Direct Marketing, Stamm Rd., Wroxham, Norwich NR2 8DH, England; 011-44-01603-739-543; workingholidays@smtp.ntrust.org.uk, www.

nationaltrust.org/uk/volunteers.

National Trust, P.O. Box 84, Cirencester, Gloucestershire GL7 1RQ, England; www.nationaltrust.org/uk/volunteers. Long-term volunteering, 3-, 6-, or 12-month placements. Accommodations often available.

Scottish Conservation Projects Trust, Balallan House, 24 Allan Park, Stirling FK8 2QG; 011-44-1786 479697. Organizes residential conservation breaks throughout Scotland between March and November.

TASIS England American School, Coldharbour Ln., Thorpe, Surrey KT20 8TE, England; 011-44-1932-565252; www.tasis.com. EFL teaching vacancies for qualified Americans and jobs for sports monitors to work at children's summer camp.

Thistle Camps, National Trust for Scotland, 28 Charlotte Sq., Edinburgh EH2 4ET, Scotland; 011-44-131-243-9470; conservation-volunteers@ nts.org.uk, www.nts.org.uk. Similar to National Trust but in Scotland. Includes archaeological digs. Two- or 4-week projects; fee of £50-£110. Application deadline is February for overseas applicants. Sponsored by the Bank of Scotland.

Trees for Life, The Park, Findhorn Bay, Forres, Scotland IV36 3TZ; 011-44-1309 691292; trees@findhorn.org, www.treesforlife.org.uk. Volunteers needed to restore the native Caledonian Forest in Scotland. One-week camps cost £65.

Trident Transnational, Saffron Court, 14B St Cross St., London EC1N 8XA, England; 011-44-207-440-9190; info.transnational@ trid.demon.co.uk, www.trident-transnational.org. Offers unpaid work placements lasting 4 weeks to 6 months in U.K. companies. Participants aged 18-26.

UsitNow, 19 Aston Quay, Dublin 2, Ireland; 011-353-1-602-1777. Advice on job opportunities for Council Exchange participants.

Winant & Clayton Volunteers, 109 E 50th St., New York, NY 10022; 212- 378-0271. Since 1948, has arranged for U.S. citizens to volunteer for 7 weeks during the summer in community social service agencies in Britain, followed by independent travel for 2 weeks. Application deadline is January 31.

Youth Hostels Association, National Recruitment Dept., P.O. Box 11, Matlock, Derbyshire DE4 2XA, U.K. Seasonal assistant youth hostel wardens for 240 U.K. hostels. Interviews required.

UNITED STATES

WWOOF USA, S 18, C.9, Nelson, BC, Canada VIL 5P5; 250-354-4417; wwoof@usa.com, www.wwoofusa.com. Volunteer your time on farms in the U.S. and receive accommodations, meals, and an interesting experience in return. Descriptive booklet and membership is $30.

WORLDWIDE

Accord Cultural Exchange, 750 La Playa, San Francisco, CA 94121; 415-386 6203, fax 415-386-0240. Family placements in France, Germany, Spain, Austria, and Italy. $1,200 placement fee ($750 for summer positions).

AFS USA 310 SW 4th Ave., Suite 630, Portland, OR 97204-2608; 800-AFS-INFO; www.afs.org/usa. Students aged 18-29 spend 6 or 12 months in one of 10 countries (in Latin America, Africa, Thailand, Russia, or France) living with a family and working voluntarily on a social project. Participants must fundraise before program begins.

Agriventure (International Agricultural Exchange Association), 1000 1st Ave. S, Great Falls, MT 59401; 800-272-4996, fax 406-727-1997; iaea@sofast.net, www.usa@agriventure.com. Agricultural/horticultural exchange program for participants 18-30 years of age. Trainees are placed with a host family in Australia, New Zealand, Japan, and parts of Europe where they receive room, board, and allowance. Trainees learn first hand agricultural/horticultural techniques in a different country, have time to travel and see the sights, as well as make new, life long friends.

AIESEC (International Association for Students in Economics and Business Management), 135 W 50th St., 17th Fl., New York, NY 10020; 212-757-3774, fax 212-757-4062; aiesec@us.aiesec.org, www.us.aiesec.org. Business-related jobs available in over 80 countries. Highly qualified interns must apply through an AIESEC chapter in the U.S.

AIFS (American Institute For Foreign Study), 38 Queen's Gate, London SW7 5HR, England; 011-44-171-590-7474. U.S. office: River Pl., 9 West Broad St., Stamford, CT 06902; info@aifs.com, www.aifs.com. One hundred tour managers needed to lead educational tours of Europe for North American students.

Alliances Abroad, 702 West Ave., Austin, TX 78701; 888-6-ABROAD; info@alliancesabroad. com, www.alliancesabroad.com. Range of programs include teaching in Mexico, Africa, and the Far East; unpaid internships and volunteer work in many countries including Ireland, Germany, Jamaica, Guatemala, and Ecuador. Fees vary; samples are $1,200 for up to 5 months of teaching in Mexico, and for 2-month internship in Dublin.

Amity Volunteer Teachers Abroad (AVTA), 10671 Roselle St., Suite 101, San Diego, CA 92121-1525; 858-455-6364; mail@amity.org, www.amity.org. Voluntary teaching opportunities in Latin America, Africa (Senegal and Ghana), and France while living with local families.

Association for International Practical Training, 10400 Little Patuxent Pkwy., Suite 250, Columbia, MD 21044-3519; 410-997-2200, fax 410-992-3924; aipt@aipt.org, www.aipt.org. Short- and long-term placements in more than 70 countries through the International Association for the Exchange of Students for Technical Experience (IAESTE) available to students in science, engineering, math, agriculture, or architecture.

Au Pair in Europe, P.O. Box 68056, Blakely Postal Outlet, Hamilton, ON L8M 3M7, Canada; 905-545-6305; aupair@princeent. com, www.princeent.com/aupair. Au pairs placed in 21 countries including Australia. Airfare reimbursement plan operates in Holland, Sweden, and Iceland. Administrative and referral fee $425.

CCUSA/Work Experience Outbound, 2330 Marinship Way, Suite 250, Sausalito, CA 94965; 415-339-2728; outbound@ workexperienceusa.com, www.workexper ienceoutbound. com. Work programs in Russia (summer camp counseling), Brazil (4-12 weeks conservation volunteering), Australia, and New Zealand.

CDS International, 871 United Nations Plaza, 15th Fl., New York, NY 10017-1814; 212-497-3500; info@cdsintl.org, www.cdsintl.org. Arranges paid internships in Germany, Switzerland, Turkey, Argentina, and Singapore for students or recent graduates in business, engineering, technical, and other fields. Placements are 3-18 months.

CHELON, Viale Val Padana 134B, 00141 Rome; 011-39-06-812-5301; chelon@tin.it. Italian research organization active in Italy, Greece, Thailand, etc. Self-funded volunteers help with taking a census of loggerhead turtle nests, helping to tag turtles, and doing observation studies.

Communicating for Agriculture Exchange

Program, P.O. Box 677, Fergus Falls, MN 56537; 218-739-3241; http://ca.cainc.org. Work abroad program in 23 countries from Chile to Latvia for people aged 18-28 with at least one year of practical experience in agriculture, horticulture, equine husbandry, or oenology.

Council Exchanges, 633 3rd Ave, 20th Fl., New York, NY 10017-6706; 888-COUNCIL (268-6245); www.councilexchanges.org. Coordinates a working holiday program for U.S. college students to Ireland, France, Germany, Canada, New Zealand, Australia, and Costa Rica. The participation fee ranges from $300 to $425. Participants receive work documentation and access to job-finding assistance in the destination country. The Canadian equivalent is the Student Work Abroad Program (SWAP) administered by the Canadian Federation of Students, 45 Charles St. E, Suite 100, ON, M4Y 152, Canada.

ELS Language Centers, 400 Alexander Park, Princeton, NJ 08540; smatson@els.com. International chain of language schools. U.S. office is a clearinghouse of recruitment for ELS's 55 overseas franchise schools. Applicants must have prior teaching experience or related training.

Explorations in Travel, Explorations in Travel, 2458 River Rd., Guilford, VT 05301; 802-257-0152; explore@volunteertravel.com, www. volunteertravel.com. Rainforest conservation, wildlife projects, etc. in Ecuador, Costa Rica, Belize, Puerto Rico, Guatemala, Mexico, Nepal, Australia, and New Zealand. Language classes and homestays also arranged.

Global Routes, 510-848-4800; www.global routes.org. Places volunteers with families in rural communities in Costa Rica, Ecuador, Thailand, India, Kenya, Ghana, and the Navajo Nation to teach in local schools. Training, support, and adventure travel are integral parts of the program. Information on scholarships, fundraising, and academic credit is available. Program fee is $3,950 for summer semester and $4,250 for fall and spring semesters.

Greenforce, 11-15 Betterton St., Covent Garden, London WC2H 9BP, U.K.; 011-44-870-770-2646, fax 011-44-207-470-8889; greenforce@btinternet.com, www.greenforce. org. Recruits volunteers to join conservation aid projects for a minimum of 10 weeks in Zambia (and the Amazon, Borneo, and Fiji). All training provided.

Horizon Cosmopolite, 3011 Notre Dame O.,

Montréal, QC, H4C 1N9, Canada; 514-935-8436, fax 514-935-4302; info@horizon cosmpolite.com, www.horizoncosmopolite.com. Offers volunteer work or service learning abroad in about 25 countries. No experience required, open to all nationalities from 18 to 78 years old. Enrollment fee of CAN255-CAN450, and participation fees vary. Guarantees placement.

InterExchange Program, 161 6th Ave., New York, NY 10013; 212-924-0446; info@interexchange.org, www.interexchange.org. Work placements in Germany, France, Scandinavia, Switzerland, Belgium, the U.K., and Eastern Europe. Also au pair placements in France, Germany, Netherlands, and Spain. Teaching English in Spain, Bulgaria, and Poland. Fees are $400-$450 for most programs.

Interlocken International, RR 2, Box 165, Hillsboro, NH 03244; 603-478-3166, fax 603-478-5260, kim@interlocken.org, www.interlocken.org/jobs.htm. Experienced leaders needed for small group travel programs for teens worldwide. Minimum age is 24. Ten-day orientation held in June.

International Cooperative Education, 15 Spiros Way, Menlo Park, CA 94025; 650-323-4944; info@icemenlo.com, www.icemenlo.com. Arranges paid summer work for 2-3 months in Germany, Switzerland, Belgium, Finland, Singapore, Japan, and Luxembourg. Jobs include retail sales, banking, computer technology, hotels and restaurants, agriculture, offices, etc.; most require knowledge of relevant language. Placement fee is $600 plus application fee of $200.

International House, 106 Piccadilly, London W1J 7NL, U.K.; 011-44-207-518-6970, fax 011-44-207-518-6971; worldrecruit@ ihlondon.co.uk, www.ihworld.com. With 120 schools in 30+ countries, IH is one of the largest English teaching organizations in the world. The Recruitment Services Dept. does much of the hiring of teachers—who must have an ELT certificate after completing a 4-week Cambridge CELTA, RSA/Trinity TESOL or equivalent

International Schools Services, See where education can take you! Applicants for overseas teaching positions in private American international schools are able to interview in the states at one of our U.S.-based International Recruitment Centers. Applicants must have a Bachelor's degree and 2 years of current K-12 teaching experience; 609-452-0990, fax 609-452-2690; edustaffing@iss.edu, www.iss.edu.

Internships International, P.O. Box 480, Woolwich, ME 04579-0480; 207-443-3019, fax 207-442-7942; intintl@aol.com, http://rtp-net.org/~intintl. Internships (unpaid) arranged in London, Glasgow, Dublin, Paris, Dresden, Florence, Budapest, Santiago, Bangkok, Shanghai, and Melbourne. Must be college senior or graduates. Application fee from $700.

i-to-i, 9 Blenheim Terrace, Leeds LS2 9HZ, U.K.; 011-44-870-333-2332, fax 011-44-113-242-2171; info@i-to-i.com, www.i-to-i.com. TEFL and voluntary placements in Africa, Latin America, Asia, and Australia.

LEAPNow: Lifelong Education Alternatives and Programs, P.O. Box 1817, Sebastopol, CA 95473; 707-829-1142, fax 707-829-1132; info@leapnow.org, www.leapnow.org. Consulting service aimed primarily at preuniversity and university students looking to tailor experiences in the U.S. and abroad. 20,000 plus internships, work exchanges, and programs. College and high school credit.

People to People International, 501 E Armour Blvd., Kansas City, MO 64109-2200; 816-531-4701; internships@ptpi.org, www.ptpi.org. Two-month unpaid internships in Brazil, Denmark, England, Ireland, Spain. Interns can receive 6 hours of academic credit.

Taking Off, P.O. Box 104, Newton Highlands, MA 02161; 617-630-1606, fax 617-630-1605; Tkingoff@aol.com. Gives clients access to a database with 2,500 options worldwide.

Teaching & Projects Abroad, Gerrard House, Rustington, W Sussex BN16 1AW. U.S. address: 19 Cullen Dr., West Orange, NJ 07052; info@teaching-abroad.co.uk, www.teaching-abroad.co.uk. Short-term unpaid teaching and other voluntary positions in Ukraine, Moscow, China, Ghana, India, Mexico, Mongolia, Nepal, Peru, South Africa, Thailand, and Togo.

Travellers, 7 Mulberry Close, Ferring, West Sussex BN12 5HY, U.K.; Tel./fax 011-44-1903 502595; info@travellersworldwide.com. Volunteers can teach conversational English and/or other subjects in a growing range of countries including India, Nepal, Sri Lanka, Russia, Cuba, South Africa, Ukraine, and Malaysia. Sample charge for 2-3 month stay in India/Sri Lanka is £925 excluding airfares.

Wall Street Institute International, Sylvan Learning Systems, Rambla Catalunya 2-4, 08007, Barcelona, Spain; 011-34-93-301-0029, fax 011-34-93-301-0954; www.wallstreet institute.com. Chain of 164 commercial language institutes for adults that employ approximately 350 full-time EFL teachers in Europe and Latin America. In some countries such as Spain the "Master Center" acts as a clearinghouse for teacher vacancies.

World Wide Opportunities on Organic Farms (WWOOF), P.O. Box 2675, Lewes, Sussex BN7 1RB, England; www.wwoof.org. Connects members with organic farmers throughout Britain and the world, annual membership £15.

YMCA Go Global, International YMCA, 71 W 23rd St, Suite 1904, New York, NY 10010; 888-477-9622, fax 212-727-8814; jpsewavi@ ymcanyc.org, www.ymcanyc.org. Range of outbound programs lasting up to 3 or 6 months worldwide. Most consist of teen leadership, English teaching, camp counseling, computer training and community development.

Work Abroad as an Au Pair
A Guide to Employment in Europe

By Susan Griffith

Au pairing (literally "living on equal terms") provides single women and men aged 18-27 the chance to study a language and culture while living as part of a family abroad. The demand for live-in childcare is huge. A good source of agency addresses is the web site of the International Au Pair Association, www.iapa.org, though a number of member agencies operate outgoing programs only (i.e., they send their nationals abroad, primarily to learn English).

Austria. The tradition of au pairing is well established in Austria and prospective au pairs are served by several agencies (see below), all of whom are accustomed to dealing with direct applications from foreigners. Requirements are not strenuous, and many inexperienced 18-year-olds are placed. The agencies can take a long time to reply and may need some follow-up faxes and phone calls.

The main Vienna agency Auslands-Sozialdienst runs an au pair club among other services. Officially, au pairs from outside Europe must obtain both a work and residence permit *(Beschäftigungsbewilligung).* Almost no one succeeds. The majority of non-European au pairs leave the country every three months, re-registering on their return.

Belgium. Regulations governing the employment of au pairs from outside Europe in Belgium have tightened up in the last year or two, so it is now more difficult for non-Europeans to find a family placement. One disincentive for families to employ a non-European au pairs is that they are required by law to pay very high wages of Euro 450 a month (more than $500) in addition to other compulsory benefits.

If you intend to look for a family after arrival, check the ads in *The Bulletin,* the English-language magazine for the huge expatriate community in Belgium.

Non-European citizens must obtain an authorization of provisional sojourn from the Belgian Embassy in their home country before arriving in Belgium. Their contract with their host family (minimum 12 months) must be approved by the *administration communale* to get a one-year "B" work permit from the regional Office National de l'Emploi. To qualify, the applicant must show proof of having registered in a language course in Belgium.

France. Au pairing has always been a favored way for young women to learn French and, increasingly, for young men too. The pocket money for au pairs in France is currently Euro 270 per month (in Paris a little more plus the *carte orange* or travel pass).

North Americans can fix up au pair placements directly with a French agency, but bear in mind that you may have to pay the high placement fees (typically over $100) in advance and that in some cases very little advance information about the family is available. Enrollment in a French language course is compulsory for non-European au pairs.

In Paris, the notice board at the American Church (65 Quai d'Orsay) is crammed with announcements of live-in positions. Unless you especially like small children, it might be better to look for a free room in exchange for minimal babysitting.

Germany. Dozens of independent agents have recently popped up all over Germany, many of them members of the Au Pair Society e.V., Erlenweg 4, 53881 Euskirchen, Germany (011-49-2255-959804; info@au-pair-society.org). The Society's web site www.au-pair-society.org carries contact details for its nearly 50 members with links to agency websites if available. Commercial au pair agencies do not charge a placement fee to incoming au pairs.

Non-EU citizens no older than 24 can become au pairs through a German agency. A special au pair visa must be obtained before leaving the U.S., a process that takes up to three months.

The monthly pocket money for an au pair in Germany starts at Euro 205 ($230) plus a monthly travel pass and other benefits such as a contribution to course fees of Euro 100 per semester and up to Euro 155 for return travel at end of year. For this expect hard work that usually involves more housework than au pairs normally do.

Greece. Ads appear in the *Athens News*, usually placed by families in the wealthy suburbs of Athens. The agency Nine Muses accepts postal applications from young European and American women and also can place candidates after arrival in Athens. The Athenian Nanny Agency keeps detailed dossiers on vacancies, most of which tend to be for experienced nannies though there are some for au pairs. Most families ask their live-in staff to work longer hours and reward them accordingly. For the limited number of summer positions available application should be made by April.

Israel. Plenty of Israeli families, especially in Tel Aviv, Jerusalem, and Haifa, are eager to employ mother's helpers, even those who lack experience but are prepared to work very long hours. Many stories circulate of exploitation and ill treatment of live-in helpers. A considerable amount of housework will be expected of mother's helpers, and plenty of evening babysitting. Au pairs should receive a day-and-a-half off per week, though these are not always consecutive. Virtually all au pairs work in Israel on tourist visas.

In return for all this hard work, wages are moderately high. Those who stay for an entire year have a chance of having their fare home paid by the family as well as a two-week paid holiday. In some cases, families will give their employee a week's holiday after six months work. The standard starting wage is the shekel equivalent of $700-$750 a month.

Ads appear constantly in papers like the *Jerusalem Post*. Note that many ads that sound attractive are placed by agencies; when you ring, they say that the advertised job has been taken but they have others on their books. You should be prepared to learn how to keep a kosher kitchen.

Italy. It is possible to apply independently through an Italian agency, but first make sure that you won't be liable to pay a hefty registration fee. There are many opportunities for au pairs during the summer holidays when most Italians who can afford au pairs migrate to the coast or the mountains and take their helpers with them. The weekly pocket money for au pairs is about average for Europe, i.e. Euro 60-65 for working 30 hours a week or Euro 70-75 for 36 hours.

Netherlands. Americans and Canadians do not have to apply for any special permits before they arrive in the Netherlands. They simply register with the immigration police (*Vreemdelingenpolitie*) within eight days of arrival in the municipality where they will be au pairing. Once the forms are in order, a one-year residence permit (*Verblijfsvergunning*) will be granted.

Scandinavia. Until recently, the au pair system has not been popular in the countries of Scandinavia, probably due to the excellent state-sponsored childcare and the limited appeal for young foreigners to learn the languages. However, the concept is catching on and some of the many agencies which send Scandinavian au pairs abroad are also placing young foreigners as au pairs in Scandinavian homes, incidentally providing one of the few ways to afford an extended stay in this very expensive region.

The situation in Norway is most promising for English speakers of all nationalities, though the red tape for North Americans is still considerable. Atlantis Youth Exchange runs the largest program for au pairs in Norway. Applicants must be aged 18-30 and willing to stay between six months and two years. The first step is to fill out an information sheet and application forms. Atlantis charges foreign au pairs a substantial registration fee of 1,000 Norwegian Kroner ($110).

For many years the Finnish Family Program accepted young people who wanted to spend the summer months helping a family with household chores and English conversation. However, this program, formerly administered by the Centre for International Mobility (CIMO, P.O. Box 343, 00531 Helsinki, Finland; www.cimo.fi), has been drastically reduced and is open only to students studying the Finnish language at university. Openings for au pairs still exist but must be arranged independently through contacts or advertisements.

Interest in au pairing in Iceland is increasing, and Americans can find a family through Au Pair Vistaskiptiin Reykjavik (the only mediating agency for au pairs licensed by the Ministry of Social Affairs). Families cover half the travel costs (if you stay six to nine months) and the full cost if you stay nine to 12 months, to a maximum of KR50,000.

Spain. The chance of arranging an au pair placement in Spain is very good. The majority of jobs are in the cities and environs of Madrid and Barcelona, though jobs do pop up in glamorous resorts like Marbella and Tenerife from time to time. Several au pair agencies in Spain are associated with language schools such as Centros Europeos Galve.

The average pocket money for au pairs at present is Euro 55-60 a week. There are also opportunities for young people to stay with Spanish families in exchange for speaking English with the children without having any domestic or childcare duties, for example through the Vallodolid agency Castrum. Americans and Canadians who wish to work as au pairs should apply for a student visa before leaving home. Officially, the Embassy requires both an offer of employment from the family and a letter from the school where the au pair is enrolled (or will enroll) to study Spanish.

Switzerland. Those interested in a domestic position with a Swiss family should know the rules laid down by each Swiss canton. You must be a female between the ages of 17 (18 in Geneva) and 29 from Western Europe, North America, Australia, or New Zealand, stay for a minimum of one year and a maximum of 18 months, and attend a minimum of three hours a week of language classes in Zürich, four in Geneva. Families in most places are required to pay half the language school fees of SFR500-SFR1,000 for six months.

Au pairs in Switzerland work for a maximum of 30 hours per week, plus babysitting once or twice a week. The monthly salary varies among cantons but the normal range starts at SFR800 from which compulsory deductions are made for tax and health insurance.

Au Pair Placement Placement Agencies

NORTH AMERICAN AGENCIES

The following North American agencies have outgoing au pair programs in Europe:

Accord Cultural Exchange, 750 La Playa, San Francisco, CA 94121; 415-386-6203, fax 415-386-0240; leftbank@hotmail.com, www.cogni text.com/accord. Au pairs sent to France, Germany, Spain, Austria, and Italy.

Au Pair Canada, 15 Goodacre Close, Red Deer, Alberta T4P 3A3, Canada; Tel./fax 403-343-1418; aupaircanada@shaw.ca. Au pairs to France, Netherlands, Switzerland, and Germany.

Au Pair in Europe, P.O. Box 68056, Blakely Postal Outlet, Hamilton, Ontario, Canada L8M 3M7, Canada; 905-545-6305, fax 905-544-4121; www.princeent.com/aupair. Au pairs placed in France, Switzerland, Netherlands, Belgium, Germany, Spain, Austria, Belgium, Italy, Greece, Finland, Norway, Denmark, Sweden, Iceland, England, Bermuda, Australia, and New Zealand.

E.L.J.A. International, 6235 Des Erables, Montreal, Quebec H2G 2M7, Canada; 514-722-5911, fax 514-481-8933; info@elja.qc.ca, www.elja.qc.ca. Au pairs as well as language assistants, work and travel program for Canadians in U.K., U.S., France, Spain, Germany, Denmark, Iceland, and Netherlands.

InterExchange Au Pair USA Program, 13th Fl., 161 6th Ave., New York, NY 10013; 212-924-0446, fax 212-924-0575; info@interex change.org, www.interexchange.org. Au pairs to Austria, Finland, Netherlands, Italy, Norway, and Spain.

Le Monde Au Pair, 7 rue de la Commune Ouest, Bureau 204, Montréal, Québec H2Y 2C5, Canada; 514-281-3045, fax 514-281-1525; aupair@generation.net, www.genera tion.net/~aupair. Au pair placements in Denmark, France, Germany, Italy, Netherlands, Norway, Spain, Switzerland, U.K., and U.S.

Scotia Personnel Ltd., 6045 Cherry St., Halifax, Nova Scotia B3H 2K4, Canada; 902-422-1455, fax 902-423-6840; scotiap@ns.sym patico.ca, www.scotia-personnel-ltd.com. Au pairs to U.S., England, France, Holland, Germany, Australia, Spain, Switzerland, Denmark, Ireland, etc.

World Wide Au Pair & Nanny, 2886 Davison St., Oceanside, NY 11672; Tel./fax 516-764-7528; info@worldwideaupair.com, www.world wideaupair-nanny.com. Places American and Canadian au pairs with families in the Netherlands, France, Switzerland, Italy, etc.

COUNTRY-BY-COUNTRY AGENCIES

Austria

Auslands-Sozialdienst, Johannesgasse 16/1, 1010 Vienna; 011-43-1-512-7941, fax 011-43-1-513-9460; www.kath-jugend.at/aupair.

Irmhild Spitzer, Sparkassenplatz 1, 7th Fl., 4040 Linz; Tel./fax 011-43-732-73-78-14.

Au-Pair4You, Hasnerstrasse 31/22, 1160 Vienna; 011-43-1-990-1574; www.au-pair4you.at.

For-Future Au Pair Agentur, Postfach 20, 2431 Kleinneusiedl; 011-43-676-314-3160; for-future@netway.at.

Belgium

Stufam, Vierwindenlaan 7, 1780 Wemmel; 011-32-2-460-33-95; aupair.stufam@pi.be.

Services de la Jeunesse Feminine, 29 rue Faider, 1050 Brussels; 011-32-2-539 3514.

Denmark

Exis, P.O. Box 291, 6400 Sonderborg; 011-45-74-42-97-49, fax 011-45-74-42-97-47; info@exis.dk, www.exis.dk.

France

Accueil Familial des Jeunes Etrangers, 23 rue de Cherche-Midi, 75006 Paris; 011-33-1-42-22-50-34; accueil@afje-paris.org.

Butterfly et Papillon, 5 Av. de Genève, 74000 Annecy; 011-33-4-50-46-08-33/50-67-01-33; aupair.france@wanadoo.fr.

Europair Services, 13 rue Vavin, 75006 Paris; 011-33-1-43-29-80-01; europairservices@wanadoo.fr.

Institut Euro Provence, 69 rue de Rome, 13001 Marseille; 011-33-4-91-33-90-60; euro.provence@wanadoo.fr.

Soames **International Services,** 6 route de Marlotte, 77690 Montigny-sur-Loing; 011-33-1-64-78-37-98; soames.parisnannies@wanadoo.fr.

Germany

In Via, Ludwigstr, 36, 79104 Freiburg; 011-44-761-200206; www.invia.caritas.de. Has branches throughout Germany.

Verein für Internationale Jugendarbeit, Goetheallee 10, 53225 Bonn; 011-49-228-69-89-52; www.vij-Deutschland.de. Part of the German YWCA with 23 offices in Germany.

Au Pair Interconnection, Staufenstrasse 17, 86899 Landsberg am Lech; 011-49-8191-941378; aupairscp@t-online,de; www.aupair-interconnection.de.

GIJK/Au Pair in Germany, Baunscheidtstrasse 11, 53113 Bonn; 011-49-228-95-73-00; www.gijk.de. Part of GIJK, a cultural exchange organization.

Greece

Nine Muses, P.O. Box 76080, 17110 Nea Smyrni, Athens; 011-30-210-931-6588; www.ninemuses.gr.

Aiolos Employment Agency, 8 Piraeus St, 10552 Athens; 011-30-210-520-0081; aiolos@otenet.gr.

Iceland

Au Pair Vistaskipti, Bankastraeti 10; 011-354-562-2362; www.vistiskipti.is.

Israel

Hilma's Au Pair Intermediary, 5 Moholiver, P.O. Box 91, Rishon le Zion; 011-972-3-965-9937; hilma@netvision.net.il.

Au Pair International, 2 Desler St., Bnei Brak 51507; 011-972-3-619-0423, shulmitg@zahav.net.il, www.aupair-international.co.il.

Italy

Au Pair International, Via S. Stefano 32, 40125 Bologna; 011-39-51-267575, fax 011-39-51-236594; www.au-pair-international.com.

L'Aquilone, Via Giovanni, Pascoli 15, 20129 Milan; 011-39-2-2952-96-39; www.s.snf.it/aquilone.

ARCE, Via Settembre 20/124, 16121 Genova 011-39-010-583020, arceita@tin.it.

Aupairitaly.com, Via Demetrio Martinelli 11/d, 40133 Bologna; 011-39-051-383466; www.aupairitaly.com.

The Netherlands

Activity International, P.O. Box 7097, 9701 JB Groningen, Netherlands; 011-31-50-31-30-666, fax 011-31-50-31-31-633; www.activity.aupair.nl.

Travel Active Programmes, P.O. Box 107, 5800 AC Venray; 011-31-478-551-900; www.travelactive.nl. Euro 145.

House o Orange Au Pairs, Noordeinde 134, 2514 GN The Hague; fax 011-31-70-324-5913; www.house-o-orange.nl.

Norway

Atlantis, Kirkegata 32, 0153 Oslo; 011-47-22-47 71 70; post@atlantis-u.no; www.atlantis-u.no. 1,000 kroner registration fee for 8-12 month stay.

Spain

Centros Europeos Galve, Calle Principe 12-6ºA, 28012 Madrid; 011-34-1-532-72-30; ccprincipe@inicia.es.

GIC, Pintro Sorolla 29, 46901 Monte Vedat; Tel./fax 011-34-96-156-5837; gic@eresmas.net.

Club de Relaciones Culturales, Calle Ferraz 82, 28008 Madrid; 011-34-91-5417103; spain@clubrei.es.

S&C Asociados, Avda. Eduardo Dato 46, 2ºB, 41005 Seville; 011-34-95-464-2447; idiomas@supercable.es.

Sweden

Au-Pair World Agency Sweden, Box 356, 461 27 Trollhättan; 011-46-520-30950; www.interteam.se/au-pair.html.

Scandinavian Institute, Box 3085, 200 22 Malmo; 011-46-40-93 94 40; info@scandina vianinst.com; www.scandinavianinst.com. Place au pairs in Sweden, Norway, Denmark, and Finland.

Switzerland

Compagna, Reckenbuhlstrasse 21, 6005 Lucerne; 011-41-41-312 11 73; compagna-Luzern@bluewin.ch. For the French part of Switzerland (Geneva and Lausanne), contact Compagna Lausanne, Rue du Simplon 2, 1006 Lausanne; 011-41-21-616-29-88, fax 011-41-21-616-29-94.

Pro Filia, Nationalsekretariat, Beckenhofstr. 16, Postfach, 8035 Zurich; Tel./fax: 011-41-1-361 53 31.

Heli Grandjean Placements Au Pair, Chemin de Relion 1E, Case Postale 4, 1245 Collonge-Bellerive; Tel./fax 011-41-22-752-38-23; grandjean@geneva.link.ch.

Perfect Way, Steigweg 12B, 5303 Würenlingen; 011-41-56-281 39 12; perfect-way@pop.agri.ch.

Perspective

Crewing a Boat
The Secrets to Finding Work on a Yacht

By Robert Hein

In my more than 20 years as a yacht sailor many people have said, "I always want-ed to take a voyage on a small boat; I wish I could get a job like yours." Practically all of them thought that crewing was impossible unless they had years of expe-rience, but this is not the case. Captains routinely sign on people who have no sail-ing experience.

The secrets to finding a berth on an ocean-going yacht is to know where, when, and how to search. There is no shortage of opportunities. Thousands of private yachts are currently sailing on years-long extended cruises and have crew require-ments that change from port to port. Some moor in foreign ports for months, hir-ing live-aboard maintenance or delivery crews to sail them home.

The qualities most desired in crew members are compatibility, a positive attitude, and reasonably good health. Stamina, not brute strength, is the physical require-ment, so age and gender are not limiting factors. Men and women, from teens to retirees, are sailing the high seas as crew on cruising yachts.

Yachts crossing the South Pacific follow the southeast trade winds. Although they take various courses as they filter through Oceania, the great majority call at the inexpensive and friendly island nation of Fiji.

In Fiji, the best time to look for a crew position is from August through October. This is the last half of the sailing season and many yachts will stop for provisions and repairs before heading for New Zealand or Australia. Plan to arrive in Fiji in August or September and you have an excellent chance of getting a crew position. (The cost of living there is very reasonable: food and accommodations are as low as $10 a day.)

Find the captains at the Royal Suva Yacht Club near the capital and main port,

Suva, or at the Tradewinds Marina a few miles out of town at the Tradewinds Hotel. Both places are easily accessible by city bus. Yacht marinas are also located at several large resorts near the town of Nadi and the International Airport and nearby Lautoka. Yacht clubs always have bulletin boards listing want ads for crew.

Just visit yacht clubs or marinas, have a drink, and meet the yachties who gather for the "sundown hour" when they are returning from day trips or just getting off the boat for the first time that day. Introduce yourself and tell them you are looking for a crew position. Don't be discouraged if offers don't come right away; it takes a little while to build up your credibility.

Have a simple resume ready in advance. This shows that you are serious about crewing and gives the skipper a sketch of your background. Keep it simple. Just list your name, home address, and a contact person with address and phone number. Paste a passport-size photo near the top. If possible, list a few people as references. Local ones are best, but anyone who can be easily contacted by phone will do.

Next, give a brief history of your activities or occupation for the past few years. Then list your skills and hobbies. Can you cook or play a musical instrument? Seagoing cooks are always in demand and entertaining people make great shipmates. Finally, include a copy of your passport data and photo pages.

Some boats offer an airline ticket back to the port where you signed on. Some pay the crew. Others offer a free ride but the crew members pay for their own upkeep at the end of the voyage. Still others charge a few dollars a day.

Perspective

Work in New Zealand

By Todd Hewett

When I applied for a New Zealand work visa I knew that only 150 were granted each year. The chirpy voice on the line at BUNAC (www.bunac.org), the agency that issues work visas for Americans to Australia, Britain, and New Zealand, informed me that I just made the cut. I chose New Zealand because it was the longest available period for a work visa—12 months instead of the typical four—and I had heard many good and not a single bad word about the country.

So I got everything arranged and boarded the flight to the "Land of the Long White Cloud," as the Maoris called New Zealand. I called it 12 months in paradise.

Back home I had worked in advertising, and my plan was to find a similar job in Zealand. In Auckland, I contacted several ad agencies. Initially people were positive-sounding, but when they asked what kind of work visa I had ("The one that lets me work here for 12 months"), the conversation would change to the polite "don't-call-us, we'll-call-you" tone. Criss-crossing the country over the next few months wasn't exactly what was expected from a perfect employee. Some suggested I look for temporary office or seasonal work.

So I left Auckland on a 4-month tour of the rest of the country. Sure enough, the traveling workers I met along the way were usually picking fruit or temping in an office. In the cities I heard the same story as in Auckland: "We're looking for employees who will stay with us for a minimum of three years." I could understand this, but I couldn't accept it.

So I devised Plan B on the spot. I would attend every advertising and marketing function I could and then network-just like I did in the U.S. Only I couldn't find any functions. Didn't these people meet?

Plan C was even simpler: find the largest ad agencies, walk through the front door, and offer my services—gratis. Then, once they saw me contributing, they would inevitably want to take me on as part of the staff. Who could turn down free service? The receptionist, that's who. Her job as gatekeeper is to keep everyone who didn't have an appointment out of the office. Which she did. Quite well.

Plan D was the simplest of all. Stalking. Find the decision makers as they leave the building and thrust my CV at them. It worked! The result was that I worked on a few projects, and one eventually turned into a paid position. I was happy I had found a way to use my skills and contribute. Looking back, the work visa really does have something for everyone. You just have to be creative.

Perspective

The Best Job in the World
Write for an English-Language Paper

By Gregory Benchwick

The first step in finding a job at an English-language newspaper is getting to know a little bit about the country. The next step is to find out who runs the paper and the paper's web address. You can find the URLs for worldwide newspapers at www.escapeartist.com/media.htm. Read the online version of the paper before you send your letter. After six months at the *Bolivian Times* I was promoted to managing editor and I read tons of letters from people looking for work. The only people I responded to were those who mentioned something about a recent article in the paper.

Your application should include three to five writing samples, your resume, a synopsis of your experience with the language of the country you plan to work in, and any other pertinent information about your experience.

Generally, papers will only consider paid positions for college students or graduates with some experience with the native language. Only the top guns get paid, but papers will often give unpaid internships to people who lack the language skills.

The key to finding a job at a newspaper abroad is not your skills but your willingness to go out on a limb to get the job. When people showed up in our office with no Spanish or journalistic skills, I said to them, "Go out on the streets, find me a story we haven't covered, and write it." The people who could do this eventually worked their way into paid positions.

Follow your heart in deciding where to go, but beware of editors who say, "Yeah, come down, we can probably find you some work."

Once you arrive, the editor of the paper will usually help you find a place to live and help you get a visa. As you are normally paid under the table, a tourist visa will generally suffice. Read the local dailies and try to get the lay of the socio-political landscape. The *Latin American Journalism Handbook* at www.planeta.com/eco travel/period/period.html may help.

Being a journalist is as much about research and marketing as it is about writing. Introduce yourself to everyone, make calls, don't be afraid to ask questions, and ask the other writers for help.

Most English newspapers in South America do not pay enough to survive on. I was paid $200 as a staff writer for the *Bolivian Times*. My wage doubled when I became the managing editor, but still I couldn't make ends meet. Most of the staff had at least one second job. Some taught English, others wrote for American and European newspapers and magazines. In the end we all got by.

Being a journalist in a foreign country is quite possibly the best job in the world. For me, it is the only job for a traveler: not only does it allow you the freedom to travel where and when you want, it also gives you a unique vantage point from which to gain the kind of intimate knowledge of a foreign land that you would never have been afforded otherwise.

For More Info: Latin American Journalism Handbook: www.planeta. com/ ecotravel/period/period.html. Writers Workshop offers an excellent research library: www.writerworkshops. com. World's Newspapers: www. escapeartist. com/media/media.htm.

Perspective

Working in War Zones

Dangers Abound Yet the Work Satisfies the Soul

By Jeff Morris

War leaves countries in ruins. To make matters worse, many countries, like Afghanistan, are in trouble before war breaks out. The international community often comes to the rescue, and, fortunately for Americans looking for adventurous and meaningful work abroad, American organizations make up much of that community.

Have you done any volunteer work? Military service? Foreign travel? Do you speak another language? Anything helps, and the more you can put on your resume, the better your chances.

The United Nations should be the first place a potential war zone worker looks for a job. Currently there are over 34,000 UN military, police, and civilian personnel working in 15 different war zones. The application process can be slow, but the personal and financial rewards are worth the effort it takes to get hired. Many

UN war zone workers make over $100,000 tax-free per year. Contact: United Nations, Personnel Management and Support Services, Field Administration and Logistics Division, Department of Peacekeeping Operations, Room S-2280, New York, NY 10017.

The Operation for Security in Central Europe (OSCE) is probably the second largest war zone employer. It employs most human rights and elections supervision workers and most of the American attorneys working in war zones. The U.S. State Department oversees official war zone employment for Americans working for OSCE. Contact: OSCE Secretariat, Kärntner Ring 5-7, 4th Fl., 1010 Vienna, Austria; 011-43-1-514-36180, fax 011-43-1-514-36105; info@osce.org, www.osce.org. You can find additional information on OCEA at www.pae-react.com.

The International Rescue Committee was founded during WWII to help those who were displaced because of the war. It provides medical services, food, shelter, and refugee assistance among other things. Contact: International Rescue Committee (IRC), 122 E 42nd, St., New York, NY 10168; www.intrescom.org. You can fax a resume to 212-551-3710. The IRC also offers intern and volunteer positions if you need to strengthen your resume before you apply for your desired war zone job.

DynCorp employs most of the American police officers working in war zones. It also hires medics, security officers, logistics coordinators, pilots, aircraft mechanics, and computer technicians. Their web site has information on their many different divisions and fields as well as employment sections and a job search engine (www.dyncorp.com.)

While you're checking out these organizations' web sites, also check search engines like Yahoo, Google, Lycos, and job search engines like www.monster.com for overseas employment. Fill out as many online resumes and applications as possible; new war zone positions open up every week.

Life in a War Zone

The lack of electricity, water, food, supplies, or telephones can make the simplest things difficult. Imagine trying, with no telephone, to find housing for a family of 11 before the rapidly approaching winter hits. But then imagine how you'll feel after you find those 11 people a warm place to live.

War zone workers' work schedules include a 4- to 8-day break at the end of the month, and many of the world's top travel destinations are often an inexpensive plane or train ride away. Even if you don't take off for Amsterdam or Paris, you can immerse yourself in learning about local life. The average war zone assignment lasts 9 to 12 months, leaving you plenty of time get to know the country you work in as well as nearby countries. People take you into their home, make you part of their family. You will not have a problem finding someone willing to trade language lessons.

There is of course a catch. The reason war zone workers are paid well is because of the dangers they face. There would not be war without hate, and to think that hate disappears after the war is a deadly mistake. Being in the wrong place at the wrong time has killed several war zone workers. By studying the war zone you plan to work in ahead of time and paying attention during orientation, you should be able to avoid this danger.

Then there's the bad food and health conditions. Medical facilities may be limited and far away. Make sure you get a physical and dental exam prior to leaving; if there is something wrong, get it fixed.

Even if you don't make a lifelong career in war zone work, when you return home from the most challenging and rewarding period in your life, you'll be a stronger and wiser person.

The Best Web Sites
Internet Resources for Short-Term Jobs Abroad

Selected and Reviewed by William Nolting

Organizations in this section offer work permits and placements into short-term paid jobs or on-site assistance in finding them—jobs typically lasting a summer or semester, though some programs offer permits for up to 18 months. These programs are allowed to operate on the basis of official reciprocal agreements between the U.S. and foreign governments.

Web sites in this section are some of the most useful for students and graduates. They list internships, volunteer, work abroad, and study abroad programs with or without academic credit. The rating codes are as follows: ** *Essential;* * *Outstanding and of broad interest.*

(I) Informational site with directories or databases listing
(P) Site for a specific work abroad program
(S) Scholarships or fellowships

*(P) AIESEC-USA, www.us.aiesec.org.** AIESEC (from the French acronym for the International Association of Students in Economic & Business Management) is an international student-run organization which offers approximately 5,000 paid internships each year in business and other fields in over 80 countries. Site has links to chapters worldwide. Note that application for AIESEC internships is possible only through campus chapters.

****(P) AIPT** (Association for International Practical Training) / **IAESTE** (International Association for the Exchange of Students for Technical Experience) **www.aipt.org/pro grams.html.** Nonprofit organization offers several different programs:

• **IAESTE, www.aipt.org/iaeste.html,** offers engineering & science internships in over 60 countries for students (apply by January 1).

• **Work permit service / US Reserved Offer Program, www.aipt.org/subpages/iaeste_ us/students,_reserved_offer_program.html,** provides work permits in numerous countries for non-technical and technical fields for students who find their own internships.

• **Career Development program, www.aipt. org/subpages/iaeste_us/students_index.html,** provides work permits for up to 18 months in Austria (11 month limit), Britain (12 month limit), Finland, France, Germany, Hungary, Ireland, Japan, Malaysia, Mexico, Slovak Republic, Sweden, and Switzerland for university graduates who find their own placements.

*(I, P) American-Scandinavian Foundation,** **www.amscan.org.** Web site of this nonprofit organization includes a comprehensive directory of study, language, and work abroad programs in all the Scandinavian countries. ASF offers internship placements as well as English-teaching positions. ASF can also assist with short-term work permits in Scandinavian countries for those who have job offers.

****(P) BUNAC: Work in Britain & Australia Programs, www.bunac.org.** Nonprofit organization BUNAC (British Universities North

115

American Club) operates the Work in Britain program—with 6,000 U.S. participants, the largest of all work abroad programs. The program provides a work permit and job-search assistance. Also offers a Work in Australia and New Zealand program. The BUNAC handbook has a great selection of addresses for potential internships in Britain, which can be used to arrange interviews when they arrive. For students and very recent graduates (within one semester of graduation) only.

*(P) Camp Counselors USA, Outbound Program, www.ccusa.com. Nonprofit organization offers programs for American students and non-students: Work in Australia, Work in New Zealand, as well as programs which offer placements to serve as camp counselors in Russia.

*(P) CDS International, www.cdsintl.org. Nonprofit organization offers several paid internship programs in Germany, Switzerland, and Singapore for students, graduates and professionals. Web site provides program information and listings of new internship openings. CDS can also assist with short-term work permits in Germany for those who have job offers.

• **The Congress-Bundestag Youth Exchange for Young Professionals, www.cdsintl.org/cbyxintro.html** consists of two months of intensive German, four months attending a technical school, and a five-month internship. All expenses paid; no application fee. Specified age of participants is 18-24. Application deadline is mid-December for the following academic year.

• **The CDS Internship Program, www.cdsintl.org/intintro.html** is for seniors or graduates and is of three or six months duration.

• **The Bavarian American Center Professional Internship Program, www.cdsintl.org/bacintro.html** is for graduate students in public administration, political science, or international relations.

• **The Robert Bosch Foundation Fellowship Program, www.cdsintl.org/rbfpintro.html** offers high-level internships for those holding graduate degrees. Internship Program is for seniors or graduates and arranges paid internships for 6-24 months in Germany or Singapore, **www.cdsintl.org/fromus.html**.

• **Summer Internship Program in Germany, www.cdsintl.org/sipintro.html** offers paid 3-month internships to juniors, seniors, and recent graduates.

• **Summer Internship program in Turkey, www.cdsintl.org/sitintro.html** offers paid 3-month internships to juniors, seniors, and recent graduates.

• **Summer internship Program in Argentina, www.cdsintl.org/sipaintro.html** offers unpaid 3-month internships to juniors, seniors, and recent graduates or a combination 1-month Spanish language course followed by a 2-month internship.

**(P) Council Work Abroad Program, www.councilexchanges.org. The nonprofit Council Work Abroad program, one of the largest work abroad programs, offers short-term work permits and job search support for France, Germany, Ireland, Canada, Costa Rica, Australia, and New Zealand. Also offers a Teach in China program and volunteering abroad in around 30 countries. For students and very recent graduates (within one semester of graduation) only.

**(P) InterExchange, www.interexchange.org. Nonprofit organization offers a variety of placements for students and non-students. Apply four months in advance of desired departure date. English Teaching in Bulgaria, Spain, and Poland. Paid summer jobs in Germany and Belgium, unpaid internships in England and France. Agricultural work in Norway. Au pair (child care) placements in France, Germany, Spain, and The Netherlands. Volunteering in Russia and the Ukraine.

**(P) International Cooperative Education Program, www.icemenlo.com. Program provides paid summer internships in Switzerland, Germany, Belgium, Finland, Japan, or Singapore for students and recent graduates who have studied the appropriate language: German, French, Italian, Finnish, Dutch, Japanese, or Chinese. Apply by January.

VOLUNTEERING ABROAD

*While volunteering means giving, it also means
receiving—friendships, knowledge of oneself, insight
into another culture, and the relationship
between that society and our own. For some
it can be a catalyst towards lifelong work for social
change at home or abroad.*

Volunteer Work Abroad

Introduction: Working to Provide for Unmet Needs

By William Nolting

Volunteering abroad is defined not so much by earnings, since volunteer programs may or may not provide some form of reimbursement, as it is by service, working to provide for unmet needs, including social (poverty, hunger,
illiteracy), environmental, or educational. Traditionally, volunteering has been seen
as helping others. Today, it is often seen as helping persons or groups achieve their
goals as they themselves define them, building local self-reliance.

Why Volunteer?

"Before making a commitment, it is important to clarify your motives. You may be
drawn to voluntary service by a desire to help impoverished people. You may be
interested in learning about another culture and society. You may wish to be part of
a process of positive social change. Or you may wish to gain experience which will
help you find employment. Each of these motivations will direct you to distinct
options for voluntary service." — Alternatives to the Peace Corps

Some Characteristics of Volunteer Work

Skills required: These run the gamut from unskilled through professional, in areas
such as teaching, business, health sciences, environment and natural resources,
engineering, special education, math and sciences, and many more.

• Time commitment: From a few weeks to two or three years.

• Pay or cost: A few long-term (two or more years) volunteer programs cover all
expenses plus a stipend. Many provide for room and board but not for transportation or personal expenses. Some require volunteers to cover their own expenses.
Short-term programs that provide training, on-site support, and sometimes academic credit usually charge a fee, but are still generally less expensive than study
programs or simply traveling.

- Location and type of work: You can volunteer virtually everywhere in the world. In wealthier areas such as Western Europe (or the U.S.), volunteering may be the only way for nonspecialists to work for social, educational, or environmental causes. In most countries with developing economies, volunteering is often the only work for foreigners (except for experienced professionals working for major governmental and non-governmental organizations).

- Sponsoring organizations: These include the U.S. government (e.g., the Peace Corps), large multigovernment organizations such as the United Nations, smaller non-governmental organizations (known as NGOs), and religious organizations. The latter may have either a social-activist or a proselytizing orientation, or both.

Funding Your Experience

The best way to find funds is to go directly to people or organizations for support. In exchange, the volunteer can provide reports from abroad or presentations upon return. Possible sources include service clubs such as Rotary or Kiwanis, religious organizations, and relatives. Other fundraising events include raffles, providing services for contributions, etc. Most organizations will assist volunteers with suggestions for raising funds. See the article on Tips for Fundraising on the WorldTeach website, at www.worldteach.org/fundraising2.html.

Choosing a Volunteer Placement Organization

By Joseph Collins, Stefano DeZerega, and Zahara J. Heckscher

The number of international volunteer programs is growing, and it can be difficult to make your way through all the brochures and web sites describing the myriad of options. But it is worth taking the time to carefully consider the various programs available. Many past volunteers offer the following advice: "Don't just select the first program that comes along, as I did. Investigate the different options." The following tips will help you heed their advice and make an informed decision about which international volunteer program is right for you.

1. Assess your interests. Before you start exploring different volunteer options, take the time to explore your own interests. Consider the major issues in choosing a program such as where you want to go and for how long, the type of work you want to do, your living situation, and whether you want a rural or urban placement.

2. Think about your special needs and aspirations. Consider the various components of your identity—including age, ability, race, and sexual orientation—and identify the factors that are most important to you. Also think about your vision of volunteering. How much staff support do you need? What are you looking for in your daily work environment? Do you want to volunteer alone or in a group?

3. Create a vision. List the characteristics you are looking for in an organization. Include logistics such as costs and length of volunteer stay as well as more philosophical issues such as the organization's approach to development. Since you prob-

ably won't find an organization that matches your vision perfectly, circle the qualities that are most important to you.

4. Refer to the listing of organizations. For example, if your goal is to work in Africa for a year or more in the educational field, create your own list of groups that have all at your specified characteristics. See www.volunteerinternational.org for a searchable database of programs.

5. Begin your research. Conduct preliminary research by visiting the organizations' web sites. Also try a general web search to find "unofficial" information.

6. Narrow your list. Figure out the top two to four organizations. If you don't find any groups that meet your specifications, you may want to broaden your search by focusing on one or two primary factors to judge organizations.

7. Create a list of questions. Based on any concerns you have from the web sites, your personal values, and any special needs, create a list of questions for staff and or alumni.

8. Contact the organization to ask your questions. These days, email may be the best way to communicate. Ask your questions and request contact information for program alumni as well as information regarding the application process. Verify that the organizations still operate in the country where you want to go, and note any changes in fees or programs.

9. Contact alumni. Ask them hard questions about their experiences and try to get contact information for people who they volunteered with who might be more critical of the program than they are.

10. Choose. Select the organization that matches your interests and aspirations most closely and begin the application process.

11. Get it in writing. No matter how nice the people you talk to are, get a written document explaining fees, benefits, insurance issues, and refund policies.

Volunteer Placements
Coping With Potential Problems

By Susan Griffith

Many potential volunteers aspire to serve humanity or are motivated by some similarly grand ambition. Many past volunteers have discovered that the world is wider and their role smaller than they previously thought.

While most volunteers return from a project abroad buzzing with excitement and their lives enriched, others have experienced disillusionment. Either way, they have gained. The process of shedding illusions, though sometimes uncomfortable, is enlightening and ultimately positive. When starting your research for a stint abroad as a volunteer, it is important to maintain realistic expectations. Think about potential problems and how you would cope.

Begin with the Key Resources and Best Web Sites on volunteering abroad at the end of this chapter, which introduce you to the range of possibilities. Then go to the list of programs for details on the ethos and what the work involves, along with dates and costs. Ideally, your research should begin at least a year in advance of your intended departure so that applications can be lodged, sponsorship money raised, language courses and other preparatory courses attended, and so on.

When you receive a placement organization's literature, consider the tone as well as the content. For example, the glossy brochure of a U.K.-based agency that arranges short stints of volunteer English teaching reads almost like a tour operator's hard sell: "Choose your destination—colorful Ghana, exhilarating Mexico, the grandeur of Ukraine or Siberia, mystic India, lively Brazil or magical China." Sure enough, volunteers must pay from $1,350 for arrangements in the Ukraine to more than $2,000 for short placements in Ghana or Mexico, not including travel to the destination country. These contrast sharply with the cheaply produced directories sent by the main U.S. workcamps coordinators like Volunteers for Peace. For a modest contribution of $240 (plus travel costs), VFP volunteers can join anything from an environmental project in rural Italy to a community center for Aboriginal people in the center of Sydney.

To illustrate further the diversity of cost, even among projects working towards broadly similar ends, the book *Green Volunteers* edited by Fabio Ausenda includes many conservation organizations looking for volunteers (the book is available for $22 including postage from 1 Greenleaf Woods Dr., #302, Portsmouth, NH 03801; info@greenvol.com). Of the three operating exclusively in Peru, one runs eco-safaris and charges volunteer naturalists nothing at all; another collects data on marine wildlife and charges volunteers $5 a day for food and a mattress in a shared house; and the last, which monitors the macaw population, charges $50 per day (for a minimum of four weeks). Predictably, the ones charging very little expect their volunteers to have an appropriate background or degree, previous fieldwork experience, and computer skills (in the case of the marine wildlife project). The expensive program requires nothing apart from good health.

For pre-arranged placements, much depends upon the efficiency and commitment of the representative or project coordinator on the ground. Promises of expert back-up are easier to make than to keep if the sending organization's local agent is more interested in his or her own prestige than in attending to the day-to-day problems of foreign volunteers. Few steps can be taken to guard against clashes with other individuals. The archaeologist for whom you are cleaning shards of pottery may turn out to be an egomaniacal monster. Fellow participants may not always be your cup of tea either. Voluntary projects attract a diverse range of people of all nationalities and ages, from the wealthy and pampered who complain about every little discomfort to the downright maladjusted. Assuming you fall outside both categories, you may have to call on every ounce of tolerance.

Anticipate the Unexpected

Even when good will predominates, things can go wrong. One young volunteer who arranged a stay with a small grassroots development organization in Sri Lanka felt isolated and miserable when she was billeted with a village family who knew no English. She was given very little to do apart from menial office tasks. When she asked for something more to do, she was told to visit nursery schools, but had to refuse on the grounds that her embassy had advised foreigners not to leave the main roads. Perhaps someone with a little more travel experience might not have felt so daunted by these circumstances, difficult as they were.

A more mainstream example of differing expectations comes from Israel where every year thousands of young people continue to work as volunteers on kibbutzim. In exchange for doing primarily manual work, volunteers are given free room and board, quite a bit of time off, and the chance to make a set of new international friends—all of which are sufficient rewards for most foreign volunteers. But others question the arrangement. In an era when the ideals behind the original communal societies of Israel have been replaced by a more hard-nosed business approach, some young people can't justify working for eight hours a day picking fruit or working on a factory production line for no pay.

In many cases, the longer a volunteer stays, the more useful he or she becomes, and the more interesting the jobs assigned. Of those organizations that charge volunteers by the week, some have introduced a progressively decreasing scale of charges. In some cases, long-stay volunteers who have proved their usefulness do not have to contribute toward expenses. However, red tape sometimes gets in the way of this arrangement. Most countries of the world impose a maximum period of stay for foreigners, and it can be very difficult to renew visas in countries like Nepal and Uganda after the original tourist visa has expired. In other cases, there may be a hefty fee for visa renewals and a lot of tiresome form filling by both volunteer and sponsor.

Volunteer vacations are very different from normal vacations, though the difference in cost may be negligible. Restoring historic buildings or teaching classes is just as much work as it would be if you were still at home. Jobs are jobs wherever you do them, and there may be little chance to see the sights or sample the nightlife. Provided you are prepared for such eventualities, you will in all likelihood have a thoroughly interesting and rewarding experience.

Perspective

The Cost of Volunteering
Secrets from Behind the Nonprofit Desk

By Daniel Weiss

I am the director of Amizade, a nonprofit organization that puts together short-term volunteer programs. Many people call our office looking for volunteer possibilities that do not cost an arm and a leg.

First of all, you should know that volunteering costs money. Even when you volunteer for an organization in your community, you have expenses. For example, when you volunteer at a local animal shelter or literacy program, does the organization pay for your transportation? Your meals? Your rent? Your health insurance? Probably not. When you volunteer overseas, you cannot expect the organization to pay for these things either. When looking for a volunteer opportunity, keep in mind you will probably have to pay for your own airfare and room and board.

A variety of sources are available to help you find volunteer opportunities. The best are your library, the Internet, and *Transitions Abroad* magazine. *Alternatives to the Peace Corps, Volunteer,* and *International Exchange Directory* are good resource books that you can find at most libraries. They list a variety of organizations looking for volunteers of all types. Explain to your local librarian what you want to do, and he or she should be able to provide you with plenty of information.

Some of the best sources of volunteer information on the Internet include: Action Without Borders, **www.idealist.org**; Empower Web, **www.SFtoday.com/empower. htm**; GuideStar, **www.guidestar.org**; Volunteer Match, **www.volunteermatch.org**; SERVEnet, **www.servenet.org**; Vancouver Community Net, **www.vcn.bc.ca**; Volunteering Abroad, **www.cie.uci. edu/~cie/iop/voluntee.html**; Volunteer Vacations, **www.mel.lib.mi.us/health/health-vol-vacations.html**; International Volunteer Programs, **www.volunteerinternational.org**.

Other sources include your local church or temple. Also, talk to your local Rotary, Lions, Kiwanis, and Optimists clubs. They do a lot of international work and have connections overseas. Furthermore, many provide financial assistance to volunteers abroad. If you don't have the time to do the research yourself, organizations including the **Overseas Development Network**, 415-431-4204, and the **Catholic Network of Volunteer Service**, 800-543-5046; volunteer@cnvs.org will help you find a volunteer placement for a nominal fee.

When applying to volunteer with an organization, be very specific about the kind of service you can provide them. Many people call me up and say, "I just want to help." This is a very pleasant sentiment, but when I ask, "What can you do?" many respond with, "I don't know, what do you need?"

Just because you want to help doesn't mean that you can. Many nonprofit organizations are underfunded, understaffed, and overworked. You must prove to the organization that you will be an asset—and not a drain—by convincing them that you understand their needs and have the skills and ability to truly help them.

It is not a wise idea to quit your job with the idea of volunteering right away. Finding a volunteer position overseas takes time. You must be persistent and patient. There is a reason why there is such a long period of time between when you apply, get accepted, and actually join the Peace Corps. Wisely, they want to ensure that your commitment to volunteering is genuine and not just a whim. It is neither fair to the people you are volunteering with nor to yourself if you are not serious about your commitment to serve.

If you have already made plans to travel, work, or study abroad, and you want to volunteer as well, I suggest bringing your resume and a generic cover letter with you. To find volunteer opportunities when in a foreign country, go to the local church or synagogue. Even though you may not be of the same faith, these institutions are often familiar with local health, education, and welfare organizations. Again, you may want to try the local Rotary, Kiwanis, and Lions Clubs—international organizations with chapters all over the world.

Volunteering should be fun and rewarding. Go with an open mind and an open heart; you will return enriched with a better understanding of yourself and the world around you.

Perspective

International Monitoring

Helping with Transitions from Conflict to Peace

By Kara C. McDonald

As the international community attempts to respond to the changing nature of conflict in the post-Cold War era, government and international organizations have looked to peacekeeping and monitoring missions to deliver various kinds of assistance—from traditional humanitarian aid to democracy building. While monitoring missions may be dangerous, monitors have the opportunity for meaningful involvement with a society that is making the transition from conflict to peace.

Assignments

The tasks of international monitors range from elections observation to human rights reporting to community development and civic education. The specific nature of the job depends upon the degree of stability in the country. The work may include visits to field sites to report on events, interview locals, and correspond with civilian and government counterparts. Elections often involve working with a local staff in a particular region to prepare for upcoming votes. Community and civic development could involve working as an intermediary between local groups and the international community. All assignments involve working with locals, international organizations, the military, and NGOs (nongovernmental organizations) in the field.

Skills

Depending upon the nature of the mission, you may be required to have a professional degree (law, political science, international relations). Many missions are staffed through a government seconding process to an international organization, and governments vary in the skill levels they require of their volunteers.

Because these missions arise at short notice, do not pay a salary, and offer only short-term opportunities, professionals often cannot leave their full-time work. Volunteers have included graduate students, retirees, and part-time workers with varying backgrounds. International experience isn't always necessary if you have functional experience in social work, community development, human rights, etc.

Besides job-related experience, all missions require inordinate amounts of patience and flexibility. You must be ready to deploy at a moment's notice or to wait with your bags packed for days, sometimes weeks, while bureaucrats make the necessary arrangements. You must also be willing to serve anywhere in the country of assignment. Not knowing where you will be placed requires packing lightly for all kinds of weather. Finally, monitors often travel in large groups and in clumsy operations, so mental flexibility and physical stamina are crucial.

It goes without saying that you must be in good health. Access to Western-style hospitals may be limited.

Compensation

While the U.S. government usually does not provide a salary to its volunteers, the per diem package ranges from approximately $45-$110 per day (depending on the country of assignment) and usually allows volunteers to take some cash home. The rates are meant to cover Western-style lodging and three hotel meals per day. You will most likely have a much cheaper housing arrangement. In the end, you may find that volunteering pays better than many jobs back home.

Finding a Mission

The first place to start looking for mission opportunities is the Internet. Check the web sites of the State Department and international organizations like the OSCE, OAS, and OAU (see below). Keep up with foreign affairs. When news sources start mentioning a "possible monitoring mission," get on the phone to the regional officer at the State Department or to an officer with USAID and ask about the staffing of the mission: Will the U.S. be sending a contingent? Who will be responsible for hiring the volunteers?

Once you've found the personnel contact, you will most likely be asked to send a resume. Don't be surprised if government officers are a bit curt—if the deployment of a peacekeeping mission is underway in their region, they will be extremely busy. Also, don't be discouraged if they don't call you back. Hiring for missions depends upon unpredictable funding. Check weekly on the status of the hiring. Timing is everything. The decision to begin deployment of staff may be made with as little as 24 hours notice, and a government worker won't have the time to search diligently through a stack of 500 resumes.

Picking a Mission

Before you accept an offer to leave on an international monitoring mission, ask the following questions: Will health insurance (including emergency evacuation) be covered? What is the per diem rate? What kind of training will you receive? Training will be invaluable, especially if this is your first international mission.

In areas that are conflict-ridden, tense, or politically hostile to Americans, take appropriate precautions. Ask about the security situation in-country. Who is directly responsible for your safety (your hosting government or the international organization)? Ask about evacuation procedures. Peacekeeping missions don't need martyrs or war heroes, so don't apply if you are looking for a front-line adventure. On the other hand, don't let tense conditions scare you off.

Long-Term Opportunities

Many civilian peacekeeping missions look for volunteers who can stay in-country beyond the period of assignment to help with the logistics of repatriating other volunteers, wrapping up mission projects, and paving the way for a new round of monitors. Get to know the breadth and activities of the mission while you are out there and set up informational interviews. By being a willing and able body, you can often find ways to extend your work with the mission.

Working with an international mission can be a most rewarding job. In fact, it will probably change your life. You will gain practical experience, but, most importantly, you will have the chance to work alongside locals who want peace.

Useful Websites

International Organizations: the Organization for Security and Cooperation in Europe, www.osce.org; the Organization of American States, www.oas.org; the United Nations, www.un.org; United Nations Development Programme, www.undp.org; UN Volunteers, www.unv.org.

U.S. Government: the State Department, www.state.gov; The Peace Corps, www.peacecorps. gov; USAID, www.usaid.gov.

Perspective

Work for Peace

Workcamps Maintain Tradition from WWI

By April Thompson

For good-hearted paupers, workcamps offer an attractive alternative to volunteer projects requiring large amounts of time and money. "The typical 'Third World program' covers everything from inoculations to airfare, but it can cost as much as $4,000 for a month-long program," says Peter Coldwell, founder of Volunteers for Peace (VFP), in Belmont, VT. The largest of three U.S. organizations linking volunteers to workcamps, VFP has placed over 10,000 Americans abroad since 1982.

VFP's small program fee of $175 to $300 per camp covers organizational expenses. "I still can't believe that for $175 I lived, ate, played, and worked in a remote village in central France in the heart of a valley summer," said Angela Kolter, a former VFP volunteer.

Worldwide, roughly 150 organizations coordinate more than 2,200 projects. Each group places volunteers abroad in exchange for receiving foreign volunteers into its domestic programs. By virtue of a body-for-body swap, money never needs to change hands between groups. Any local organization—be it a church, arts group, or state park branch—can coordinate a camp to help with a community project. The local host group provides everything from tools to leaders, often with financial support from the community and government.

The work varies widely from site to site. A group may excavate a medieval Jewish necropolis in Spain, plant mango trees in Thailand, or set up a summer music festival in Norway. Projects often involve the environment, arts, social services, archeology, construction, and historic preservation. Volunteers may sleep in a school, church, private home, community center, or even a tent. Some groups cook and clean for themselves; others eat meals donated by a local family or restaurant. Most camps arrange evening and weekend excursions to local attractions, whether a city cultural tour or a trip to a national park.

Workcamps are for a mature audience only, Coldwell cautions. Volunteers must make their own travel arrangements and inform themselves about their host countries. Because camp conditions vary so widely, volunteers must come with an open mind as well as an open heart.

"None of us realized we would be giving 100 percent for 14 hours a day, yet we loved it," said Sandy Stefanowicz, who volunteered with a children's program in Ireland.

Work Not War

Workcamps originated with Pierre Ceresole, a Swiss pacifist and Quaker. In 1920 Ceresole led a small international team in reconstructing a French village destroyed during World War I. He hoped that such projects would provide an alternative to military service.

Ceresole's efforts evolved into Service Civil International (SCI), a volunteer service organization that now has 33 branches worldwide. SCI's volunteer-run U.S. branch sends about 50 Americans abroad each year, according to Traudi Krausser, volunteer coordinator.

Workcamps are well established in Western Europe, where service projects have continued since Ceresole's postwar effort. The region is now saturated with workcamps—several hundred in Germany alone. European camps often recruit unemployed youth to help organize projects, Krausser said.

In the 1980s VFP concentrated on exchanges across the Iron Curtain. Today, not only Eastern and Central Europe but developing nations in Asia, Africa, and Latin America abound with new projects, according to Coldwell. Several countries hosting camps, such as Azerbaijan, Israel, and Northern Ireland, face political turmoil that can lead to violence. Volunteers in these areas sign up at their own risk.

"We rely on information from our partners. If a country's residents feel an area is safe, that's what we tell our volunteers," explained Coldwell.

"Here was this place so devastated and destroyed and yet the people were the most beautiful I ever met," said Hau Truong, a volunteer in Bosnia. "They seemed more real to me, unspoiled by the things we take for granted in the West."

A Transforming Experience

Ultimately, volunteers get back much more than the time and tiny amount of money they give. By working, living, and playing with people from a variety of countries and cultures, volunteers transcend a country's tourist facade and transform their own sense of the world.

"People cared enough to travel around the world to help a small town called Allemont," said Patrick Nolen of his camp in France. "Through our experiences, we created a magic that penetrated the boundaries not only of our minds but also our countries."

Molli Grant, who volunteered in the Czech Republic, summed it up: "When representatives from 10 different countries get together and hold hands and pitchforks for two weeks, I call that peace. Mission accomplished."

Perspective

Volunteer in Northern Thailand

By Kenneth Champeon

Northern Thailand is a center of volunteer activity, in part because of its many problems: AIDS, poverty, the plight of hill tribes and Burmese refugees, deforestation, and drug abuse, to name a few. A number of non-governmental organizations (NGOs), their work supplemented by volunteers, operate solely in this region. The ones below stand out because of their past accomplishments and need your support.

Chiang Mai Disabled Center concentrates on making the disabled more employable.

Helping Hands provides support for Thai and hill tribe people, refugees, the handicapped, and other minorities, chiefly by providing education, educational materials, and scholarships for AIDS orphans and underprivileged children. Needed are teachers of English, French, computers, and music; nurses; administrators; writers; midwives; community health workers; illustrators; and translators.

Huen Nam Jai provides free shelter and education to a small group of street children, mostly from the hill tribes, lest they fall prey to drugs, prostitution, or AIDS. All are enthusiastically encouraged to come to teach the children and, says Khun Chananwat of the Home, "share love for them."

Volunteers at **Elephant Nature Park** are selected on the basis of their knowledge, experience, and interest in caring for elephants.

Vieng Ping is one of the area's best-known orphanages and nursing homes for homeless, abandoned, neglected, and HIV-positive children. Its mostly foreign volunteers help caretakers attend to the children's material, medical, educational, and emotional needs. They also teach English classes to those orphans slated for adoption.

TVS supports volunteers working in NGOs. It helps villagers promote and manage tourism to their areas.

Raintree Resource Center (RRC) is a library of books, videos, and CDs for the children and adults of Chiang Mai. Foreign volunteers maintain the resource center, lead English conversation classes as well as preschool craft and story hours, and coordinate other special events.

Contacts:

• **Chiang Mai Disabled Center,** 133/1 Rajapakinai; 011-66-213-941; assist@loxifo.co.th, www.infothai.com/disabled. Contact: Don Wilcox

• **Helping Hands** Social Projects, c/o Eagle House, 16 Chang Moi Gao Rd., Soi 3, Chiang Mai 50300, Thailand; 011-66-53-874126 or 011-66-53-235387, fax 011-66-53-874366; mail@eaglehouse.com, www.eaglehouse.com. Contact: Annette Kunigagon.

• **Huen Nam Jai Home,** Chang Kham Church, Hang Dong, Chiang Mai, Thailand; 011-66-53-433571. Contact: Mr. Tonkhum, Director.

- **Elephant Nature Park,** 29 Chareonpratet Rd., Soi 6, Chiang Mai, Thailand; 011-66-53-272855, fax 011-66-53-271680; lek@thaifocus.com, www.thaifocus. com/elephant. Contact: Lek (Ms Sangduen Chailert).

- **Vieng Ping Children's Home,** 63/3 Moo 4, Tambon Donkaew Amphoe Mae Rim, Chiang Mai 50180, Thailand; 011-66-53-211877, fax 011-66-53-220802. Contact: Pim.

- **Thai Volunteer Service,** 409 TVS Bldg., 2nd Fl., Soi Rohit-sook, Pracharat-bampen Rd, Huaykhwang, Bangkok 10310, Thailand; 011-66-2-6910437, fax 011-66-2-6910438; ngotvs@samarts.com. Contact: Kannika Kuankachorn, Director.

- **TVS-REST,** 409 Soi Rohitsook, Pracharaj-Bampen Rd., Huay Khwang, Bangkok 10320, Thailand; 011-66-2-6902796, 011-66-2-6929786, fax 011-66-2-6902796; tvs-rest@ecotour.in.th.

- **Raintree Resource Center,** 3 Charoen Muang Rd., P.O. Box 18, Chiang Mai 50000, Thailand; 011-66-53-262660; bclark@chmai.loxinfo.co.th. Contact: Judy Clark, Volunteer Coordinator.

Volunteer Work Abroad
The Key Print Resources

Selected and Reviewed by William Nolting

Volunteering abroad is the best option for working in developing countries or for social causes anywhere. Many volunteer positions do "pay," at least room and board, and it may be possible to defer educational loans during the volunteer assignment. Typical locations include Africa, Eastern and Western Europe, Latin America, and North America (with international volunteer organizations). For summer workcamps, apply March–May. For long-term options like the Peace Corps, apply six to nine months in advance.

**Essential; *Outstanding and of broad interest.

For ordering information, if not included below, see Key Publishers, page 13.

**Alternatives to the Peace Corps: A Directory of Third World and U.S. Volunteer Opportunities by Joan Powell. 2001. 128 pp. $9.95 plus shipping from Food First Books; foodfirst@foodfirst.org, www.foodfirst.org. Order online or from LPC Group, 1436 Randolph St., Chicago, IL 60607; 800-243-0138. Thoroughly researched guide to voluntary service, study, and alternative travel overseas and in the U.S. that "addresses the political and economic causes of poverty."

Archaeological Fieldwork Opportunities Handbook compiled by Margo Muhl Davis. 2000. 154 pp. $15 ($12 members of AIA) plus $4 s/h from Kendall/Hunt Publishing Co.,

Order Dept., 4050 Westmark Dr., Dubuque, IA 52002; 800-228-0810. A comprehensive list compiled by the Archaeological Institute of America of almost 300 archaeological field schools, volunteer positions, and programs throughout the world with openings for volunteers, students, and staff. AIA also publishes *Archaeology* magazine, which lists volunteer opportunities in the Old World (Mar/Apr) and the New World (May/Jun). For membership in AIA or subscriptions, call 617-353-9361 or fax 617-353-6550.

Archaeology Abroad, 31-34 Gordon Square, London WC1H 0PY, U.K.; archabroad@ucl.ac.uk, www.britarch.ac.uk/

archabroad/index.html. Two bulletins each year in April and November. Lists worldwide projects for volunteers and professionals.

CCIVS Publications Lists. Available from: Coordinating Committee for International Voluntary Service (CCIVS), c/o UNESCO, 1 rue Miollis, 75732 Paris, Cedex 15, France; 011-33-1-45-68-49-36, fax 011-33-42-73-05-2; ccivs@unesco.org, www.unesco.org/ccivs. *Running a Workcamp.* A practical guide for workcamp organizers. *How to Present a Project.* A guide for NGOs and individuals who want to draw up and present their projects to international organizations. *The Volunteer's Handbook.* A practical guide for volunteers who wish to participate in workcamps. *Volunteering in Conflict Areas, The Leader Trainer Handbook, National Service, What Are the Options?* Discussion and information on civilian and youth service worldwide. Price of one publication is seven International Reply Coupons.

*Global Work: InterAction's Guide to Volunteer, Internship and Fellowship Opportunities. 2000. 95 pp. (oversize). $10 plus $4 shipping from Interaction, Publications Department, 1717 Massachusetts Ave. NW, Suite 801, Washington, DC 20036; 202-667-8227, fax 202-667-8236; publication-sia@interaction.org, www.interaction.org. Describes opportunities in the US and abroad with over 70 major organizations working in international relief and development. Most require professional skills, though some are open to students. Indexes for location and type of work.

Green Volunteers: The World Guide to Voluntary Work in Nature Conservation edited by Fabio Ausenda. 1999. Vacation Work (U.K.). Available for $19.95 from Seven Hills. Information on conservation organizations which accept volunteers and how to apply.

**How to Live Your Dream of Volunteering Abroad by Joseph Collins, Stefano DeZerega, and Zahara Heckscher. 2002. 467 pp. $17. Penguin-Putnam (available through bookstores). www.volunteeroverseas.org. New book provides a comprehensive overview of volunteering abroad, by three American authors with extensive experience. It includes in-depth profiles of over 100 volunteer placement organizations and evaluations to help volunteers assess whether the organization is right for them. Twelve chapters cover topics such as: Is Volunteering Overseas Right for You, Pros and Cons of the Peace Corps, Doing it Without a Program, Overcoming Financial Obstacles, How to Be an Effective International Volunteer, and Staying Involved When You Get Back.

How to Serve and Learn Effectively: Students Tell Students by Howard Berry and Linda A. Chisholm. 1992. 77 pp. $7.00 from Partnership for Service Learning, 815 2nd Ave., Suite 315, New York, NY 10017; 212-986-0989, fax 212-986-5039; pslny@aol.com, www.ipsl.org. Reality-testing and exploration of motivations for students considering volunteering overseas. Not a directory of opportunities.

*International Directory of Voluntary Work by Louise Whetter and Victoria Pybus. 2000. 319 pp. Vacation Work (U.K.). $15.95 from Peterson's. Directory of over 700 agencies offering volunteer jobs and how to apply. Most comprehensive listing of volunteer opportunities in Britain and Europe of any directory, plus worldwide listings.

*International Volunteer Projects (Council). Free brochure from Council Exchanges, 633 3rd Ave., 20th Fl., New York, NY 10017; 888-COUNCIL, fax 212-822-2649; info@coun cilexchanges.org, www.councilexchanges. org/vol. Describes over 600 short-term summer voluntary service options available through Council in over 25 countries of Europe, Africa, and North America.

*International Workcamp Directory: A Listing of Hundreds of Volunteer Projects Located in 50 Countries (SCI-IVS). Updated each Apr. $5 postpaid (or free on their web site) from SCI-International Voluntary Service, 814 NE 40th St., Seattle, WA 98105; 206-545-6585; sciinfo@sci-ivs.org, www.sci-ivs.org. Describes short-term volunteer options in Europe, Africa, Asia, and North America available through SCI-IVS. Their web site has links to many other volunteer organizations.

*International Workcamper (Volunteers for Peace). Free brochure available from Volunteers for Peace (VFP), International Workcamps, 1034 Tiffany Rd., Belmont, VT 05730-0202; 802-259-2759, fax 802-259-2922; vfp@vfp.org, www.vfp.org. *The VFP International Workcamp Directory* (280 pp.), available each Apr. for $20 from VFP (or free on their web site), describes over 2,000 short-term voluntary service placements in over 70 countries available through VFP for the summer and fall of the year of publication.

Just Act — Working For Global Justice: A Directory of Progressive Organizations, 333 Valencia St., #101, San Francisco, CA 94110; 415-431-4204, fax 415-431-5953; info@

129

justact.org, www.justact.org. This directory includes information on global justice organizations working in the US and internationally ($8). Also available: *Pros and Cons of the Peace Corps,* a compilation of articles and interviews with former Peace Corps volunteers ($7).

Kibbutz Volunteer by Victoria Pybus. 2000. 223 pp. Vacation Work (U.K.). $17.95 from Seven Hills. The most up-to-date and comprehensive resource on volunteering in Israel. New edition lists over 200 kibbutzim at different sites in Israel; also includes information on work on a moshav and other employment opportunities in Israel.

Nepal Volunteer Handbook. 2001. $10 hard copy from Scott Dimetrosky (free for members), Himalayan Explorers Connection, P.O. Box 3665, Boulder, CO 80307-3665; 303-998-0101, fax 303-998-1007; info@hec.org, www.hec.org. Publication by nonprofit organization offers potential volunteers everything they will need to know about volunteering in Nepal, including a personal skills assessment, background on the history of foreign assistance in Nepal, tips for ensuring a worthwhile experience, and information on over 50 volunteer leads.

**The Peace Corps and More: 175 Ways to Work, Study, and Travel at Home and Abroad by Medea Benjamin and Miya Rodolfo-Sioson. 2002. 126 pp. $8.95 from Global Exchange.

**Peace Corps Information Packet, The Peace Corps, 1111 20th St., NW, Rm. 8436, Washington, DC 20526; 800-424-8580; www.peacecorps.gov. Peace Corps seeks individuals to serve as volunteers in overseas communities in the areas of education, small business development, the environment, health, youth development, and agriculture. Tour is 27 months with $6,075 readjustment allowance upon completion of service. Must be U.S. citizen, over 18, in good health, and have education and/or experience relative to programs.

*Response: Directory of Volunteer Opportunities by the Catholic Network of Volunteer Service. 2002 (revised annually).

100 pp. Free (donations accepted) from CNVS, 1410 Q St., NW, Washington, DC 20009; 800-543-5046 or 202-332-6000, fax 202-332-1611; volunteer@cnvs.org. Directory also online at www.cnvs.org. Directory of lay mission opportunities in the U.S. and abroad. Indexes by type of placement, location, length of placement, whether married couples or parents with dependents are accepted, age requirements, etc.

*South American Explorers Volunteer Opportunities Information Packet. Latest update: May 2001. 50 pp (oversize packet, not a book). Updated 3-4 times a year. $6 for non-members, $4.50 for members, postpaid from South American Explorers, 126 Indian Creek Rd., Ithaca, NY 14850; 607-277-0488, fax 607-277-6122; explorer@samexplo.org, www.samexplo.org. Directory of volunteer possibilities located mainly in Ecuador, Peru, and Bolivia, some in Brazil, Chile, and Costa Rica, with local and U.S.-based organizations. Divided into categories of environment, education, arts and culture, agriculture, human rights, general, working with children, and working with women.

**So, You Want to Join the Peace Corps...What to Know Before You Go by Dillon Banerjee. 2000. 178 pp. $12.95 from Ten Speed Press, P.O. Box 7123, Berkley CA 94707; 800-841-BOOK or 510-559-1600; www.tenspeed.com. By a former Peace Corps volunteer, this new book provides comprehensive information in a question & answer format on topics ranging from applying and training to "living like the locals," health concerns, and returning home. A must-read for anyone considering Peace Corps, and valuable for others considering volunteering abroad.

**Volunteer Vacations: Short-Term Adventures That Will Benefit You and Others by Bill McMillon. 1999. 390 pp. $16.95 from Chicago Review Press, 814 N Franklin St., Chicago, IL 60610; 312-337-0747. Describes more than 250 organizations sponsoring projects in the U.S. and abroad. Indexed by cost, length of time, location, type of project, and season. Opportunities from 1 weekend to 6 weeks.

Volunteer Vacations

Directory of Programs

By Transitions Abroad Editors

The following listing of volunteer programs was supplied by the organizers. For the most current information check the *Transitions Abroad* web site www.TransitionsAbroad.com, or contact the program directors. Please tell them you read about their program in this book. Organizations based in more than one country are listed under "Worldwide."

AFRICA

Combat AIDS in Africa

Educate with knowledge and actions; work with schools and families; make a difference in Mozambique, Botswana, and Zambia.

Dates: Terms start May, Aug, Sep, and Nov. Programs last 11-14 months. Cost: Grants available to help with cost. Contact: 530-467-4082.

AUSTRALIA

Conservation Volunteers Australia

CVA is a national, nonprofit, nonpolitical organization undertaking practical conservation projects including tree planting, seed collection, flora/fauna surveys, endangered species projects, coastal restoration, habitat protection, track construction, and weed eradication. Volunteers work in teams of 6-10; all training is provided.

Dates: Year round in all states and territories; choose any Friday throughout the year as starting date. Cost: Six-week Conservation Experience Package: AUS$966 includes all food, accommodations, and project-related transport within Australia. Contact: CVA, P.O. Box 423, Ballarat, Victoria 3353, Australia (please include IRC); 011-61-3-5333-1483, fax 011-61-3-5333-2166; info@conservationvolunteers.com.au, www.conservationvolunteers.com.au.

Willing Workers on Organic Farms (WWOOFING)

Learn organic growing while living with a host family — 1,500 hosts in Australia or travel the world with over 600 hosts worldwide, on every continent, where you work in exchange for food and board.

Dates: Year round. Cost: AUS$50 single, AUS$60 double (add $5 for postage outside of Australia). Contact: WWOOF Australia, Buchan, Victoria 3885, Australia; 011-61-3-5155-0218, fax 011-61-3-5155-0342; wwoof@wwoof.com.au, www.wwoof.com.au.

CANADA

WWOOF-Canada (Willing Workers on Organic Farms)

In exchange for your help (4-6 hours per day, 5-5 1/2 days per week) you receive accommodations, meals, and an interesting and valuable experience. Host farms/homesteads in every region of Canada, East to West. Over 400 hosts.

Dates: Year round. Most opportunities early spring to late fall. Cost: $30 per person includes membership. Contact: WWOOF-Canada, 4429 Carlson Rd., Nelson, BC, V1L 6X3, Canada; 250-354-4417; wwoofcan@uniserve.com, www.wwoof.ca.

CARIBBEAN

Historic Preservation

CVE recruits volunteers to work on historic preservation projects throughout the Caribbean. We work with local agencies: national trusts, museums, and historical societies.

Dates: One-week trips throughout year: Dominica Feb 3-10, Nevis Slave Research Mar 17-27, Virgin Gorda Mar 31-Apr 7, Nepal Sep. Cost: $500-$1,000 per week. Contact: CVE, Box 388, Corning, NY 14830; 607-962-7846; ahershcve@aol.com, www.cvexp.org.

CENTRAL AMERICA

Cultural and Volunteer Programs in Belize

Belize has a variety of cultures living side by side and intermingling, yet keeping their individual identities (Kriol, Spanish, Garifuna, Mayan, Chinese, Lebanese, British, and more). This is an opportunity to learn about different cultures and lifestyles while contributing something of value, developing skills, and recognizing the inner voice of empowerment.

Dates: Year round, 3-week sessions, and long-term commitments. Cost: $549 and up. Varies according to program and length of stay. Contact: Kara

Johnson, Cornerstone Foundation of Belize, 90 Burns Ave., San Ignacio, Cayo District, Belize, Central America; 011-501-824-2373; sweetmaryk@btl.net, www.peacecorner.org.

CENTRAL AND EASTERN EUROPE

Bridges for Education, Inc.

Bridges for Education sends volunteer teachers to teach conversational English in summer. Three weeks teaching. 1 week travel. Educated adults (including families) and college students pay roundtrip airfare and BFE administrative expenses. Since 1984 about 850 teachers to 8 countries, serving 8,500 students from 34 countries with Ministry of Ed., UNESCO. Tax deductible, earn college credit.

Dates: Summer, Jul, and Aug. Cost: Approx. $2,000, depending on departure and destination points. Contact: Margaret Dodge, Applications Coordinator 8912 Garlinghouse Rd., Naples, NY 14512; 716-534-9344; mdodge@frontiernet.com, www.bridges4edu.org.

Central European Teaching Program

English conversation teachers urgently needed! Provide an essential service to public schools in Central Europe by teaching English (or German, French, Literature, or History) in Hungary, Poland, Romania, and other countries. No foreign language skills required. Extensive support plus free housing, health insurance, and local salary provided.

Dates: Sep-Jun or Jan-Jun. Cost: Placement fee ranges from : $2,000-$3,450. Contact: Amy Berigtold, CETP, Beloit College, Box 242, 700 College St., Beloit, WI 53511; 608-363-2619; cetp@beloit.edu, www.beloit.edu/~cetp.

COSTA RICA

Affordable Spanish Programs: CRLA Costa Rican Language Academy

Costa Rican owned and operated language school offers first-rate Spanish instruction in a warm and friendly environment. Teachers with university degrees. Small groups or private classes. Volunteer opportunities. Included free in the programs are airport transportation, coffee and natural refreshments, Internet, excursions, Latin dance, Costa Rican cooking, and conversation classes to provide students with complete cultural immersion.

Dates: Year round (start anytime). Cost: $155 per week or $235 per week for program with homestay. All other activities and services included at no additional cost. Contact: Costa Rican Language

Academy, P.O. Box 1966-2050, San José, Costa Rica; fax 011-506-280-2548. In the U.S.: 866-230-6361; crlang@racsa.co.cr, www.learn-spanish.com, www.spanishandmore.com.

COSI (Costa Rica Spanish Institute)

COSI offers high quality instruction with a very professional and organized staff. We provide the unique possibility of taking Spanish classes in San José and at Manuel Antonio National Park (beach and rainforest).

Dates: Year round. Cost: Prices start at $315 per week including 20 hours of instruction in mini groups of a maximum of 5 students, books, homestay, cultural activities, access to email, airport pickup. Contact: COSI, P.O. Box 1366-2050, San José, Costa Rica; 011-506-234-1001, fax 011-506-253-2117; office@cosi.co.cr, www.cosi.co.cr.

Learn Spanish While Volunteering

Assist with the training of Costa Rican public school teachers in ESL and computers. Assist local health clinic, social service agencies, and environmental projects. Enjoy learning Spanish in the morning, volunteer work in the afternoon/evening. Spanish classes of 2-4 students plus group learning activities; conversations with middle class homestay families (1 student or couple per family). Homestays and most volunteer projects are in a small town near the capital, San José.

Dates: Year round, all levels. Classes begin every Monday (except Mar 25-29 and Dec 14-Jan 5), volunteer program is continuous. Cost: $345 per week for 26 hours of classes and group activities including Costa Rican dance and cooking classes. Includes tuition, meals, homestay, laundry, all materials, weekly 3-hour cultural tour, and airport transportation. $25 one-time registration fee. Contact: Susan Shores, Registrar, Latin American Language Center, P.M.B. 123, 7485 Rush River Dr., Suite 710, Sacramento, CA 95831-5260; 916-447-0938, fax 916-428-9542; lalc@madre.com, www.madre.com/~lalc.

Sustainable Living Center

Rancho Mastatal is a 219-acre environmental center bordering La Cangreja Rainforest Reserve. Offers customized educational programs for all ages, workshops in natural building, renewable energy systems, and tropical agriculture. Organic farming, gardening, and natural building methods practiced. Internships and volunteers encouraged. Beautiful waterfalls and swimming holes. Birds galore. Community focus.

Dates: Year-round. Custom. See web site for details. Cost: Varies. See web site for details. Contact: Timothy O'Hara, Rancho Mastatal, Apdo.185-6000, Puriscal, San Jose, Costa Rica; 506-416-6359 (Spanish only), fax 506-416-6359 (Attn: Rancho Mastatal).

ECUADOR

Academia Latinoamericana

Proud to be the friendliest Spanish school you have ever known. Family owned and operated. The program offers language study at 9 levels, from complete beginners through advanced. Experienced staff, native Ecuadorians. Carefully selected host families within walking distance of school. Exclusive "Cloud Forest and Galápagos" extension program, volunteer program. U.S. college credit available.

Dates: Year round. Cost: $255 per week. Includes 20 hours of lessons, 7 days with host family, 2 meals per day, transfer, services at the school, and teaching material. Contact: Suzanne S. Bell, Admissions Director, USA/International, 640 E 3990 S, Suite E., Salt Lake City, UT, 84107; 801-268-4608, fax 801-265-9156; ecuador@access.net.ec, www.latinoschools.com.

EUROPE

World PULSE Young Ambassadors

World PULSE is a scholarship-based international volunteer program for young adults in the San Francisco Bay Area. Participants do volunteer work and attend workshops in the Bay Area from February-June. In the summer, they travel abroad to join peers from around the world for 2-3 weeks on a volunteer 'workcamp.'

Dates: February to August. Apply by November. Cost: $350-$500 World PULSE sponsors the rest. Contact: Bettina Mok, Director World PULSE, 663 13th St., Oakland, CA 94612; 510-451-2995, fax 510-451-2996; info@worldpulse.org, www.worldpulse.org.

FRANCE

Archaeological Excavations

Excavations, drawing, and mapping in a medieval town.

Dates: Jul-Sep. Cost: Contact organization for details. Contact: Service Archaeologique de Douai, 191 rue Saint Albin, F59500 Douai, France; 011-33-3-2771-3890, fax 011-33-3-2771-383; arkeos@wanadoo.fr.

Restoration of Medieval Buildings

Volunteers restore and maintain medieval buildings and sites, including 2 fortified castles at Ottrott, Alsace, destined as cultural and recreational centers. We provide participants with both cultural enrichment and physical exercise.

Dates: Jul, Aug (1999). Cost: Approx. Euro 85 (1999). Contact: Chantiers d'Études Médiévales, 4 rue du Tonnelet Rouge, 67000 Strasbourg, France; 011-33-88-37-17-20; chateaux-forts@libertysurf.fr, http://castrum.chez.tiscali.fr.

ISRAEL

Kibbutz and Israel Volunteers

Kibbutz volunteers live and work on a kibbutz in Israel. Work can vary: agriculture, services, education, or industry. The volunteer program is for 2-6 months. Ulpan students live on kibbutz for 5 months where they work 3 days and study Hebrew 3 days a week. The program offers trips and tours in Israel as well as social and educational activities. It is a great way to explore your Jewish heritage and get connected with your Jewish roots. Kibbutzim are located throughout Israel. Magen David Adom Program: 2 months of volunteering with other volunteers on ambulances. Program offered in the winter and the summer. Qualifications: age 19-35, prerequisite: EMT. Internships Program: 2 6-month internships designed according to individual requests of students and young professionals.

Dates: Ulpan: 5 months, starting every month. Volunteers live and work-full week on a kibbutz in return for room and board. Volunteer: minimum 2 months, all year. Magen David Adom: registration $50, program fee $400. Internsips program: $50 registration. Cost: Ulpan: $250 registration fee, $600 program fee and $80-$145 insurance. Volunteer: $150 registration and insurance. Magen David Adom: registration $50, program fee $400. Internships program $50 registration. Contact: Tal Lifshitz, Director of Admissions, Kibbutz Program Center, 633 3rd Ave., 21st Fl., New York, NY 10017; 800-247-7852, fax 212-318-6134; ulpankad@aol.com, www.kibbutzprogramcenter.org.

Volunteering at Archaeological Digs

A listings of digs recruiting volunteers can be found on the web site of the Israel Ministry of Foreign Affairs: www.mfa.gov.il/mfa/go.asp?MFAH00wk0.

Dates: Spring and summer. Cost: Vary. Contact: Addresses on the web site, www.mfa.gov.il/mfa/go.asp?MFAH00wk0.

LATIN AMERICA

Volunteer and Internship Positions

In Costa Rica, Mexico, Guatemala, Ecuador, Argentina, Peru, Bolivia. Various positions in the fields of health care, education, tourism, ESL, business, law, marketing, administrative, environmental, and social work. Additional customized options available. Four weeks to 6 months. Inexpensive lodging in homestays or dorms. Some positions provide free room and board.

Dates: Year round. Flexible start dates. **Cost:** $350 placement and application fee. Travel insurance and pre-departure preparation included. Lodging costs depend on location. **Contact:** AmeriSpan Unlimited, P.O. Box 40007, Philadelphia, PA 19106; 800-879-6640, fax 215-751-1100; info@amerispan.com, www.amerispan.com.

MEXICO

Development, Indigenous People, and Ecology

The center, located in Oaxaca in southern Mexico, offers tailor-made programs focusing on environment and indigenous people in Oaxaca, Mexico. They provide a mix of language training, academic classes by experts and local activists, and field trips where students become involved in our research, environmental and cultural activities.

Dates: Flexible. **Cost:** Generally around $400 per week, including room and board, local transportation, and all program activities. **Contact:** Gustavo Esteva/Oliver Froehling, Centro Intercultural de Encuentros y Diálogos Interculturales, Azucenas 610 Col. Reforma, Mexico; 011-52-951-4-6490; dialogos@terra.com.mx.

Mar de Jade Ocean-front Center, Chacala, Nayarit

Celebrating our 20th year as a center for responsible tourism, we are located in the fishing village of Chacala on its beautiful beach north of Puerto Vallarta. For 15 years, our volunteer/study program has been offering opportunities to guests to learn Spanish and put it to use in rural community volunteer projects, including a medical clinic, an after school program for children, a community kitchen and garden project, ESL classes, and house construction. Guests gain insight into local culture through volunteering. Surrounded by lush jungle with the warm, clear Pacific at our door, they enjoy swimming, surfing, hiking, horseback riding, snorkeling, kayaking, whale-watching, and other excursions. Our calendar of retreats include yoga and meditation, among others, as well as our teen summer camp.

Dates: Year round. **Cost:** All rates are per person per night and include accommodations and 3 meals daily. Rates start at $70 per person per night for shared accommodations (up to 4 in a room), or $1,200 for 21 day/20 night optional volunteer program. Doubles, singles, suites, master suites, and apartments available. Add 15 percent tax to all rates.Reduced 3-week rates available in May, June,

September, October. Children welcome. Optional Spanish classes: $80 per week with minimum of 6-night stay. Group rates available. **Contact:** In Mexico, Tel./fax 011-52-322-222-1171; Tel. 011-52-322-222-3524. U.S. mailing address: P.M.B. 078-344, 705 Martens Ct., Laredo, TX 78041-6010; info@marde jade.com, www.mardejade.com.

MONGOLIA

Restore a 300-Year-Old Temple

Travel to the "Land of Blue Skies" and the birthplace of Genghis Khan to help restore an 18th century Buddhist temple. Volunteers live and work alongside local Mongolians, while enjoying the lush beauty of the Khentii countryside. Work with CRTP in one of the least-traveled destinations on earth: Mongolia.

Dates: May-Sep (1- to 2-week tours). **Cost:** $930-$2,325. **Contact:** Mark Hintzke, Cultural Restoration Tourism Project, 410 Palamo Ave., Pacifica, CA 94044; 415-563-7221.

NEPAL

Volunteer Nepal Himalaya

The Himalayan Explorers Connection places volunteer English teachers in Nepal to teach conversational English for 3 months in the spring and fall. Volunteer teachers receive intensive teacher and language training. Qualifications: 18 years and older; some travel/camping experience, willingness to learn and give.

Dates: Fall (Sep-Dec), and spring (Feb-May). **Cost:** $1,000 donation to the Himalayan Explorers Connection 501(c)(3) plus travel and homestay expenses. **Contact:** Jane Sabin-Davis or Scott Dimetrosky, Himalayan Explorers Connection; 888-420-8822; scott@hec.org, jsd@vcinet.com, www.hec.org.

PACIFIC REGION

Kalani Oceanside Retreat

Located on the lush, tropical southeast coast of Hawaii, the Aloha State's "Big Island," our Oceanside Retreat uniquely celebrates nature, culture, and wellness by providing a variety of eco-adventures, events, and comfortable accommodations. Kalani currently offers 2 programs: Resident Volunteers (3-month, 30 hours per week commitment; and Volunteer Scholars (1 month, 20 hours per week commitment), allowing time to participate in our ongoing educational activities. Kalani Oceanside Retreat also offers individual and group opportunities to experience Kalani, utilize our facility or participate in yoga, adventure, and other programs. Please visit www.kalani.com/volunteer.htm.

Dates: Year round for Resident Volunteers and Volunteers Scholars. Cost: $900 for Volunteer Scholar Program (1 month, 20hrs/week commitment). Meals and camping fee included. Private rooms available for additional fee. $900 for Resident Volunteer Program (3 months, 30hrs/week commitment). Lodging and meals included. Contact: Volunteer Programs, Kalani Oceanside Retreat, RR2, Box 4500, Pahoa-Beach Rd., HI 96778-9724; 800-800-6886 or 808-965-7828, fax 808-965-0527; volunteer@kalani.com, www.kalani.com.

ROMANIA

Child Development Program

Romanian Children's Relief sponsors experienced, degreed professionals in child development (OT, Ed, MSW, etc.) fields to go to Romania and train caregivers in pediatric hospitals and orphanages. Programs are in Bucharest and Bistrita, Romania.

Dates: Vary. Minimum 2-year commitment. Cost: RCR pays for housing, living stipend, transportation, and health insurance. Contact: Eileen McHenry, Romanian Children's Relief, P.O. Box 107, Southboro, MA 01772; 508-303-6299; emmc2@aol.com.

UNITED KINGDOM

Worcestershire Lifestyle

Full-time volunteer workers are required to act as the arms and legs of people with physical disabilities who wish to live independently in their own home. Duties include personal care, household tasks, and sharing leisure interests. Free accommodations are provided in Worcestershire or Herefordshire and £58.88 per week.

Dates: Vacancies are on-going. Cost: Contact organization for details. Contact: Worcestershire Lifestyles, Woodside Lodge, Lark Hill Rd., Worcester WR5 2EF, U.K.; 011-44-1905-350686, fax 011-44-1905 350684.

Work on Organic Farm in Scotland

Daily help with dairy goats, friendly sheep, and in organic kitchen garden in stress-free, beautiful countryside near Sea (Dornoch Firth). Home-produced food (vegetarian), comfortable caravan, pocket money. Can take paying guests.

Dates: Any time throughout summer. Cost: Getting there (North of Inverness). Contact: Pam Shaw, The Rhanich, Edderton, Tain Rossshire, Scotland, 1V19 1LG; 011-44-1862-821-265.

UNITED STATES

Rethinking Tourism Project

The Rethinking Tourism Project, an Indigenous organization based in Minnesota, offers volunteer opportunities for students and others to work with us in our home office. Volunteers learn about responsible tourism and international development issues from the Indigenous perspective. Non-paid positions and require a 3-month commitment.

Dates: Contact organization for details. Cost: Contact organization for details. Contact: Rethinking Tourism Project, 366 North Prior Ave., Suite 203, St. Paul, MN 55104; 651-644-9984, fax 651-644-2720; RTProject@aol.com, www.rethinking tourism.org.

TEFL Programs in Boston

Explore the World through Teaching! Full-time and part-time teaching training programs; no previous teaching experience required, practical classroom experience before you leave, career guidance, certificate recognized internationally.

Dates: Sep 10, Oct 15, Nov 26. Cost: $2,495. Contact: The Boston Language Institute, TEFL, 648 Beacon St., Boston, MA 02215; 617-262-3500 ext 288, fax 617-262-3595; tefl@boslang.com, www.teflcertificate.com.

WORLDWIDE

Amity Institute - AVTA Program

Amity Volunteer Teachers Abroad (AVTA) Program offers opportunities to serve as a teacher or teaching assistant in Germany, Latin America, Africa, and Chinese-speaking countries. Programs range from 1 month to a full academic year; room and board is provided. Candidates must be a university graduate or have experience teaching ESL.

Dates: Year-round. Cost: $500-$1,200. Contact: Karen Sullivan, Amity Institute, 10671 Roselle St., Suite 100, San Diego, CA 92121-1525; 858-455-6364, fax 858-455-6597; avta@amity.org, www.amity.org.

Amizade Volunteer Programs

Amizade is a nonprofit organization dedicated to promoting volunteerism, providing community service, encouraging collaboration, and improving cultural awareness in locations around the world. Amizade offers programs for individuals and customizes programs for groups in Brazil, Bolivia, Australia, Nepal, Thailand, as well as the Navajo Nation and the Greater Yellowstone Region, USA.

Dates: Contact Amizade for specific dates. Cost: Ranges from $450 to $2,000, airfare not included.

Fee is tax deductible. **Contact:** Michael Sandy, Executive Director, 367 South Graham Street, Pittsburgh, PA, 15232; 888-973-4443, fax 412-648-1492; volunteer@amizade.org, www.amizade.org.

BTCV-Conservation Holidays

Program of practical conservation holidays at locations around the U.K. and worldwide. No experience necessary, just energy and enthusiasm. You could be drystone walling in the English Lake District or turtle monitoring in Thailand.

Dates: Year round. **Cost:** From £45-£1,000 includes food and accommodations. **Contact:** BTCV, 36 St. Mary's St., Wallingford, Oxfordshire OX10 0EU, U.K.; 011-44-1491-821600, fax 011-44-1491-839646; information@btcv.org, www.btcv.org.

Conservation Research

Frontier is an international conservation and research NGO which works in threatened tropical environments to protect endangered habitats and wildlife through research and practical projects. Offers self-funding volunteers the opportunity to work on overseas projects for 10 or 20 weeks or to participate on expeditions for 28 days. Full training is provided, leading to a level 3 BTEC qualification.

Dates: Projects depart Jan-Mar, Apr-Jun, Jul-Sep, and Oct-Dec of each year. Expeditions depart Jul, Aug, and Jan of each year. **Cost:** Volunteers must raise approx. £2,500 for 10 weeks or £1,850 for 28 days (excluding airfare and visa). **Contact:** Research Assistant Coordinator, Frontier, 50-52 Rivington St., London EC2A 3QP, U.K.; 011-44-20-7613-2422, fax 011-44-20-7613-2992; enquiries@frontierprojects.ac.uk, www.frontier.ac.uk.

A Cultural Immersion Experience

Live with local families! Serve communities in need! Study the language and put it to use! Learn about the culture through seminars and local exploration! A comprehensive orientation sets the stage for a deeper and more intimate cross-cultural experience. Make friends and make a contribution through these extraordinary immersion programs in Nepal, Peru, and India.

Dates: Summer: 6 weeks (Jun 15-Jul 26, Jul 8-Aug 18); semester: 3-5 months (Jan-May and Sep-Dec). **Cost:** Summer programs: from $1,900; semester programs: from $2,650. **Contact:** David, Program Director, International Cultural Adventures; 888-339-0460; icadventures@usa.net.

Franciscan Mission Service

FMS prepares and sends Catholic women and men for extended assignments among oppressed and poor peoples of Africa, Asia, and Latin America. Volunteers are needed to work in the areas of health care, social service, education, agriculture, and community organizing. Allow a different culture to expand your worldview.

Dates: Jan-Apr 2003; Sep-Nov 2002-2003. **Contact:** Megeen White, Co-director, Franciscan Mission Service, P.O. Box 29034, Washington, DC 20017; 877-886-1762, fax 202-832-1778; fms5@juno.com.

Global Service Corps (GSC)

A project of Earth Island Institute, creates opportunities for adult participants to live in homes in Tanzania and Thailand while volunteering for health, education, sustainable agriculture, HIV/AIDS awareness and environment community service and development projects. These service-learning programs emphasize grass-roots collaboration on the local level, mutual transfer of skills, and cross-cultural understanding. Undergraduate and Graduate level credits qualifying for financial aid available.

Dates: Year round. Contact GSC office or check the web site for specific starting dates **Cost:** Approx. $1,900-$2,000 for 23-28 day project trips; $3,255-$4,305 for summer and semester college internships. Long-term 3-6 month placements also available. Includes pre-departure preparations and in-country expenses (hotel and homestay room and board, orientation, training, language lessons, project expenses, transportation, and weekend safari). Airfare not included. **Contact:** Global Service Corps., 300 Broadway, Suite 28, San Francisco, CA 94133; 415-788-3666 ext 128, fax 415-788-7324; gsc@earthisland.org, www.globalservicecorps.org.

International Service-Learning

The International Partnership for Service-Learning, founded in 1982, is an incorporated not-for-profit organization of colleges, universities, service agencies, and related organizations united to foster and develop programs linking volunteer service and academic study for credit. The International Partnership administers 13 undergraduate programs in 12 nations, and offers an MA degree program in International Service. Program locations include the Czech Republic, Ecuador (Guayaquil and Quito), England, France, India, Israel, Jamaica, Mexico, the Philippines, Russia, Scotland, and South Dakota (with Native Americans). Students earn 12-18 college credits per semester and serve up to 15-20 hours per week. The programs are based at accredited universities and all aspects of the programs are conducted by in-country professionals. More than 4,000 students from 400 colleges and universities in U.S. and 25 other nations have participated in IPS-L programs.

Dates: Summer, semester, year, or intersession. **Cost:** Vary. **Contact:** The International Partnership for Service-Learning, 815 2nd Ave., Suite 315, New York, NY 10017; 212-986-0989, fax 212-986-5039; pslny@aol.com, www.ipsl.org.

International Volunteer Program

IVP provides 6-week summer volunteer placements in nonprofits in France and the U.K. Volunteer placements include work with at-risk youth, elderly, handicapped, and homeless individuals. The administrative fee covers roundtrip airfare and room and board during the whole 6-week program.

Dates: Jun 20-end of July **Cost:** $1,500. **Contact:** Rebecca Jewell, International Volunteer Program, 210 Post St., Suite 502, San Francisco, CA 94108; 415-477-3667, fax 415-477-3669; rjewell@ivpsf.com, www.ivpsf.com.

Jewish Volunteer Corps

The Jewish Volunteer Corps sends skilled Jewish men and women to provide technical assistance and training in the fields of health, agriculture, business, and education to communities in the developing world. JVC volunteers work with local grassroots nongovernmental organizations throughout Latin America, Asia, and Africa from 1 to 12 months.

Dates: Year round, minimum 1 month. **Cost:** JVC covers airfare, emergency evacuation insurance, volunteers cover all other costs. **Contact:** American Jewish World Service, 45 W 36th St., 10th Fl., New York, NY 10018; 212-736-2597, fax 212-736-3463; jvcvol@jws.org, www.ajws.org.

Overseas Action Program (Nepal and Kenya)

World Youth International is a nonprofit, non-religious, nonpolitical organization that runs a number of overseas volunteer programs for people of all ages and creates overseas community development projects. We are currently offering our Overseas Action Program, which is a 3-month program for 18-to-30-year-olds in Nepal, Kenya, and Brazil, for volunteers from all over the world. Programs for each country run twice a year.

Dates: Programs run twice a year to Kenya (Jun and Nov), Nepal (Mar and Nov). **Cost:** $1,500-$2,000. **Contact:** Anita Adlam, World Youth International, 18 3rd St., Brompton, South Australia, Australia 5007.

Research/Conservation Expeditions to Canada and Nepal

In Canada help monitor population trends and changes on record and document flora and fauna species. Live the life of a field biolo-gist and learn. In Nepal visit rural areas in the Central-Hill region to document and record the use of rare and endangered medicinal plants. Results will be used to help establish protected areas.

Dates: Canada: Jun-Aug (2 weeks). Nepal: Mar-Aug (2 weeks). **Cost:** Canada $425-$499 per person (14 days). Nepal $999 per person (14 days). **Contact:** Dave Jolly, Executive Director, EARTHQUEST (Canada) for the Environment, P.O. Box 24142, London, Ontario, Canada N6H SC4; 519-642-9988; earthquest@hotmail.com, www.geocities.com/earthquestcanada.

Teach in Africa, Asia, Latin America

WorldTeach. Based at Harvard Univ. for 15 years, WorldTeach provides opportunities for individuals to make a meaningful contribution to international education by living and working as volunteer teachers in developing countries in Africa, Asia, Latin America, and Pacific Islands. Offers 8-week summer teaching programs to qualified adults 18 years of age and older, involving either English or basic computer/Internet instruction. WorldTeach also offers 1 year and semester teaching placements for college graduates.

Dates: Jun 20-Aug 20 (summer); long-term programs depart through the year. **Cost:** Summer $3,990; year/semester $4,990-$5,990. Includes international roundtrip airfare, health insurance, orientation and training, room and board, and full-time in-country staff support. **Contact:** WorldTeach, Center for International Development, Harvard Univ., 79 John F. Kennedy St., Cambridge, MA 02138; 800-483-2240 or 617-495-5527, fax 617-495-1599; info@worldteach.org, www.worldteach.org.

Volunteer and Cultural Exchange

Cross-Cultural Solutions offers life-changing volunteer programs and "insight" cultural tours in Asia, Africa, Latin America, the Caribbean, and Eastern Europe. Volunteers typically work in the areas of education, healthcare, and community development for 1 week to 6 months. Cultural tours range from 7 to 18 days.

Dates: Year round. **Cost:** Programs begin at $1,200 and vary depending on duration and country. **Contact:** Volunteer Coordinator, Cross-Cultural Solutions, 47 Potter Ave., New Rochelle, NY 10801; 914-632-0022 or 800-380-4777, fax 914-632-8494; info@crossculturalsolutions.org, www.crossculturalsolutions.org.

Volunteers for Peace

Over 2,200 voluntary service projects in over 80 countries. An opportunity to complete meaningful community service while abroad. Most programs last 2-3 weeks; work includes construction, renovation, environmental and social work, refugee programs, education, arts, etc. Some medium- to long-term programs available.

Dates: May-Sep; some programs run all year. **Cost:** $200 (some camps have extra fee). Volunteer pays transportation costs. **Contact:** Volunteers for Peace, 1034 Tiffany Rd., Belmont, VT 05730; 802-259-2759, fax 802-259-2922; vfp@vfp.org, www.vfp.org.

World Wide Volunteer Services

Volunteering? WWVS is a personalized service locating challenging volunteer positions and negotiating placements to meet your special interests and skills. Opportunities are global, of long or short duration (including summers). Placements usually provide free room and board.

Dates: Year round. **Cost:** Varies. **Contact:** Director, WWVS, P.O. Box 3242, West End, NJ 07740; 732-571-3215; worldvol@aol.com, http://welcome.to/volunteer_services.

Youth International

An experiential education program focusing on international travel and intercultural exchange, adventure, community service, and homestays. Teams of 14, aged 18-25, travel together for 1 semester of 3½ months to Asia (Vietnam, Thailand, and India) or Africa (Kenya, Tanzania, Botswana, and Namibia) or South America (Bolivia, Peru, and Ecuador, including the Galapagos islands). Assist refugees, hike the Himalayas or the Andes, live with and help an African tribe, scuba dive in the Galapagos, and much more.

Dates: Every year, early Sep-mid-Dec, and early Feb-late May. **Cost:** $7,500 including airfare. **Contact:** Brad Gillings, Youth International, 1121 Downing St., #2, Denver, CO 80218; 303-839-5877, fax 303-839-5887; director@youthinternational.org, www.youthinternational.org.

Volunteer Work Abroad
The Best Web Sites

Selected and Reviewed by William Nolting

Volunteering may be the best option for working in less-developed countries, or to work for social causes anywhere. And volunteering does not necessarily mean unpaid work—see the Peace Corps, for example. Duration of volunteer abroad programs may range from two weeks to two years or more. ****Essential; *Outstanding and of broad interest.**

(I)   Informational site with directories or databases listing many programs

(P)   Site for a specific work abroad program

(S)   Scholarships or fellowships

(I) Directory on International Voluntary Service, www.avso.org/en/links/links.htm. Site provides extensive links to volunteer organizations worldwide; hosted by the Association of Voluntary Service Organizations (based in Belgium).

**(I) Idealist (a resource by Action Without Borders), www.idealist.org. This site's claim of tens of thousands of non-profit organizations "under one roof" says it all. Excellent search provisions give useful results using "internship" or "volunteer". Also has lists of volunteer, internship and job opportunities. Search possible by country, type of work, and many other variables. The "browse by country" section lists organizations according to their work focus. Note, however, that not every volunteer abroad program is listed here, so you'll still want to

check hard-copy volunteer directories such as *The Peace Corps and More.* Site includes organizations worldwide, not only U.S.-based ones.

**International Volunteer Programs Association (IVPA), www.volunteer international.org by Christine Victorino. IVPA is a professional association for administrators of international volunteer programs, as well as advisers and students interested in this type of international experience. Their web site lists programs for volunteering abroad, some of which offer academic credit, and has extensive links to relevant resources.

(Videos) Making a Difference: College Volunteers Abroad, and **Making a Difference: American Volunteers Abroad by Bob Gilner. 2000. $39.95 (individuals) or $79.95 (institutions) for each video from: Bob Gilner Productions, P.O. Box 596, Boulder Creek, CA 95006; fax 831-338-7381; bgliner@hotmail.com, www.docmakeronline.com/VolunteersAbroad.html. These outstanding videos, made onsite by an award-winning filmmaker, provide first-hand insight into the rewards and realities of volunteering abroad through programs offered by established U.S.-based organizations. College Volunteers Abroad looks at programs intended for college students, while American Volunteers Abroad is about programs for adult volunteers. Each hour-long video profiles several different programs in Africa, South America, and Europe.

(P) Peace Corps, www.peacecorps.gov. Sometimes overlooked because of its designation as a volunteer program, Peace Corps is one of the largest work abroad programs for U.S. citizens. It provides some of the best-paid opportunities in over 90 countries in less-wealthy regions such as Africa, Latin America, South and Southeast Asia, and even Eastern Europe and the former USSR. Program is funded by the US government, while projects are determined by the host countries. Volunteers receive all expenses paid, training, health insurance, and a "resettlement allowance" of over $6,000 after completing the two-year assignment. Even if you're not interested in the Peace Corps, this website has lots of information about international work and careers — see Peace Corps Career TRACK, www.peacecorps.gov/rpcv/career/index.cfm.

*(I) **PCORPS-L** (a listserv discussion group) Free to join. Send message "sub PCORPS-L yourfirstname yourlastname" to: listserv@cmuvm.csv.cmich.edu. Discussions by former and prospective Peace Corps volunteers of interest to anyone interested in studying or working in developing countries. This group is unofficial.

(I, P) Quaker Information Center, www.afsc.org/qic/oportnty.htm by Peggy Morscheck. This very comprehensive website includes links to hundreds of organizations sponsoring overseas volunteer, internship, and study programs with a focus on social justice, relief, and development.

*(I) **Response,** www.cnvs.org/vo-rdir.htm. Response, a comprehensive directory to Catholic and other Christian overseas volunteer organizations (most focus on areas such as social justice, relief and development), is online and searchable.

(I) **University of Minnesota ISTC, www.istc.umn.edu. This site has several searchable databases. Each one produces lots of listings by using the term "volunteer". Searches possible by country and many other variables.

(P, I) **Volunteers for Peace, www.vfp.org. VFP offers over 1,000 low-cost, short-term (a few weeks) volunteer abroad programs. The VFP site also has extensive links to other international volunteer organizations.

www.spanish.com.mx

Learn,
Live
& Love
Spanish where it is spoken!

Universidad Internacional is pleased to invite you to participate in its Study Abroad programs in beautiful Cuernavaca, Mexico.

Over 20 successful years of experience in teaching Spanish to speakers of other languages

Recognized as quality programs through a formal agreement with SUNY-Brockport

Exchange programs with more than 60 educational institutions throughout the U.S.

Intensive Spanish Courses designed for students and professionals of all levels

Semester and Internship programs available

Academic Credits available.

Courses taught by native teachers and instructors

Housing with Mexican families for a complete immersion experience

Courses for every level begin each Monday of the year

Intensive Spanish programs designed for executives

Universidad Internacional
The Center for Bilingual Multicultural Studies

For more information contact us at:
Admission@bilingual-center.com
Toll free From U.S. (800) 932 20 68
From Canada 1(877) 4-MEXIC-8
Fax 52 (777) 3 15 05 33

CHAPTER 5

TEACHING ENGLISH ABROAD

As the world rushes to acquire English, the new lingua franca of international commerce, diplomacy, and higher education, the bulk of overseas teaching opportunities abroad are for English teachers. Your "credential" is simply being a native speaker of the English language. That may be all you need to obtain a job and a work permit in areas such as Asia and Eastern Europe.

Teaching Jobs Abroad: Overview
The Most Accessible Employment for Those Without Special Training or Skills

By William Nolting and Anthony Hand

The most readily-available overseas teaching opportunities are for English teachers. As people worldwide rush to acquire the new lingua franca of international commerce, diplomacy, and higher education, the main credentials you'll need for many positions are to be a native speaker of English and to have a college degree.

Some programs are now requesting experience in Teaching English as a Foreign (or Second) Language, known by the acronyms TEFL, EFL, TESL, ESL, or even TESOL (Teaching English to Speakers of Other Languages). Formal credentials in TEFL can be gained in a 1-month course. This could open doors in competitive areas like Western Europe. Those with a master's in TEFL, available through a 1-year program at many universities, can teach virtually anywhere.

Qualified teachers have still another range of options. Yet, other teaching possibilities, some of which we list here, exist for those with knowledge of special fields such as business, health, math or science (through the Peace Corps and Teachers for Africa) or for graduate students (through the Civic Education Project).

Earnings can be good in relatively wealthy countries like Japan, South Korea, and Taiwan. In China, Eastern Europe, Russia, and the Newly Independent States, pay may be high by local standards but not sufficient for savings. Africa and Latin America are primarily served by volunteer organizations. Western Europe presents dim prospects for Americans (with some notable exceptions, such as Austria, Finland and France, for which there are official placement programs), because British and Irish teachers do not need work permits as members of the European Union.

In general, if your main motivation in teaching is to make a lot of money, you will likely be disappointed. In some cases the experience may even cost you more than you earn, but this is usually still far less than the cost of study or travel abroad. (Student loans can sometimes be deferred during volunteer work; inquire through your loan and program sponsors.)

Before You Begin

Before you begin your search, determine what you hope to gain from your overseas experience. Are your goals to experience a different culture? Gain language proficiency? Try out teaching as a career? How important is money—do you hope to make a lot of money, is it okay to break even, or can you spend more than you might make for the sake of the cross-cultural experience?

The answers to your money questions may limit your choices. The highest number of well-paying teaching jobs are in Asia.

Next, try to narrow down your geographic preferences to a few countries or regions. Do you hope to tie your experience to career objectives? How does this affect the money issue?

About a year before you begin teaching abroad, think about getting TEFL experience or a certificate. You will be glad you did the first time you face a class thousands of miles from home. Opportunities are available as a literacy volunteer or through local ESL programs for international students or refugees offered by colleges, schools, and religious organizations almost everywhere.

Finding a Job

One way to find an overseas teaching position is to apply through a U.S.-based organization. These usually arrange placement and provide for logistical matters, such as housing and a work permit.

The second strategy is to write directly to overseas schools. Chances of success are limited without going to that country for an interview.

The third strategy is to go to the country where you want to work and apply in person. The major downside to this is cost: airfare, housing (possibly paying several months' rent up front), and the need to travel to a third country to get a work permit once you land a job. The total up-front investment required by this last approach could easily be $2,000-$3,000 or more—something to keep in mind when evaluating program fees.

We generally recommend applying through U.S.-based organizations rather than seeking a job on-site because of the uncertainty and expense of the latter two strategies. Most U.S.-based teaching placement organizations are small nonprofits, some staffed by volunteers. All (except for private language schools) view their primary mission as cultural exchange, not as placement agencies for well-paid overseas jobs.

Choosing a Placement Program

Programs vary widely in the fees, services, and assistance they offer. When choosing a program, inquire about: fees, salary, job placement, work permit, health insurance, housing, teacher training and materials, whether there is an orientation, and level of on-site support. It is better to be clear about these basics before you apply than to turn up and find you do not have a legal work permit.

Fees. What exactly do they include?

Placement. Find out who you will be teaching (elementary, high school, university students, or adults?) and where (a state school, private school, or for-profit language institute?).

Salary. How much and how often will you be paid? Compare your salary with the local cost of living.

Health insurance may not be provided by program fees, or you may be covered by socialized medicine available only in-country. Get an International Teachers' ID Card for $22 from STA Travel (800-777-0112, www.statravel.com) which includes a minimal health insurance policy and gives access to student-rate airfares. Consider special comprehensive coverage for educators provided by such companies as HTH Worldwide (800-242-4178, www.hthworldwide.com, Seabury and Smith (800-282-4495 or 800-331-3047, www.maginnis-ins.com, or Wallach and Company (800-237-6615, www.wallach.com). Costs begin at approximately $50 per month.

Materials and training. If they don't provide materials, what do they recommend to bring with you? Even if some training is provided, would it still be useful to get experience teaching or tutoring in the U.S.?

For comprehensive listings of worldwide placement organizations, see the article "Teaching Without Certification" on Univ. of Michigan web site www.umich.edu/%7Eicenter/overseas/work/teach_no_cert2.html.

Preparing to Teach
Pick the Training Course That Best Suits You

By Erika Weidner

For college-educated native English speakers looking to finance extended travel abroad, teaching English as a foreign language (TEFL) is often the first thing that comes to mind. The question is, how does one prepare?

Most TEFL training courses prepare you to teach English to non-native speakers using a method commonly called European-direct. The variations in courses are worth investigating to find the course that best suits you.

But before you start researching the different TEFL schools you should determine if you need one at all. First, decide what part of the world you wish to work in, the length of time you wish to work there, and how important it is that you work legally.

If you want to work for only six months to a year it may be smarter to put your money toward living expenses—especially if you are going someplace where the dollar is relatively strong and there is ample opportunity for private tutoring without a certificate. However, if your intention is to work in a private school, you should be aware that most reputable schools require previous training.

If you are determined to teach in Western Europe you should also be aware that you will face stiff competition from legal EU residents who possess an RSA/Cambridge certificate. You may want to arm yourself with the same credential, although this course is considerably more costly than a noncertificate course. RSA/Cambridge courses are monitored by exams from Cambridge and thus their standards are uniform throughout the world. This is not to say that other courses cannot offer you a jump start for teaching English and give you the same fundamental training based on the same methodology.

If you are only interested in teaching in Asia you may not need a certification course: most recruiters who place teachers in Japan and Korea have their own training sessions. In fact, for those seeking structure and direction in teaching, Japan and Korea may be good choices. But the better your credentials, the greater your opportunities.

Certification Courses

Certification courses differ in that some are 100-hour crash courses offered through specialized schools like New World Teachers and St Giles, while others are offered through universities in degree programs.

Intensive part-time classes are excellent for working students. Such courses give you the tools to effectively interact with a class full of non-native speakers using the European-direct method of teaching. Rather than spending a lot of time studying linguistics, you learn how to teach on a day-to-day basis. Learning to teach through teaching is highly effective and also fun.

University-based courses, on the other hand, may be taught in a more traditional way. You study linguistics and history of language, but that may not prepare you to teach a classroom full of teenaged Argentines or a group of Hungarian businesspeople. Compare the syllabus of university-based courses with that of an intensive program to determine which will give you the appropriate practical tools for teaching. Short courses offered in major metropolitan areas with large immigrant communities may offer you the best chance to teach actual classes of non-English speakers while being critiqued by trainers, an invaluable experience.

Another consideration is your long-term goal. If you plan to travel from country to country for a few years, a certificate with strong emphasis on practical skills is essential. If you are considering a career in ESL, a university-based degree program may be more appropriate.

Schools break down the 100 hours of training differently. Some may spend five hours on practice teaching; others may spend none. In some schools the education trainers hold masters degrees. In other schools the trainers have no more qualifications than you would have after a few years of teaching. If the level and field of education of your trainer is a concern, you may want to ask. You may also want to inquire how long the school has been in business and if it is licensed by the state in which it operates.

What About Placement?

One of the most important factors to consider when choosing a course is placement assistance. Be aware that schools do not place you in jobs (unless you are going through a volunteer organization). When a school says they have job placement assistance, it simply means that they have materials available for you to do your own research—binders filled with feedback from previous students and bulletin boards with available job openings at language schools around the world. The school provides you with guidance and resources, but you are on your own when it comes to an actual job search.

Carefully check out the school's placement services before enrolling. Some may offer Internet access at no extra charge. Some send you lists of schools with job openings (for a small fee) once you have graduated.

Ask specific questions when comparing schools. Find out the total cost including books, tests, etc. Some schools that offer RSA/Cambridge certification may charge extra for the exam. Other courses offer discounts of up to $300 if you sign up with a friend.

The cost of living in the city in which the course takes place is also an important consideration. So is housing. Some courses may have dorm-like housing–essential in cities like San Francisco where the competition for rentals is fierce and the cost comparable to New York.

Teaching ESL Training Courses

For a directory of training courses by country leading to the RSA/Cambridge Certificate (CTEFLA) see Susan Griffith's *Teaching English Abroad* (Peterson's Guides) and the "Key Resources" in the Introduction to this book.

For a guide to academic courses in the U.S. (but not short courses) see the *Directory of Teacher Education Programs in TESOL in the U.S. and Canada 2002-2004* available from TESOL, Inc., 1600 Cameron St., Suite 300, Alexandria, VA 22314-2751; 703-836-0774, fax 703-836-7864; place@tesol.edu, www.tesol.org.

For a current directory of TESOL training and placement programs, both academic and short-term, see the end of this chapter.

Ten Tips for EFL Teachers

By Jann Huizenga

Here are some tips to help you avoid classroom culture clash in those heady first months of teaching abroad:

1. **Dress right.** Jeans, sneakers, and just-out-of-bed hair may be okay for teachers in the U.S., but in many parts of the world, a neat appearance counts far more than credentials. In Korea dark clothes lend an air of authority. Red is to be avoided at all costs. In Morocco female teachers don't wear pants, sleeveless blouses, or short skirts.

2. **Behave appropriately.** When Judith Johnson asked 250 students at the Sichuan Institute of Foreign Languages in China what they liked and disliked about native speaker English teachers, the students' main gripe was the informality of foreign

teachers, who often seem to undermine their own authority by acting in undigni-fied ways. In the U.S. teachers go on a first-name basis with students, sit on their desks, sip coffee, and even bounce off the walls without causing student discomfort or losing prestige. But these behaviors don't export well.

3. **Don't worry if students seem unresponsive at first.** Americans are used to par-ticipatory classrooms with plenty of teacher-student dialogue. Elsewhere, students are often trained to be silent, good listeners, and memorizers. In my classes in Poland, the Balkans, and Mongolia, students wore impassive classroom masks the first few weeks of class. It's disconcerting to stand in front of a sea of blank faces, but expecting it reduces the shock. Introduce new concepts, such as discussion and role-play gradually. You'll be surprised at how students will come to embrace the change.

4. **Choose topics carefully.** In the 1980s in totalitarian Yugoslavia I made the mis-take of asking students to debate the pros and cons of capital punishment. A painful silence fell over the room. What discussion was possible, someone pointed out to me later, when the government's position was clear? There are still many countries in the world where people are hesitant to voice opinions because of a fear of reprisal. If you're conducting a classroom debate, remember that there's a distaste for Western-style argumentation in Middle-Eastern societies, and in Japan it's offensive for an individual to urge others to accept his opinion.

Certain topics may be taboo for cultural reasons: Most Americans don't want to discuss their salaries or religious beliefs; Japanese may be disinclined to talk about their inner feelings; the French think questions about their family life are rude.

5. **Don't ask, "Do you understand?"** In China and Japan, students will nod yes, even if they're totally lost, in an attempt to save face for the teacher. Even in a country as far west as Turkey, yes often means no.

Nor should you expect students to ask questions in class if they don't understand something. A former student of mine told me: "In China, a student who asks ques-tions is considered a pain in the neck." Check understanding by asking students to paraphrase or write questions they have in groups.

6. **Avoid singling students out.** Our society fosters a competitive individualism which is clearly manifested in our classrooms. American students are not shy about displaying their knowledge. In classrooms outside the U.S., however, showing soli-darity with classmates and conforming to the status quo is often more important than looking good for the teacher. In Turkey and Montenegro students told me they disliked volunteering answers too often because it made them look like show-offs and attracted the evil eye of envy. This holds true in Japan and China, too, where proverbs express the cultural idea in a nutshell: "The clever hawk hides its claws" and "The nail that stands up must be pounded down."

If you want to play a game, make the competition among groups rather than among individuals. If you need to discipline a student, do so in private.

7. **Be aware of cross-cultural communication styles.** French students appreciate wit. Venezuelan students like boisterous rapid-fire exchanges. In Japan, where debate is not as valued as in the U.S., students appreciate long pauses in discussions and silent "think time" after you ask a question. "Hollow drums make the most

noise" goes a Japanese proverb, and Japanese students are uncomfortable blurting out the first thing that comes to mind. American teachers, who are uncomfortable with silence, tend to anticipate the student's words or repeat their original question—both irritating interruptions for the Japanese student.

8. **Present a rationale for what you do in class.** Your pedagogy is going to be very different from what students are used to. They'll conform much more eagerly to new classroom content and procedures if they understand the benefits.

9. **Expect the best of your students.** They'll be serious about learning English because their economic advancement often depends upon mastering it.

10. **Relax and enjoy yourself.** Happiness in the classroom is contagious.

Work in Europe
Teaching English Offers the Most Opportunities

By Susan Griffith

Whatever transatlantic trade agreements now exist or might exist in the future, one thing is sure: there will be no free exchange of labor between North America and Europe. As the ties between European nations strengthen, particularly among the 15 members of the European Union, the employment opportunities for non-Europeans decline. Yet thousands of Americans live and work in Europe at this moment. Many of them have arrived in the past year and have found a niche, comfortable or otherwise.

The business of teaching English absorbs a considerable percentage of these temporary European residents. North Americans with a professional background in language teaching (e.g., a degree in applied linguistics and some relevant experience) might find an employer willing to sponsor them for a work visa. Even more desirable in many cases is a solid background in the business world, since the majority of language teaching in Europe is to businessmen and women who want practical language tools for the workplace and prefer to be taught by someone with experience of this world than by a free-faced modern languages graduate. Opportunities for non-Europeans are more plentiful in some countries than others—easier in Germany and Portugal than Italy and Spain, for example. The alternatives are to work for an employer who is not bothered about officialdom (this often implies a similarly casual approach to pay and working conditions) or to work on an informal or freelance basis. In European cities of any size the pool of native speaker teachers on the spot is so large that language school proprietors almost always have a choice of hopeful applicants to interview. In most cases a speculative application and resume sent from the U.S. will not meet with a favorable response.

Freelancing
The majority of language North American teachers and trainers in Europe work on a freelance basis. This can take the form of private tutoring whereby a native speaker goes it alone, finding private clients independently by advertising, etc. The more

common way of freelancing, however, is to do it through an agency that provides language teaching, primarily to businesses. Freelancers work on short-term contracts or on an hourly basis. They are paid by the course or by the hour, but are not eligible for paid holidays or the other benefits of long-term employment. They must also worry about paying their own taxes plus they may have to pay compulsory contributions into a pension scheme (as in Germany) or to cover social security.

Independent freelance tutors will find it difficult to start teaching without contacts and a good working knowledge of the language. When they do get started, it may be difficult to earn a stable income because of the frequency with which pupils cancel. It is unrealistic for a newly arrived freelancer to expect to earn enough to live on in the first six months or so.

Getting clients for private lessons is a marketing exercise, and all the avenues that seem appropriate to your circumstances have to be explored. Here are some ways you can market yourself:

• Put a notice up in schools and universities, supermarkets or corner shops, and run an advertisement in the local paper if you have the use of a telephone.

• Send neat notices to local public schools, announcing your willingness to ensure the children's linguistic future.

• Compile a list of addresses of professionals (lawyers, architects, etc.) who may need English for their work and have the resources to pay for it. Then contact them.

• Call on export businesses, distribution companies, perhaps even travel agencies.

These methods should put you in touch with a few hopeful language learners. If you are good at what you do, word will spread and more paying pupils will come your way, though the process can be slow.

Working solo has disadvantages. Everyone, from lazy Greek teenagers to stressed Barcelona businessmen, cancels or postpones one-on-one lessons with irritating frequency. Since your clients are paying for your flexibility, you can't afford to take too tough a line. Unless your place is suitable for teaching, you will have to spend time traveling to your clients.

If you are more interested in integrating with the local culture than making money, exchanging conversation for board and lodging may be an appealing possibility. This can be arranged by answering (or placing) small ads in appropriate places. The American Church in Paris notice board is famous for this.

Language Schools

When you arrive in a likely place your initial steps might include some of the following: copy a list of schools from the yellow pages (many are now available on-line such as the *Pages Jaunes* in France or the *Gelbe Seiten* in Germany; read the classified columns of the local papers; check notice boards in likely locations such as universities, TEFL training centers, English language bookshops (where you should also notice which EFL materials are stocked), or places frequented by expatriate teachers.

After putting together a list of potential employers, get a detailed map and guide to the public transport network so you can locate the schools. Phone the schools and try to arrange a meeting with the director or academic director of studies. Even if an initial chat does not result in a job offer, you may learn something about the local TEFL scene that will help you at the next interview, especially if you ask lots of questions.

France: French Majors Encouraged to Apply

Advanced TEFL qualifications seem to be less in demand in France than business qualifications and experience or even just "commercial flair." Anyone who has a BA and is comfortable in a business setting has a chance of finding teaching work, particularly if they have a working knowledge of French.

The Cultural Service of the French Embassy (4101 Reservoir Rd., NW, Washington, DC 20007; assistant@frenchculture.org; www.frenchculture.org/education/support/assistant/index.html) runs an English Teaching Assistantship Program for US citizens. Postings last 6-9 months and are in primary or secondary schools or teacher training colleges. Assistants give conversation classes, provide classroom support and teach pupils about the U.S. A working knowledge of French is required so French majors are encouraged to apply. Assistants receive approximately Euros 900 gross per month. Work in France program participants who are in France under the auspices of **Council Exchanges** (112 ter, rue Cardinet, 75017; www.councilexchanges-fr.org) often work as English teachers though they are at liberty to work in any capacity.

Work permits must be obtained before leaving home, which is simply impracticable unless you have spent time in France and developed a working relationship with a cooperative employer. (Note that the long-established Paris training organization, **WICE**, at 20 boulevard du Montparnasse www.wice-paris.org, can advise on how to get working papers, though it warns of the difficulties.) Foreigners on a student visa are permitted to work 10-20 hours a week (after their initial year of study) or full-time in the vacations. At a more casual level, language exchanges for room and board are commonplace in Paris; these are usually arranged through advertisements or word of mouth. You can also offer English lessons privately in people's homes starting at Euro 15-20 a session.

Expatriate grapevines can be found all over Paris and are very helpful for finding teaching work and accommodations. The one in the foyer of the **CIDJ** at 101 Quai Branly (Métro Bir-Hakeim) is good for occasional student-type jobs, but sometimes there are ads for a soutien scolaire en Anglais (English tutor). It is worth arriving early to check for new notices (the hours are Monday-Friday 9:30 a.m. to 6 p.m. and Saturday mornings).

Other meccas for job-hunters include the **American Church** at 65 Quai d'Orsay (Métro Invalides) and the **American Cathedral in Paris** (23 av. George V; www.us.net/amcathedral-paris). Both have notice boards crammed with employment opportunities, courses and housing listings. The Cathedral even offers career forums for job-seekers.

Highly qualified TEFL teachers from the U.S. might approach some of the important Paris companies such as **Le Comptoir des Langues** (63 Re la Boetie, 75008 Paris; 011-33-1-45-61-53-56), and **Executive Language Services** (20 rue Sainte Croix de la Bretonnerie, 75004 Paris; 011-33-1-44 54 58 71; www.els-france.com), who between them employ over 100 teachers on a short- or long-term basis.

Most expat meeting places in Paris distribute the free bilingual newsletter *France-USA Contacts* www.fusac.org that comes out every other Wednesday. Its classified ads are best followed up on the day the paper appears. It is also a good place to put your own "Work wanted" ad, which will cost $20 for 20 words. You can do this ahead of time by contacting FUSAC in the U.S. at P.O. Box 115, Coopers Station, New York, NY 10276 (212-777-5553, fax 212-777-5554).

An interesting development in the TEFL world is teaching by telephone, which is becoming more and more popular among language learners both for its convenience and for the anonymity. For many people, making mistakes over the phone is less embarrassing than face to face. Apparently this method of teaching is great fun for teachers since the anonymity prompts people to spill out all their secrets. It is not necessary to be able to speak French, though you will need to have access to a computer and telephone. One company which specializes in this is Telab Cours de Langues par Telephone www.telab.com.

Germany: Business and IT Experience Can Help

Although Germany is a Eurocentric country, it is generally more tolerant of U.S. nationals working in certain sectors than its neighbors are, and that includes English teaching. People with a strong business or IT background and a knowledge of German might find their applications acceptable to the hundreds of language training companies in every German city, like **Leipzig Language Service,** Paul-List-Str. 8, 04103 Leipzig; Tel./fax 011-49-341-211-12 82; artes@planet-interkom.de which employs a substantial number of native speakers. Both the **Inlingua** and **Linguarama** groups have an extensive network of schools and frequently post vacancies on their web sites www.inlingua.com and www.linguarama.com. For example, the Inlingua school in Munich employs about 30 native speaker teachers for whom the minimum requirement is a university degree; Inlingua, Sendlinger-Tor-Platz 6, 80336 Munich; 011-49-89-231-15-30; muenchen@inlingua.de. The central contact address for **Lingarama Spracheninstitut Deutschland** is Rindermarkt 16, 80331 Munich; 011-49-89-260 7040 where again the emphasis is on teaching business English.

Speakers of American English will obviously have a better chance of finding teaching hours at an institute which caters to that market, like the **German American Institute** in Tubingen, Karlstrasse 3, 72072 Tubingen; 011-49-7071 795260; www.dai-tuebingen.de.

Adult education courses are offered throughout Germany at about 1,000 Volkhochschulen. English teachers must apply to the individual centers whose addresses are listed on the central web site www.vhs.de. Another major employer is **Carl Duisberg Centren** (Hansaring 49-51, 50670 Cologne; 011-49-221-1626-258; fki@cdc.de.) Students of German who would like to spend a year as an English language assistant in a German secondary school can contact the German organization that oversees the exchange, the **Padagogischer Austauschdienst** (Postfach 22 40, 53012 Bonn; 011-49-228-0228 501-0; www.kmk.org/pad/home.htm) distributes information on the teaching assistant program in Germany, which is also available through the Institute of International Education, 809 United Nations Plaza, New York, NY 10017-3580.

Greece: Permits Required, Difficult to Obtain

Fewer Americans teach in Greece because of visa difficulties. Non-European teachers need a teacher's license plus work and residence permits, and the Ministry of Education delays and often refuses to grant them. Americans of Greek extraction might consider claiming citizenship (while bearing in mind that this might make them liable to compulsory national service). A prospective teacher must obtain a letter of hire from the employer sent to an address outside Greece. The teacher then takes the letter to the nearest Greek consulate and applies for a work permit, a procedure that takes at least two months. Detailed information about obtaining the correct documents are posted in the U.S. Embassy site www.usembassy.gr/consular/residency.htm. Yet a number of schools, especially small ones in remote locations, may be prepared to tackle the bureaucratic procedures. Decisions are often based more on whether or not you hit it off with the interviewer than on your qualifications and experience, though a good university degree is essential.

The best times to look are early September, or possibly again at the beginning of January. Finding work in the summer in Athens is impossible.

It is normally necessary to knock on the doors of *frontisteria*, the private language crammers attended by the vast majority of secondary school students outside school hours. To find out about local *frontisteria*, contact the local branch of PALSO, the Pan-Hellenic Association of Language School Owners. By asking enough questions (try the local English language bookshop) you can find individual school addresses. The current monthly wage is the Euro equivalent of $650 gross. It should be possible to supplement wages with private tutoring at a rate of about $13-$15 an hour.

Spain: Market for English Teachers May Have Peaked

Recent years have seen unprecedented economic growth in Spain as business and industry forged ahead in the wake of European economic unification. Few job interviews would have omitted the question, "Can you speak English?" It seems now the market has peaked and the boom in English is over.

Work permit applications must be lodged in the applicant's country of residence and collected there as well, sometimes months later. Although teachers from outside the E.U. are occasionally hired on the spot by "storefront" schools and paid cash, the wage will normally be below the going rate. The area of the market that continues to grow is the teaching of children, starting with the pre-school age group. A knowledge of Spanish is virtually essential if you are going to teach young children (with whom the total immersion method is not really suitable).

The probable scenario for the new arrival is that he or she will elicit mild interest from one or two schools and will be told to contact the school again at the beginning of term when a few hours of teaching may be offered. Spanish students sign up for English classes during September and into early October; consequently, the academies do not know how many classes they will offer and how many teachers they will need until quite late. It can become a war of nerves; if you can afford to stay you have an increasingly good chance of becoming established.

Jobseekers in Madrid mainly rely on the *Yellow Pages* and the *Madrid Blue Pages* (a directory organized by street address). It is possible to pick out language schools in neglected neighborhoods this way, i.e., near where you are staying. It is also worth checking advertisements in the press, like *La Vanguardia* in Barcelona (especially the Sunday edition) and *El Pais* in Madrid. Alternatively, of course, you can simply wander the streets looking for schools. The density is so high that you are bound to come across them. Wherever you are looking for work, you can consult the Yellow Pages online at www.paginas-amarillas.es.

Several independent TEFL training organizations train large numbers of North Americans and acquiring an English language teaching certificate through one of these would be a good way of getting to know the local scene in Madrid or Barcelona (though the work permit problem persists). Investigate for example **Via Lingua** www.benedictinternational.co.uk/ctefl who runs training courses in Madrid, Barcelona and Malaga; ITC English www.itc-training.com and **Passport TEFL,** www.passportTEFL.com. Because schools run the whole gamut from prestigious to cowboy, every method of job-hunting works at some level. The big chains like **Berlitz** are probably a good bet for the novice teacher because of the stability of hours they can offer. Anyone hired by Berlitz receives a free week-long training course in the Berlitz Method. Similarly the **Wall Street Institutes** with scores of academies in Spain and a head office in Barcelona (Rambla de Catalunya 2-4, 2a Planta, 08007 Barcelona; www.wsi.es) are always looking for teachers whom they train in their own method. Another major chain is **Opening Schools** also headquartered in Barcelona (www.openingschool.com). One of the few organizations to favour U.S. nationals over Europeans is the **IEN Institut Nord-america** (Via Augusta 123, 08006 Barcelona; www.ien.es) but to work for them you need at least two years of experience in teaching both adults and children and you must be prepared to wait 6-8 months for the work permit to be processed.

Many language schools and youth organizations run summer schools and camps for children and adolescents. For voluntary work as an English assistant on summer camps, try **Relaciones Culturales,** a youth exchange organization at Calle Ferraz 82, 28008 Madrid; 011-34-91-541-7103, fax 011-34-91-559-1181; www.clubrci.es, which also places native speakers with Spanish families who want to practice English in exchange for providing room and board. Another agency involved in this sort of live-in placement is **Castrum,** Ctra. Ruedas 33, 47008 Valladolid; 011-34-983-222213; info@castrum.org; their placement fee is Euro 160.

Portugal: Demand for Teachers Mostly in North

Unlike in Spain, some schools in Portugal claim to be willing to hire non-European nationals. According to official sources, once an American finds a teaching job in Portugal he or she can apply for the appropriate permits locally. After arrival, take the contract of employment to the local aliens office (Serviço de Estrangeiros e Fronteiras—in Lisbon the SEF is at Avenida António Augusto Aguiar 20; 011-351-21-315-9681) or to the local police. The permit obtained here is sent off together with the contract of employment to the Ministry of Labor. The final stage is to take a letter of good conduct provided by the teacher's own embassy to the police for the work and resident permit.

Outside the cities, where there have traditionally been large expatriate communities, schools cannot depend on English speakers just showing up and so must recruit well in advance of the academic year. The demand for English teachers is mostly in the north. Apart from in the main cities of Lisbon and Oporto, jobs crop up in historic provincial centers such as Coimbra and Braga and in small seaside towns like Aveiro and Póvoa do Varzim. The small group **Royal School of Languages** (Av. Lourenco Peixinho 92-2°, Andar and Rua Jose Rabumba 2, 3800 Aveiro; www.royalschooloflanguages.pt) employs about 30 teachers with TEFL certificates in their nine schools in small towns. These can be a welcome destination for teachers burned out from teaching in big cities or first-time teachers who want to avoid the rat race. Both the main cities of Lisbon and Oporto have American Language Institutes which prefer to employ teachers from the U.S.; the ALI in Lisbon can be contacted on ali@mail.telepac.pt.

Italy: Work Permits Difficult to Obtain

Red tape is most daunting in Italy, and work permits are virtually impossible for non-E.U. citizens to obtain. There is a pronounced bias towards hiring Britons as indicated by the names of the main language school chains, the **British Schools Group, British Colleges, British Institutes, Oxford Schools**. Yet there are also those willing to hire qualified Americans, such as the **Interlingue School of Languages** in Rome (Via E. Q. Visconti 20, 00193 Rome; 011-39-06-321 5740).

Yet enrollment in English language schools continues to increase at a dramatic rate among ordinary Italians, and there will always be schools that choose not to comply with the very strict labor regulations. Milan is considered a promising destination, even for unqualified non-Europeans. Yet it is not just the sophisticated urbanites of Rome, Florence, and Milan who long to learn English. Small towns in Sicily and Sardinia, in the Dolomites, and along the Adriatic all have more than their fair share of private language schools and institutes. As in Spain, a number of organizations run language summer camps, among them **ACLE Summer & City Camps,** Via Roma 54, 18038 San Remo; tel./fax 011-39-0184 506070; www.acle.org. Summer counsellors must enrol in a short training course for Euro 150 and are paid Euro 170-190 per week plus board and accommodation. Summer counsellors and language tutors aged 19-28 are recruited for Italian camps by the Canadian company Scotia Personnel Ltd., www.scotia-personnel-ltd.com.

Italy has a complete range of language schools, as the heading Scuole di Lingue in any Yellow Pages will confirm; the Pagine Gialle can be consulted on www.pagine-gialle.it. At the elite end of the market, there is a handful of schools (35 at present) which belong to AISLI, the Associazione Italiana Scuole di Lingua Inglese, administered from Via Campanella 16, 41100 Modena; www.eaquals.org linked to AISLI. Strict regulations exclude all but ultra-respectable schools.

Another possibility is to set up as a freelance tutor, though a knowledge of Italian is even more an asset here than is knowing the local language elsewhere in Europe. You can post notices in supermarkets, tobacconists, and primary and secondary schools. It may be worth advertising in a local paper.

Perspective

Teach English in Spain?

It's Possible, But Only if You Have *Ganas*

By Kate Doyle

For several years it's been illegal for language academies and companies in Spain to hire non-E.U. residents; however, many still hire North Americans and Australians without proper papers. While finding a job is about four times as difficult for an American as it is for a Brit, it is entirely possible if you have *ganas* (gumption) and the energy and savings for a possibly long job search. If you must teach in Spain, here are some suggestions:

Research your destination. Think about the city size that you'll be most comfortable with and the surrounding areas you'd like to visit. In general it's better to start off in a city where the number of schools and companies gives you better odds. Keep in mind that the cost of living is generally lower in southern Spain and highest in Madrid and Barcelona.

Enroll in a teacher-training course in your desination city. This is particularly important if you've never taught before. One-month intensive courses, offered by several large organizations, are rigorous and notoriously difficult. But having a certificate makes getting work easier, and, more importantly, it gives you some know-how in the classroom. Having English as your mothertongue and a great personality does not necessarily make you a good English teacher.

While the course will keep you incredibly busy, you will inevitably become friends with other students in the school. Business contacts develop quickly this way. Bulletin board postings in the language schools are vital, too. It's unlikely that you'll have much time to fax or hit the pavement till your course is over, but with minimum effort you could have a list of leads to explore upon finishing.

Another good option or complement to a teacher-training course is a short Spanish class—especially if you have never studied it. You will need Spanish for everything you do here when you're not teaching English, and it's another good way to meet people in and around a school. Through either course you can do a family homestay or share an apartment with young Spaniards. Both options can lead to English teaching job leads.

Save money. Academies only offer jobs onsite, so you'll have to job search here. While the peseta-dollar exchange rate is favorable for Americans, you should still aim to have several thousand dollars at your disposal to cover a basic U.S. healthcare plan while you are away, a teacher training course, and living expenses while you find a job and an apartment. Everyone here, regardless of profession, is paid once a month, so you'll want to have the first of couple months of rent before you start working. And, of course, you won't get rich teaching English anywhere, so it's nice to have some dollars for occasional luxuries.

The job hunt. Prepare a special seeking-English-teaching-job resume. Most training courses will advise you on the contents and the accepted European style. Academies receive hordes of resumes; the more succinct and clear yours is, the more you will stand out. Visiting schools in person is best. Be prepared for automatic rejection if you don't have proper papers, but pay attention to how emphatically the schools say no. In the mad rush of early October, many administrators change their tune. The same holds for employment agencies that place English teachers in companies. If you appear at the right time, they make exceptions.

Working illegally has few disadvantages. It means you don't sign a contract, and in theory the stability factor is lower. But it also means you don't pay taxes. In some cases you will be paid in cash, while some schools and agencies will give you a monthly pay-to-bearer check cashable at a designated bank.

When to go. The end of September is the best time to look for work, since hires are made at the last minute possible. August and September, then, are the months to arrive and get settled here so that you're ready to teach when most schools begin in October.

Language schools offer few classes during the summer, and companies offer none. And, of course, cities slow to a crawl in August, the traditional month of vacations. All this makes it nearly impossible to find work without proper papers.

So yes, a bit of a *lio* (trouble) awaits you if your American heart is set on teaching on the Iberian penninsula (or in other E.U. countries for that matter), but Americans without credentials can teach in Spain—if they come with enough time and money and inform themselves upon arriving.

On Being Legal

The tourist time limit throughout the E.U. is three months. To stay longer, technically you must have either a work/residency visa or a student visa.

To obtain a work visa, find a school, employment agency, or company that is willing to petition the Spanish government for your residency/working papers. The employer must prove that a Spanish native cannot do the job adequately. With a huge number of Brits, Scots, and Irish looking for work, very few schools are willing to do this. It takes up to 12 months to complete the process, in which time you must fly to the U.S. to obtain and sign documents.

A student visa, which must be obtained before leaving the U.S., allows you stay a minumum of six months. You must apply in person at a Spanish consulate. You will need a passport valid for a minimum of six months, four recent passport photos, original letter from a school or university saying you are a full-time paid-up student, a letter typed on doctor's stationery saying that you are in good health, and one of the following: $350 in traveler's checks per month of stay in Spain, a bank account in a Spanish bank with a minimum balance of $350 per month of stay in Spain, a letter from a study abroad program assuming full financial responsibility for tuition, room, and board for the length of stay in Spain and proof of having received financial aid covering expenses for tuition, room, board and personal expenses ($350 per month).

For more visa information, visit www.spainconsul-ny.org.

The Eastern Mediterranean

English Teachers in Demand

By Susan Griffith

Turkey: Middle Class Eager to Learn

The increasingly prosperous Turkish middle classes are more eager than ever to learn English. Dozens of private secondary schools *(lises)* and a few universities use English as the language of instruction, and many secondary schools hire native speaking teachers. Among the main indigenous language teaching organizations (see addresses below) are **Interlang** (employs about 40 native speakers in three schools), **Dilko English,** and **The English Centre,** all in Istanbul. Although Istanbul is not the capital, it is the commercial, financial, and cultural center of Turkey, so this is where most of the EFL teaching goes on. For less competition, consider Ankara and other inland cities.

A TEFL qualification may not be a prerequisite, but a university degree and a commitment to stay for a year usually are. Private language schools will expect you to work the usual unsocial hours and may chop and change your timetable at short notice, while lises offer daytime working hours plus (sometimes onerous) extracurricular duties such as marking tests, attending school ceremonies, etc.

Wages and working conditions often leave much to be desired. Teachers complain that the accommodations supplied by employers may be worse than mediocre and far from the workplace. Teachers have had difficulty collecting promised wages on time. Rampant inflation can cause a salary that seems reasonable at the beginning of the year worth far less at the end of nine months.

Egypt: Prosperous Residents Employ Private Tutors

Institutions like the American Univ. in Cairo and the International Language Institute Heliopolis have very exacting standards. At the other end of the spectrum there are plenty of commercial language institutes, often located in the back streets of Cairo, which are less fussy about the backgrounds of their teaching staff.

In prosperous residential areas like Heliopolis, Mardi, and Zamalek anyone who can cultivate contacts may be able to set up private lessons. If you have no acquaintances among affluent Cairenes you will have to advertise with notices written in Arabic and English or in the expatriate press. A simpler way to advertise your availability might be to place an ad in the expatriate monthly *Egypt Today* or try the notice board at the **Community Services Association** (No. 4 Road 21, Maadi, Cairo; www.csa-egypt.com) where expats sign up for adult education courses.

Partly because inflation is very high in Egypt, expenses are low. This is also true for the TEFL training course offered by the American Univ. in Cairo and the International Language Institute.

Most teachers enter Egypt on a tourist visa (which you can purchase at the airport), then ask their school to obtain a work permit for them from the Ministry of the Interior. Work permits are not processed abroad.

Morocco: English Gaining Prominence

Although Morocco is a Francophone country, English has gained prominence in both academic and business circles. Ten American Language Centers in all the main cities (see below) employ a number of native speakers—some as part of a Visiting Teachers Program.

The Moroccan Ministry of Labor stipulates that all foreign teachers have a university degree to qualify for a work permit. Permits are obtained after arrival. Although knowing French is not a formal requirement, it is a great asset for anyone planning to spend time in Morocco. The hourly rate of pay is between $9 and $12. Net salaries for contract teachers are 8,000-9,000 dirhams per month.

Eastern Mediterranean Language Schools

Turkey

Active English, Ataturk Bulvari 127/701, Selcan Hanbakanliklar, 06640 Ankara; 011-90-312-418-4975; www.acteng.com.

Antik English, Bakirkoy, Istanbul; 011-90-212-570-4847; Taksim, Istanbul 011-90-212-293 5600; antiktaksim@hotmail.com.

Best English, Bayinder Sokak No. 53, Kizilay, Ankara; 011-90-312-417-6063; www.bestenglish.com.tr.

Dilko English, Hatboyu Caddesi No. 16, 34720 Bakirkoy, Istanbul; 011-90-212-570-1270; info@dilko.com.tr. Sixty teachers for 4 centers in Istanbul.

The English Centre, Rumeli Caddesi 92/4, Zeki Bey Apt., Osmanbey, Istanbul; 011-90-212-247-0983; www.englishcentre.com. Also in Ankara.

English Time, Karokolhane Cad. No. 4, Kadikoy, Istanbul; 011-90-216-330-3055; www.englishtime.com. Five branches in Istanbul.

Interlang, Istanbul Cad., Halkei Sok, Yalcinlar Han. No. 4, Kat 2-5, Bakirkoy, Istanbul; Tel./fax 011-90-212-418-3910; www.interlang.com.uk.

Istanbul Language Centre, Yakut Sok. No. 10, Bakirkoy, Istanbul; 011-90-212-82 84-94; ilm@ilm.com.tr. Forty teachers in 4 branches.

Egypt

American Univ. in Cairo, Division of Public Service, English Language Program, Room 108, Falaki St., Cairo; 011-20-2-354-2964-9/354 6870; in the U.S., 420 5th Ave., 3rd Fl., New York, NY 10018-2729; 212-730-8800; www.aucegypt.edu.

ELS Language Centres/Middle East (ELSME), P.O. Box 3079, Abu Dhabi, United Arab Emirates.; 011-971-2-651516; Elseme@emirates.net.ae, www.elsme.com. "Minimum requirements BA, TEFL Certificate and 2 years experience."

International Language Institute, 2 Mohamed Bayoumi St., off Merghany St., Heliopolis, Cairo; ili@idsc.net.eg. Offers RSA/Cambridge Certificate course seven times a year.

Amideast American Cultural Center, English Teaching Program, 3 El Pharana St., Alexandria; Tel. 011-20-3-483-1922, fax 011-20-3-483-9644; www.amideast.org.

Morocco

American Language Center, rue des Nations-Unies, Cite Suisse, Agadir; 011-212-48-821589.

American Language Center, 1 Place de la Fraternite, Casablanca 2000; 011-212-22-277765; casa_dir@aca.org.ma; http://casablanca.aca.org.ma.

American Language Center, Rue de Sebta, Complexe Mont Joli, 2nd Fl., Apt/15, Mohammedia; 011-212-23-326870.

American Language Center, 4 Zankat Tanj, Rabat 10000; 011-212-37-766121, fax 011-212-7-767255; alcrabat@mtds.com. Has 25 full-time and 20 part-time teachers.

Business and Professional English Centre, 74 rue Jean Jaurès, Casablanca; 011-212-22-470279, fax 011-212-22-296861. Several qualified teachers needed to teach professionals and executives.

EF English First, rue du Marche, Residence Benomar, Maaris, Casablanca; 011-212-22-255-174.

Tunisia

Amideast Tunisia, 22 Rue Al Amine Al Abassi, B.P. 351, Cité Jardins 1002, Tunis, Tunisia; 011-216-71-790559; tunisia@amideast.org.

Work in Egypt
Get a Tourist Visa and Take Your Time Looking

By Jane E. Cuccia

Finding a teaching job in Egypt is a bit more difficult now than in the past. Private K-12s, where the language of instruction is English, now annually produce graduates fluent in both English and Arabic who go on to take positions previously filled by native speakers. Since most adult students want to know enough English to understand business and acquire computer skills, Americans who want to teach in Egypt will do better if they are specialized in one of these two fields rather than in general language skills.

Plenty of jobs do exist, but it will be easier to find what you want if you are already in Egypt and have enough funds to see you through two or three months. Come on a tourist visa and take your time looking around.

Cairo American College is a private K-12 school totally American in its system and therefore in the qualifications of its teachers. It caters to the children of diplomats and of other expatriates living in Egypt for a limited time. The tuition is extremely high, and teachers are paid on an American salary scale. For more information check out their web site, www.cac.edu.eg.

The Center for Adult and Continuing Education (CACE) of the American Univ. in Cairo hires a limited number of teachers to teach English as a second language. Interviews are granted to five applicants a month. Only teachers with long experience or an internationally recognized certificate in teaching English to adults are hired. More information about the CACE can be found at their web site http://CACEstudent.aucegypt.edu or at www.aucegypt.edu.

The internationally famous **Berlitz School of Languages** usually hires full-timers, trains them in their methodology, and pays well. Their web site, www. berlitz.com, lists vacancies here and in their branches worldwide.

Amideast, www.amideast.org promotes intercultural understanding between the U.S. and countries of the Middle East. It hires only very qualified teachers.

The British Council, www.britishcouncil.org.eg, another intercultural organization, favors British English speakers and insists on British certification. The **International Language Institute (ILI)** offers an instructor training course but no guarantee of a job upon completion of the course.

Numerous nursery schools around Cairo are looking for native speakers to work with preschool children. A love of children is more important than certification.

Tutoring Egyptian language school students is another possibility, but I don't advise it unless you know the people you'll be getting involved with or they come highly recommended. Strangers might set up appointments with you out of curiosity or with ulterior motives.

Job Information

A very useful publication is the *Maadi Messenger,* published by volunteers and available at English-speaking churches and in districts with expatriate communities, such as Maadi, Zamalek, and Heliopolis. Jobs, such as babysitting and tutoring of

American children, are often listed. *The Middle East Times* also occasionally lists jobs. Many jobs are not listed anywhere, however; it is up to the person to find one by applying at the human resources or personnel office of a company or school and wait for results.

The *Cairo Yellow Pages,* listing many businesses both in the capital and in Alexandria, is available online at www.egyptyellowpages.com.eg. Searching under "Schools" and "Language Training" will lead you to updated contact information.

Learning "survival Arabic" will make your stay much easier. Taxi drivers and store employees do not always speak English. The institutions mentioned above offer all levels of Arabic at competitive prices.

Tourists report that Egyptians are the friendliest people they have ever met; they constantly help friends, acquaintances, or total strangers. So if you decide to visit Egypt for an extended period of time, you need never feel alone or isolated.

New Destinations

ESL Teaching Jobs in Central and Eastern Europe

By Susan Griffith

The dramatic changes which took place in the former Communist bloc more than a decade ago mean that over the past decade native speakers of English have flooded the major population centers, taking advantage of the unprecedented demand for Western input. Americans, Britons, and other foreigners have been hired by companies, boards of education, tourism authorities, and governments from Kraków to Kiev. Thousands of joint ventures have been launched and academic alliances forged between East and West, almost all of them underpinned by the English language.

The stable Central European states of Hungary, Poland, the Czech Republic, and Slovakia have largely found their democratic feet. The situation for prospective English teachers has settled down so that now it is almost essential to have some ESL training and/or experience, or at the very least friends and contacts in situ, in order to get a full-time job as an English instructor in Prague or Budapest. Vacancies tend to be in the less appealing industrial cities and provincial towns.

The demand for native speakers of English—with or without qualifications—is still increasing in the less developed parts of Eastern and Central Europe, especially in the Baltic states and other former satellite republics of Russia. In many of these regions, economic hardship prevails, which means that relatively few paid opportunities exist for expatriate teachers. Although ordinary people are very keen to learn English, they cannot afford to pay for a course of English lessons. These countries are desperate to develop economic links with the West; yet their economies are not strong enough to attract commercial language schools from the U.S. and Britain.

In other former Eastern bloc nations huge strides have been made in turning around the state-controlled economies and there will be a great demand for native EFL teachers for many years. And though these may not be the best-paid EFL jobs,

Eastern Europe offers historic and beautiful cities, gregarious and open-minded people, and a unique chance to experience life in the "other Europe."

A number of independent placement organizations and commercial companies in the U.S. and U.K. send teachers to Eastern and Central Europe. Such programs (some are listed below) are designed primarily for individuals in search of a cultural experience who don't mind financing themselves.

Anyone with a relevant resume should contact the well-established schools in East European cities. To find the smaller schools on the spot, check the English language press, look for notices in English language bookshops or at universities, try to meet teachers in their favorite watering holes, or ask the U.S. Embassy if it can offer any advice.

Russia and the Newly Independent States: A TEFL Boom

Due to the political and economic difficulties Russia has been undergoing in recent years, some private schools have closed or, at best, reduced their teaching staffs. But the mainstream academic institutes and international language chains continue to recruit teachers abroad. Anyone with contacts anywhere in the (no longer) Newly Independent States, or who is prepared to go there to make contacts, should be able to arrange a teaching niche on an individual basis, always assuming money is no object.

The development of the oil industry in the Caspian Sea has resulted in an unexpected economic boom (and therefore a TEFL boom) in the former Soviet republics of Kazakhstan, Azerbaijan, Uzbekistan, and Turkmenistan. The U.S. investment in infrastructure may gradually result in a switch from Russian to American English as the language of commerce.

In the mid-1990s, the Soros Foundation moved into the region, recruiting a number of ELT professionals to introduce modern methodology in English teaching to local schools. Since the Central Asian republics became independent, the old Soviet order has quickly evaporated. For example, Almaty, the capital of Kazakhstan—the ninth largest country in the world—is now a relatively cosmopolitan city with international hotels and private language schools. Yet it is still impossible to enter the country without an official invitation from a sponsor.

Petro-Teach has nothing to do with the petroleum industry. This teaching internship program based in St. Petersburg places teachers and students of Russian in the state education system for an academic year. Fee-paying participants must be college graduates and apply by June 1 for a September starting date or by December 1 for the spring program. Accommodations are with Russian families. Information is available from Dr. Polly Gannon, Westport, P.O. Box 109, Lappeenranta, Finland 53101; gannon@online.ru, www.petroteach.com.

The Teacher Internship Program run by Project Harmony in Vermont which arranged for college graduates to work in host schools in Russia and the Ukraine ceased operating in 2000. A new possibility is to apply to the Svezhy Veter Travel Agency, P.O. Box 2040, 426000 Izhevsk, Russia (3412-512500/fax 3412-752268; www.sv-agency.udm.ru which runs a number of programs in the seldom-visited city of Izhevsk between Moscow and the Urals. Native speakers can be placed at a local secondary school to teach 15 hours a week in exchange for homestay accommodation, meals and visa support. The agency is also working to develop a program to place English-speakers on summer camps and in work experience.

Applicants for a visa to teach in Russia need a letter of invitation from their employer and an official document issued by the Russian Ministry of Foreign Affairs. The invitation procedure may take up to a month, unless a premium fee is paid to hasten the process.

Baltic States: Looking Toward the West

Arguably the most westernized of the old Russian states, Lithuania, Latvia, and Estonia are looking toward a future as part of Western Europe. Estonia seems to be the most progressive while Latvia has changed the least and at present can offer very few paid TEFL possibilities. However, there are some volunteer opportunities.

The International Exchange Center (2 Republic Sq., 1010 Riga, Latvia; 011-371-2-327476; info@iec.lv) invites volunteers to work as counselors in summer camps for children in Latvia (and also Russia, Ukraine and Belarus), though these are not primarily English language summer camps. There is a registration fee of $120. By all accounts the living conditions at these camps are extremely spartan.

Lithuania, on the other hand, desperately needs English teachers, especially in Kaunas, the second largest city. The Ministry of Education and Science will try to place anyone with a degree by calling schools to arrange interviews. The very low pay can be supplemented with private tutoring. Accommodations with a family follow easily. No background in teaching is required, but a week's preparatory course on teaching in Vilnius is offered. Contact the Teacher Training Office, Ministry of Education and Science, Volano Gatve 2/7, 2600 Vilnius, Lithuania; 011-370-2-622483, fax 011-370-2-612077; www.smm.lt.

The American Professional Partnership for Lithuanian Education (APPLE), 1114 Golfside Dr., Winter Park, FL 32792; 401-671-0189; www.applequest.org places English teachers from the U.S. in Lithuanian high schools each academic year.

Ukraine: Serious Shortage of Teachers

Ukraine has a serious shortage of English teachers, among other things. In addition to the placement organizations already mentioned which send volunteers to the Ukraine, several emigré organizations in the U.S. recruit volunteers, warning that teachers must be prepared to accept a modest standard of living.

The Ukrainian National Foundation, 2200 Route 10, P.O. Box 280, Parsippany, NJ 07054; 973-292-9800; mylsko@unamember.com sends volunteer teachers to scores of Ukrainian cities during the summer.

Czech and Slovak Republics: Opportunities in Small Towns

More than a decade after the Velvet Revolution of 1989, Western-backed language schools have been joined by many private schools run by locals in both the Czech and Slovak republics. While there seems to be an equal demand for English in both republics, the majority of TEFL teachers tend to gravitate to the Czech Republic, partly because there are more established language schools in Prague than Bratislava.

Unless you have a recognized TEFL qualification, it remains very difficult to obtain employment in the Czech capital because of the competition from other foreigners. Some of the smaller Czech towns, including the Moravian capital Brno, offer teachers more opportunities.

Qualified EFL teachers are being recruited to teach in primary and secondary schools, usually on a 1-year contract with low-cost or free accommodations and a salary of at least 8,000-11,000 crowns (about $220-$300) net per month. The centralized contact is the **Academic Information Agency** (AIA) in Prague, part of the Ministry of Education. The AIA simply acts as a go-between, circulating resumes and applications to state schools, which then contact applicants directly. Its web site includes updated school vacancies with contact details.

The English language *Prague Post,* www.praguepost.com carries classified advertisements including some job vacancies. In Bratislava, check the *Slovak Spectator* published every other Thursday.

Academic Information Agency, Dum Zahranicnich sluzeb MSMT, Senovázné nám. 26, P.O. Box 8, 110 06 Prague 1, Czech Republic; 011-420-2-24-22-96-98; www.dzs.cz/aia/lektori.htm.

Akademia Vzdelavania, Gorkého 10, 815 17 Bratislava, Slovak Republic; 011-42-12-544 10033; www2.aveducation.sk. Has many adult education centers around Slovakia.

Akademie J. A. Komenskeho, Trziste 20, Mala Strana, 118 43 Prague 1, Czech Republic; 011-4290205753 1476; akademie@login.cz; www.akademie.cz. Many posts available as English lecturers in 50 adult education centers and schools throughout the Czech Republic.

Akcent International House Prague, Bítovská 3, 14000 Prague 4, Czech Republic; 011-420-2-6126 16 38; info@akcent.cz. Positions for qualified teachers in and outside Prague.

Anglictina Expres, Korunni 2, 12000, Prague 2, Czech Republic; Tel./fax 011-420-2-2251 3040; www.anexpres.cz. Employs up to 20 teachers.

Caledonian School, Vltavska 24, 150 00 Prague 5, Czech Republic; jobs@caledonianschool.com. Employs over 100 teachers with TEFL background to teach English in Prague and Bratislava to professionals, many working for American companies. North American Director of Professional Recruitment may be contacted by fax at 416-231-1730.

Poland: More Jobs Than Other Central European Countries

Prospects for English teachers in Poland remain more promising than in the rest of Central Europe. Even the major cities like Warsaw, Wroclaw, Kraków, Poznan, and Gdansk are hopeful destinations for the job-seeking teacher, though the job hunt is predictably easier in the lesser-known cities and towns. As in the Czech and Slovak Republics, possibilities exist in both state and private schools. Any number of school directors are delighted to interview native English speakers who present themselves in a professional manner. But it must be borne in mind that although the reverence for native speakers of English still runs high, the EFL public in Poland has slowly become more selective. Interested teachers should not expect to be snapped up by every high-quality school to which they apply unless they have at least a TEFL certificate and some sort of teaching experience.

Contacting private schools ahead of time may produce some interest, though it is much easier to find a job on the spot. Would-be teachers should dutifully do the rounds of the *Dyrektors*.

The current average wage in the private sector is the zloty equivalent of $10 an hour (gross). The standard deduction is 21 percent for taxes and contributions. As long as there's subsidized or affordable housing, this is enough for teachers working at least 20 hours a week, though most foreigners supplement this income with tutoring.

Albion Language Services, Noakowskiego 26/26, 00-668 Warsaw, Poland; Tel./fax 011-48-22-628-89-92; languages@albion.com.pl. Teachers receive assistance with accommodations and visas. Local interviews essential.

English School of Communication Skills, ul. Agnieszki 2/Ip, 31-068 Krakow, Poland; Tel./fax 011-48-14-621-37-69; www.escs.pl. Private language schools that employ teachers, also runs summer language camps.

English Unlimited, ul. Podmlynska 10, 80-885 Poland; Tel./fax 011-48-58-301-3373; kamila@eu.com.pl. A large English language school with seven centers around Gdansk, Sopot, and Gdynia.

JDJ College, ul. Bninska 26, Poznan, Poland; 011-48-61-827-71-24; irosiak@jdj.com.pl. 35-45 experienced teachers for 16 language schools throughout Poland. Employer has flats available in some towns.

Profi-Lingua, ul. 3 Maja 10/2, 40-096 Katowice, Poland; 011-48-32-253-05-19; www.profi-lingua.pl. Up to 20 teachers who must have a TEFL certificate and a year's experience.

Target Professional English Consultants, ul. Polna 50, 7th Fl., 00-644 Warsaw, Poland; fax 011-48-22-870 35 57; jobs@target.it.pl. Large language provider employing 50 teachers.

York School of English, ul. Mackiewicza 12, 31-213 Krakow, Poland; 011-48-12-415 1818; www.york.edu.pl. Employs teachers of many nationalities.

Hungary: Opportunities Are Mostly in Provinces

Partly because the Hungarian language is so difficult to master and partly because of the success of the program to retrain teachers who taught Russian in the bad old days, many schools prefer native Hungarians as English teachers. Despite this, a demand for qualified native speakers still exists, especially in the business market. For example **In2itiv Language Services in Budapest** (Kardow u. 3, 1028 Budapest; 011-36-30-999-86-64) employs native speakers of all nationalities who can make language lessons fun.

The invasion by foreigners of Budapest was never as overwhelming as it was (and is) in Prague, but Budapest still has a glut of teachers. More opportunities exist in the provinces though, even in the more remote parts of the country, formal academic qualifications are important.

Central Europe: English Schools and Placement Organizations

Bridges for Education, Applications Coordinator, 94 Lamarck Dr., Buffalo, NY 14226; 716-839-0180, fax 716-839-9493; mdodge@frontiernet.com, www.bridges4edu.org. Sends groups of teachers and unskilled teaching assistants to summer language camps in Eastern Europe.

Central European Teaching Program, Beloit College, 700 College St., Beloit, WI 53511; 608-363-2619; cetp@beloit.edu, www.beloit.edu/~cetp. About 90 placements in state schools in Hungary, Romania, Poland. The program offers "cultural immersion through teaching" and is open to anyone with a university degree, some experience of TEFL, a strong interest in the region, and $3,450 for the placement fee and return airfares. The deadline for a fall start date is mid-March.

EF (English First) Education, Human Resources, 1 Education St., Cambridge, MA 02141; 617-716-1775; Careers@ef.com. European office: Teacher Recruitment Centre, EF House, 1-3 Farman St., Hove, East Sussex BN3 1AL; 011-44-1273 747308; recruitment.uk@englishfast.com. Expanding group of schools worldwide with vacancies for TEFL-trained teachers in Russia (mainly Moscow), Lithuania, Poland, Azerbaijan, and Slovenia.

International TEFL Certificate, Kaprova 14, 110 00 Prague 1; 011-420-2-2481 4791; info@itc-training.com. Agency matches clients (mainly graduates of the ITC TEFL course) with suitable posts in the Czech Republic and elsewhere in Eastern Europe. Candidates must have a university degree and either a TEFL certificate or relevant experience. Assistance fee charged.

International House, 106 Piccadilly, London W1V 7NL, U.K.; 011-44-207-518 6970, fax 011-44-207-518 6971; hr@ihlondon.co.uk, www.ihworld.com/recruitment/index.htm. One of the first language teaching organizations in Eastern Europe, IH continues to be one of the most active and has expanded into the Central Asian Republics. Open only to teachers with a Cambridge CELTA certificate or equivalent.

i-to-i, 1 Cottage Rd., Headingley, Leeds LS6 4DD, U.K.; 011-44-870-333-2332, fax 011-44-113-274-6923; info@i-to-i.com, www.i-to-i.com. TEFL training company places graduates in short-term voluntary teaching posts in Russia (St. Petersburg), $1,495 for 3 months excluding airfares.

Language Link, 21 Harrington Rd., London SW7 3EU, U.K.; 011-44-207-225-1065; languagelink@compuserve.com, www.languagelink.co.uk. Mainly active in Russia and Slovakia but also has positions in their network of schools. Contracts for new teachers from September pay $500 per month.

Peace Corps, Rm. 803E, 1111 20th St., NW, Washington, DC 20526; 800-424-8580. Electronic application forms are available online at www.peacecorps.gov/assignments/education.cfm. Formal TEFL training is not required though volunteers must have at least 3 months experience of 1-on-1 ESL tutoring or classroom teaching.

Saxoncourt & English Worldwide Recruitment, 124 New Bond St., London W1Y 9AE; 011-44-207-491-1911; recruit@saxoncourt.com. Frequently advertise to fill teacher vacancies in Moscow, Siberia, Poland, and many other countries.

Services for Open Learning, North Devon Professional Centre, Vicarage St., Barnstable, Devon EX32 7HB, U.K.; 011-44-1271-327319, fax 011-44-1271-376650; info@sol.org.uk. U.K. charity recruits graduates to teach in state schools in Belarus, Bulgaria, Croatia, Czech Republic, Hungary, Poland, Romania, Slovenia, and Slovakia for local salaries and accommodations.

Soros Professional English Language Teaching (SPELT) Program, Open Society Institute, 400 W 59th St., 4th Fl., New York, NY 10018; 212-548-0136; spelt@sorosny.org, www.soros.org/spelt. Instructors placed in universities and teacher colleges in most Russian republics from Azerbaijan to Kyrgyzstan. An MA in Linguistics or TESOL is required in most cases.

Teachers for Central and Eastern Europe (TFCEE), 21 V 5 Rackovski Blvd., Dimitrovgrad 6400, Bulgaria; Tel./fax 011-359-391-24787; tfcee@usa.net, www.tfcee.8m.com. Sixty teachers for English language secondary schools in Bulgaria, Czech Republic, Hungary, Poland, and Slovakia.

Teaching & Projects Abroad, Gerrard House, Rustington, W Sussex BN16 1AW, U.K.; 011-44-1903-859911, fax 011-44-1903-785779; info@teaching-abroad.co.uk, www.teaching-abroad.co.uk. Self-funding volunteers are placed in schools in Russia (mainly Moscow), the Ukraine, and Romania, as well as many other countries worldwide. No TEFL background required. Packages cost from £795 for 3 months in Kiev. Volunteers should be prepared to be self-reliant during their stay. Flexible starting dates.

Travellers, 7 Mulberry Close, Ferring, W Sussex BN12 5HY, U.K.; 011-44-1903 700478; teach@travellersworldwide.com. Paying volun-

teers teach conversational English in Russia (Moscow, St. Petersburg and Siberia) and the Ukraine (Kiev and Crimea). Placements last from two months; £1,095 for Moscow excluding airfares.

Perspective

Cobbling in Prague
Jobs Are Here, Just Come and Look

By Nicole Rosenleaf Ritter

To hear the "old" Prague expatriates tell it, the early 1990s were a time when any American, Canadian, Brit, or Australian could arrive in Prague and have a dirt-cheap flat and an outsized income by lunchtime. They worked when they wanted during the day and partied all night on 10-cent beer. Finding a job in Prague that you can live on is no longer so easy.

That said, even with the changes in the residency permit laws, there are jobs here, and the easiest way to find them is still to come here and look. While it's possible to get hired for some positions via email, you run a real risk of tying yourself to something that may not be at all what you had in mind. Best to see the whites of your potential employer's eyes before committing yourself.

Getting Legal

While you must apply for a residency permit outside of the Czech Republic, it's probably not practical to apply from your home country, especially if your home country lies across an ocean.

Some companies will hire you without a residency permit, but beware. If they don't pay, you have no recourse—and I know plenty of expats who have found themselves in just that situation. Once you find a job you feel you can live with for a while, start the legalization process. And be prepared with some savings to live on while you wait to get the permit and get paid.

The Job Hunt

Most expats started out doing whatever work they could find and went from there. Expect to spend a good deal of time, especially if you don't speak Czech, working as a "cobbler"—picking up some English classes here and there or answering an ad for part-time proofreading help or even web design. *The Prague Post,* www.praguepost.cz, the weekly English-language newspaper, is the best place to look for possibilities.

In any given week, 95 percent of the jobs listed in *The Prague Post* are for English teaching positions. While finding a position without a TEFL certificate is not difficult, the training will help you to know what to do on that first day in front of a new class.

Teaching private classes can be more lucrative, but it will be difficult to get your residency permit without an actual employer to back you up. If you do work illegally, just be sure you cross a border before your tourist visa expires.

What's Hot

High-tech skills will take you far—there are numerous Internet start-ups and old veterans in the city. Look for job postings in *The Prague Post,* and also on Monster.com. English-language publications and multinational companies also often advertise for editors, writers, and people with business, marketing, and accounting skills.

Like everywhere, getting the job you want depends upon who you know. I found my current dream job as an editor for an Internet news magazine because I interned for them virtually several years ago and volunteered to do some projects when I first got to Prague. The more people you meet in Prague—not just expats, but especially locals—the better your chances of finding something you're satisfied with.

Until you do, it can be fun to be a cobbler. When I was teaching for three schools and freelancing as an editor and writer, I set my own schedule. Now that I have a more traditional job, my income is steadier but so is the routine. I love what I do, but I also enjoyed my initial Prague lifestyle as a cobbler. Don't be afraid to take similar risks.

Work in Asia
Where and How to Find ESL Jobs

By Susan Griffith

D espite the rumors, a native's knowledge of the English language is not an automatic passport to employment anywhere abroad. It can, however, be put to profitable use in many Asian countries. In Korea, Taiwan, Japan, Thailand and, increasingly, China a high proportion of the population are eager for tuition from English speakers. A university degree in any subject is the only prerequisite, though in some cases just a degree of enthusiasm will suffice.

Most foreign teachers work as employees of privately-run language institutes whose owners are often much more interested in maximizing profits than in maintaining high educational standards. Working as a self-employed private tutor is more lucrative than teaching at an institute but normally requires considerable experience of the market and suitable premises from which to work.

Teachers must be prepared to face a range of problems and disappointments—from the high cost of housing in Japan to ingrained racist attitudes in many quarters—and a resistance to innovation. However, with tact and perseverance it is possible to overcome some of the obstacles encountered by new arrivals.

Persuading shy or under-confident students to speak in class will be a challenge in many Asian contexts. Like teachers the world over, those who can make their classes fun and can encourage students to use the English they already know, however limited, get the best results and find the job more rewarding.

China: An Explosions of Private Language Schools

The Chinese nation is huge and hungry for the English language. For two decades there has been a flow of native speakers from the West to teach at schools and academic institutions around the country. But the past few years have seen a remarkable explosion in the number of private language institutes and companies, something that would have been unthinkable just a few years ago. The emerging middle class aspires to send their children for private tuition just as in the capitalist countries of Taiwan, Korea, and Japan. So a great many opportunities are opening up and are being advertised abroad especially via the Internet. For example the web site www.teach-in-china.com is a goldmine of up-to-date job vacancies—just short of one thousand at the time of writing—and the service is free. Check also wwww.chinatefl.com. The eagerness to import English teachers continues unabated in provincial academic institutes. Many middle schools and normal schools (teacher training colleges) have trouble filling teaching posts and turn to foreign recruitment organizations like **Council Exchanges** which place about 100 U.S. nationals in their Teach in China Program, 633 3rd Ave., 20th Fl., New York, NY 10017; 888-268-6245; teachinchina@councilexchanges.org, www.councilexchanges.org/work/ticfacts. htm. Application deadlines fall on May 1 for a late August departure and early November for departures in mid-February. **The Chinese Education Association for International Exchange (CEAIE),** 37 Damucang Hutong, Beijing 100816; 011-86-10-664 16582, fax 011-86-10-664 16156; www.ceaie.edu.cn recruits for institutes of higher education. CEAIE cooperates with Chinese embassies in the west. A private recruitment agency worth contacting is **China English TeacherLink,** Asian Games Garden No. 2-6A, 12 Xiaoying Lu, Chao Yang District, Beijing 100101; 011-86-10-8463-4451; expats@cbwchina.com.

Requirements for teaching posts in China are not always stringent: a university degree is often sufficient and teaching experience counts for more than formal training. In many cases teachers receive free airfare, a local salary, and perks. Wages are best in the big cities (Beijing, Guangzhou, and Shanghai) where there are scores of English schools. But many teachers feel that the drawbacks of Chinese city life are so great that they prefer to work in the provinces for less money. The western provinces like Yunnan are more pleasant and less money-mad than the east coast cities. Once you get a job make sure the school sorts out the various permits for which you are eligible, particularly a teacher's card that permits half-price rail travel. Ask for help in obtaining a temporary residence so you can avoid the tedious and expensive necessity of renewing your visa.

Indonesia: Foreign Teachers Receive Ten Times Local Wage

The world's fifth most populous nation, Indonesia, has been rapidly recovering from the political and economic instability that rocked the country at the end of the 1990s. The major language schools survived the crisis and continue to be staffed by foreign teachers. Big companies and rich individuals support about a dozen large schools that can afford to hire trained foreign teachers and pay them about ten times the local wage. Unlike in Thailand and Korea, beginners lacking the appropriate background or training will have to confine their job search to the locally-run back-street schools. The best teaching prospects in Indonesia are for those who have completed some TESL training and are willing to sign a 12- or 18-month contract. Contracts tend to start in July or October. Most jobs are in Jakarta, though there are also schools in Surabaya, Bandung, Yogayakarta, and Solo (among others). Jobs are occasionally advertised in the *Jakarta Post* or *Indonesian Observer*. Schools are willing to hire teachers with either a British or North American accent.

Visas are an issue whatever the nationality. Work permit regulations are rigidly adhered to in Indonesia, and all the established schools will apply for a visa permit on your behalf. You must submit your CV, teaching certificate, and other documents to the Indonesian Ministry of Education, the Cabinet Secretariat, and the Immigration/Manpower Developments. English teachers must have English as their first language and be nationals of the U.S., Canada, Britain, Australia, or New Zealand. With more informal teaching positions it is necessary to leave the country every two months (normally a day trip to Singapore).

Most schools pay between six and eight million rupiahs (net) per month ($700-$900) and some offer free accommodation alongside the salary, which permits a comfortable lifestyle.

Japan: The Financial Rewards Can Be Considerable

For decades, North Americans have been tempted to spend a year or two working in the land where English commands an almost reverential respect. The demand for language tuition remains strong, although recession in the late 1990s resulted in the closure of some major companies when fewer Japanese people were willing to pay for expensive English lessons. Consequently, competition for teaching jobs has become more acute. Be prepared to spend a sizeable sum of money while conducting the job hunt because of the high cost of living in Japanese cities. But many people persevere because of their commitment to an extended stay in Japan and also because of the potential earnings. Once established, the financial rewards can be considerable.

Japanese people of all ages eagerly sign up for lessons, especially evening classes, held in schools, town halls, and offices. "Conversation lounges" or "voice rooms" are popular among young adults who simply want to converse or socialize with a native speaker. These can have a relaxed and pleasant atmosphere, though they do not pay well and are probably unsatisfactory for serious English teachers.

The most common means of recruitment after the internet—on websites such as www.ohayosensi.com—is by advertising in English language newspapers, especially the *Japan Times* on Mondays and, to a lesser extent, *Kansai Time Out* magazine www.kto.co.jp and *Metropolis* www.metropolis.co.jp.

To shine over the competition, you must be prepared when you present yourself to a potential employer. Dress as impeccably and conservatively as possible. Take along (preferably in a smart briefcase) your undergraduate diplomas plus any other education certificates you have earned and a well-produced resume that does not err on the side of modesty. Be prepared at the interview to be tested or to be asked to teach a demonstration lesson.

Anyone arriving in Tokyo to conduct a speculative job hunt should go straight to one of the dozens of "gaijin houses," relatively cheap long-stay hostels for foreigners, listed in guidebooks or the glossy monthly *The Tokyo Journal*. Popular gaijin houses will be full of new or nearly new arrivals chasing teaching jobs. Because rents in Tokyo are virtually prohibitive, some foreign teachers stay in gaijin houses throughout their stay.

Most Americans enter Japan on a 90-day tourist visa and then begin the job hunt. The best times are late March and August. The key to obtaining a work visa is to have a sponsoring full-time employer in Japan. If you are hired by a school or company able to offer a full timetable, your employer must take your documents to the Immigration Office for processing within six weeks. Technically, you are not supposed to work until this process is complete, but most schools seem to get you working immediately. Once your visa is confirmed, you must leave the country and apply to a Japanese embassy abroad for your tourist visa to be changed. You can do this in 48 hours in Seoul. The government of Japan will not give work permits to anyone without a university degree.

A third visa option is a "cultural visa." To qualify, you must be able to prove that you are studying something Japanese like flower arranging, Shiatsu massage, martial arts, or the Japanese language.

If you want to arrange a teaching job in advance, the best bet is the government's JET (Japan Exchange and Teaching) Program. Each year, more than 6,000 foreign language assistants from 40 countries receive 1-year renewable contracts to work in private and state junior and senior high schools. Anyone with a university degree who is under 40 is eligible to apply. The program is fairly competitive, partly because of the generous salary of ¥3,600,000 (about $29,000) in addition to a free return air ticket on completing a contract. Americans, who make up about 40% of the total of JET participants, should contact their nearest Japanese consulate or the embassy in Washington (JET Office, 2520 Massachusetts Ave., NW, Washington, DC 20008; 800-INFO-JET or 202-238-6772, fax 202-265-9484; eojjet@erols.com, www.embjapan.org/jet.)

A number of large private organizations recruit abroad. Most pay at least ¥250,000 ($2,000 per month). A few of the major chains to look out for are GEOS, Nova, and ECC (for these and others see below).

Korea: Competition for Jobs Less Acute Than in Japan

The demand for native speaker English teachers in Korea far outstrips the supply, so competition for jobs is much less acute in Korea than in Japan. More than two-thirds of the work available is teaching young children and adolescents so any native speaker with experience of or just enthusiasm for working with children will have a large choice of job offers. Language institutes advertise for teachers on a host of websites such as www.teachkorea.com and www.teachabroad.com/KoreaSouth.cfm and also in the English language press, principally the *Korean Times* and *Korean Herald*. The bias in favor of North American accents helps in the job search and Canadian teachers are particularly in demand, with several recruitment agencies based in Canada actively looking for university graduates willing to give teaching a go for a year, for example **Asia-Pacific Connections Ltd** (Suite 2703, 1128 Alberni St., Vancouver BC V6E 4R6; 604-408-3760; jobs@asia-pacific-connections.com), **Russell Recruiting** (#207,-35 E 16th Ave., Vancouver, BC V5T 2T1; russellrecruiting@yahoo.ca); **Goal Asia** (243, Oak Park Ave., Toronto, ON M4C 4N4; 416-200-2074; apply@goalasia.com); and **SKA Overseas Agency** (530 Palmerston Boulevard, Toronto, ON M4G 2P4; www.skaoverseas.org). Goal Asia works with language institutes in Thailand, Taiwan, and Japan as well as Korea.

A typical package available through recruiters in exchange for signing a contract to teach a minimum of 120 hours a month is a salary of 1,800,000-2,000,000 won ($1,450-$1,600), return airfare, free accommodations, paid holidays, medical insurance, and a bonus on completion of the contract. It is a requirement of the E2 visa that teachers have a four-year degree or a 3-year degree plus TEFL Certificate.

Jobs are easiest to find at *hogwons* (language schools) in the Chongro district of Seoul, in Pusan, and in the smaller cities. The minimum qualifications are fluency in English, a bachelor's degree, and a positive attitude. Berlitz Korea hires dozens of teachers at its schools, while Ding Ding Dang Children's English also hires 50 native speaker teachers for 18 franchised schools throughout Korea. The U.S.-based chain of English language schools, ELS operating under the name YBM, has a major operation in Korea, including five institutes in different cities and affiliated ECC Language Institutes in Seoul and throughout the country; www.ybmhr.com is a fully operational recruitment web site. Another important group of language schools goes under the name Wonderland Language Institutes which hires most of its teachers via North American recruiting agents like Russell Recruiting. The English in Korea Program (EPIK) is a scheme run by the Ministry of Education to place more than 1,500 native speakers in schools and education offices. The monthly salary is between 1.7 and 2.1 million won plus accommodations, roundtrip airfare, medical insurance, and visa sponsorship. Contact the nearest Korean Consulate, check the web site http://epik.knue.ac.uk, or contact the office in Korea 011- 82-43-233-4516/7; epik@cc.knue.ac.kr.

Some neophyte teachers who arrange their jobs while still in North America wish they had waited until arrival in Seoul before committing themselves to a school. Often better wages and working conditions can be negotiated in person. Twelve-month contracts normally include a sizeable bonus, so it is in the teacher's interest to complete the contract. For new arrivals who have not prearranged a job, a good place to pick up information is from Dave's ESL Café (www.daveseslcafe.com) which has a link to the "Gray Page" with specific warnings about bad employers. The U.S. embassy in Seoul issues a free guide, *Teaching English in Korea* (American Citizen Services, 82 Sejong Rd., Chongro-ku, Seoul) which is posted on the Internet http://usembassy.state.gov/ seoul/wwwh.3550.htm.

Private tutoring normally requires traveling to the clients, though in Seoul this is less stressful than in Japan since the subway stops are announced in English. Most people who have taught in Korea report that the students are friendly and eager to learn but the hogwan owners are more interested in profit than in honoring their promises and even contracts with native speaker teachers. As a general rule be suspicious of anything that sounds like a dream contract. Lessons are not generally strenuous since the emphasis is on conversation rather than grammar.

Taiwan: Only Requirements Are College Degree and a Pulse

It has been said that the only requirements for being hired as an English teacher in Taiwan are a college degree and a pulse. Despite changes in immigration legislation which have made it more difficult for foreigners to undertake private tutoring, the demand for college-educated native speaking teachers who are prepared to stay for at least one year is huge. Many of the hundreds of private children's language institutes (as in Korea, the children's ESL market predominates), cram schools (called *buhsibans*) and also some state secondary schools are keen to sponsor foreign teachers for the necessary visas.

The requirements for a working permit include the original of your university diploma, health certificates issued in Taiwan (including an HIV test and chest X-ray), and a 1-year contract signed by your employer. This must be done within the 60-day validity of your Visitor Visa. With the working permit you can obtain a resident visa and ARC (Alience Resident Certificate). The American accent is invariably preferred, especially in the capital Taipei. Yet not everyone wants to stay in Taipei where the air pollution is second only to that of Mexico City; the traffic congestion is appalling, and the rents are high. Jobs are plentiful in the other cities of Taiwan such as Kaohsiung, Taichung, and Tainan. The majority of schools pay at least NT$550 ($16) per hour, and quite a few pay NT$700 after a teacher has proved him or herself. Fees for private tuition are considerably higher.

To see which schools are hiring, check web sites such as www.globalesl.net or www.workabroad.esl.com, ads in the daily *South China Post* and notice boards at travelers' hostels and the Mandarin Training Center of Taiwan Normal Univ. on Hoping East Rd. Recruiting agents can be tracked down though they do not proliferate as is the case of Korea. Try Taiwan-Teachers www.taiwn-teachers.com — they can arrange interviews in Boston and Canada as well as Kaohsiung. North American graduates can fix up a 1-year job ahead of time with the Overseas Service Corps of the YMCA (see below). You might also make useful expat contacts in Taipei at the **Community Services Center,** 25 Ln., 290 Chung Shan Rd., North Rd., Sec. 6, Tien Mu (011-886-2-2833-7444). One organization worth investigating if you want to teach English while studying Mandarin is ESL House www.eslhouse-online.com which runs a pre-arrival teacher placement service for a fee of $150.

Thailand: Teaching Jobs Are Virtually Guaranteed

While Bangkok absorbs an enormous number of English teachers, both trained and untrained, there is also demand in the other cities such as Hat Yai, Chiang Mai in the north, and Songkhla in the south, where there is less competition for work. Not much teacher recruitment takes place outside Thailand. Even Thai universities and teachers' colleges, as well as private business colleges, all of which have EFL departments, depend on finding native-speaking teachers locally.

In short, anyone who is determined to teach in Thailand and prepared to go there to look for work is virtually guaranteed to find opportunities. Finding language schools to approach is not a problem. Most new arrivals in Bangkok start with the English language yellow pages. Job vacancy notices appear in the English language press: *The Bangkok Post* and *The Nation.* Popular hostels often have bulletin boards with job notices and other information for foreigners. The best place to start the actual job hunting is around Siam Square and the Victory Monument where language schools and institutes abound. Check the Teaching in Thailand web site www.ajarn.com for inside information on potential employers.

First impressions are important throughout Asia. Dress smartly for interviews. A professional-looking resume and references help. University graduates (ajarn) are highly respected in Thailand and are expected to look respectable. At your interviews, be prepared to undergo a grammar test. As usual, it may be necessary to start with part-time and occasional work with several employers, aiming to build up 20-30 hours in the same area to minimize traveling in the appalling traffic conditions of Bangkok (smog masks are cheap and a wise investment).

The busiest season for English schools is mid-March to mid-May during the school holidays, when many secondary school and university students take extra tuition in English. This coincides with the hot season. The next best time to look for work in private schools is October. The worst time is January and February.

Working as a self-employed private tutor pays better than working for a commercial school, but tutoring jobs are hard to set up until you have been settled in one place for a while and found out how to tap into the local elite community. Placing an ad for private pupils in English language papers often works. Possible venues for would-be teachers include hotels where a native speaker is needed to organize conversation classes for staff.

The vast majority of EFL teachers in Thailand do not have a work visa, and this seems to cause no serious problems. At present, foreigners mostly teach on a tourist visa or (preferably) a non-immigrant visa. So far a crackdown, threatened by the authorities, has not happened. Universities and established language schools may be willing to apply for a work permit on behalf of teachers who have proved themselves successful in the classroom and who are willing to sign a 1-year contract. To be eligible for a work permit you must have a minimum of a BA and, in most cases, a relevant teaching certificate. However, most teachers simply cross the border into Malaysia every three months where a new visa can quickly and easily be obtained from the Thai consulate.

In a country where teaching jobs are so easy to come by, there has to be a catch—low wages. The basic hourly rate in Bangkok is only about 250-300 baht (less than $6), with a few schools paying less and some promising considerably more, especially if travel to outside locations is required. Rates outside Bangkok are lower.

By the same token, living expenses are also low. Out of an average monthly salary of 25,000 baht ($600) teachers can expect to pay 4,000 baht ($95) in rent, even in Bangkok. Tasty food can be had from street stalls for a few baht, and more substantial and exciting meals exploiting the area's marvelous fresh fish and fruit cost about $2. There is no reason why even part-time teachers should not be able to afford to travel around the country, including to the islands, where life is slow and the beaches are wonderful.

South Asia: Jobs Scarce Because of Poverty

In contrast to Thailand and Indonesia, it is generally not easy to find work as an English teacher in countries between Pakistan and the Phillipines. Poverty is the main reason for the small market for expatriate teachers. Singapore, Malaysia, and Brunei, which are relatively wealthy, mainly turn to Britain for teachers.

However, those foreigners prepared to finance themselves and volunteer their time can find eager students simply by asking around in Sri Lanka, India, and (especially) Nepal. Vietnam, Cambodia, Laos and even the pariah state of Myanmar are developing a range of commercial institutes devoted to English language teaching. In Vietnam, the daily paper *Nguoi Vet* publishes its Thursday edition in English, so check for ads (or consider placing your own). **World Universities Service of Canada** (WUSC), Recruitment Section, P.O. Box 3000, Ottawa, ON K1Y 4M8, Canada (613-798-7477; recruit@wusc.ca) recruits Canadian ESL teachers for a range of countries, especially Vietnam. Two private language institutes to try are **ILA Vietnam** (recruitment@ilavietnam.com) and **New Star ELT** in Hanoi (newstar@fpt.vn).

A handful of private language schools have opened in the Laotian capital of Vientiane. The longest established English teaching center is **Vientiane Univ. College,** P.O. Box 4144; (011-856-21-414-873/414052; vtcollege@laopdr.com, www.geocities.com/vientianecollege), which employs 25 teachers on seasonal and 1-year contracts. Visas can be a problem since countries understandably want to control the number of long-stay foreigners. For example, with very few exceptions the Nepali government does not allow foreigners to stay for more than three months in any 12. One possibility in India is to become a volunteer teacher with **Jaffe International Education Service** (Kunnuparambil Buildings, Kurichy, Kottayam 686549, India; Tel./fax 011-91-481-430470), which tries to place young volunteers in English medium high schools and training institutes for short periods.

Nepal is a more promising destination than India for short-term English teachers willing to work for low wages. **Insight Nepal** (P.O. Box 489, Pokhara, Kaski; insight@mos.com.np) has a Placement for Volunteer Service Work program in which volunteers are allocated to primary and secondary schools in different areas of the country for between three and four months to teach English, science, and sports. Starting dates are in February, August, and October. The participation fee of $800 covers pre-orientation and a one-week village or trekking excursion; the host village provides food and accommodations. Another alternative for volunteers wishing to teach in Nepal is to apply to the **New International Friendship Club Nepal** (P.O. Box 11276, Maharajgunj, Kathmandu; 011-977-1-427-406; fcn@ccsl.com.np). **The Himalayan Explorers Connection** (P.O. Box 3665 Boulder, CO 80307; info@hec.org) sends teaching volunteers to mountain villages. The program costs $150 per month excluding airfare.

China

Amity Foundation, 71 Han Kou Rd. Nanjing, Jiangsu 210008; 011-86-25-331-4118; amityed@jlonline.com. Christian organization which places native speaker teachers in schools and colleges.

Appalachians Abroad Teach in China Program, Marshall Univ., Center for International Programs, 1 John Marshall Drive, Huntington, WV 25755; 304-696-6265, fax 304-696-6353; gochina@marshall.edu, www.marshall.edu/gochina. Thirty graduates per year teach English at public and private K-12 schools and higher education institutions mainly in Shanghai and Beijing.

Beijing New Bridge Foreign Language School, Chao Yang Qu Yong An Nan Li, Jiao Yu Xue Yuan, Chao Yang Fen Yuan Xin Qiao, Yu Yan Zhong Xin, Beijing 100022; Fax 011-86-10-6592-8135; www.newbridgeschool.com. Private language school employing native speakers for conversational English in six branches.

Buckland International Education Group, Buckland ESL Hostel, P.O. Box 555, Yanshuo Guilin 541900; 011-86-773-882-7555; buckland@china.com, www.bucklandgroup.net. Casual conversation classes.

Colorado China Council, 4556 Apple Way, Boulder, CO 80301; 303-443-1108; alice@asiacouncil.org. From 20-35 American graduates are placed in institutes throughout China and Mongolia.

IEF Education Foundation, 18605 E Gale Ave., Suite 230, City of Industry, CA 91748; 626-965-1995; teachers@ief-usa.org. University graduates teach junior high and high schools students in many Chinese cities for a minimum of six months.

Prolegion Language Center Beijing, c/o Prolegion Training, 1072 S de Anza Blvd., Suite 508, San Jose, CA 95129; fax 408-252-8861; prolegion.cn@prolegion.com, www.prolegion.com. Fifteen teachers with North American accents needed in downtown Beijing.

Ready to Learn, Administrative Office, 1st Fl., 4 W Ng Sing Ln., Yau Ma Tei, Kowloon, Hong Kong; 011-852-2388-1318; www.readytolearn.net. Employs 30 native speakers with college degrees.

Western Washington Univ., China Teaching Program, MS-9047, 516 High St., Bellingham, WA 98225-9047; 360-650-3753, fax 360-650-2847; ctp@www.edu, www.wwu.edu/~ctp.

WorldTeach, Center for International Development, Harvard Univ., 79 John F. Kennedy St., Cambridge MA 02138; 800-4-TEACH-O; www.worldteach.org. Summer teaching program at language camps for Chinese high school students (participation fee $3,990) and 6-month opportunities in Yantei (fee $4,990).

Indonesia

EF English First-Menteng, Jl. Timor No. 25, Menteng, Jakarta 10350; 011-62-21 3148815. One of many EF franchised schools in Indonesian cities. Try also Surabaya branch: Plaza Surabaya, Jl. Pemuda 31-37, Surabaya 60271; 011-62-31-548-4000; teachers@rad.net.id, www.geoctieis.com/efjatim. Employ 40 foreign teachers for 2 schools in Surabaya and one in Melang. Application can be made through EF office in Boston.

English Education Center (EEC), Jalan Let. Jend. S. Parman 68, Slipi, Jakarta 11410; 011-62-21 532 3176/532 0044; eec@vision.net.id, www.indodirect.com/eec. Thirty teachers for 3 schools in Jakarta. Also U.S. recruiting office: c/o Kiyomura & Associates, World Trade Center Bldg., 350 S. Figueroa St., Suite 501, Los Angeles, CA 90071; 213-626-8170; ecc@kiyomura.com.

Executive English Programs (EEP), Jalan. Ir. H. Juanda 77, Bandung 40155; 011-62-22-420 5153; eepbdg@bdg.centrin.net.id.

International Language Centre, Jl. Samanhudi No. 22, Medan 20151; 011-62-61-451 5766; ilc@mdn.centrin.net.id, www.ilc-medan.com. Airfare and shared housing provided for teachers with one year's experience willing to stay for 12 months.

KELT, Jalan Jawa 34, Surabaya 60281, Jawa Timor; 011-62-31-502 3333; ilp101@sby.dnet.net.id or jawa@k-elt.com. Twenty-five native speaker teachers.

School for International Training (SIT), Jalan Sunda 3, Menteng, Jakarta Pusat 10350; 011-62-21-390, 011-69-20-337240/336238. Twenty teachers for this branch plus two in Jakarta and one in Surabaya.

Japan

AEON International USA, 1960 East Grand Ave., #550, El Segundo, CA 90245; 310-414-1515, fax 310-414-1616; aeonla@aeonet.com, www.aeonet.com. Recruits throughout the U.S. for 270+ branches in Japan. Other North American recruiting offices: 203 North LaSalle St., #2100, Chicago, IL 60601; 312-251-0900, fax 312-251-0901; aeonchi@aeonet.com. 230 Park Ave., #1000, New York, NY 10169; 212-808-3080, fax 212-599-0340; aeonnyc@aeonet.com. 145 King St., #1000, Toronto, Ontario, Canada M5H 1J8; 416-364-8500, fax 416-364-7561; aeontor@aeonet.com.

Adler Recruiting Service, 424-301 Maude Rd., Port Moody, BC, Canada V3H 5B1; 604-461-5131, fax 604-461-5133; aeoncanada@attcanada.net.

American Language School, 7-11 Honchiba-cho, chuo-ku, Chiba City, Chiba 260-0014; 011-81-43-224 0099; als_recruit@syd.odn.ne.jp, www.americanlan guageschool.co.jp. About 90 North American teachers, preferably experienced teaching children.

Berlitz, hr@lc.berlitz.co.jp. Hires native speaker teachers year round.

ECC Foreign Language Institute, 15th Fl., San Yamate Building, 7-11-10 Nishi-Shinjuku, Shinjuklu-ku, Tokyo 160-0023; 011-81-3-5330 1585; www.ecc.co.jp. Offices in Osaka and Nagoya also. Over 300 teachers recruited in Japan only.

GEOS Language Corporation, Simpson Tower, Suite 2424, 401 Bay St., Toronto, ON M5H 2Y4, Canada; 416-777-0109, fax 416-777-0110; geos@istar.ca; www.geoscareer.com. Recruits 1,800 graduates to teach at 450 schools.

Institute for Education in Japan, Earlham College, 801 National Rd. West, D-202, Richmond, IN 47379; 888-685-2726; www.earlham.edu/~aet. Two-year contracts in Japanese junior high schools for college grads interested in learning Japanese.

Interac Co Ltd, Fujibo Bldg. 2F, 2-10-28 Fujimi, Chiyoda-ku, Tokyo 102-0071; 011-81-3-3234-7857, fax 011-81-3-3234-6055; recruit@interac.co.jp, www.interac. co.jp/recruit. Nine branches recruit most of their 280 teachers locally.

Interact Nova Group, 2 Oliver St., Suite 7, Boston, MA 02110; 617-542-5027 or 601 California St., Suite 702, San Francisco, CA 94108; 415-788-3717; www. teachinjapan.com. Has 390 schools throughout Japan; teachers recruited through-out the year.

Yokohama YMCA, 1-7 Tokiwa-Cho, Naka-Ku, Yokohama 231-8348; 011-81 45 662 3721, fax 011-81 45 664 4018; ymjohn@yokohama-ymca.or.jp. Two hundred full-time and part-time positions for graduates with TESOL training.

Westgate Corporation, 1173-1 Aza Hikakida Hagiwara, Gotemba, Shizuoka 412-0042; 011-81-550-84-0880' recruiter@westgate.co.jp. Provides native-speaking lan-guage trainers to businesses and public schools in Gotemba near Mount Fuji.

Korea

Berlitz Korea, Sungwoo Academy Building 2F, 1316-17 Seocho-Dong, Seocho-Gu, Seoul 137-074; 011-82-2-3481-5324; gerald.drabick@berlitz.com.sg.

Ding Ding Dang Children's English, 1275-3 Bummel-dong Soosung-gy, Taegu 706-100; 011-82-53-782-5200; dings@korea.com.

EFZ World, 88-1 Freezone B/D Sadangdong Dongjakgu, Seoul 156-090; 011-82-2-595-8222. English language franchise group with about 40 schools in Seoul and throughout Korea.

English Friends Academy, 733 Bang Hak 3 Dong, Do Bong Ku, Seoul 132-885; 011-82-2-956-9777; recruiter@tefa.net, www.tefa.net. Up to 30 teachers hired by email.

English Program in Korea (EPIK), Training Center for In-Service Education, Korea National University of Education, Chongwon, Chungbuk, 363-791, Korea; 011-82-43-1233-4516/4517, fax 011-82-43-1233-6679; epik@cc.knue.ac.kr. North American applicants for teaching posts in schools and education offices through the Ministry of Education should contact their nearest Korean Consulate for information. Scheme is not usually over-subscribed.

John's Consulting Canada, 394 Brown's Line, Toronto, Ontario, Canada M8W 3T8; 416-226-9787; www.iloveesl.com. Recruits teachers on behalf of some of the 90 Wonderland Language Institutes. Another Canada-based agent is EasterSchool. com; 203-2588 Nanaimo St., Vancouver, BC V5R 6C5; 604-454-1587; esl_Korea@hotmail.com.

Kim's Agency, 5th Fl., 28-8 Noryangjin 2 dong Dongjakgu, Seoul 156-052; 011-82-2-812-8262; www.kimsagency.com.

Se Jong Seo Jeog ESL Recruitment Company, B Dong Sang Ga, 10 Sam lk 1 Cha, Gae Shin dong, Cheongju Shi, Chungbuk; 011-82-43-211-3466; fax 011-82-43-211-9060.

YBM Education/ELS, Recruiting Office, 55-1 Chongno 2 Ga, chongno Gu, 3rd Fl., Seoul 110-122; 011-82-2278-0509, fax 011-82-2269-0275; teach@ymbsisa.co.kr, www.ybmhr.com. Recruit hundreds of teachers for around 10 language schools throughout the country (branch contact details on website). Division for children's language schools is called YBM/Sisa or YBM/ECC; www.ybmsisa.com.

Taiwan

Kojen English Language Schools, 6F, #9, Lane 90, Sung Chiang Rd., Taipei; 011-886-2-2581-8511; www.kojenenglish.com.tw. From 200-300 teachers in 3 main cities.

Hess Educational Organization, 235 Chung Shan Rd., Chung Ho City, Sec. 2, No. 419, Chung Ho City, Taipei County; 011-886-2-3234-6188 ext 1053; hesswork@hess.com.tw, www.hess.com.tw. Specializes in teaching children. Over 250 teachers for 100 schools and 40 kindergartens.

International Avenue Consulting Company, 16F-1 No 499, Chung Ming South Rd., Taichung City; 011-886-4-2375 9800; www.iacc.com.tw. Currently expanding number of teachers to 150.

Jump Start, 6F, 3 Lane 334, Chein-kwo South Rd, Sec 2, Taipei; 011-886-2-2369 4128; www.jumpstart.com.t. English immersion schools for kids.

Noble American Children's School, No. 850 Ta-Ya Rd, Sec. 1, Chiayi 600; 011-886-5-275 9951; shereed@telusplanet.net. Teachers for young children's English classes.

Overseas Service Corps, c/o YMCA International Services, 6300 Westpark, Suite 600, Houston, TX 77057; www.ymca.net/yworld/taiwan. Twenty-five English teachers needed for minimum of a year in Taiwan.

Shane English Schools, 5F, 41 Roosevelt Rd., Sec. 2, Taipei; 011-886-2-2351 7755; www.saxoncourt.com/taiwan.htm. Over 50 qualified or experienced TEFL teachers.

Thailand

American University Language Centre, 179 Rajadamri Rd., Bangkok 10330; 011-66-2-252-8170. Employs 80 plus teachers in central Bangkok and about 100 at other branches in 11 provinces, mainly at universities. Applicants should have a BA and be able to commit themselves to a six-week stint. Also try Chiang Mai branch: 73 Rajadamnern Rd., Amphur Muang, Chiang Mai 50200; 011-66-53-211973.

Bell Language Centres, 204/1 Ranong 1 Rd., Samsen, Dusit, Bangkok 10300; 011-66-2-644-9310; teach@loxinfo.co.th, www.bell-centres.com. Over 60 teachers, preferably with qualifications.

ECC (Thailand), 430/17-24 Chula Soi 64, Siam Sq., Bangkok 10330; 011-66-2-253-3312; jobs@ecc.ac.th. Around 500 native speakers teaching at 60 branches (40 in Bangkok).

Elite Training Institute, 2nd Fl., Kongboonma Building, 699 Silom Rd, Bangkok 10500; 011-66-2-635-3319/20; elite@eliteinstitute.com. EFL teachers for schools in downtown Bangkok.

Nava Language Schools, 34 Payolyothin 7, Phayathai, Bangkok 10400; 011-66-2-617-1500; navaoperations@nls.ac.th, www.nls.ac.th. Group of schools that claims to teach 13,000 students each week.

Siam Computer and Language Institute, 471/19 Ratcha Withi Rd., Victory Monument, Ket Ratcha Tevi, Bangkok 10400; 011-66-2-247-2345 ext. 370-373; www.siamcom.co.th. Over 70 branches in Bangkok and the provinces.

Thai Youth Hostelling Association, International Community Service Program, 25/14 Phitsanulok Road, Si Sao Thewet, Dusit, Bangkok 10300; 011-66-2-628 7413-5; bangkok@tyha.org, www.tyha.org. 'Giving English for Community Service' program involves foreign volunteers with some basic experience of English teaching spending three to five months teaching English to classes of low-paid local people.

Teach in China
Do-It-Yourself Steps to Finding a Job

By Daniel Walfish

If you want to join the growing number of Westerners teaching English in mainland China, all you really need is a college degree and native fluency in English. Training in ESL is useful and you might feel at a loss without it, but a certificate is not necessary to convince a Chinese university or private language school to hire you as a teacher of English.

If you're not eligible for a university exchange program and you're unwilling to pay the fee for an independent sending organization, you can go on your own. But apply early: While some positions are open as late as July or August, try to make contact by March. (Occasionally, positions are open for the second semester, too, which begins in February.) Here's what to do:

1. **Learn about China and the experience of teaching English in China.** Indispensable for these purposes is *Living in China* (Rebecca Weiner, Margaret Murphy, and Albert Li, China Books & Periodicals, 415-282-2994, $19.95). The book provides incredibly useful advice on many aspects of living and teaching in China, and also contains a virtually complete directory of Chinese schools of higher education.

2. **Decide on a list of universities to apply to.** Use the directory in *Living in China* or the sidebar to this article.

3. **Contact someone at the school responsible for hiring foreign teachers.** No other individual, no matter how important or friendly they seem, is likely to have the

authority to hire. So who is the right person? Individual academic departments—usually foreign languages or English—hire their own foreign teachers, so the right person is usually the chair or vice-chair of that department. The foreign affairs office is often useless for getting job offers. However, larger universities might have other departments (e.g., "Public English") which need teachers, and you won't find out about them unless you ask someone.

One way to get in touch with the right person is to be in China while you're looking. Bring application materials with you. But keep in mind that if you do line up a job as a student or tourist you will probably have to leave the country or go to Hong Kong to get your visa changed.

International dialing from the U.S. can be cheap. For example, from a residential phone you can use the company PT-1 www.pt-1.com by dialing 101-6868 and the phone number. The cost for China is 39 cents per minute. Your phone bill might get quite large, but it's still cheaper than paying thousands of dollars to a sending organization. Most of the people you reach by phone will know English. If the right person isn't in, say you're calling from abroad and you need the right person's home number. But don't call after 9:30 p.m. China time (12 hours ahead of Eastern Standard Time).

4. Send a resume. Highlight any teaching or tutoring experience. You may also want to include references and a letter of explanation. Keep in mind that anyone reading these materials is likely to have very good English reading ability but may not understand Western resume jargon.

5. If you are ultimately offered a position you like, you may want to try a little negotiating. But you're unlikely to be successful if the school has a standard contract. In public universities, compensation for inexperienced foreign teachers is never very much. Expect to get housing, anywhere from RMB1,400 to RMB2,200 ($169-$266) a month, and sometimes a one-way ticket home as well.

Chinese universities rarely require foreigners to teach more than 14 or 15 hours of English classes each week. If the department wants you to do more, ask if some lessons can be converted to optional office hours. Also, if you're teaching any writing or "content" courses, you should have significantly fewer classroom hours.

6. When you consider a job offer, ask for the names of foreigners who are currently teaching or have recently taught at that school so you can get the real scoop on the university and its treatment of foreigners.

Other Teaching Jobs: A master's degree or a doctorate may qualify you to work as a "Foreign Expert" in a university and to teach more advanced courses for much more pay than a "Foreign Teacher" receives.

Private language schools and companies also recruit foreigners. These organizations pay better but are not really service experiences. A few possibilities are the **English First** language schools, with various locations throughout mainland China, Hong Kong, and Taiwan (www.ef.com). **Dave's ESL Café,** www.eslcafe.com is a great starting point to search for private school openings. **China's State Bureau of Foreign Experts** (Friendship Hotel, 3 Bai Shi Qiao Rd., Beijing 100873; 011-86-10-6849-9753; sbfe@chinaonline.com.cn.net) has been known to match applicants with jobs in universities and state-owned companies.

Perspective
The New South Korea
Securing a Good Teaching Job Is a Snap

By Lavinia Spalding

In the mid-'90s, South Korea became known as a country where one could earn a small fortune teaching English and it quickly became a hot spot for ESL instructors. In late 1997, however, the Asian economic crisis caused a mass exodus of Westerners, leaving Korea desperate for English education but unable to afford it. The country has not yet fully recovered, but it is well on its way. A renewed, almost palpable, optimism has spread through Korea

Hogwans, or private institutes, the easiest places to find work, have earned a reputation for being on the shady side. However, if you look carefully, plenty of reputable ones do exist and hiring packages have become increasingly attractive. A 1-year contract typically includes roundtrip airfare to Korea, a relatively competitive salary (the equivalent of $1,500-$1,700 per month for a 25- to 30-hour work week), housing, two weeks' paid vacation, and severance pay equal to one month's salary upon completion of your contract.

Do Your Homework
The basic rule for securing a good teaching position in Korea is to do your homework. Begin with Dave's ESL Café (www.eslcafe.com) and ESL Worldwide (www.eslworldwide.com), where you can sift through countless job advertisements. At www.lifeinkorea.com, you'll find a wealth of general information on Korea. These sites also offer invaluable links to numerous other sites.

If you want to facilitate the process and truly immerse yourself in Korean culture, try www.Komestay.com, a homestay placement service for international visitors. www.Pusanweb.com is a rich source of practical info. For answers to specific questions, join a discussion board on any Korea-related site.

Whatever you do, don't jump at the first job offer you receive. It's wise to search the Internet for blacklists (sometimes called greylists) that warn against schools best avoided. Before deciding to accept a job offer, try to contact another Westerner employed at the school so you can get the inside scoop.

Finally, remember that there's no lack of job opportunities—so if a school sounds even slightly sketchy, take a pass. Once you've signed a contract, getting out of it and changing jobs can be a colossal pain in the neck.

The Logistics
The traditional method of finding work in Korea is to secure employment in advance, but many teachers now head to Korea first and find a job after they arrive. A 3-month tourist visa is available to Americans and a 6-month visa to Canadians. Immigration officers who might wonder why you have no return ticket are usually mollified with an explanation that you plan to travel on to Japan via ferry.

Once in Korea, finding accommodations is painless and fairly cheap. Most people take a room at a *yogwan* (motel). These are ubiquitous and cost approximately $15-

$30 a night. Finding temporary teaching work while searching for a permanent position isn't difficult. Short-term institute jobs abound and are most easily located on the Internet or by word of mouth.

The most significant benefit of arriving in Korea jobless is that you have the luxury of looking around for the position that offers the best teaching and living conditions. You'll be able to see the school and accommodations (insist on this), negotiate with the director, and consult other teachers at the school before signing a contract. Once you are hired, most institute directors will pay your way to Japan so you can obtain a work visa.

The Pay-Offs

While most people who move to Korea are enticed by the possibility of financial gain (saving $10,000 to $20,000 a year), that's certainly not the only reason to come here. Koreans are exceptionally warm and generous. Students are polite and respectful. And the culture is fascinating. One of the greatest rewards of life in Korea is the opportunity—around virtually every corner—to take classes and acquire knowledge. Koreans, particularly those living in smaller cities and towns outside of Seoul, welcome any chance to share their culture with foreigners. This means teachers can study everything from Korean language and cooking to meditation, traditional drumming, and martial arts at a truly minimal charge, in exchange for English lessons, or even for free.

Studying Tae Kwon Do or another martial art in Korea might cost you no more than $30 a month for intensive daily classes. Institutes and restaurants in most towns and cities offer lessons in Asian and international cooking. One such institute is La Cuisine in Seoul (02-3444-5861-2). On the other hand, convincing a Korean friend or student to teach you to prepare your favorite local dishes usually takes little more than a request. Volunteer groups across the country, offer Korean classes to foreigners at no charge. The Busan Buddhist mission (busanmission@orgio.net) offers free classes every other Sunday. Foreigners and Koreans are taught to make green tea, perform mask dances, meditate, fashion lotus lanterns, and learn a variety of other cultural crafts and traditions.

Korea can of course be a challenging place to live from day to day: cities are crowded, traffic tends to be nightmarish, and, at first, Koreans might seem somewhat brusque or pushy. But once you've lived here a while and learned to navigate the cultural differences, the greatest challenge often lies in staying only a year or two. Countless expatriates fall so deeply in love with Korea that they wind up making it their permanent home.

Perspective

Teach in Thailand

A New Home With an Array of Choices

By Dave Abernathy

My first 28 years, most of them spent in a small town in Oregon, did not prepare me for Bangkok. The first night I didn't sleep at all. I wandered the streets, amazed by the strange mix of the ancient and modern, Thai and Western. My obscure goal was to find an elephant. And believe it or not I found one—complete with a flashing red light attached to its tail.

After a few days of exploring Bangkok I heard about a language school called **TEFL International** (www.teflintl.com) in a small coastal town called Ban Phe, about 120 miles from Bangkok. After signing up on their web site, I spent four weeks learning how to teach English to non-native speakers. In the process I realized just how much fun teaching could be and began to acquaint myself with Thai language and culture. I made new friends and began to understand what it was I was really looking for—and what I was beginning to find.

After graduating, I spent a few agonizing weeks weighing job offers. There were many jobs to choose from all over Thailand; some of my classmates were choosing more lucrative posts in Japan, Taiwan, and Korea. I could have gone virtually anywhere in the world, but I finally decided to accept a position at a small school in Rayong, a town not far from Ban Phe.

I worked mainly weekday evenings and all day Saturday—a total of about 20 hours per week. I became friends with the local motorcycle taxi drivers. I spent time with an ice cream vendor who spoke English quite well from his days working for the U.S. Army during the Vietnam War. I met a local English teacher who had received her master's degree in Australia. And I was befriended by a wealthy student who is the CEO of a successful Thai company. All of these new friends gave me a perspective on the world and on myself that I had never had before.

After my first year came and went, when, according to my initial plan, I should be returning to my home in Oregon, I found that I had a new home—a home I had no great desire to leave. So I have spent the last few years exploring. From the rugged terrain and rich history of the North, to the gorgeous islands and beaches of the south, to the friendly countrysides of the Northeast. Despite four years of teaching, I still feel that I have learned more than I taught. Here's wishing you the same grand adventure.

For More Info: TEFL International offers a TESOL certification in an intensive, 4-week course. I chose them because they are the largest school of TESOL in Asia, because of the many positive comments by graduates of the program, because of their low price (which even includes a private air-conditioned room with private bath), and because of their location—only 100 meters from the beach and a short ferry ride from Samet Island. Contact: Tel./fax 011-66-38-652-280; info@teflintl.com, www.teflintl.com.

Work in Latin America
English Language Links Visitors and Residents

By Susan Griffith

The vast continent of South America holds an almost infinite range of opportunities for anyone who wants to share their native English. From the specialized training for the business communities of Santiago and Brasilia to the informal conversation exchanges with Mexican fishermen and Venezuelan waiters, the English language provides a link between visitors and residents.

Apart from a few popular cities, seldom do you find the glut of teachers you find elsewhere in the world, possibly because South America is often pictured as a place of poverty and crime, danger and corruption, dictators and drug barons. In fact, South America is home to a staggering variety of charming and generous people from café-culture urbanites to street kids, many of whom are eager to meet travelers and improve their knowledge of the gringos' native tongue. The stampede to learn English seems unstoppable.

In the big cities the greatest demand for English comes from the business community. And because of the strong commercial links between the two American continents, the demand tends to be for American English. The whole continent is culturally and economically oriented towards the U.S.

Among the most important providers of English language training are American binational centers and cultural centers—in Brazil alone there are 23 Brazilian-American Cultural Institutes ICBEUs) and 235 bi-national centers. Information on the centers, including email addresses, can be found on the web at http://exchanges.state.gov/education/engteaching. While some want teachers with a degree in TESL from a U.S. university, others require only a good command of English and a tidy appearance. For example the **Centro Venezolano Americano** (addresses below) takes interns for a minimum of six months to teach English to children and adolescents in Caracas, Maracaibo and Merida. **The International Institute for Teachers Exchange (IICA)** in Brazil is affiliated to Brazil's bi-national centers and runs a program whereby about 30 native speakers from the U.S., Canada and Great Britain are placed in host schools. In exchange for helping with English tuition, they receive $400 a month plus room and board with a local family. See their web site at www.mgt.com.br/icbeu.

Career TEFL teachers should contact **LAURELS,** the **Latin American Union of Registered English Language Schools,** which currently has over 70 members in Brazil and a number of others in Uruguay. Contact LAURELS at International House Goiania, Rua 4, 80 Setor Oeste, Goiania 74110-140, GO, Brazil; 62-224-0478, fax 62-223-1846; inthouse@nutecnet.com.br. Novice teachers are more likely to be employed by one of the language school chains like **English First** and **Wall Street Institutes** which at first offer part-time contracts and relatively low wages. For contact details for indigenous schools in a number of South American countries see the web site www.inglesnet.com.

Several South American nations have American- or British-style bilingual schools and colegios. Although they normally hire state-accredited teachers, a number take on students and university graduates looking for brief periods of work experience.

Voluntary and international exchange organizations which arrange for young people to do English tutoring include **WorldTeach,** www.worldteach.org, with programs in Costa Rica and Ecuador, and **Amity Volunteer Teachers Abroad,** www.amity.org which place Spanish-speakers over 21 in schools in Argentina, Peru, Mexico, Brazil, Venezuela and the Dominican Republic. An increasing number of language schools offer Spanish instruction to fee-paying foreigners in the mornings and arrange a community volunteer program in the afternoons, for example, **CIS-MAM** in El Salvador). **The Native English Center** in Bogotá employs native-speaking English teachers on official contracts and also offers more casual positions to those who do not want to embark on the laborious visa chase. People can barter English lessons for Spanish lessons plus housing for two to four months, www.nativeenglishcenter.com.

TEFL training colleges in the U.S. like Transworld and the Boston Language Institute send large numbers of their graduates to posts in Latin America.

Even the poorest of Latin American nations offer possibilities to EFL teachers, provided they are prepared to accept a low wage. In contrast to the an hourly wage of $10-$30 in Europeanized cities like Buenos Aires and Santiago, the wages paid by language schools in la Paz and Quito may be closer to $2.

Picking up Casual Work

Many aspiring teachers find that the response to sending their resumes to addresses abroad is disappointment. It is better to present yourself in person although having sent a "warm-up" resumé beforehand can do your cause no harm. Finding casual teaching work is a matter of asking around and knocking on enough doors. Check ads in the English language press such as Mexico City's *The News* or the *Caracas Daily Journal.* The *Buenos Aires Herald* has been a promising source in the past but Argentina's economic crisis means that jobs are scarce at present. English language bookstores are another possible source of teaching leads; try for example the English Book Center in Guayaquil Ecuador or Books and Bits in Santiago. Many foreign teachers are simultaneously learning Spanish, so a good place to link up with people in the know is to visit the local Instituto de Lengua Espanola para Extranjeros or its equivalent. Check the telephone directory for schools or agencies. In Lima and Quito the clubhouses of South America Explorers (see following page) keep a list of language institutes and the expat staff will be happy to share information with members.

Credentials Not Required

Teachers tend to agree that Latin American students are a joy to teach because they love to talk. If you have plenty of enthusiasm in addition to a good education, are carrying references and diplomas, and are prepared to stay for an academic year, it should be possible to fix up a contract with a well-established language institute. Many institutes offer their own compulsory pre-job training.

The academic year begins in February or early March and lasts until December. The best time to look for work is a few weeks before the end of the summer holidays. However, many institutes run 8- to 12-week courses year round and will hire a native speaker whatever the time of year.

In-company teaching usually takes place early in the morning; a popular starting time is 7 a.m. People learning English outside their workplaces usually sign up for evening lessons. Most teachers enjoy the off-site teaching more than classroom teaching, which tends to be more textbook-based.

Work visas require gathering a battery of documents—including notarized and officially translated copies of teaching qualifications, a police clearance, etc.—and paying a hefty fee. Consequently, a high percentage of teachers work on tourist visas. These must be kept up-to-date by applying for an extension from the immigration department or by crossing into and back from a neighboring country.

Not only will a stint of teaching be good for learning a language, it will give you the chance to experience the Latin zest for life.

Teaching Contacts in Latin America

Argentina

The American Training Company, Viamonte 577, 7° 59, 1053 Buenos Aires; 011-54-11-5031 3939; contactenos@americantrainingco. com.ar. Must have TEFL certificate.

CAIT (Capacitacion en Interpretacion y Traducciones), Maipu 863, 3rd Fl., C, 1006 Buenos Aires, Argentina; 011-54-11-4311 8544/4314 2583; cait@ciudad.com.ar. About 30 freelance teachers for in-company language training, must be available for local interview.

Interchange Language Service, Peru 84-5to. Piso, Of 74, 1084 Buenos Aires; 011-54-11-4345 3132; www.Interchangels.com.ar.

Bolivia

Centro Boliviano Americano (CBA), Parque Iturralde Zenon 121, Casilla 12024, La Paz; 011-591-2-431779; cbalp@caoba.entelnet.bo. The Binational Centers in Bolivia are the largest English language provider in Bolivia with four locations in La Paz plus schools in Sucre, Santa Cruz de la Sierra, and other cities.

Pan American English Center, Avenida 16 de Julio 1490, Edificio Avenida 7 piso, Casilla 5244, La Paz; Tel/fax 011-591-2-340796. Reputable language school with branch in Cochabamba, 011-591-42-97027.

Brazil

Britannia Schools, Central Department, Av. Borges de Medeiros 67, Leblon, Rio de Janeiro RJ); Tel/fax 011-55-21-511 0143; recruitment@britannia.com.br, www. britannia.com.br. Also: Rua Garcia D'Avila 58, Ipanema; 011-55-21-2511 0940. Employ 20 native speaker teachers for schools in Rio de Janeiro and Porto Alegre. Despite name, North American teachers are hired.

IICA Brazil, Instituto de Intercambios e Cultura Americana, Ituiutaba, Minas Gerais 38300-114; 011-55-34-3269 6099. Runs a trainee teacher scheme lasting 6 or 12 months for candidates aged over 20 with some teaching experience. Homestay accommodation is provided and a monthly salary of $600 is paid.

Lex English Language Services, Rua Humberto 1, No. 318, Vila Mariana, Sao Paulo 04018-030, SP; 011-55-11-5-84 4613. Looking especially for lawyers or law students to teach legal English.

New Start Comunicacoes Ltda., Av. Rio Branco 181/702, Centro, 20040-007 Rio de Janeiro, RJ; 011-55-21-240 5807; stephanie@newstart.com.br, www.newstart.com.br. TEFL certificate required and preferably professional experience in a non-teaching area.

Schutz & Kanomata ESL, Rua Galvao Costa 85, Santa Cruz do Sul 95810-170; 011-55-51-3715 3366; www.sk.com.br. Exchange program of ESL teaching for Portuguese learnng.

Wizard, Rua Marechal Henrique Lott 120/107, Barra da Tijuca, 22631 390 Rio de Janeiro; www.wizard.com.br. Dozens of branches listed on web site, though most employ local teachers.

Chile

Typically these schools may offer a newcomer no more than a few hours of teaching work, gradually working up to a full timetable after a probationary three months. American job-seekers, especially those with a TEFL background, should approach one of the Institutos Chileno Norteamericano which are located in Concepcion, Arica, Curico and Valparaiso as well as the capital.

Berlitz, Av Pedro de Valdivia 2005, Providencia, Santiago; 011-56-2-204 8076.

Bridge-Linguatec International, Av. Los Leones 439, Providencia, Santiago; 011-56-2-233 4356 ext 15; www.bridgelinguatec.com.

Large branch of U.S.-based teaching organization; head office 915 S Colorado Blvd., Denver, CO 80246; 303-777-7783. Compulsory 1-week training course for all accepted teachers which is unpaid but guarantees the offer of some hours of work on completion.

Fischer English Institute, Cirujano Guzman 49, Providencia, Santiago; 011-56-2-235 6667). Teaches both on- and off-site. Offers plenty of structure in planning lessons.

Impact English, Rosa O'Higgins 259, Las Condes, Santiago; 011-56-2-211 1925, fax 011-56-2-211 6165. Fluctuating demand for freelance American ELT teachers for client companies.

Polyglot, Villavicencio 361 Of. 102, Santiago; 011-56-2-639 8078; application@polyglot.cl, www.polyglot.cl. Employs 40-50 teachers a year.

Sam Marsalli, Av. Los Leones 1095, Providencia, Santiago; 011-56-2-231 0652; marsalli@entelchile.net. Hires only North Americans on one-year contracts at one of 3 institutes in Santiago.

Tronwell S.A., Apoquindo 4499, 3er Piso, Las Condes, Santiago; 011-56-2-246 1040; www.tronwell.com, 40-50 teachers for a minimum of 1 year. Degree in English or ELT Certificate preferred.

Wall Street Institute, Av. Apoquindo 3502, Las Condes, Santiago 011-56-2-335 6256; wsichile@netline.cl. Master franchise in Chile for other branches.

Colombia:
Colombia is even more strongly oriented towards the U.S. than elsewhere in South America with an extensive network of Colombian-American Cultural Centers around the country including the following which teach English:

Centro Cultural Colombo Bogotá, Avenida 19 No. 3-05, Santafé de Bogotá; 011-57-1-334-7640, fax 011-57-1-282 3372; colombo@colomsat.net.co.

Centro Cultural Colombo Barranquillo, Carrera 43, No. 51-95, Apartado Aereo 2097, Barranquilla; 011-57-5-340 8084, fax 011-57-5-340 8549; colombo@b-quilla.cetcol.net.co.

Centro Cultural Colombo Cali, Calle 13 Norte 8-45, A.A. 4525, Cali; 011-57-2-667 3529; www.colombocali.edu.co. BA plus 6 months teaching experience needed.

Centro Cultural Colombo Medellin, Cra. 45 No. 53-24, A.A. 8734, Medellin; 011-57-4-513 4444, fax 011-57-4-513 2666; www.colomboworld.com.

Other prominent schools include:

EF English First, Calle 76, No. 9-66, Santafé de Bogota; 011-57-1-347-8055; centrosidiomas.co@ef.com. Also Carrera 43 A #16A sur 38, Medellin; 011-57-4-266 8433.

Native English Center, Cra 6 No 49-56, Bogotá; 011-57-1-548 4146; www.nativeenglishcenter.com.

Praxis, Calle 79, No. 39-30, Medellin; 011-57-4-250 0515, fax 011-57-4-250 8239. 2 schools which hire native speakers for 3 months and pay $300 a month for a full-time timetable.

For a list of schools in Medellin, a mountain city considered by official sources to be potentially dangerous because of its association with drug barons, see www.poorbuthappy.com/colombia.

Costa Rica:
CIESA (Consultoria Internacional de Educacion), P.O. Box 383-4005, San Antonio de Belen, Heredia; 011-506-221-4100; arauz_jose@hotmail.com. Graduates with some teaching experience can spend 10 months staying with a family and learning Spanish in exchange for English tutoring.

Ecuador
The market for English, particularly American English, continues to thrive despite grave economic difficulties in the country. The devaluation of the currency means that almost no school can pay more than the equivalent of $2 an hour. Dozens of language academies and institutes can be found in Quito, the second city Guayaquil, and in the picturesque city and cultural center of Cuenca in the southern Sierra.

Benedict Schools of Languages, P.O. Box 09-01-8916, Guayaquil; 011-593-5-444 4418, fax 011-593-5-444 1642; www.benedictquito.com. 15 teachers in various branches plus 10 more for the Quito branch at Edmundo Chiriboga N47-133 y Jorge Paez, Quito; Tel./fax 011-593-2-432729; benedict@accessinter.net. College degree needed.

CEDEI Centro de Estudios Interamericanos, Casilla 597, Cuenca; 011-593-7-839003; English@cedei.org, www.cedei.org. Needs 18 university-educated native speakers to teach for at least 6 months. Recruitment information available online.

Genesis Exchange Program, Horacio Gostalle 402 and Padre Laenen St, Bahia de Caraquez, Manabi, Ecuador; 011-593-5-692400; vladirv@hotmail.com). Volunteers teach English to children aged 4-7 for 2 hours a day

185

for a minimum of 2 weeks between April and January, in exchange for free accommodation in an adjoining house near the beach. Program cost of $10 per day includes meals.

Inlingua, Arroyo del Rio y Manuel Maria Sanchez 320, Quito; 011-593-2-243 788; www.inlingua.com. Seeks 30 native speakers. Preference given to those with inlingua experience.

Key Language Services, Alpallana 581 y Whymper, Quito Casilla 17-079770, fax 011-593-2-220956; kls@hoy.net. Up to 15 native speaker teachers needed.

South American Language Center, Amazonas 1549 y Santa Maria, Quito; 011-593-2-544715, fax 011-593-2-226348; sudameri@impsat. net.ec. Needs 15 native speakers.

El Salvador

CIS Centro de Intercambio y Solidaridad (MAM Language School), Boulevard Universitario, Casa No. 4, Colonia El Roble, San Salvador, El Salvador; Tel./fax 011-503-226-2623; cis@netcomsa.com, www.cis-elsalvador.org. Volunteer teachers to give evening English lessons to members of the Salvadorean opposition. Training provided, and also Spanish classes and a political-cultural program.

Guatemala

Casa Guatemala, 14th Calle 10-63, Zona 1, 01001 Guatemala City; 011-502-232 5517; casaguatemal@guate.net. Runs an orphanage in the Petén region that needs volunteer teachers and nannies, among other tasks.

Modern American English School, Calle de los Nazarenos 16, Antigua; 011-502-932-3306, fax 011-502-932-0217. Experienced teachers can be interviewed by telephone. Board and lodging provided.

Mexico

One of the most important language training organizations with 22 franchise schools is Wall Street Institutes, Presidente Masaryk #49, Mezzanine, 11570 Mexico D.F.; 011-52-5-545 23 53; ggv@wsimex.com.

ABC English, 1616 Suite 6 Blvd, Ruiz Cortines Fracc. Palmas, Poza Rica 93300 Veracruz; Tel./fax 011-52-29-782 23981.

American School of Veracruz, Progresso 52 Jardinas de Mocambo, Boca del Rio, Veracruz 94298; 011-52-29-21 97 78. Package includes immigration clearance, (shared accommodation females only), contribution to airfare and approximately $650 per month.

Anglo American, Campos Eliseos No. 111,

Col. Polanco 11560 Mexico D.F.; 011-52-5395 6779; www.angloamericano.com.mx. 5 locations.

Arizona School of English, Blvd 1 Rosales y Ortega, Deco Plaza, Loc. 7, Col. Centro, Los Mochis, Sinaloa 81200; 011-52-68-18-56-71; azschool@bigfoot.com.

Berlitz Mexico, Ejército Nacional 530 2 Piso, Col. Polanco, 11550 Mexico D.F.; 011-52-55-3531-4353.

Centro Mexicano Internacional, CMI Institute, Calz. Fray Antonio de San Miguel 173, Morelia 5800; 800-835-8863, fax 011-52-43-13 98 98; cmi@spanish-language.com. Range of voluntary internships including some as English teachers.

English First Mexico, Col. Juarez 06600, D.F. Mexico; 011-52-5514 3333, fax 011-52-5514 1362; www.englishfirst.com or www.englishtown.com. Twelve teachers for 4 schools. Must be certified. Twenty-six contact hours per week; visa, return flight, paid holiday, bonus, ongoing teacher training and medical insurance provided as well as salary of 7,000-9,500 Mexican pesos per month.

English Unlimited, Valentin Gama #800, Colonia Jardin, San Luis Potosi, SLP 78270; tel/fax 011-52-4-833 1277; teaching@ englishunlimited.com, www.englishunlimited. com. No special qualifications requested.

Glen Internacional Instituto Superior de Idiomas, Viena No. 71-301 Col. Del Carmen, Coyoacan 04100 Mexico D.F.; 011-52-59 37 74; www.solucion.com/glen.

Harmon Hall, Puebla No. 319. Col. Roma, 06700 Mexico; 011-52-11 60 60; www.harmonhall.com.mx. Has numerous branches around Mexico City and elsewhere.

IMARC Instituto Mexicano Norteamericano de Relaciones Culturales, Pres. Cardenas 840, Saltillo, Coahuila 25000; 011-52-84-14 84 22, fax 011-52-84-12 06 53. Interviews can be carried out at TESOL conferences in U.S.

Furthermore, many universities, institutes of higher education, and bilingual schools hire teachers. If you have a specific destination in mind, you might wish to purchase the relevant back issue of the "Teach English in Mexico Newsletter" for $5; see their online catalog www.employnow.com/2000back.htm. An alternative route to finding a job in Mexico is via the Internet Works web site www.teach-english-mexico.com which operates a guaranteed placement program for a fee of $925.

Peru

Centro de Idiomas, Cuzco 784, Piura, Peru; globalingua@viabcp.com. Must have relevant experience. High wages for Peru ($500 per month).

Instituto Cultural Peruano Norteamericano, M. M. Izaga #807, Chiclayo; 011-51-74-231241; icpnachi@mail.udep.edu.pe. Wants to double the number of native-speaking teachers at present.

Venezuela

The number of opportunities for in-company language trainers through Caracas-based agencies has declined in the wake of the failed coup and economic instability, but Venezuela is still a promising destination for English teachers.

Centro Venezolano Americano, Av. José Marti, Edf. CVA, Urbanizacion Las Mercedes, Caracas 1060-A; or: Apartado 61715 Del Este, Caracas 1060-A; 011-58-2-993 7911, fax 011-58-2-993 8422; www.cva.org.ve. Combined work/study internships open only to U.S. citizens.

Centro Venezolano Americano del Zulia, Calle 63, No. 3E-60, Apartado 419, Maracaibo; 011-58-911880; www.cevaz.org. Also CVA Merida, Prolongacion Av. 2, Lora Esq. 43, No. 1-55, Urb. El Encanto, Merida; cevam@icnet. com.ve. Native speakers given pre-service training.

IFISA Instituto de Formacion Idiomatica. D.A., Calle 4 Cruce con Carrera 4, 6016 Lecharia; 011-58-281-7651; www.ifisa.com.ve. Undergraduates to teach ESL to all age groups.

Iowa Institute, Avenida Cuatro con Calle 18, Mérida Edo. Mérida; 011-58-74-526404. Teaching opportunities for trained TEFL teachers and for Americans with camp counseling experience to teach children.

Venusa, Program at the Instituto de Estudios Internacionales, Merida. U.S. contacts: 6342 Forest Hill Bouolevard, P.M.B. 308, West Palm Beach, FL 33415; venusa@earthlink.net, www.home.earthlink.net/~venusa. Work-study positions, mainly for American graduates and undergraduates studying English/Spanish. Minimum stay 3 months.

U.S. and U.K. Placement

American Friends Service Committee, 1501 Cherry St., Philadelphia, PA 19102-1479; 215-241-7295, fax 215-241-7247; www.afsc.org. A Quaker organization which recruits Spanish-speaking volunteers aged 18-26 to work in Mexico for 7 weeks in the summer, some on teaching projects programme fee $1,250 plus travel expenses. Mexican partner organisation

is SEDEPAC, Apartado Postal 27-054, 06760 Mexico DF; http://sedepac.org.mx.

AmeriSpan Unlimited, P.O. Box 40007, Philadelphia, PA 19106; 800-879-6640, fax 215-751-1100; info@amerispan.com, www.amerispan.com. Spanish language travel organization that offers unpaid volunteer placements and internships as English teachers in Bolivia, Brazil, Costa Rica, Ecuador and Mexico. One-month immersion language program followed by 1-6 month volunteer placements. Application and placement fee is $350 including travel insurance. Lodging with local family provided.

Amity Volunteer Teachers Abroad (AVTA), 10671 Roselle St., Suite 101, San Diego, CA 92121-1525; 858-455-6364; www.amity.org. Sends volunteers to teach in Argentina, Mexico, Brazil, Venezuela, Dominican Republic and Peru. Volunteers must be over 21, in their final year or two of a degree course or a graduate, have a working knowledge of Spanish and be able to stay for 8/9 months months from January/February or August/September. Homestay accommodations and a small allowance ($15-$25 a week) are provided.

Association of American Schools in South America (AASSA), 14750 NW 77th Ct., Suite 210, Miami Lakes, FL 33016; 305-821-0345, fax 305-821-4244; info@aassa.com, www.aassa.com. Coordinates teacher recruitment for 25-30 international schools in 11 South American countries. Candidates who attend a recruiting fair in November/December must be state-certified teachers and pay a placement fee of $200 if hired (which is usually reimbursed by employer).

Caledonia Language Courses, The Clockhouse, Bonnington Mill, 72 Newhaven Rd., Edinburgh EH6 5QG, U.K. 011-44-131-621 7721; www.caledonialanguages.co.uk. Spanish language and voluntary work programmes organized in Peru and Costa Rica year round.

ELTAP English Language Teaching Assistant Program), Univ. of Minnesota, Morris, MN 56267; 320-589-6464; jkuechle@mrs.umn.edu, www.eltap.org. Placement of university students for 11 weeks at various times of year in one of several Latin American countries: Brazil, Chile, Guyana, and Panama. Volunteers pay $300-$600 placement fee plus travel and living expenses.

i-to-i, 1 Cottage Rd., Headingley, Leeds LS6 4DD, U.K.; 011-44-0870 333 2332, fax 011-44-

113 274 6923; www.i-to-i.com. TEFL teacher training and travel organization which accepts North American participants for 3-month voluntary teaching placements in Bolivia, Costa Rica, and Honduras. Fees respectively $1,795, $1,695 and $2,195 excluding airfares.

Office of English Language Programs, U.S. State Department, SA 44, Room 304, 301 4th St. SW, Washington, DC 20547; 202-619-5892; http://exchanges.state.gov/education/engteaching. Part of the State Department, this office runs a network of overseas field offices based in U.S. Embassies, many of which have English teaching programs employing native speakers of American English. Binational Centers offer English instruction in most of the countries of Latin America; contact details are available online.

South America Explorers, 126 Indian Creek Rd., Ithaca, NY 14850; 607-277-6122; explorer@samexplo.org, www.samexplo.org. Annual membership costs $50. Allows access to SAE clubhouses with useful notice boards and contacts. Each of its three clubhouses in Lima, Cusco and Quito have an Explorers Volunteer Resource section, a database of volunteer opportunities to which members can gain access.

Teaching & Projects Abroad, Gerrard House, Rustington, West Sussex BN16 1AW, U.K.; 011-44-1903-859911; info@teaching-abroad.co.uk, www.teaching-abroad.co.uk. Volunteer English language teaching assistants placed in Mexico, Chile and Peru and many countries worldwide. No TEFL background required. Self-funded packages cost from £795-£1,595 ($1,150-$2,300) excluding airfares.

WorldTeach, Center for International Development, Harvard Univ., 79 John F. Kennedy St., Cambridge, MA 02138; 617-495-5527, 800-4-TEACH-0; info@worldteach.org, www.worldteach.org. Nonprofit organization which places several hundred graduates as volunteer teachers of EFL or ESL in several countries including Costa Rica and Ecuador for the summer or for 1 year, and Mexico for 6 months. The inclusive cost is about $4,000 for the summer program and $5,000 for a year.

Perspective

Teach English in Colombia

Grappling with Grammar, Gold, Guns, and Guayaba

By Larry M. Lynch

Americans avoid Colombia for good reasons. A virtual civil war has been waged for nearly 40 years. Rates of crime and violence are among the world's highest. And then there's the "drug problem." Why would anyone consider coming here to teach English?

"I came because a friend who was working in Cali liked it here and recommended it," says Glenn Yates, a teacher now in his second year at a bilingual school. Tired of Canada's frigid winters, he fled to a land of year-round warm weather and an even warmer welcome.

Colin Jacobs, weary of gloomy days and drizzle, found his way to teaching English in Cali from his native England more than 20 years ago and hasn't left since. "I don't think I could live in London again," he says. "After adjusting to the near-perfect weather, the food, and the easy-going lifestyle here, I'm not really keen to go back. I'm spoiled for life."

So am I. Hundreds of varieties of flowers perfume the air, even in winter. Pantries abound with exotic fruits like *guayaba* and *carambolo*. The year-long growing season allows papayas to reach nearly the size of watermelons; mangoes can weigh up to two pounds each. Colombia's strong, black coffee, considered the world's richest, is served everywhere.

But Is It Safe?

There are problems, yes, but not of "run-screaming-to-the-hills" intensity. Most conflicts occur in the countryside. While this can make inter-city travel risky at times, residents inside major cities like Bogotá, Cali, and Medellin feel little impact and live quite normally. Adjusting to power failures, phone or water outages, and rainy season flooding is more of a nuisance than life-threatening. Larger cities are reasonably well policed and usually safe, if you're careful.

Drugs? Most illicit production is for export, so, except for warring drug factions in the coca-growing areas, there's not much everyday impact. During major holidays the government steps up military patrols of principal highways and vacation resort areas to insure protection and safer travel for vacationers.

Quality of Life

Cali, with two million residents, is known as the "Salsa capital of the world," rivaling Cuba. The two largest shopping malls house multi-cinema complexes featuring first-run U.S. films in English with Spanish subtitles. English publications are readily available at bookstores and newsstands. Material in English can be borrowed free from the Universidad Santiago de Cali and for a $3 annual fee from the Centro Cultural Colombo Americano. The Municipal Theatre, Tertulia Arts Complex, and Jorge Isaacs Theatre offer regular productions in Spanish. Ethnic restaurants specializing in Latin American and Mediterranean cuisines continually tempt Caleño palettes. Holiday celebrations take place year-round. Check them out online at www.holiday festival.com/Colombia.html. You will never be bored in Cali.

Jobs

Native-speaking English teachers are scarce here. Salaries reflect the high demand. Most teaching positions require an applicant to be a native speaker of English and have a university degree. A teaching certificate and some experience are a definite plus. Work is available at bilingual colegios, language institutes, and universities. Sending out a dozen or so resumes in English should land you half that number of interviews, culminating in several on-the-spot job offers.

No hablas español? Interviews are typically in English, but as a working resident you'll likely want to pick up more than just tourist Spanish. The Universidad Santiago de Cali and the Pontifica Universitaria Javeriana have Spanish programs for foreigners. Berlitz (www.berlitz.com) has offices in Cali with Spanish classes. A private tutor is fairly easy to come by.

"It hasn't been a problem to find someone to help me when I need something done in Spanish," said Glen Yates, who, with his limited Spanish, has found Colombians to be very friendly and sociable.

So, don't worry needlessly about the news reports. Call, write, or email the schools and institutes to get a feel for their needs and requirements. Check out the web sites. Assemble your diplomas, certificates, and reference letters. Don't forget to collect materials like maps, postcards, flyers, magazines, and memorabilia from your hometown. These will be invaluable for your conversations with students.

English Teaching in Cali

Kiss English Academy, Cra. 42 No. 5B-105, Barrio: Tequendama; 011-57-53-6534; kisseng@telesat.com.co. Contact: Anthony Kiss, Director.

Learn English School, Cra. 100 No. 15-14, Barrio: Ciudad Jardin; 011-57-680-3080; learnenglish@andinet.com, www. learnenglishschool.com.co.

Colegio Bolivar, Av. 10 de Mayo, Pance, Cali, Colombia; 011-57-555-2039, www.colegio bolivar.edu.co.

Colegio Bennett, Calle Alférez Real A. A. 7948, Barrio: Ciudad Jardín, Cali, Colombia; 011-57-332-2353; fbennett@telesat.com.co, www.telesat.com.co/bennett.

ELS Language Centers, Av. Roosevelt Transversal, 5a, #5E-80, Tequendama, Cali, Colombia; 011-57-2-553-6397; elstequendama@telesat.com.co, www.els.com.

Centro Cultural Colombo Americano, Calle 13N No. 8-45, Barrio: Granada, Cali, Colombia; 011-57-667-3539. Contact: Beth Barlett, Academic Director,

www.colombocali.edu.co.

Universidad Santiago de Cali, Institute of Languages, Calle 5 at Cra. 62, Pampalinda Campus, Cali, Colombia, Contact: Marilyn Molano, Director; 011-57518-3000 ext 411, fax 011-57-552-5250; coorpost@usaca.edu.co, www.usaca.edu.co.

Universidad San Buenaventura, La Umbría, Carretera a Pance, A.A. 7154, Cali, Colombia. Contact: Juan Carlos Muñoz, English Department Director; 011-57684-7200, 011-57555-2007, 011-57318-2200, www.usb.edu.co.

Universidad ICESI, Calle 18 No. 122-135, Cali, Colombia; 011-57555-2334. Contact: Esperanza Ferreira, English Dept. Director; fmartine@icesi.edu.co, www.icesi.edu.co.

Universidad Autonoma, Calle 25 No. 115-85 (km. Via Jamundi), Cali, Colombia; 011-57-318-8000. Contact: Cristina Peñafort, English Dept. Director; buzon@cuao.edu.co, www. cuao.edu.co.

Teaching English Abroad
The Key Print Resources

Selected and Reviewed by William Nolting

Teaching English may not require any special credentials other than having English as your native language and a year's commitment (and usually a college degree). Typical locations: Eastern Europe and Asia. Apply as early as December prior to the fall you want to start.

*Essential; *Outstanding and of broad interest. For ordering information, if not included below, see Key Publishers, Page 13.*

The ELT Guide. 1999. 9th ed. 271 pp. TESOL. Order #683GAZ. $28.95 (member $24.95). Comprehensive reference for English language teaching worldwide. Primarily intended for ESL teachers with professional credentials. Country-by-country guide with recruitment information, school listings, and training courses.

French Cultural Services: English Teaching Assistant Program. Applications available from: Cultural Services of the French Embassy, 972 5th Ave., New York, NY 10021; fax 212-439-1455; info-france-usa.org/culture/

education/index.html. Several hundred academic-year positions available for Americans under 30 with a college degree and working knowledge of French. Stipend is paid which covers living expenses.

*Fulbright English Teaching Assistantships.** Applications free from Dept. of State Fulbright, IIE/U.S. Student Programs Division, 809 United Nations Plaza, New York, NY 10017-3580; 212-984-5330; www.iie.org/fulbright. Enrolled students must apply through own college; graduates apply "at-large" to regional IIE offices. English teaching options for graduates in Belgium/Luxembourg, France, Germany, Hungary, Korea, Taiwan, and Turkey. Application deadline for current students is in mid-September (or mid-October for "at-large" applicants) for teaching in the following academic year. Also available are Fulbright scholarships for study abroad in over 100 nations.

**Japan Exchange Teaching Program (JET). Free applications from Office of the JET Program, Embassy of Japan, 2520 Massachusetts Ave. NW, Washington, DC 20008; 800-INFO-JET or 202-939-6772; www.jet.org, or contact any Japanese consulate. This is the largest program for teaching English abroad, with more than 6,000 participants annually. Offers 2 types of paid positions in Japan: English-teaching assistantships in secondary schools or Coordinator for International Relations (latter requires Japanese proficiency). Application deadline early December.

*Make a Mil-¥en: Teaching English in Japan by Don Best. 1994. 176 pp. $14.95 plus $3 (book rate) or $3.95 (first-class) shipping from Stone Bridge Press, P.O. Box 8208, Berkeley, CA 94707; 800-947-7271, fax 510-524-8711; sbp@stonebridge.com, www.stonebridge.com. Guide has information on everything from the job search to settling in. The experts at O-Hayo Sensei consider this to be the best book on Japan from an American perspective currently available.

*More Than a Native Speaker: An Introduction for Volunteers Teaching Abroad by Don Snow. 1996. 321 pp. (Order #641). $29.95 (member $24.95) plus $4.50 shipping from TESOL. Covers classroom survival skills for teaching English as a second or foreign language from lesson planning to adaptation to life in a new country, with detailed discussions of how to teach listening, speaking, reading, writing, grammar, vocabulary, and culture.

Native Speaker: Teach English and See the World by Elizabeth Reid. 1996. 96 pp. In One Ear Publications. $7.95 plus $3 s/h from Book Clearing House, 46 Purdy Street, Harrison NY 10528; 800-431-1579. A basic guide guide to teaching English as a second language, finding a position, and setting up private classes, by an American who taught in Latin America.

*O-Hayo Sensei: The Newsletter of Teaching Jobs in Japan edited by Lynn Cullivan. Twice-monthly by email, $12 for 12 issues. Single issue free, check web site. To subscribe, send check or money order payable to O-Hayo Sensei, to: O-Hayo Sensei, Subscription Dept., 1032 Irving St., PMB 508, San Francisco, CA 94122; fax 415-731-1113; editor@ohayosensei. com, www.ohayosensei. com. Lengthy lists of current job openings for English teachers, university-level teachers and others. Classifieds, Japan info, and lists of schools.

Opportunities in Teaching English to Speakers of Other Languages by Blythe Camenson. 1999. 160 pp. $20 hardcover/ $11.95 paperback from VGM Career Horizons. Overview of the professional field of Teaching English as a Foreign/Second Language.

*"Teaching Abroad Without Certification" by William Nolting. Available free on the Univ. of Michigan International Center's web site, www.umich.edu/~icenter/overseas. A well-researched listing of U.S.-based organizations which can place teachers of English abroad.

**Teaching English Abroad: Teach Your Way Around the World by Susan Griffith. 2001. 544 pp. Vacation Work (U.K.). $17.95 from Peterson's. The only book with extensive worldwide coverage (including Western and Eastern Europe, the Middle East, Africa, Asia, and Latin America), this outstanding volume gives in-depth information on everything from preparation to the job search. Many first-hand reports from teachers. Extensive directories of schools, with full contact information including email addresses and web sites.

*Teaching English in Asia: Finding a Job and Doing it Well by Galen Harris Valle. 1995. 178 pp. $19.95 plus $3 s/h from Pacific View Press, P.O. Box 2657, Berkeley, CA 94702; 510-849-4213, fax 510-843-5835; pvp@sirius.com. Detailed yet lively overview of teaching English in East and SE Asia, with comprehensive teaching tips, by a professional teacher. However, it provides few job search addresses.

TESOL Placement Bulletin. TESOL members: $50 (not offered to non-members). Monthly bulletin lists position openings for qualified ESL/EFL teachers and administrators. TESOL, 700 S Washington St., Suite 200, Alexandria, VA 22314; 703-836-0774, fax 703-836-6447; info@tesol.org, www.tesol.org.

Teaching English as a Second Language

Directory of Training and Placement Programs

By Transitions Abroad Editors

If you lack experience or credentials, you may want some formal study before heading overseas in search of an English language teaching position. Virtually all positions require only a bachelor's degree. However, candidates with advanced training and either a certificate or a master's degree in TESOL will have greater flexibility and command more pay. For the most current information see the *Transitions Abroad* web site www.TransitionsAbroad.com or contact the program directors. And please tell them you read about their programs in this book. Organizations in more than one country are listed under "Worldwide."

ASIA

TEFL Int'l. TESOL Certificate

TEFL International is an internationally recognized 4-week course which trains you to be an English teacher. As the largest organization of its kind in Asia, we pride ourselves in providing a supportive course with lifetime job placement assistance. We operate courses all year long in Thailand, China, and Morocco. Accommodations are included in the course fee.

Dates: Monthly. **Cost:** $1,590. **Contact:** TEFL Int'l., 38/53-55 Moo1, Saunson Rd., Klaeng, Muang, Rayong 21160; Thailand; Tel./fax 011-66-38-652-280; info@teflintl.com, www.teflintl.com.

CANADA

Cambridge CELTA

The Certificate in English Language Teaching to Adults (CELTA) is the world's most widely recognized entry-level certificate for teaching English as a second or foreign language and is the credential employers ask for by name. CELTA at ILI is now offered as a 4,000 level university credit.

Dates: 2002: May 27-Jun 24, Jul 22-Aug 16, Aug 19-Sep 1, Sep 16-Oct 1; 2003: Apr **Cost:** Registration fee $75. Course fee $1,500. **Contact:** Registrar, International Language Institute, 5151 Teminal Rd., 8th Fl., Halifax, NS, B3J 1A1, Canada; 902-429-3636, fax 902-429-2900; study@ili-halifax.com, www.ili-halifax.com/celta.

Teacher of English (TESOL) Certification

Travel and teach English around the world. Five-day intensive TESOL certification courses in-class across Canada and Australia, or worldwide online or by correspondence. Learn hands-on skills and theory. Employment contacts and job guarantee included. Over 15,000 successful graduates. Government accredited. Other specialized TESOL courses available (grammar, business English, TOEFL, etc.). No prerequisites or experience rquired.

Dates: Year round across Canada; worldwide online or correspondence. **Cost:** CAN$1,000 in-class; U.S.$800 by correspondence. **Contact:** Canadian Global TESOL Training Institute, Travel and Teach English Center, 10762-82 Ave., Suite C, Edmonton, AB T6E 2A8, Canada; 888-270-2941, 780-438-5704, fax 780-435-0918; tesol@canadianglobal.net, www.canadianglobal.net.

CENTRAL AND EASTERN EUROPE

Bridges for Education, Inc.

Bridges for Education sends volunteer teachers to teach conversational English in summer. Three weeks teaching, 1 week travel. Educated adults (including families) and college students pay roundtrip airfare and BFE administrative expenses. Since 1984 about 850 teachers to 8 countries, serving 8,500 students from 34 countries with Ministry of Ed., UNESCO. Tax deductible, earn college credit.

Dates: Summer, Jul, and Aug. **Cost:** Approx. $2,000, depending on departure and destination points. **Contact:** Margaret Dodge, Applications Coordinator 8912 Garlinghouse Rd., Naples, NY 14512; 716-534-9344; mdodge@frontiernet.com, www.bridges4edu.org.

Cambridge/CELTA

Four-week intensive course for those wishing to enter ELT or experienced teachers seeking recognized qualification. Highly practical, including seminars and workshops, observed teaching practice, and feedback. Assessment of teaching and written work throughout course. Help provided with accommodations. (Also DELTA, YL extension, Teaching English for Business).

Dates: Jul, Aug. **Cost:** £650 course fee (including Cambridge registration fee). **Contact:** Eliza Jaroch, International House, ul. Leszczynskiego 3, 50-078 Wroclaw, Poland; Tel./fax 011-48-71-7817-293 or 011-48-71-372-3698; ttcentre@ih.com.pl, www.ih.com.pl.

Central European Teaching Program

Teach conversational English (or German, French, and other subjects) in schools in Hungary, Poland, and Romania. Live and work for a year in this rapidly changing part of the world, and immerse yourself in a new culture. Salary, housing, and health insurance are provided. Program support services.

Dates: Sep-Jun or Jan-Jun. **Cost:** Placement fee ranges from: $2,000-$3,400. **Contact:** Amy Berigtold, CETP, Beloit College, 700 College St., Beloit, WI 53511; 608-363-2619; cetp@beloit.edu, www.beloit.edu/~cetp.

CHINA

China Teaching Program

A training and placement program for those wanting to teach at institutions of higher education or at secondary schools throughout the P.R.C. Most opportunities are in TEFL, some in business or law. Five-week summer training session held on WWU campus. Participants study Chinese language and culture, TEFL methodology, etc. Minimum requirements: BA, native speaker of English. (Placement-only option may be possible.) TESOL certification option also offered.

Dates: Application deadline for Summer Session is in early February. **Cost:** Approx. $1,200 (includes tuition and placement). **Contact:** Catherine Barnhart, Director, China Teaching Program, Western Washington Univ., HSH6, 516 High St., Bellingham, WA 98225-9047; 360-650-3753; ctp@wwu.edu, www.wwu.edu/~ctp.

Teach in China

Teach English, history, economics, etc. for 1 year in Chinese universities. Minimum BA. All majors considered, Chinese language not necessary. Placements in February and September. Chinese schools provide salary (good by Chinese standards), free housing, medical care, paid 3-4 week vacation. Fabulous opportunity to teach, travel, and learn Chinese. Professionals encouraged to apply, as well as couples.

Dates: Feb-Jun or Aug-Jun, with option to renew. **Cost:** Application, placement, assistance with all forms, visa and travel arrangement, medical evacuation insurance, teaching and orientation materials, 3-week intensive Chinese language study and Teacher Training Institute in Shanghai (tuition, private room) sightseeing, airport pickups and backup support: $2,950. Application, placement, medical evacuation insurance, orientation and teaching materials, backup support, and assistance with all official forms for spring placement only (no Institute training): $1,350. Many schools reimburse airfare home after 1 year. Professionals fee is $2,950—Institute extra. **Contact:** Alice Renouf, Director, 4556 Apple Way, Boulder, CO 80302; 303-443-1108, fax 303- 443-1107; alice@asiacouncil.org, www.asiacouncil.org.

CZECH REPUBLIC

TEFL Diploma Teacher Training

Teach English abroad! The Boland School, located in Brno, capital of the beautiful wine region of Moravia, Czech Republic, offers high-quality intensive 4-week teacher training courses to those interested in starting a career teaching English as a foreign language. The course focuses on the practical with lots of real teaching practice opportunities, in-house language school, comprehensive job placement assistance for jobs all over the world. Free internship in Czech secondary school upon completion of course. The Boland School is accredited by the Czech Ministry of Education.

Dates: Once monthly. **Cost:** $1,095 includes all fees and materials. **Contact:** The Boland School, Palackeho 148a, 612 00 Brno, Czech Republic; 011-420-5-41-24-16-74, fax 011-420-5-41-24-16-74; boland@mbox.vol.cz, www.boland.cz/tefl.

EGYPT

The American Univ. in Cairo

Graduate Master's degree program and fellowship for teaching English as a foreign language are offered at the American Univ. in Cairo. Courses essential for effective teaching are given by a supportive, skilled faculty. The master's degree program requires 2 years and the intervening summer for completion. Program starts in Sep only.

Dates: Sep-Jun; Jun-Aug. **Cost:** Without fellowship: year $11,525; summer $2,858. **Contact:** Matrans

Davidson, American Univ. in Cairo, 420 5th Ave., 3rd Fl., New York, NY 10018-2729; aucegypt@aucnyo.edu, www.aucegypt.edu.

EUROPE

English Language Teaching

Certificate and diploma courses for English language teaching to adults and younger learners, certified by Cambridge Univ. Part-time and intensive courses available.

Dates: Intensive 2002: Sep 2-29. 2003: Jan 23-Feb 19; May 20-Jun 25; Jun 30-Jul 25; Sep 1-26. Part-time 2002: Oct 3-Dec 19. 2003: Feb 27-May 22. **Cost:** Euro 1,291.00 plus Univ. Cambridge fee Euro 118,000 . **Contact:** Teacher Training Dept., International House, Viale Manzoni 22, 00185 Rome, Italy; 011-390-6-70476894, fax 011-390-6-70497842.

FRANCE

French in France

The French American Study Center was founded 25 years ago in the U.S. Students of any age or any level can be at home in Normandy to study French in real immersion.

Dates: Spring: Mar-May; summer: Jun-Aug; fall: Sep-Oct. **Cost:** From $490 per week (tuition, room and board, and excursions). **Contact:** Dr. Alméras, Chairman, French American Study Center, 12, 14, Blvd. Carnot, B.P. 4176, 14104 Lisieux Cedex, France; 011-33-2-31-31-22-01, fax 011-33-2-31-31-22-21; centre.normandie@wanadoo.fr, http://perso.wanadoo.fr/centre.normandie.

JAPAN

Japan Exchange and Teaching (JET) Program

Sponsored by the Japanese Government, the JET Program invites over 1,300 American college graduates and young professionals to share their language and culture with Japanese youth. One-year positions are available in schools and government offices throughout Japan. Apply by early December for positions beginning in July of the following year.

Dates: One-year contracts renewable by mutual consent not more than 2 times. **Cost:** Participants receive approx. ¥3,600,000 per year in monthly payments. **Contact:** JET Program Office, Embassy of Japan, 2520 Massachusetts Ave. NW, Washington, DC 20008; 202-238-6772, fax 202-265-9484; eojjet@erols.com, www.embjapan.org.

Teaching English in Japan

Two-year program to maximize linguistic and cultural integration of participants who work as teachers' assistants. Placements twice yearly in Apr and Aug. Most positions are in junior high schools in urban and rural areas. Bachelor's degree and willingness to learn Japanese required.

Dates: Hiring for positions every Apr and Aug. Applications accepted year round. Potential applicants are encouraged to submit applications between Oct-Feb. **Cost:** No application fees. **Contact:** Institute for Education in Japan, Earlham College, 801 National Rd. W, D-202, Richmond, IN 47374; 888-685-2726, fax 765-983-1553; sebener@earlham.edu, www.earlham/edu~aet.

LATIN AMERICA

Bridge-Linguatec TEFL & CELTA

Whether you select the 4-week international TEFL Certificate program or the world-renowned CELTA, your training will give you the fundamentals needed to be an effective English Language teacher from the start. In addition, graduates of either of these training programs will be given preference in hiring to teach at any of Bridge-Linguatec Centers.

Dates: Year round. **Cost:** $1,500. **Contact:** Bill Arnold, tefl@bridgelinguatec.com.

Teach in Latin America

Recruits college graduates for year-long programs in Costa Rica and Ecuador to teach English at various levels. Specialized summer programs for volunteers who are at least 18 years old in both countries.

Dates: Jan departure for Costa Rica; Apr and Sep for Ecuador; summer programs Jun 20-Aug 20. **Cost:** $4,990 (year); $3,990 (summer). Includes international roundtrip airfare, health insurance, orienation and training, room and board, and full-time in-country staff support. **Contact:** WorldTeach, Center for International Development, Harvard Univ., 79 John F. Kennedy St., Cambridge, MA 02138; 800-483-2240 or 617-495-5527, fax 617-495-1599; info@worldteach.org, www.worldteach.org.

SPAIN

Cambridge CELTA, Cambridge DELTA

The CELTA (Certificate in English Language Teaching to Adults) is an initial training course in the teaching of English as a foreign language. The DELTA (Diploma in English Language Teaching to Adults) is intended for practicing ELT teachers with substantial experience. Accommodations can be arranged by the center.

Dates: CELTA 4-week intensive: 10 times a year; DELTA full-time from Sep-Nov. **Cost:** CELTA Euro 1,150; DELTA Euro 1,900 ; Accommodations Euro 360 per 4 weeks. **Contact:** Teacher Training Dept.,

CLIC International House, Mendez Nuñez, 7, 41001 Sevilla, Spain; 011-34-954-500316, fax 011-34-954-500836; training@clic.es, www.clic.es.

TAIWAN

Hess Educational Organization

Largest private children's language school in Taiwan specializing in Teaching English as a Foreign Language (TEFL). Over 120 schools and 50 kindergartens island-wide, we offer 3 contract options. The curriculum has been tried, tested, and constantly updated to provide the most successful programs for teaching English to learners of all ages. Requirements: a bachelor's degree, a passport from an English-speaking country, a 1-year commitment, and being a native English speaker. For more information and an application form, check out the web site, www.hess.com.tw.

Dates: Application accepted anytime. Deadlines are Jan 31 for Jun 1; Apr 30 for Sep 1; Jul 31 for Dec 1; and Oct 31 for Mar 1. **Cost:** No fee. We recruit only for our own schools. **Contact:** Hess Educational Organization, English Human Resource Dept., 419 Chung Shan Rd., Sec. 2, Chung Ho City 235, Taiwan, ROC; 011-886-2-3234-6188 ext. 1053, fax 011-886-2-2222-94-99; hesswork@hess.com.tw, www.hess.com.tw.

Overseas Service Corps YMCA

BAs to PhDs placed in ESL teaching positions in community-based YMCAs in Taiwan. No Chinese language necessary. Preference given to applicants with teaching experience, either general or ESL, or degree in teaching. This conversational English program provides an opportunity for cultural exchange. Must reside in North America and be a citizen of an English-speaking country. 20 to 30 openings.

Dates: Call anytime for a brochure and application. Placement ends Sep through following Sep, 1-year commitment. **Cost:** $50 application fee. Benefits include: housing, health insurance, international air travel, paid vacation, bonus, orientation, sponsorship for visa, and monthly stipend. **Contact:** Patty Schnabel YMCA International Services, 6300 Westpark, Suite 600, Houston, TX 77057; 713-339-9015 ext 338; kpsmile@flash.net.

UNITED KINGDOM AND IRELAND

Cambridge/RSA CELTA and DELTA Courses

CELTA 4-week preparatory certificate in teaching English, the most widely accepted qualification for teaching English in the world. Also DELTA, an 8-week intensive course for teachers with a minimum of 2 years experience teaching English as a second/foreign language (vital for more responsible posts e.g., D.O.S., Director, etc.).

Dates: CELTA every 6 weeks; DELTA Jan/Feb and July/Aug every year. **Cost:** CELTA £945; DELTA £1,400. **Contact:** Trevor Udberg, Director, International House Newcastle, 14-18 Stowell St., Newcastle Upon Tyne; NE1 4XQ, England; 011-44-191-232-9551, fax 011-44-191-232-1126; info@ihnewcastle.com, www.ihnewcastle.com.

UNITED STATES

CTESOL and Advanced CTESOL

Transworld Schools is internationally recognized and approved by the state of California to offer both the CTESOL and Advanced CTESOL training courses. All courses include teacher practice, grammar and skills training, teaching children and adults, business English, and computer assisted language learning. Lifetime job placement is provided in the U.S. and worldwide. Continuing education credits awarded.

Dates: Year round. Full-time every 2 weeks from Jan 6, part-time every 6 weeks from Jan 7. **Cost:** Comprehensive CTESOL $1,900, CTESOL $1,700. $100 application fee. All course materials included. **Contact:** Ceri Rich-Odeh, Director, Transworld Schools, 701 Sutter St., 2nd Fl., San Francisco, CA 94109; 415-928-2835, 888-588-8335; transwd@aol.com, www.transworldschools.com.

ESL Intensive Institute

Learn English pronunciation, listening comprehension, conversation, reading and writing. Includes an orientation to American culture and weekly field trips. By Univ. of New Hampshire in Durham (hour north of Boston and 15 minutes from ocean). For students wanting to learn English before college or who want to improve TOEFL scores (4-12 credits, 4 hours per day).

Dates: Take 1 session or more. Sessions 4-, 8-, or 12-week study. Sessions run year round. **Cost:** Tuition varies depending on length of study. Room and board available at a moderate additional cost. **Contact:** H. Smith, UNH Continuing Education, ESL Institute, 24 Rosemary Ln., Durham, NH 03824; 603-862-2069; learn.dce@unh.edu, www.learn.unh.edu/ESL.

Hamline TEFL Certificate Course

The Graduate School of Education at Hamline Univ. offers an internationally recognized TEFL certificate course to prepare individuals to teach English overseas. An interactive approach enables participants to discover the practices of language teaching. Courses include lectures, workshops, and practice teaching. Career counseling provided. Graduates can complete 3 additional online courses for an Advanced TEFL Certificate or apply their course work to an MA in ESL.

Dates: Three 1-month intensives: Apr, Jul, and Aug; evening extensive: Oct-Mar. On-campus room and board available except in Aug. **Cost:** All courses are $2,400 beginning June 2002. Participants receive 8 graduate semester credits upon completion of the program. Materials: approx. $80. Rates valid through June 2003. **Contact:** Betsy Parrish, Associate Professor/Coordinator, or Julia Reimer, Assistant Professor/Summer Coordinator TEFL Certificate Program, Graduate School of Education, Hamline Univ., 1536 Hewitt Ave., St. Paul, MN 55104; 800-888-2182, fax 651-523-2489; bparrish@gw.hamline.edu, jreimer@gw.hamline.edu, www.hamline.edu/tefl.

IELI at Humboldt State Univ.

Intensive English with part-time university academic courses in a congenial and safe community in northern California. Small classes, personalized instruction. Housing in homestays, student apartments, and on campus. A complete recreational and activity program. Airport pickup and assistance in getting settled.

Dates: Jan, Mar, May, Aug, and Oct—8-week sessions. **Cost:** Tuition $1,440 for 21 hours per week. Room and board $1,320 for 8 weeks. **Contact:** IELI, Humboldt State Univ., Arcata, CA 95521-8299; 707-826-5878, fax 707-826-5885; ieli@humboldt.edu, www.humboldt.edu/~ieli.

Lado TEFL Certificate

Four-week intensive, 10-week night/Saturday classes. Highly successful placement services. Recognized by ACE (American Council on Education).

Dates: Year round. **Cost:** $1,850 includes registration fee, textbooks, and other materials. **Contact:** Suzanne Matula, Lado TEFL, 2233 Wisconsin Ave., NW, Washington, DC 20007; 202-333-4222, fax 202-337-1118; teachertraining@ladoent.com, www.lado.com/home_t.htm.

Master of Arts in Intercultural Service, Leadership and Management

The School for International Training (SIT) offers academic curriculum integrated with field-based practice, reflection, and application including professional practice. SIT offers master's degrees in Teaching (ESOL, French, Spanish), Intercultural Relations, International Education. Sustainable Development, Organizational Management, Conflict Transformation, and a self-design option. SIT also offers undergraduate study abroad programs in over 45 countries.

Dates: Call for details. **Cost:** Call for details. **Contact:** Admissions, School for International Training, P.O. Box 676, Kipling Rd., Brattleboro, VT 05302; 800-336-1616, fax 802-258-3500; admissions@sit.edu, www.sit.edu.

Master's Degree in TESL

Successful program graduates have a strong background in descriptive English linguistics; an appreciation for the influence of culture on language learning; broad knowledge of past and current language learning theories and teaching approaches; and experience creating syllabi and lessons, selecting and creating teaching materials, and adapting instruction to students' needs.

Dates: Spring: Jan 14 (international student orientation Jan 9); fall: Aug 21 (international student orientation Aug 14); summer: Jun 17 (international student orientation Jun 12). **Cost:** U.S. citizens $175 per credit hour; international students $348 per credit hour. **Contact:** Graduate Coordinator, MA-TESL Program, Central Missouri State Univ., Martin 336, Warrensburg, MO 64093-5046; 660-543-8507, fax 660-543-8544; eason@cmsu1.cmsu.edu.

Midwest Teacher Training Program

Earn a TEFL certificate in a 5-week intensive teacher training program that prepares you to teach English worldwide. Hands-on approach incorporates course work, practice teaching, and ESL observation in a unique observation theater. No foreign language or teaching experience required. Job placement assistance and career workshops included.

Dates: Jan 21-Feb 21, Mar 17-Apr 18, May 12-Jun 13, Jul 7-Aug 8, Sep 15-Oct 17, Nov 10-Dec 12. **Cost:** $2,325 includes books. **Contact:** Renee Lajcak, Program Director, Midwest Teacher Training Program, 19 N Pickney St., Madison, WI 53703; 800-765-8577, fax 608-257-4346; info@mttp.com, www.mttp.com.

St Giles Language Teaching Center

Training courses leading to the prestigious, internationally recognized Cambridge Certificate in English Language Teaching to Adults (CELTA). The CELTA is the TEFL qualification required by many employers worldwide. Successful candidates also earn a graduate credit recommendation of six hours toward an MA TESOL. Each course is externally moderated by Cambridge Univ. We also offer lifelong job guidance to our graduates.

Dates: Jan 7, Feb 11, Mar 11, Apr 15, May 20, Jun 24, Jul 29, Sep 9, Oct 14, Nov 18. **Cost:** $2,695 ($2,495 in Jan and Feb). **Contact:** St Giles Language Teaching

Center, 1 Hallidie Plaza, Suite 350, San Francisco, CA 94102; 415-788-3552, fax 415-788-1923; sfstgile@slip.net, www.stgiles-usa.com.

TESL Degree Courses

Western Kentucky Univ. provides courses in TESL leading to the BA or MA degree in English or in education.

Dates: Aug-Dec, Jan-May. **Cost:** $3,000 out-of-state tuition per semester. **Contact:** Dr. Ronald D. Eckard, English Dept., Western Kentucky Univ., Bowling Green, KY 42101; 270-745-6320; Ronald.Eckard@wku.edu.

Training and Placement Programs

Online and onground classes. Since 1985 a pioneer of intensive ESOL training in the U.S. Prepare to teach in the U.S. as well as overseas. Receive 900-level education credits and the Certificate in Teaching English as a Second or Foreign Language. Credits also apply to Washington State ESL Supporting Endorsement, and to various Seattle Univ. Master's Programs. Graduates currently teaching and administrating in the U.S. and more than 58 other countries. On-site ESL class. Well-qualified and experienced instructors. Lifetime job information. Internet discussion list for graduates. International applicants welcome (I-20s available). We work with VISTA, Americorps, and other government agencies for tuition payment.

Dates: Eleven starting dates per year for the 4-week intensive sessions. Evening non-intensive program and online classes are on the Seattle Univ. quarterly schedule. **Cost:** $2,460 for the 12-credit certificate training for the 2001-2002 academic year. Low-cost housing on-site. **Contact:** School of Teaching ESL, 2601 NW 56th St., Seattle, WA 98107; 206-781-8607, fax 206-781-8922; hasegawa@seattleu.edu, www.seattleu.edu/soe/stesl.

The Univ. of Arizona

The Dept. of English MA in ESL emphasizes leadership development and is designed for experienced teachers with a strong academic record and leadership experience. Specialized courses are offered in language program administration, comparative discourse, teaching language through literature, sociolinguistics, language testing, and technology. PhD in SLAT.

Dates: Applications due by Feb 1 for the following fall semester. Two years are normally required to complete the program. **Cost:** $1,132 registration for 7 or more units, plus approx. $275 per unit for nonresident tuition. **Contact:** Director, English Language/Linguistics Program, English Dept., P.O. Box 210067, The Univ. of Arizona, Tucson, AZ 85721-0067; 520-621-7216, fax 520-621-7397; maes1@u.arizona.edu, www.coh.arizona.edu/ell.

Univ. of Cambridge CELTA-DELTA

The most widely recognized initial qualification for teaching English as a foreign language to adults, the CELTA is offered at our Portland, San Francisco, Santa Monica, and San Diego centers year round. You need to be at least 20 years old, have a good standard of education and recent foreign language learning experience to be qualified.

Dates: Year round. **Cost:** $2,250 CELTA; $4,145 DELTA (includes enrollment fee). **Contact:** Conrad Heyns, International House-San Francisco, 49 Powell St., 2nd Fl., San Francisco, CA 94102; 415-989-4473, fax 415-989-4440; teachertraining@ih-portland.com.

WORLDWIDE

Amity Institute - AVTA Program

Amity Volunteer Teachers Abroad (AVTA) Program offers opportunities to serve as a teacher or teaching assistant in Germany, Latin America, Africa, and Chinese-speaking countries. Programs range from 1 month to a full academic year; room and board is provided. Candidates must be a university graduate or have experience teaching ESL.

Dates: Year-round. **Cost:** $500-$1,200. **Contact:** Karen Sullivan Amity Institute, 10671 Roselle St., Suite 100, San Diego, CA 92121-1525; 858-455-6364, fax 858-455-6597; avta@amity.org, www.amity.org.

Berlitz General English Courses

Offers year round General English, Business English, and Junior English, Easter and summer vacation courses, and Management English courses for nonanglophone managers, Heritage tours of the U.K.'s historical towns of interest for U.S. senior citizens, church, and youth organizations. General English group or individual study. Full- and half-day group, student group, and charter group full- and half-day individual, semi-private, and total immersion instruction. Residential English Language Courses for Teenagers. Homestay and hostel accommodations arranged for students.

Dates: Year round. **Cost:** From £149 (approx. $225) per week includes books, materials, and excursions. **Contact:** Paul Corcut, Berlitz Language Centre, 20 Queens Rd., Brighton BN1 3XA, E. Sussex, U.K.; 011-44-1273-322-700, fax 011-44-1273-322-701; info@berlitz-brighton.co.uk, www.berlitz-brighton.co.uk.

English as a Second Language

The program consists of an integrated core curriculum and a number of electives. Students are able to create their own program by focusing on academic English, business writing and communication, and general communication. Conversation partners, and short-term customized courses available.

Dates: 2003: Jan 8-Apr 4 (winter); Apr 16-Jun 13 (spring); Jun 25-Aug 22 (summer); Sep 10-Dec 5, 2003 (fall). **Cost:** Winter/fall $2,290. Spring/summer $2,010. **Contact:** Ruth Heinrichs (Acting Head), English as a Second Language Centre, Univ. of Regina, Rm. 211, Language Institute, Regina, SK S4S 0A2, Canada; 306-585-4585, fax 306-585-4971; esl@uregina.ca, www.uregina.ca.

International Expeditions

Conservation Expeditions, Teaching Projects and Independent Voluntary Work Opportunities around the world. Train as a Safari Field Guide, Teach in Nepal, or join pioneering Conservation Expeditions in the Amazon or Africa. Additional programs in Brazil, Ecuador, Costa Rica, and Panama. Full international support and training is provided for all programs. From 3 weeks to 12 months.

Dates: Year round. **Cost:** From $500 per month. **Contact:** Global Vision International, 781-740-1170; info@gvi.co.uk, www.gvi.co.uk.

International Schools Services

Learn about teaching opportunities in private American and international schools around the world and discover how you can carry your education career overseas. The Educational Staffing program of International Schools Services has placed over 17,000 K-12 teachers and administrators in overseas schools since 1955. Most candidates obtain their overseas teaching positions by attending our U.S.-based International Recruitment Centers (IRCs) where ISS candidates interview with overseas school heads seeking new staff. Applicants must have a bachelor's degree and 2 years of current K-12 teaching experience. The experience may be waived for those who have overseas living or working experience, teaching certification, and a motivation to work in the developing world. IRC registration materials are provided upon approval of your completed ISS application. See web site for more information or to fill out an application.

Dates: International Recruitment Centers in Feb, Mar, and Jun. **Cost:** $150; International Recruitment Center registration: $200. There are no placement fees charged to candidates who are placed through the work of ISS. **Contact:** Educational Staffing, ISS, P.O. Box 5910, Princeton, NJ 08543; 609-452-0990 or 609-452-2690; edustaffing@iss.edu, www.iss.edu.

Passport TEFL

Internationally recognized Trinity College Certificate in TESOL. Train in Prague or Barcelona, teach worldwide. Four-week intensive sessions are year round on a monthly basis. No second language required, English-only method. College degree not mandatory. Practical training with foreign students. Job guaranteed at Prague location.

Dates: Jul 1-27, Aug 5-31, Sep 2-28, Sep 30-Oct 26, Oct 28-Nov 23, Nov 25-Dec 21. Dates for 2003 TBA. **Cost:** Prague $1,250, Barcelona $1,000. Includes tuition, airport greeting, orientation, guaranteed job in Czech Republic, assistance with work visa, lifetime international job guidance. Housing in Prague is $400, Barcelona $250. **Contact:** Passport TEFL, 655 Powell St., Suite 505, San Francisco, CA; 415-544-0447; info@itc-training.com, www.itc-training.com.

Teach in Africa, Asia, Latin America

WorldTeach. Based at Harvard Univ. for 15 years, WorldTeach provides opportunities for individuals to make a meaningful contribution to international education by living and working as volunteer teachers in developing countries in Africa, Asia, Latin America, and Pacific Islands. Offers 8-week summer teaching programs to qualified adults 18 years of age and older, involving either English or basic computer/internet instruction. WorldTeach also offers 1 year and semester teaching placements for college graduates.

Dates: Jun 20-Aug 20 (summer); long-term programs depart through the year. **Cost:** Summer $3,990; year/semester $4,990-$5,990. Includes international roundtrip airfare, health insurance, orientation and training, room and board, and full-time in-country staff support. **Contact:** WorldTeach, Center for International Development, Harvard Univ., 79 John F. Kennedy St., Cambridge, MA 02138; 800-483-2240 or 617-495-5527, fax 617-495-1599; info@worldteach.org, www.worldteach.org.

TESOL Career Services

Use TESOL's Career Services to find the best ESOL teaching positions worldwide. The TESOL **Placement E-Bulletin (PEB)** has job listings and job searching resources for ESOL professionals. The PEB, free to all members, provides the latest job listings in biweekly email updates and is posted on TESOL's Online Career Center searchable job bank. The Employment Clearinghouse at TESOL's annual convention and exposition in April is the world's largest TESOL job fair. Jobs will be posted and interviews are conducted on site.

Dates: Call for details. **Cost:** Contact TESOL for more information. **Contact:** Career Services, TESOL, 700 S Washington St., Suite 200, Alexandria, VA 22314; 703-836-0774, fax 703-836-6447; career@tesol.edu, www.tesol.org.

The Best Web Sites

Internet Resources for Teaching English Abroad

Selected and Reviewed by William Nolting

Teaching abroad is one of the most accessible options for longer-term work abroad, typically for a year, though some programs offer short-term placements. Teaching English as a second or foreign language (TESL, ESL, TEFL, EFL) may be an option for college graduates without TESL credentials. Alternatively, other options are strictly for professionals with at least a Masters in Teaching English. ***Essential *Outstanding and of broad interest.*
(I) Informational site with directories or databases
(P) Site for a specific work abroad program
(S) Scholarships or fellowships

**(I) Dave's ESL Cafe, www.eslcafe.com, ESL Cafe's Web Guide, www.eslcafe.com/search, ESL Cafe's Web Guide: Jobs, www.eslcafe.com/search/Jobs by Dave Sperling. This site has a staggering amount of well-organized information about teaching English as a second language, either abroad or in the U.S., as well as job databases. Useful for those with and without TESL credentials. A highly recommended resource for anyone interested in working abroad.

**(P) Fulbright English Teaching Assistantships, Fulbright Student Programs, Institute of International Education, www.iie.org/fulbright. Program for recent university graduates to serve as English Teaching Assistants in Belgium/Luxembourg, France, Germany, Hungary, Korea, Taiwan and Turkey. The Fulbright Student Program also offers scholarships for study abroad.

**(P, I) Japan Exchange and Teaching Program (JET), www.jet.org. JETAA site by Michael McVey. The Japan Exchange and Teaching Program is administered by the Japanese government, and is the largest single program for teaching English. Graduating seniors and university degree holders eligible. Also offers positions for those who have studied Japanese as Coordinators of International Relations. This website, by the JET Alumni Association (JETAA), has links to the JET program site. It also has extensive information about international jobs (great links to job search sites worldwide, www.cheno.com/job/) and a good discussion about career choices after teaching abroad. You can also subscribe to JET-L, a discussion group by participants (returned, current and prospective), from this site—useful for anyone interested in teaching abroad.

(I) O-Hayo Sensei, www.ohayosensei.com. Listings of ESL and other types of teaching positions in Japan.

**(P, I) Peace Corps, www.peacecorps.gov. Sometimes overlooked because of its designation as a volunteer program, Peace Corps is one of the largest work-abroad programs for U.S. citizens. It provides some of the best-paid teaching opportunities in less-wealthy regions such as Africa, Latin America, South and Southeast Asia, and even Eastern Europe and the former USSR.

*(I) Teachers of English to Speakers of Other Languages (TESOL), www.tesol.org. Web site of the largest U.S. professional association for ESL teachers. An essential resource for qualified professionals, though less useful for students.

**(I) Univ. of Michigan, International Center's Overseas Opportunities Office, www.umich.edu/~icenter/overseas. See article on "Teaching Abroad Without Certification" which lists U.S.-based programs for teaching abroad that do not require professional TESL credentials.

*(I) U.S. State Department, Office of English Language Programs, http://exchanges.state.gov. Official information about U.S.-sponsored programs for teaching English abroad. Includes links to job search sites, of use especially to qualified ESL teachers (MA in TESL).

CHAPTER 6

K-12 AND UNIVERSITY TEACHING

Teachers with K-12 certification have a wide range of options for teaching abroad. The types of schools can be viewed in terms of the amount of integration into the host culture that the teacher is likely to experience. The following are listed in an order that proceeds from culturally less-integrated to more-integrated settings.

Key Programs and Organizations
Teaching K-12 and University

By William Nolting

Department of Defense Schools. Located at military bases in 19 countries around the world, some 200 DOD schools employ around 13,000 U.S. citizens. The teaching environment is roughly similar to that of U.S. public schools. Contact with host-country nationals is relatively limited. Contact: 4040 North Fairfax Dr., Arlington VA 22203-1634; (703) 696-3269; www.state.gov. Publishes free brochure *Overseas Employment Opportunities for Educators*. Available from Department of Defense, Office of Dependent Educational Activity, Office of Personnel, Dependents Schools, 4040 N Fairfax Drive, Alexandria, VA, 22203; 703-696-1352. Includes application.

The **U.S. Dept. of State** publishes the free brochure *Overseas American-Sponsored Elementary Schools Assisted by the U.S. Department of State.* Order from Office of Overseas Schools, U.S. Dept. of State, Rm. 245, SA-29, Washington, DC, 20522; 703-875-7800, fax 703-875-7979. Information on 192 private schools.

Private International Schools. Located worldwide, nearly 1,000 private English-language K-12 schools educate the children of diplomats and businesspeople and of wealthy host country nationals. The teaching environment is similar to that of elite U.S. private schools. Although one can apply directly, the most efficient way to apply is through recruitment fairs in the U.S. (see below), most of which take place in February (apply early since some fill up by December).

Volunteer Organizations. Despite the name, most volunteer placements, if long term (two years), usually cover expenses and provide a stipend. Options range from the government-sponsored Peace Corps to religious organizations (from non-proselytizing to traditional missionaries).

Unlike private schools, pupils in these schools will be the children of ordinary people from the host country. Contact: **Peace Corps**, Rm. 8500, 1990 K St. NW, Washington, DC 20526; 800-424-8580; www.peacecorps.gov. Contact religious organizations directly; some recruit at the teaching abroad fairs already mentioned.

Fulbright Teacher Exchange (K-12 and Community Colleges). This program is unique in two respects: it is a one-for-one exchange of teachers between schools, and teachers are fully integrated into regular host-country schools. Applicants must currently have a full-time teaching or administrative position. Application deadline is in October for the following academic year. Contact: **Fulbright Teacher Exchange Program**, U.S. Information Agency, 600 Maryland Ave. SW, Room 235, Washington, DC 20024-2520; 800-726-0479.

University Teaching

Nearly all university positions require a PhD (or at least "ABD") or other terminal professional degree.

Teaching for Study Abroad Programs. This is generally a tough market since U.S.-sponsored programs tend to use home-campus faculty or hire local professors. One organization sometimes hires resident directors (802-258-3114) and also publishes two-page resource lists on teaching and internship opportunities abroad ($2 each): Professional Development Resource Center, **School for International Training**, Box 676, Kipling Rd., Brattleboro, VT 05302-0676; 802-258-3397, fax 802-258-3248; www.sit.edu.

Fulbrights. Information on Fulbright grants to support an academic year of teaching in an overseas university is available from the **Council for International Exchange of Scholars** (CIES), 3007 Tilden St. NW, Suite 5M, Washington, DC 20008-3009; 202-686-4000; info@ciesnet.cies.org, www.cies.org. Grants also available for international education administrators.

Special Placement Programs. Most of the organizations listed in Directory of Programs (page 192) can offer university-level positions for those who are qualified. Worth special mention are: **The Civic Education Project** (CEP), P.O. Box 205445, Yale Station, New Haven, CT 06520-5445; 203-781-0263, fax 203-781-0265; cep@minerva.cis.yale.edu, http://cep.nonprofit.net. CEP offers positions in Eastern Europe for PhDs and PhD candidates in economics, history, international relations, political science, sociology, public administration, and law. Application deadline: February 1.

Colorado China Council, 4556 Apple Way, Boulder, CO 80301; 303-443-1108, fax 303-443-1107; alice@asiacouncil.org, www.asiacouncil.org. CCC offers placements in universities in the People's Republic of China, especially in English, TESL, journalism, business, sciences, and engineering.

Regular Faculty Positions. See such standard academic job listings as those in the *Chronicle of Higher Education* (U.S. 800-347-6969 or www.chronicle.merit/edu) the *Times Higher Education Supplement* (U.K. www.timeshigher.newsint.co.uk) or the *Guardian* (U.K.), found in most university libraries.

Find a Teaching Job Abroad
Recruitment Fairs Are the Places to Get Jobs

By Clay Hubbs

The bulk of teaching opportunities abroad are for English teachers. You can obtain formal credentials in Teaching English as a Foreign (or Second) Language (variously called TEFL, TEFOL, TESL, TESOL, or ESL) in a one-month course or a two-year MA program. (See Directory of Training and Placement Programs, Chapter 5.)

Qualified K-12 teachers have another range of options: Scattered around the world are at least 800 U.S.-style international elementary and secondary schools which employ around 35,000 American educators. To find a position in one of these schools you can either conduct your own job search—using the resources at the end of this chapter—or sign up for one of the recruiting fairs listed below.

The Employment Connection (*The Source*), an online service provided by The College of Education, Placement Services, and Ohio State Univ. (address below), contains all postings received through its offices. Subscriptions cost $25 per quarter. Other web sites that catalog teaching jobs abroad (both ESL and K-12) are listed at the end of this chapter and are updated annually in the September/October issue of *Transitions Abroad*, www.TransitionsAbroad.com.

Recruiting Fairs

Attending a recruiting fair is probably the easiest way to find a teaching job overseas. Some fairs charge fees; others are free. Most charge a fee if you are offered a job. Some restrict the number of participants or have early registration deadlines.

Assn. of American Schools in South America, AASSA-Teachers Search, 14750 NW 77th Ct., Suite 210, Miami Lakes, FL 33016; 305-821-0345, fax 305-821-4244; info@aasa.com, www.aassa.com. **Fair dates:** usually late November or December; write in September for exact dates. Openings for schools in Central and South America, Mexico, and the Caribbean.

European Council of International Schools, U.S. office: 105 Tuxford Terrace, Basking Ridge, NJ 07920; 908-903-0552, fax 908-580-9381; malyecisna@aol.com, www.ecis.org. **Fair dates:** Melbourne, AUS, usually early January; Vancouver, Canada, usually mid-February; London, England, usually early February and early May. Very early deadline. Contact early.

International Schools Services, Educational Staffing, P.O. Box 5910, Princeton, NJ 08543; 609-452-0990, fax 609-452-2690; iss@iss.edu, www.iss.edu. **Fair dates:** Washington, DC in February; Miami, FL, in early March; Philadelphia, PA, in late June. Credential files must be received six weeks before fair dates.

National Assn. of Independent Schools (NAIS), 1620 L St., Suite 1100, NW, Washington, DC 20036; 202-973-9705, fax 202-973-9700; www.nais.org. **Fair date:** February 24-28. NAIS primarily serves independent schools in the U.S.

Ohio State Univ., Office of Placement Services, 110 Arps Hall, 1945 N High St., Columbus, OH 43210-2741; 614-292-2241 or 888-678-3382, fax 614-688-4612;

www.coe. ohio-state.edu/placement. Teach Ohio is an annual job fair for K-12 educators. It attracts up to 115 school districts; registration is required. **Fair date:** April.

Queen's Univ., Placement Director, Faculty of Education, Queen's Univ., Kingston, ON K7L 3N6, Canada; 613-533-6222, fax 613-533-6691; http://educ. queensu.ca/~placement//index.html. **Fair date:** Early February.

Search Associates, P.O. Box 636, Dallas, PA 18612; 717-696-5400, fax 717-696-9500; In Canada: 613-967-4902, fax 613-967-8981; www.search-associates.com. **Fair dates:** September in Cambridge, MA; February in Carmel, CA; Houston, TX. June in Bethesda, MD. Also 10 other locations worldwide.

Teacher Recruitment Int'l., P.O. Box 177, Tumby Bay, Australia; 011-02-9328-3930, fax 011-9328-3863; tiaust@ozemail.com.au, www.triaust.com. **Fair dates:** Sydney, usually early January; Melbourne, usually late March and mid-April.

TESOL, 700 S Washington St., Suite 200, Alexandria, VA 22314-2751; 703-836-0774, fax 703-836-7864; recruit@tesol.org, www.tesol.org. Primarily a convention for ESL (English as a Second Language) teachers. All levels. Good placement opportunities worldwide. **Fair date:** Varies each year. Check web site for current dates.

Univ. of Calgary, Faculty of Education, Education Tower 1302, Univ. of Calgary, 2500 University Dr., NW, Calgary AB T2N 1N4, Canada; Tel./fax 403-220-2292, fax 403-284-1755; http://external.educ.ucalgary.ca. **Fair date:** January; call for details.

Univ. of Northern Iowa, Overseas Placement Center for Educators, SSC-19, Univ. of Northern Iowa Career Center, Cedar Falls, IA 50614; 319-273-2083, fax 319-273-6998; overseas.placement@uni.edu, www.uni.edu/placemnt/overseas. **Fair date:** Usually in late February.

Perspective

Travel and Teach

Trade Your Concrete Jungle for a Real One

By T.J. Fournier

A s I gather my books for my day at school, I look out the window at the snow-capped Andes. Smoke curls from the chimneys of houses some 1,000 feet below and church bells ring in the barrio. On the bus to work I eat a warm, buttered *arepa* while we twist through the hills.

Trading my U.S. classroom in the concrete jungle for one in mountainous Colombia was not a hard choice for me. For many educators, though, teaching abroad seems only something to dream about because they may not be aware of the real opportunities to travel and teach.

"Many foreign schools have a very significant need for well-trained North American teachers," says Joe Fuchillo of International Educators Cooperative (IEC), an agency whose goal is to match teachers and administrators with South American schools. "Most U.S. teachers are unaware of the opportunities available worldwide for both short- and long-term contracts."

"Traditionally, the contracts for foreign teachers run from two to five years," he notes, "so there is constant turnover, a constant demand for new staffing."

IEC is one of the smaller headhunting agencies serving international schools. (See list of recruitment agencies and fairs above.) Most fairs are held in late February while large numbers of North American schools are closed for vacation. Attendees include administrators, teachers, and school service professionals. Many are veterans of international education. Others, like my wife and I were, are novices.

Just recently married, my wife and I began our journey over a cup of coffee. We are both former Peace Corps volunteers and perpetually afflicted with wanderlust; we were discussing whether to continue teaching in the Detroit public schools or to take a leave of absence and travel. It was evident before the coffee got cold what we were going to do.

We began by canvassing university schools of education, the Peace Corps office in Washington, and our colleagues for information regarding international schools: where they are, who hires, who gets hired, the average salary, etc. We were sent brochures, pamphlets, and applications.

The choices seemed endless. Instead of pursuing every lead, we decided what region of the world we wanted to focus on and what type of population we wanted to work with (urban or rural, native or expatriate, poor or wealthy). Our choice was South America, partly because I am fluent in Spanish. We were determined not to teach in a capital city as we were already accustomed to large populations in small spaces. Finally, we preferred teaching a native population.

Selecting an Agency

These criteria allowed us to hone our choices to a few selected agencies that deal specifically with South American schools. IEC, as a small agency, was very accommodating in responding to our questions and concerns. With our resumes and dossiers in hand, we flew to Houston for a weekend of interviewing, trading information with other applicants, and undergoing intense soul searching.

The fair began on Friday evening with an ice-breaking cocktail hour. We mingled with teachers, administrators, and conference coordinators. We were fascinated with our competition—attendees came from all parts of the world. On Saturday morning we met in a large conference room in which each school had its own table. The school directors had already reviewed our applications and posted the names of potential applicants at their stations. We were to find our names and wait in line to be interviewed. If our names were not posted anywhere, or if the school in which we were interested didn't post our names, we became second priority and were to stand in line until the preliminary interviews were finished. We were each given six interviews and received as many job offers.

Upon deciding on the Colegio Granadino in Manizales, Colombia, we returned to Detroit with new contracts in hand. Our principals accepted our announcement with good cheer, pleased that their staff members were looking to broaden their experiences. We were both offered unconditional leaves of absence and support in linking our schools in Detroit with Colombia through email pen pal exchanges.

As we begin our second term teaching at elementary schools in Manizales, we can hardly believe our luck. New experiences, new challenges, and a new perspective are benefits we find here that even the strongest of unions back home could not bargain into our contracts. Do yourselves and your classrooms a favor. Take a risk and do what few dare to do: teach abroad.

Teaching K-12 and University
The Key Print Resources

Selected and Reviewed by William Nolting

International teaching jobs in K–12 schools usually require a teaching credential. Jobs in universities often require a PhD. Major K–12 job fairs are held in February (apply in November).

** Essential; *Outstanding and of broad interest.
For ordering information, if not included below, see Key Publishers, Page 13.

Friends of World Teaching. Friends of World Teaching maintains updated listings of English-speaking schools and colleges in over 100 foreign countries where educators may apply throughout the year. For a free brochure, please send a self-addressed stamped envelope to: Friends of World Teaching, P.O. Box 84480, San Diego, CA 92138-4480; 800-503-7436, fax 619-224-5363; details@fowt.com, www.fowt.com.

*Fulbright Scholar Program: Grants for U.S. Faculty and Professionals. Free information from Council for International Exchange of Scholars, 3007 Tilden St. NW, Suite 5L, Washington, DC 20008-3009; 202-686-7877, fax 202-362-3442; scholars@cies.iie.org, www.iie.org/cies. Program offers university-level opportunities for lecturing and research abroad; most positions require doctoral degrees or master's degrees and/or equivalent professional experience. Application deadlines: May 1 (distinguished chairs program); Aug 1 (lecturing and research awards); Nov 1 (international education administrators); Jan 1 (NATO scholars); rolling deadline (senior specialists).

*Fulbright Teacher Exchange: Opportunities Abroad for Educators. Free application from the U.S. Department of State, Fulbright Teacher Exchange Program, 600 Maryland Ave. SW, Suite 320, Washington, DC 20024-2520; 800-726-0479; fulbright@grad.usda.gov, http://www.grad.usda.gov/info_for/fulbright.

cfm. Program descriptions and application for direct exchanges in over 30 countries for currently employed K-12 and community college faculty and administrators. The application deadline for 2002-2003 is October 15.

*The ISS Directory of Overseas Schools edited by Gina Parziale. 2001 (revised annually). 560 pp. International Schools Services. $34.95 from Peterson's. The most comprehensive and up-to-date directory to over 580 overseas American and international K-12 schools that hire certified teachers. For other publications and services contact: International Schools Services, 15 Roszel Road, P.O. Box 5910, Princeton, NJ 08543; 609-452-0990, fax 609-452-2690; iss@iss.edu, www.iss.edu. Available directly from ISS: *NewsLinks*, $20/year, a bimonthly news magazine for the international school community; and *Teaching and Administrative Opportunities Abroad*, free application to ISS job fairs for teaching overseas.

Overseas Academic Opportunities. Monthly bulletin. $42/year from Overseas Academic Opportunities, 72 Franklin Ave., Ocean Grove, NJ 07756; Tel./fax 732-774-1040. Openings primarily for new teachers in all K-12 subject areas for jobs where the only language needed is English and state certification is not required. Positions are regularly available in over 50 countries.

Overseas American-Sponsored Elementary Schools Assisted by the U.S. Department of State. Free pamphlet available from the Office of Overseas Schools, U.S. Department of State, Rm. H328, SA-1 Washington, DC 20522-0132; 703-875-7800, fax 202-261-8224; www.state. gov. Information on around 200 private overseas K-12 schools. *Fact Sheets* provide more detailed information, available free on www.state.gov/www/about_state/schools/ index.html.

Overseas Employment Opportunities for Educators (Department of Defense schools). Annual. Free from Department of Defense, Office of Dependent Educational Activity, Office of Personnel, Dependents Schools, 4040 N Fairfax Dr., 6th Fl., Alexandria, VA 22203; 703-696-1352; www.odedodea.edu. Application for K-12 employment opportunities in over 200 schools worldwide serving U.S. military bases. Minimum academic requirement is a BA or BS with at least 18 hours of education courses.

*Overseas Placement Service for Educators, Univ. of Northern Iowa (UNI). To order registration materials for the oldest and one of the largest U.S. international recruiting fairs for K-12 teachers, send $5 to Overseas Placement Service for Educators, Univ. of Northern Iowa, SSC #19, Cedar Falls, IA 50614-0390; 319-273-2083, fax 319-273-6998; overseas.placement@ uni.edu, www.uni.edu/placement/overseas. The fair, held each February, attracts over 100 American international schools. Fact book and newsletters are included with registration (also available as separate purchases).

The Best Web Sites

Internet Resources for K-12 and University Teaching Abroad

Selected and Reviewed by William Nolting

Teaching in international K-12 schools usually requires teaching certification. Teaching at the university level usually requires a PhD or terminal professional degree, though there are some options available for advanced graduate students. ***Essential; *Outstanding and of broad interest.*

(I) Informational site with directories or databases listing many programs
(P) Site for a specific work abroad program
(S) Scholarships or fellowships

K-12 TEACHING ABROAD

*(P) Fulbright Teacher Exchange: US State Department, Bureau of Educational and Cultural Affairs, www.grad.usda.gov/ International/ftep.html. Teaching exchanges (reciprocal) for currently employed K-12 and community college teachers.

*(P, I) International Schools Services (ISS), www.iss.edu. Non-profit organization publishes a directory of international K-12 English-language schools and organizes job fairs (IRCs) for certified teachers for these schools.

**(I) Ohio Univ., Employment Resources for Language Teachers, www.ohiou.edu/esl/ teacher/index.html. By John McVicker, this site of the Ohio Program of Intensive English (OPIE) has a comprehensive collection of websites for finding language teaching positions and courses, both abroad and in the U.S.

Site also has a guide to web resources for those studying foreign languages.

*(I) Overseas Teacher's Digest, www.overseas digest.com. Site includes overseas teaching positions and contains valuable information for Americans working abroad. Be sure to see the Better Business Bureau article made available by this site, Overseas Job Scams, http://overseasdigest.com/scams.htm.

*(I) Univ. of Northern Iowa's Overseas Placement Service for Educators, www.uni.edu/placemnt/overseas. This university-sponsored service organizes an annual job fair for certified teachers for international K-12 English language schools and publishes information about these schools.

*(I) U.S. Department of State, Teaching Overseas, www.state.gov/m/a/os/. Site describes English-language K-12 schools abroad, opportunities for teaching abroad and gives links to relevant organizations.

(I) Univ. of Michigan, International Center's Overseas Opportunities Office, www.umich.edu/~icenter/overseas. See article on "Teaching Abroad for Qualified Teachers," which lists options for K-12 and university-level teaching.

UNIVERSITY TEACHING ABROAD

(I) Chronicle of Higher Education, http://thisweek.chronicle.com/jobs/. For academicians the Chronicle is the best source of job listings. Much of site accessible only to subscribers. Also check with discipline-specific professional associations.

(P) Fulbright Scholar Program, Grants for US Faculty and Professionals, Council for International Exchange of Scholars (CIES), www.iie.org/cies. Overseas teaching and research positions for those qualified to teach or to do research in universities, as well as study tours for international education administrators.

About the Contributors

Editors

CLAY HUBBS is the founder, editor, and publisher of *Transitions Abroad*. He taught Modern European and American literature and served as Director of International Studies at Hampshire College from 1972-1998.

SUSAN GRIFFITH is the author of *Work Your Way Around the World* and *Teaching English Abroad: Talking Your Way Around the World*, both available from Peterson's Guides.

WILLIAM NOLTING is the Director of the Univ. of Michigan Overseas Opportunities Office and International Education Editor for *Transitions Abroad*.

Contributors

DAVE ABERNATHY is still teaching English in Rayong, and is an aspiring freelance author.

STEVEN AYERS spent two years teaching English in Taiwan before working as an investment research analyst in Hong Kong, New York, and Seattle.

GREGORY BENCHWICK calls Colorado home when he is not on the road. He is a frequent contributor to several guidebooks and magazines.

KENNETH CHAMPEON is an honors graduate from the Univ. of Chicago, an expatriate teacher, and a freelance writer living in Thailand. He has lived in Asia for over two years.

LORI CLOUTIER is a 1999 graduate of the Univ. of Michigan. She participated in BUNAC's Work in Britain program during the summer of 1996.

JOSEPH COLLINS, STEFANO DE ZEREGA, ZAHARA HECKSCHER have recently coauthored the book *How to Live Your Dream of Volunteering Overseas,* which includes evaluations of over 80 volunteer programs.

JANE CUCCIA is married to an Egyptian and has taught ESL in Cairo for over 20 years.

ROBERT DIEMER worked for the FSM Supreme Court and the FSM Public Defender Office for several years. He has written on Micronesia for several publications, and now lives in Paris.

BRYAN J. ESTEP founded a trading company with offices in Mexico City, San Francisco, and Santiago, Chile. He is the coauthor of the guide *Exporting to Mexico*.

T.J. FOURNIER writes from Manizales, Colombia.

VICTORIA GRISANTI, a freelance writer and English teacher currently living in Sicily, held an internship with the U.S. Department of State during the summer of 1999. Prior to her move to Italy, she worked in public relations for a Fortune 500 company.

ANTHONY HAND is a graduate student in the School of Information at the Univ. of Michigan. He is a JET program alumnus.

ROBERT HEIN has worked in Thailand for over 12 years. He recently published *The Bangkok Expat's Handbook,* a guide to living in Thailand.

TODD HEWETT is an adventure writer living in Austin, TX who loves the joys of trouble-free travel—unfortunately he's never experienced any.

LAURA HIGGINS FLORAND has been a Fulbright scholar to French Polynesia and lived, worked, and studied in Spain and France. She now teaches French at Duke Univ.

JANN HUIZENGA has taught EFL and trained EFL teachers in 20 countries since 1978. She has held three Fulbright grants to the former Yugoslavia, Turkey, and Italy.

LARRY LYNCH is a university English professor and technical copywriter and has been living in Cali, Colombia for the past seven years.

KARA C. McDONALD works at the Center for Democracy and Governance at USAID in Washington, DC. She has participated in three missions to Bosnia and was involved with efforts in Kosovo. She holds a Masters degree from the Fletcher School of Law and Diplomacy.

CHRISTOPHER MOORE has taught English in Spain and China, interned at UNESCO in Beijing, and ran from the bulls in Pamplona. He now works at the Northern Nevada International Center, and will graduate from the Univ. of Nevada, Reno. He hopes to make documentary films one day.

CHARLIE MORRIS is a writer and computer consultant. He has worked throughout Europe and lived in Switzerland, Norway, and England.

JEFF MORRIS recently spent two years working as a police officer for the United Nations in Kosovo. He is the author of *Working in War Zones*, forthcoming from Paladin Press.

DEBRA PETERS-BEHRENS is a career counselor at the Univ. of California, Santa Barbara.

MATTHEW PIERLE writes from a Permaculture microfarm and wellness center in Michigan. He spends winters in the San Francisco Bay area and is currently learning French and preparing for an around-the-world bicycle trip.

HEATHER POWERS is Program Coordinator, Field Service and Regional Affairs for NAFSA: Association of International Educators, Washington, DC.

JUDY VAN RHIJN spent three years doing seasonal work in Australia after she backpacked North America, the U.K., and Europe. She currently resides in Kitchener, Ontario.

LAVINIA SPALDING, writer, teacher, and traveler recently returned to America after five years in Korea. She is currently living in Utah, working on her first novel.

KRISTIN STEWART received her Master's degree from the Univ. of Michigan Ford School of Public Policy, after which she joined the U.S. State Department as a Foreign Service Officer.

APRIL THOMPSON covers travel, spirituality, and environmental and community issues for publications nationwide. While on a solo adventure around the world, April also published a 12-part travel series in the *San Francisco Bay Guardian.*

DANIEL WALFISH has spent over two years in China as a freelance journalist and English teacher.

ERIKA WEIDNER graduated from the Univ. of Oregon with a degree in International Studies. She interned in both Budapest and London and lives in San Mateo, CA.

DANIEL WEISS received his PhD in Educational Policy from the Univ. of Minnesota. He is the executive director of Amizade, Ltd., based in Deerfield, IL.

BECKY YOUMAN moved to Mexico City where, through a chain of contacts, she landed a job as country manager for a U.S. company in Mexico.

Index

Reader Response Page

Transitions Abroad relies on its editors for the best available information on alternative travel resources and programs. It relies on readers for first-hand reports. Please use the space below (or a separate sheet) to describe you own alternative travel and work abroad discoveries. The most useful reports will be published in Information Exchange in *Transitions Abroad*.

Send to Information Exchange, Transitions Abroad, P.O. Box 1300 Amherst, MA 01004-1300; fax 413-256-0373; info@TransitionsAbroad.com. For longer submissions, please read our Writers' Guidelines, available on our web site at [www.TransitionsAbroad.com]

Alternatives to Mass Tourism

For over 25 years *Transitions Abroad* magazine has been the #1 resource for travelers interested in alternatives to mass tourism. Bimonthly issues cover independent travel, work abroad, study abroad, living abroad and more. *"An essential publication for true travelers."* — Arthur Frommer *"The best resource around for practical, clearly stated information on travel outside the U.S."* — Rick Steves.

SHORT-TERM JOBS ABROAD (JAN/FEB)

Work your around the world—Pick up short-term jobs as you go or volunteer your services for room and board. This issue also features a directory of ESL training schools and placement programs.

SPECIAL INTEREST VACATIONS (MAR/APR)

Combine a vacation abroad with an activity you love— Whether it's hiking, sailing, bird-watching or cooking, following your own interest is much more satisfying than fighting the crowds. This issue also features information on study abroad programs.

LANGUAGE VACATIONS (MAY/JUNE)

Master a language while on vacation—In Central America, $150 a week buys room and board plus four hours a day of private tutoring. Our directory features overseas language programs throughout the world.

OVERSEAS TRAVEL PLANNER (JUL/AUG)

The best collection of alternative travel resources—This popular annual issue helps you map out an affordable strategy. Includes the best sources and programs by country and region for families, seniors, persons with disabilities, and students.

WORK ABROAD (SEP/OCT)

Live and work abroad—Our annual directory of work abroad resources, worldwide internship opportunities and volunteer programs.

RESPONSIBLE TRAVEL (NOV/DEC)

Avoid the tourist trap—This issue contains info about adventure travel tour and program operators who are committed to giving something back to the communities they visit. Our annual directory describes responsible travel programs by region and country, with an emphasis on local organizations.

Advertiser Index

Notes